Talk That Talk Some More
On the Cutting Room Floor

For Alyce Nelson Ruley

with love,

Marian E. Barnes

12-17-95

... It is clear from the readings [in *Talk That Talk Some More*] that Ms. Barnes understands that the contempt and loathing of African-Americans is non-discriminatory with respect to class, educational or any other kind of achievement, and non-discriminatory as far as admixture of or appearance of Caucasian blood.

Analysis of the themes and samplings of African-American experiences, beautifully told, offer the shock-value of the functional acceptance of African-Americans, an acceptance predicated solely on the particular function of the "accepted" Black — whether it be as a comedian (most), an athlete (next), or as a professional.

But Ms. Barnes tells us in a hundred ways that defeat dies hard. There is hope. There is hope of freedom from functional acceptance only, freedom from violence against our personhood, freedom from contempt of our physical features, freedom from contempt of our African genesis . . .

Edward W. Robinson, Jr., J.D.
Historian, educator, publisher, pioneer
instructor in the field of corrective
Black history. Philadelphia, Pennsylvania

Marian E. Barnes' book *Talk That Talk Some More: On the Cutting Room Floor* reflects upon her years of golden complex experiences. According to her own accounts of her past experiences, she could have given up the idea of ever writing again. But when the going got tough, she kept going . . .

This anthology is timely writing. Armed with courage, fortitude, and bulldog tenacity, the author of *Talk That Talk Some More: On the Cutting Room Floor* has fashioned an anthology that is informative, inspiring, humorous and instructive . . .

David A. Williams
Director, Texas African-American
Heritage Association; historian;
author; educator

TALK THAT TALK

SOME MORE!

On the Cutting Room Floor

Edited by

MARIAN E. BARNES

With an Introduction by John Henrick Clarke

EAKIN PRESS ★ Austin, Texas

FIRST EDITION
Copyright © 1993
By Marian E. Barnes

Published in the United States of America
By Eakin Press
An Imprint of Sunbelt Media, Inc.
P.O. Drawer 90159 ★ Austin, TX 78709-0159

ALL RIGHTS RESERVED. No part of this book may be reproduced in any form without written permission from the publisher, except for brief passages included in a review appearing in a newspaper or magazine.

ISBN 0-89015-895-9

Library of Congress Cataloging-in-Publication Data

Talk that talk some more: on the cutting room floor / compiled and edited by Marian E. Barnes.
    p.   cm.
Includes bibliographical references.
  ISBN 0-89015-895-9
  1. Afro-Americans. 2. Slavery – United States. 3. Slavery – Southern States. 4. Afro-Americans – Literary collections. 5. Slavery – United States – Literary collections. 6. Slavery – Southern States – Literary collections. I. Barnes, Marian E.
E185.T195   1993
398.2'089'96073–dc20   92-42419
                                                                                                CIP

Grateful acknowledgment is made for permission to publish the copyrighted works of participating authors. Every reasonable effort has been made to trace the ownership of all material included in this anthology. Any error that may have occurred is inadvertent and will be corrected in subsequent editions provided notification is sent to the publisher.

This book is dedicated to the memory of
Dr. Arthur Huff Fauset, mentor and friend,
first to believe in me as a writer;
to Dr. Edward Robinson,
first to "push" me to publish my work;
to Tony Brown,
who "pushed" a second time;
and to Priscilla Walker and
Gretchen Rasheed,
who "showed me where to fall."

Dr. Benjamin S. Carson

Astronaut Mae C. Jemison, mission specialist, appears to be clicking her heels in zero-gravity in this 35mm frame photographed in the science module aboard the Earth-orbiting Space Shuttle Endeavour. *Making her first flight in space, Dr. Jemison was joined by five other NASA astronauts and a Japanese payload specialist for eight days of research in support of the Spacelab-J mission, a joint effort between Japan and the USA.* — Photo Credit: NASA

Contents

Introduction by John Henrik Clarke	ix
Preface	xiii
Acknowledgments	xvii

COMING TO AMERICA

Tears of the Atlantic by Eartha Colson	3
Illustrations of captives	4

GONE WITH THE WIND

The Black Muslims in America After Elijah Muhammad by C. Eric Lincoln	9
Dr. C. Eric Lincoln: Early Roots by Marian E. Barnes	12
A Portrait of Segregation, Discrimination, and Degradation by John Hope Franklin	14
I Can't Forgive Her, the Way She Used to Beat Us by J. Mason Brewer	19
Reconstruction Days: Ku Klux by J. Mason Brewer	22
A Deeper Look at Aesop by Mark Hyman	23
Wade in the Water by Marian E. Barnes	24
Slavery Time Party by Marian E. Barnes	43
Enslaved: Former Captives Tell About Slavery	45
Juneteenth, First African-American Holiday by Marian E. Barnes	56
We Met a Little Tragedy on a Navasota Plantation by Ruthe Winegarten	58
Wartime Trolley by Marian E. Barnes	60
Gone With the Wind: Jessie Mae Hicks Remembers Times Past by Jessie Mae Hicks as told to Marian E. Barnes	66

OF FAMILIES AND LOVE

Grannie Jus' Come! by Ana Sisnett	72
Combing Grandma's Hair by Dorothy Charles Banks	73
What is a Grandfather? by Christine Wright	74
Warm Thoughts by Farhana Qazi	74
For Anna Mae by Rebecca Sims	74
Mother by April Parra	75
To Joan, My Loving Daughter by Marian E. Barnes	76

Grandmother's Room by Joan Barnes Stewart	77
The Crumb Snatchers by Jawara	78
Depression Love by Marian E. Barnes	79
The Wood Bowl by Marian E. Barnes	80
Urban Life and Depression Years: Thoughts of North Philadelphia by Marian E. Barnes	82
The Letter by Marian E. Barnes	85
Love and Respect Beat a Bloody Paddle by Marian E. Barnes	86

FOR YOUTHFUL MINDS

Eagles by Leon C. Anderson, Jr.	92
The Ride by Leon C. Anderson, Jr.	92
Progress . . . Or Ode to a Cynic by Jonathan Sheppard	93
To Martin by Maj. Gen. John F. Phillips	93
Doris ("Dorie") Miller: Pearl Harbor Hero by Marian E. Barnes	95
"Everyone thinks" by Sean Erickson	96
Morning Dew Drop by Jimmy Stanley	96
White Pawn by Jennifer Hansen	96
In Spite of Myself by Kyisha Diefenbach	97
A Chance for the Fire Department by Christina Mullins	98
Song of Myself: A Requiem by Colly Patton	98
Mama, What Don't White Boys Have? by Cedar Sexton	99
"The pale cloud swells" by Christina Mayne	99
Answers and Questions by Diego Prange	100
Just Another Soldier by Michelle Dion	100
Merry Go Round by Trice Ijeoma	101
Round and Round by Amanda Johnson	102
School Play Audition by Doris Barnes Polk	102
Tonka Truck by Will Angst	103
Voices by Marian E. Barnes	103
A Knife in His Hands: The Story of Dr. Benjamin Carson by Marian E. Barnes	106
East Meets West by Marian E. Barnes	109
I Like Spiders by Ada DeBlanc Simond	117
How a Horse Spoke to Me by Marian E. Barnes	118

LET'S LAUGH!

"A republican is an elephant?" by Michelle Wilkinson	120
Langston Hughes and Jesse B. Semple: The Making of a Folk Hero by John Henrik Clarke	120

Willi and Joe Joe and The Pamper Diaper by Temujin the Storyteller	122
"Goodie Two Shoes": Good Deed Makes a Barefoot Lady by Marian E. Barnes	123
Poor Sonny Boy Died in Vain by Marian E. Barnes	126
How a Hoe Became a 'Ho' and Turned Into a Rake, or How They Changed My Stories and Gave Me Other Surprises by Marian E. Barnes	129
Lessons by Marian E. Barnes	135

UNSUNG LIFESTYLES

Vaseline by Evelyn Martin-Anderson	142
Black Man by Marian E. Barnes	142
Fifty Men of Color Who Changed the World by Marian E. Barnes	143
Black Woman by Marian E. Barnes	146
Fifty Women of Color Who Changed the World by Marian E. Barnes	146
"Black women . . ." by Alli Aweusi	149
Negro by Alli Aweusi	150
Creativity by Dottie Curry	151
America's Black Holocaust Museum Founded by Near-Lynch Victim, James Cameron by Marian E. Barnes	151
Black American Cowboys and Cowgirls by Marian E. Barnes	153
Hospital Corpsman Battlefield Hero by Marian E. Barnes	154
My Day as a Migrant Farm Worker by Marian E. Barnes	161
President Johnson's Gift to Me by Marian E. Barnes	167
Scenes from the Life of Malcolm X, Martyred Muslim Leader by Marian E. Barnes	169
Exiled From South Africa, My Home by Joseph Mwalimu as told to Marian E. Barnes	170
I Must Speak Out! by Deborah L. Orr-Ogunro	172
The Death of a Kikuyu by Marian E. Barnes and Dr. Wacira Gethaiga	172
African-American Contributions Get Us Through the Day by Marian E. Barnes	183

COMMENTARIES

The Way It Is: African Words and Creative Expressions in English by Dr. Margaret Wade-Lewis	188
Language and the African-American by Marian E. Barnes	198

Notes on the Psychological Use of Language as a Tool of Oppression by Marian E. Barnes	204
Black English Expressions by Marian E. Barnes	206

NEWSPAPER COLUMNS AND LETTERS REVISITED

Minister Farrakhan Challenges Black Men, Defends Black Women: But I See Room for Improvement	224
Who Needs Richard Pryor?	225
Monster Children "Unreal" Horror Story	226
Reverse Racism: New Problem in the New South	229
White Angel Learns Her Proud Black History	231
Racist Insults Please a Listening Audience	234
"Uncle Tomahawk" — "Apple": Sad Moment in a Sad Life	237
Philly's Aframerican Youth Have Peaceful, Civilized Halloween While Young White Hoodlums Rampage in Suburbs and City	238
What's in a Name?	240
About the "Holy Spirit" Nobody Could Quench but "The Man"	242
Afro-Americans Criticize *Roots*, Docile About Insulting TV Shows	246
Modern Woman vs. "Traditional Lady": A Comparison of Roles	247
A Problem With Black Women	249
An Open Letter to Brother ———, President, *Philadelphia Tribune*, Inc.	251
Letter to the Editor, Neighbor Section, *Austin American-Statesman*	253
Letter to the Editor, *Austin American-Statesman*	254

THE ROARING BOTTOM

The Roaring Bottom by Marian E. Barnes	256
Epilogue: Rap by John O'Neal	356
Afterword by Marian E. Barnes	358
About the Authors	359
About Illustrations	364
Bibliography	367
Suggested Reading	370
Index to Authors	373
Index to Titles of Articles/Poems	374

Introduction

The book *Talk That Talk*[1] was a pioneering effort to creatively approach the humor of Black Americans. In a nation of immigrants composed of many cultures and ways of life brought from various corners of the world, the speech of the African-American is singularly unique. Nearly all immigrant groups who came to America came with language of their creation that they were able to maintain. Language is a culture carrier and a culture innovator. To the Black American in his use of language and his approach to humor, language is schizophrenic in its projection. It moves on two levels, generally, and sometimes more than two. In Black America, language and social thought are often the flip sides of the same coin. Because originally the English language was not the mother tongue of the Africans, through enforced exile in the United States learning the language was a matter of survival, and using it on two different levels simultaneously was also a matter of survival. Humor and tragedy are not very far apart.

The content of this book is, in the main, a continuation of *Talk That Talk*, and it contains some of the more serious and less humorous of the pieces left out of the first book.

In a nation of immigrants, African-Americans are the immigrants who were brought to America against their will. We are the only immigrants who came to what would become the United States with an invitation. We also came with an affirmative action program intact — guaranteed employment under a labor system

---

1. *Talk That Talk, An Anthology of African-American Storytelling*, eds. Linda Goss and Marian E. Barnes (Simon & Schuster, 1989).

called slavery. The employment paid no salary and lasted for over 200 years. This forced labor helped to lay the basis for the economic system that we now know. It also helped to make possible a great deal of the modern scientific world.

The literature of Black America is a literature of survival and celebration; not a celebration of oppression, but a celebration of survival in spite of it. This literature has a subtle message often missed by readers. The message says, "Now that we have survived, we intend to prevail." When one looks at the long stretch of history from 1492 to the present, and what Africans away from home have had to do to survive, it can be said that we have endured a holocaust lasting 500 years that is not over to this day. In spite of the condition that I have mentioned, we have not given up our laughter, our hope, and our determination. To have survived that condition is one of the great miracles of human endurance.

Africans were great storytellers long before their first appearance in Jamestown, Virginia, in 1619. In the United States, the art and literature of African people had an economic origin. Much that is original in Black American folklore, or singular in "Negro spirituals" and blues, can be traced to the economic institution of slavery and its influence upon the African soul.

After the initial poetical debut of Jupiter Hammon and Phillis Wheatley, the main literary expression of the African was the slave narrative. One of the earliest of these narratives came from the pen of Gustavas Vassa, an African from Nigeria. This was a time of great pamphleteering in the United States. The free Africans in the North, and those who had escaped from slavery in the South, made their mark upon this time and awakened the conscience of the nation.

Gustavas Vassa established his reputation with an autobiography, first printed in England. Vassa, born in 1745, was kidnapped by slavers when he was eleven years old and taken to America. He was placed in service on a plantation in Virginia. Eventually, he was able to purchase his freedom. He left the United States, made his home in England, and became active in the British anti-slavery movement. In 1790 he presented a petition to Parliament to abolish the slave trade. His autobiography, *The Interesting Narrative of the Life of Gustavas Vassa,* was an immediate success and had to be published in five editions.

At a time when slave ships were still transporting Africans to the New World, two eighteenth-century Africans were writing and publishing works of poetry in America. The first of these was Jupiter Hammon, a slave in Queens Village, Long Island. In 1760, Hammon published *An Evening Thought: Salvation by Christ, with Penitential Cries* . . . In all probability this was the first poem published by an African-American. His most remarkable work, "An Address to the Negroes of New York," was published in 1787. Jupiter Hammon died in 1800.

Phillis Wheatley (1753-1784), like Hammon, was influenced by the religious forces of Wesley-Whitefield revival. Unlike Hammon, however, she was a writer of unusual talent. Though born in Africa, she acquired in an incredibly short time both the literary culture and the religion of her New England masters. Her writings reflect little of her race and much of the age in which she lived. She was a New England poet of the third quarter of the eighteenth century, and her poems reflected the poetic conventions of the Boston Puritans with whom she lived. Her fame continued long after her death in 1784, and she became one of the best known poets of New England.

Another important body of literature came out of this period. It is the literature of petition, written by free Black men in the North, who were free in name only. Some of the early petitioners for justice were Caribbean-Americans who saw their plight and the plight of the African-Americans as one and the same.

The now flourishing literary talent of James Baldwin had no easy birth, and he did not emerge overnight, as some of his new discoverers would have you believe. For years this talent was in incubation in the ghetto of Harlem, before he went to Europe two decades ago in an attempt to discover the United States and how he and his people relate to it. The book in which that discovery is portrayed, *The Fire Next Time,* is a continuation of his search for place and definition.

Baldwin, more than any other writer of our times, has succeeded in restoring the personal essay to its place as a form of creative literature. From his narrow vantage point of personal grievance, he has opened a "window on the world." He plays the role traditionally assigned to thinkers concerned with the improvement of human conditions — that of alarmist. He calls national attention to things in society that need to be corrected and things that need to be celebrated.

Langston Hughes began to write about an urban bar-hopper

and street philosopher named Jesse B. Semple in the pages of *The Chicago Defender* and other Black American newspapers in the 1940s. The first book about this hero was called *Simple Speaks His Mind*.[1] In giving us the character of Jesse B. Semple, Langston Hughes has created a Black urban hero that will probably outlive the circumstances of his creation.

A number of attempts to compile and interpret Black humor have ended up as collected ridicule. *Talk That Talk* was a delightful exception, and so is the present volume. *Talk That Talk Some More* is a well-organized sampling of African-American humanity and literature. In our attempt to keep laughing in order to keep from crying, we have given the United States a many dimensioned literature and culture that clearly indicates our ability to prevail as well as survive.

JOHN HENRIK CLARKE   1992
Professor Emeritus, Hunter College

---

1. **Editor's note:** "Simple" is used as a variant spelling of "Semple" in the writings of Langston Hughes.

Preface

WE WEAR THE MASK

We wear the mask that grins and lies,
It hides our cheeks and shades our eyes,
This debt we pay to human guile;
With torn and bleeding hearts we smile,
And mouth with myriad subtleties.
Why should the world be overwise,
In counting all our tears and sighs?
Nay, let them only see us, while
    We wear the mask.

We smile, but O great Christ, our cries
To thee from tortured souls arise.
We sing, but oh the clay is vile
Beneath our feet, and long the mile;
But let the world dream otherwise,
    We wear the mask!
Paul Laurence Dunbar
Reprinted from *The Complete Poems of Paul Laurence Dunbar* (New York: Dodd, Mead & Co., 1913).

    The most difficult times of my days as a television reporter were spent in the cutting room, looking over the shoulder of a film editor and directing him to "save this" or "cut that out" of negatives for a story to be broadcast. Vital and vivid parts of the story often ended up on the floor with other "outtakes" or "outs" because of time limitations, government regulations, or station policy. But although television outs occasionally have been retrieved and televised for some special reason, to my knowledge the same strategy has not been employed to produce a written work.

Most of the presentations in this book were rejected at least once by a publishing or broadcast editor. But unlike my days of TV reporting, when I had to leave outtakes to their fate on the cutting room floor, I have reviewed each work presented, found it memorable, and offered it new life. Now you, the reader, and I, the collector, have the opportunity to overrule an editor and enjoy reading published works that once could be found on the cutting room floor.

Many of the stories in this book were edited out of *Talk That Talk*.[1] Impressed with their merit, I incorporated them into an anthology titled *On the Cutting Room Floor* and unsuccessfully sought a publisher. Later, during a Black Heritage Month presentation at the University of Southern Mississippi in February 1991, I spoke of our beginnings in America as a race in captivity. I described the relentless battle fought by the larger society first against enslaved Africans, and later against African-Americans for our right as a group to name ourselves, define ourselves, and control our public image.

I also recalled the history of crushing psychological warfare waged by the master class against enslaved African captives and their descendants. Language, a major weapon in the war, was skillfully employed to rename, redefine, and psychologically subjugate the enslaved population. Captured Africans were instantly degraded into "negroes," defined in the U.S. Constitution as a form of chattel, or cattle, equal to three-fifths of a human being. After being captured, they were not called captives but "slaves," a word calculated to disavow their state of captivity and conceal their ceaseless rebellion against it.

I reminded the audience that the master class had demanded "survival behavior" of African captives, insisting that they conform to an image of servile mindlessness consistent with the redefinitions. Punishment for failure to conform was swift: holed-board beatings and cat-o'-nine-tails whippings on naked flesh; permanent separation from family and loved ones; death.

I noted further that updated versions of this image have been

---

1. *Talk That Talk, An Anthology of African-American Storytelling*, eds. Linda Goss and Marian E. Barnes (Simon & Schuster, 1989).

foisted upon every era with increasingly deadly results. The media depict African-Americans as a people without historical achievement who have contributed virtually nothing to the social progress of America. Black Americans are portrayed at worst as amoral, criminal and violent, and at best as shallow buffoons who get through life in spite of themselves, sparking laughter because of their personal ineptness and verbal abuse of each other.

The grinning, lying, mouthing, singing, smiling mask of which Paul Laurence Dunbar wrote, widely promulgated through mass media, is accepted as a true reflection of African-American life by most of the world, including many Black people.[2] Few still understand that a mask exists; and film producers, artists, authors and others seeking to look beneath the mask are rarely given a platform.

That evening at the University of Southern Mississippi, I shared with the audience my personal frustration as a writer presenting realistic views of Aframerican life only to have such work ignored in favor of nonconfrontational pieces that do not challenge prevalent stereotypes. Themes that challenge accepted stereotypes vary beyond measure. To name a few: simple profiles that explore human feelings; stories that inform about Black cultures in other countries; realistic experiences of Africans and their descendants in American captivity.

I cited "Wade in the Water" as a particularly painful example. Written especially for *Talk That Talk*, it was rejected by the editor without comment. I then taped the story to be broadcast during Black Heritage Month on a radio program for which I read stories regularly. However, the producer of the show refused to air the tape, saying, "It makes slavery seem too cruel."

After my presentation at the university, I was approached by an eager group of students whose spokeswoman asked for copies of "Wade in the Water" and other stories I had mentioned. When I said I did not have them, I was fixed with incredulous stares, my own equally incredulous stare gripped by the eyes of the young woman. A wrenching moment frozen in time!

I had just challenged the audience to live up to the creed inherent in the lives of our ancestors:

---

2. In this anthology, "Black," referring to race, is considered a proper noun. See p. 254 for further explanation.

> If no one will teach me,
> I will teach myself, and then
> I will teach somebody else.
>
> If no one will help me,
> I will help myself, and then
> I will help somebody else.
>
> If no one will save me
> I will save myself, and then
> I will save somebody else.
>
> If no one will give me a job
> I will make a job for myself, and then
> *I will make a job for somebody else.*

This young woman and her friends had every right to expect that such a creed also meant:

> If no one will publish my work
> I will publish it myself, and then
> I will publish the work of somebody else.

And they told me so: by their intense eyes; by their restrained silence; by the measured tone of each voice that said, "Here is my name and address. *When* you publish the stories, please contact me."

My mother used to say, "There are some people who have to be pushed, and then you have to show them where to fall!" As I accepted the names and addresses, her words came back to me. Clearly. Overwhelmingly. Other authors had encouraged me to publish the stories, and their "pushes" had gone unheeded. These students at the University of Southern Mississippi, however, had now shown me where to fall.

Acknowledgments

Although more people than can be named assisted me in compiling this anthology and *Talk That Talk* (published by Simon & Schuster, 1989), I am grateful to every person and organization that helped. My special thanks to Melody Powers for moral support and for facilitating the reproduction and collating of manuscripts; to Joan Barnes Stewart for moral support and assistance in collecting and editing material; and to L. L. Beauman for assistance with computer input.

Austin's Public Library system and the Perry Castenada Library of the University of Texas were invaluable resources. Frank Schmitzer, administrator of the University Hills Library, was especially supportive, as were staff members Ivy V. Bradford, Ursula Brown Carter, Latisha Bowser, Pat Strieber, and Marie West. Faculty members of Austin's schools were most cooperative. They include Carol Hovland and David Meischen of A. S. Johnston High School, Margaret Roach of Covington Middle School, and staff members of Kirby Hall School.

Other Austin residents who assisted include historian Alli Aweusi; Dr. Ira Bell; artist Clarence Briscoe; Dorothea Brown, past and current president of the Austin Chapter of The Links, Inc.; Wilretta Collins, Austin Chapter, Sigma Gamma Rho Sorority; Omega Psi Phi Fraternity members Greg Caldwell, Greg Collins, and Charles Christopher, Epsilon Iota Chapter, Ninth District Representative and Supreme Council Member; Marjon Christopher, secretary, Jack and Jill of America, Inc.; computer professional Pete Daniel; Nokoa publisher Akwasi Evans; Glenda DuPrey and her daughter, young Natty DuPrey; Al Fairweather of Alpha Phi Alpha Fraternity; George Washington Carver Library administrator Clifton Griffin and library assistant Winnie Stewart; Curtis Jones, president,

Delta Chapter, Alpha Phi Alpha Fraternity; attorney Steve Fleckman; Roland Hayes, Austin Alumni Chapter of Kappa Alpha Psi Fraternity; Olden Jordan, vice-president, Austin Graduate Chapter, Phi Beta Sigma Fraternity; Lamar Kriven and David Williams of Texas African-American Heritage Organization; photographer Harold Lewis; Linda Malone, Graduate Chapter president of Alpha Kappa Alpha Sorority; poet Niobe Marshall; AKA Sorority member Cherri Mayberry; Michael Morgan, of Morgan Printing and Publishing; Angela Medearis and Michael Medearis; Gladys Miles, sister of J. Mason Brewer; African culture consultants Christopher Ologban and Prince Eromosele G. Aligbe of Out of Africa Enterprises; Gerri Pickens; Cactus Pryor; Luther Simond; Lilly Williams of Links, Inc., and Sigma Gamma Rho; Ruthe Winegarten; Ida Mae Wright; Karen Wright; B. J. Taylor; Zeta Phi Beta Sorors Annette Graham and Bernice Hart; and Austin's Alpha Kappa Zeta Chapter of Zeta Phi Beta Sorority; also members of Austin chapters of Alpha Kappa Alpha Sorority and Delta Sigma Theta Sorority; and members of Central Texas Storytelling Guild.

I deeply appreciate assistance provided by additional friends in

Atlanta:
Storyteller Baba Atu
Soror Evelyn Brown, Zeta Phi Beta Sorority
Najuma Alexander
Storyteller Akbar Imhotep

Austin:
Dr. Funsho Akingbala
Ed Eakin, publisher, Eakin Press
John Kings, associate director, office of James Michener
Melissa Locke Roberts, editor, Eakin Press
Eula Smith
Barbara Stooksberry, administrative assistant, office of James Michener

Los Angeles:
Alfreida P. Brewer

New York:
Carol Peppers, public relations assistant to Bob Law
Sharon E. Robinson, Schomburg Center for Research in Black Culture

Karen Smith, Tony Brown Productions

Philadelphia:
Editorial Consultant Cynthia Cotten Bayete and Research Assistant Caroliese I. Frink Reed; R. Sonny Driver of Scoop, U.S.A.; Loretta Lamb of ETC Printing and her staff; Larry Robin of Moonstone, Inc.; Robin's Book Store; My Solitude Book Store; members of the National Association of Black Storytellers; also PATCHWORK: A Storytelling Guild; the late Almena Monteiro, dearly loved and very much missed; Ruth Tabon and James Tabon; Zeta Phi Beta Sorors Peggy Gilmore and Barbara Younge, and Zeta Phi Beta Sorority, Beta Delta Zeta Chapter

Studio City, California:
J. Mason Brewer, Jr.

Tallahassee, Florida:
Dr. Melvin Eubanks, Florida A&M University

New Haven, Connecticut:
Dr. Melvin Wade, Yale University

COMING TO AMERICA

TEARS OF THE ATLANTIC

Eartha Colson

Souls overboard......Souls overboard

You can kill the body
But you can't kill the soul
The soul lives on

You can kill the body
But the soul lives on

Thousands boarded vessels
headed for this western world

Sickness and disease
Cast overboard souls

The Atlantic cries
African tears
of African souls

Tears of the Atlantic
The Atlantic cries for me

Souls overboard......Souls overboard
The Atlantic cries for me

The journey's long
the weak discarded
the women raped

Sick overboard
My mother overboard
My father overboard
My sister overboard
My brother overboard

You can kill the body
But you can't kill the soul
The soul lives on

The Atlantic still cries
African tears
of African souls
The Atlantic cries for me

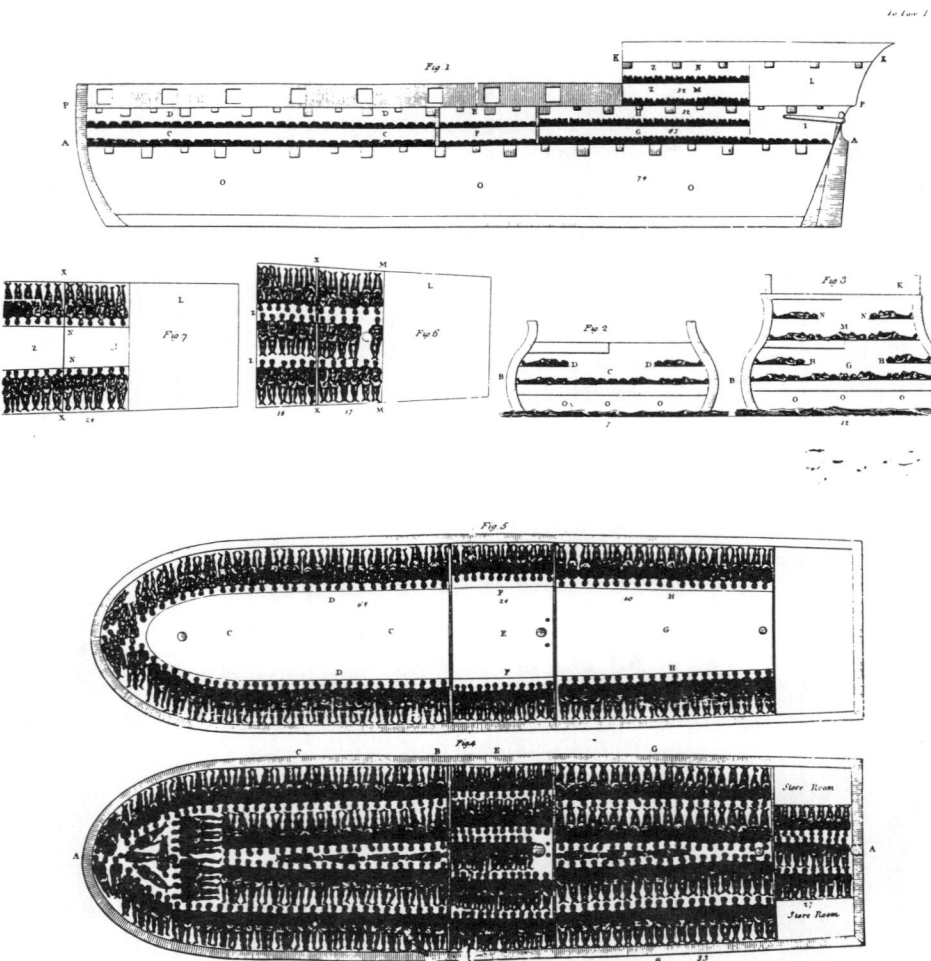

Coming to America.

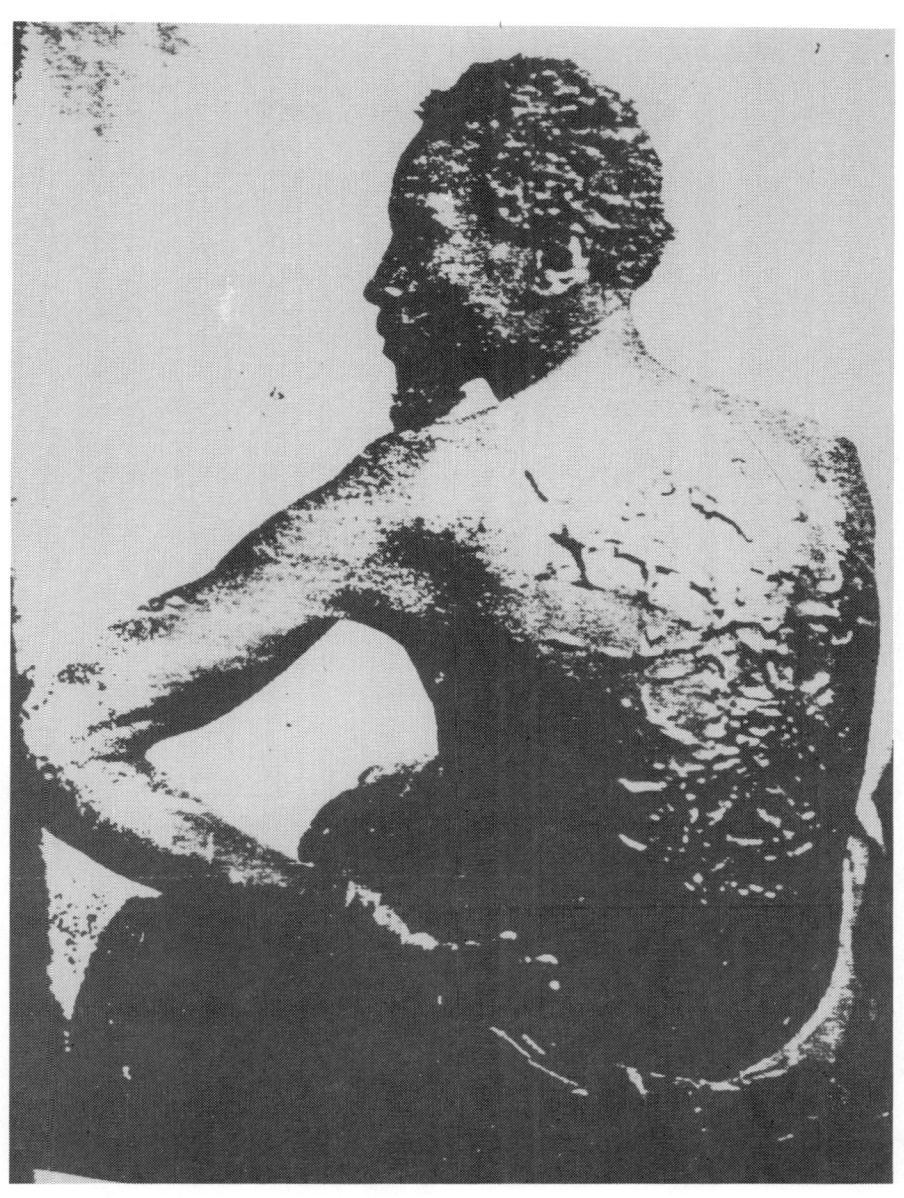

Whip-scarred flesh of a captive named Gordon.

GONE WITH THE WIND

The *Gone With the Wind* section of this volume is dedicated to the memory of my father, Elder Daniel Barnes, the memory of my mother, Mrs. E. C. Barnes, and to their generation.

Slavery fighting death
Clutched, clawed, and spat on your lives
Wrestled you down, stepped and dribbled on you
Prescribed and commanded that you stay underfoot

You, rising tall, forged a road of pride
Beauty, and overcoming
Showed me how to fight and love and live
Always looking up

. . .

Your sermon lives of service
Inched toward being free
You taught the *What* and *why* and *how*
Then passed the torch to me

Marian E. Barnes

THE BLACK MUSLIMS IN AMERICA AFTER ELIJAH MUHAMMAD

C. Eric Lincoln, Ph.D.
Professor of Religion and Culture
Duke University

Internationally recognized as an authority on the Black church, sociologist and historian Dr. C. Eric Lincoln holds five earned degrees and has authored or edited nineteen books, including the widely acclaimed best-seller study, The Black Muslims in America *(1961). Named in* Who's Who in America *and* Who's Who in the World, *his first novel,* The Avenue, Clayton City, *was a Literary Guild selection and in 1988 won the Lillian Smith prize for best fiction written on the South. Options have been purchased for the production of a television series or motion picture on the work, which is now available in paperback editions. More than a quarter of a century after his seminal study brought world attention to the Nation of Islam, and some eighteen years after the death of its celebrated leader, The Honorable Elijah Muhammad, Professor Lincoln pauses to examine the present state of the Black Muslims in America.*

* * * * *

When Elijah Muhammad died in 1975, the organization of Black Muslims in America known as the Nation of Islam was fractured — splintered, as cult movements always do. Small fragments went in various directions. One major section went to Wallace, Elijah's fifth son, who had succeeded his father as head of the Nation of Islam. Even though he was once a minister of the Nation of Islam, Wallace is an orthodox Muslim. He has studied at the world's greatest Muslim University, Al-Azhar in Cairo, and he has made his Hajj to Mecca.

When Wallace came to power, he came with the avowed intention of bringing the whole Nation of Islam into Islamic orthodoxy. He immediately began to do away with many of the rules, procedures, and practices that had structured the movement under Elijah Muhammad. As a matter of fact, he wrote a book, *As the Light Shineth from the East,* which said quite candidly that Elijah

Muhammad was not well versed in Islam, that he had been a man with limited education, that he had taught what he knew, but that some of what he had taught was inconsistent with the true religion founded by Muhammad ibn Abdullah and projected in the Holy Qur'an.

Wallace set out to correct the perceived errors, and in exactly ten years he successfully led the Nation of Islam into the orthodox faith of one billion Muslims throughout the world. Explaining that Islam was not a business enterprise but a spiritual enterprise, he did away with most of the business holdings that his father's organization owned. In the process of unloading everything that suggested a separate "Nation of Islam," he offered for sale the one-time Black Muslim headquarters building in Chicago, a huge, multimillion-dollar Greek Orthodox Cathedral purchased several years before Elijah Muhammad died with the aid of the international Muslim community. He lifted restrictions on race and redefined the role and status of women which were in effect during the long years of Elijah Muhammad's leadership. Wallace even did away with his own office, and let it be known that henceforth he was simply a Muslim Imam, which is to say a teacher; not a teacher of Black Muslims or Caucasian Muslims, but a teacher of Islam. His final act was to declare the old Nation of Islam dissolved. There were no more "Black Muslims," there were only *Muslims* of whatever color. The one-time members of the Nation of Islam were now free to worship wherever there was a masjid or mosque serving the faithful of Islam.

Following the much publicized rupture between Elijah Muhammad and Malcolm X in 1963, Minister Louis Farrakhan replaced Malcolm X as the national spokesman of the Nation of Islam and as minister of Harlem's powerful Temple Number Seven. Chastened by Elijah Muhammad for his remarks about the assassination of President Kennedy, Malcolm X – often called "The Big X" – had influenced the growth of the Nation of Islam immeasurably. He had founded most of its mosques, guided its publications, inspired its young people, visited the nation's colleges. It was Malcolm's appearances on TV, radio, and college campuses which brought the movement to public attention with the drama and excitement that seemed to follow him.

Louis Farrakhan, who had been Malcolm's most prominent protègè, was probably the best known Muslim on the scene after

Elijah Muhammad and Malcolm X, and Farrakhan was bound to be perceived as a threat to the leadership of Wallace. Consequently, when Wallace assumed leadership, Farrakhan was soon transferred to a mosque on the west side of Chicago, where any temptations he might develop toward self-aggrandizement could more easily be discouraged. But Farrakhan, who had never accepted Wallace's repudiation of the movement as it had been under Elijah Muhammad, soon became restive in his new role and spent much of his time visiting Islamic nations in Africa, including Libya and Nigeria. Once back in the United States, he soon became the leader of the largest faction of the old Nation of Islam that rejected the leadership of Wallace.

Relationships between Wallace and Farrakhan have been remarkably peaceful as far as their public postures toward each other have been noted. The apparent willingness of the two factions to live and let live is probably helped along by the fact that the families of the two leaders have intermarried, and by a common admiration of Elijah Muhammad shared by Wallace and Farrakhan.

In any case, it is safe to conclude that Wallace and Farrakhan settled their differences amicably, believing there was room in America for both denominations, and that there was no need to destroy each other. The sincerity of this accord seems illustrated by the fact that the huge mosque that Elijah Muhammad bought from the Greek Orthodox Church as his headquarters has now been sold by Wallace to Farrakhan.

The ministry of Elijah Muhammad has been expanded by both Farrakhan and Wallace; Farrakhan, by continuing a literal adherence to Elijah Muhammad, and Wallace, by building on his father's work in his successful bid toward orthodoxy.

However things go in the future, the indisputable fact is that before Elijah Muhammad and his Nation of Islam, there was no public consciousness of Islam in America. There was a handful of European Muslims mostly from Turkey in a few places like Detroit and Washington, D.C., but they had no public visibility. Elijah Muhammad, in effect, introduced Islam to this country, and in so doing he provided many other countries with a consciousness of Black America that had not existed before.

Before Elijah Muhammad, the only real consciousness people in this country had of religion was of Catholic, Protestant, and Jew. Recently, for political reasons, the United States has lowered some immigration barriers, permitting the influx of an increasing number of Islamic peoples, and raising the number of Muslims from perhaps one hundred thousand at the peak of Elijah Muhammad's movement to now about three million.

This has some very important implications. By the end of the century Islam will probably be the third major religion in America after Protestantism and Catholicism. Already some major Protestant bodies, like the Presbyterians, are preparing themselves for the new configuration expected in religion in America. Fundamentally there will be political and cultural impact too.

"Black Muslims" will probably continue to be the first contact that most Black people have with Islam for some time to come. Some of them will be content to remain in the Nation of Islam. Others will want to move on to orthodoxy. American religion is richer for its new options for personal belief in one of the world's great religions.

DR. C. ERIC LINCOLN:
EARLY ROOTS

As told to Marian E. Barnes

C. Eric Lincoln was born June 23, 1924, in Athens, Alabama, and reared by his grandparents. Grandfather, Less, owned a small farm, and Grandmother, Mattie, was a domestic who opened her home to any needy children who turned up there. Lincoln says of "Ma Matt," role model for Mama Lucy, a powerful character in his novel *The Avenue, Clayton City,* "She taught us to respect everybody, including yourself." And he vividly remembers the frequent prayer she made after she had gathered the children around her: "God, you know these are your children . . . You made them Black, Lord, because you wanted them to be the finest jewels in your crown. So bless them, Jesus, and let them be Black and beautiful."

Lincoln describes the house in which he grew up as "ancient, uninsulated, made of clapboard, built on brick stilts three feet above the ground so all the cold air would come up through the floor! Sometimes the floors were too cold to walk on."

Of the rigid rules governing behavior between the races in those days, Lincoln says, "I want to stress the importance of not only knowing the rules, but of observing them. One never knew when The Man would get offended, and whenever he got offended, he might do *anything*."

He learned the rules early. From Ma Matt, for example, when he was a teenager: "Don't you be looking at those little white[1] gals' legs!" And he learned from the outside world as he waited for a polio vaccination in a line with whites in front and African-Americans at the end. Playing with other children who were waiting, a frolicsome move suddenly placed him at the head of the line, and a nurse yelled at him, "You're out of line!"

Then the doctor rushed him. "He grabbed me by the arm, and he flung me against the wall and said, '*All niggers have to wait.*' "

Lincoln summarizes the incident: "My first lesson in race relations. I'll never forget it. 'All niggers have to wait.' "

Later he learned about a less well-known aspect of racism: that there were some white people, considered "white trash," who also had to wait at times. The lesson came on a cold morning when Ma Matt needed wood to heat the freezing house. A poor white man selling wood knocked on the front door, and Lincoln's grandmother ignored the knocks. Chilled to the bone, eagerly anticipating the warmth of a crackling fire, young Lincoln's eyes stretched in disbelief as the knocks continued to come and Ma Matt continued to do nothing. When the man finally went to the back door, Grandma Matt moved.

"My grandmother took her time. She went into the bedroom, put on a fresh apron and a fresh bandanna, then she went back into the kitchen. I'm watching all this, wondering what the hell is going on!"

What was going on taught C. Eric Lincoln and reminded the wood salesman that "white trash" were lower on the social scale than Black people; that this man was "white trash" and had no right to call his grandmother "Auntie" or to come to her front door — privileges that belonged only to upper-class whites.

At the age of fifteen, en route to a car wash job promised by an uncle in Rockford, Illinois, Lincoln stopped off in Chicago to take a look at the University of Chicago. He returned to study at the university intermittently for the next fifteen years. Today he holds a bachelor of divinity degree from the University of Chicago,

---

1. In this anthology, "white," referring to race, is an adjective (see p. 254).

a Ph.D. from Boston University, and several additional earned and honorary degrees.

A prolific writer, Professor Lincoln is published frequently in the popular press and in scholarly journals around the world. Even so, as a young man he was discouraged by his teachers from aspiring to a writing career because of the theory that no Black American of his time could make a living as a writer.

Discussing his award-winning novel, *The Avenue, Clayton City,* Lincoln says, "You can't go back to Clayton City. Clayton City was back in the thirties and forties. But you don't have to because Clayton City is still intact in a thousand small towns you know about. It has been updated a little bit; the packaging is more beguiling, but what comes out of it hasn't changed all that much. The racial attitudes which we have always known did not simply fade away with the civil rights movement. Legal access to housing, jobs and public facilities is progress, but the invisible structures which defined Clayton City continue to define America. 'The Avenue' is still intact, and the scramble to live on it is still as tragi-comic as it is predictable."

A PORTRAIT OF SEGREGATION, DISCRIMINATION, AND DEGRADATION

Dr. John Hope Franklin
James B. Duke Professor of History Emeritus
Duke University

In the autumn of 1987, a storm of controversy swirled across the United States when the administration of President Ronald Reagan nominated Judge Robert Bork, a conservative, to the Supreme Court to replace Justice Lewis Powell, a moderate, who had resigned. With the power balance of the court teetering, both conservatives and liberals thought Bork might be the key to social decisions made by the Supreme Court into the next century. Bork's supporters looked on him as a savior who would reverse the pattern of civil rights decisions that the Supreme Court had established. His opponents feared he would undo a century of social progress, and invested some $2 million to defeat his appointment.

In the forefront of the struggle, Benjamin Hooks, director of the National Association for the Advancement of Colored People, vowed the organization would battle the nomination "all the way until hell freezes over, and then we'll skate across the ice!"

Testifying before the Senate Judiciary Committee considering the Bork nomination, Dr. John Hope Franklin, one of the world's leading historians, gave the following narration. In the timeless oral tradition of Africans, he used personal-experience stories to show what life was like for African-Americans during a turbulent sixty-five-year period.

* * * * *

Thank you, Mr. Chairman and members of the Committee. I am deeply grateful to you for this opportunity to make a statement, and I will be brief.

Through the use of personal experiences, I wish to illustrate how segregation and discrimination have operated in such a way as to degrade a whole race of people who have as much right to constitutional protection as any other Americans and how the Supreme Court, viewing such degrading practices as violations of the Constitution, has effectively moved to eliminate them. Thus, Black Americans have an unusual stake in the future of the Supreme Court of the United States. That is why I, as one of them, am so concerned about any appointment to that Court and especially about this one that is under consideration by this Committee and the United States Senate.

It was in 1922 in Rentiesville, Oklahoma, the village in which I was born, that my mother flagged the incoming Katy railroad passenger train. She, my sister, and I planned to ride to Checotah, six miles away, to do some shopping. We boarded the train where it stopped, and before we could take a seat the train was moving again. We sat down in the nearest seats, at which time the conductor ordered us to go to the Negro coach, half of which, by tradition, was for baggage. My mother declined to move, asserting that we had as much right to sit there as anyone. That was not only impertinent but revolutionary. The conductor stopped the train and put us out in the woods. Disgusted and dejected, we found our way back to Rentiesville on foot. It was a searing experience that a seven-year-old lad would never forget.

I was reminded of that experience in 1945 when, after attending a college commencement in Greensboro, North Carolina, I was traveling back to Durham where I was living. We were in the final months of World War II, and the train was packed — or almost so. Negroes were uncomfortably crowded into the traditional half-baggage/half-passenger coach. When I observed to the conductor that there were only five white men in the next coach, and if they could not be accommodated in another white coach, they could be put in our coach and we could use the coach they were occupying. In such an arrangement we could all be seated. The conductor told me that the five white men were German prisoners of war and had to be left where they were. I do not know how much the Germans understood of American racial mores, traditions, and laws, but they seemed to relish our discomfort. They laughed at us all the way to Durham. They could have wondered what we had been fighting for.

If we did not derive much benefit from fighting the Nazis and the Japanese as far as equal rights in transportation at home were concerned, we fought and won that battle in the courts. Thanks to the decisions in such cases as *Mitchell v. The United States* (1941), *Morgan v. Virginia* (1946), and *Bob-Lo Excursion Company v. Michigan* (1948), the Supreme Court decreed that people such as my mother and her family and those Blacks traveling from Greensboro to Durham would never again be subjected to degradation and humiliation while traveling in the land of their birth, to which they had given so much.

When I graduated from college in 1935 and was headed for graduate school, the only gesture that my state of Oklahoma extended to me was to bar me from studying for my doctorate at the state university, and provide a portion of my out-of-state tuition expenses *if* I was successful in my course work. Thus I was not only deprived of the equal opportunity to succeed or fail at the university which was financed by taxpayers such as my parents, but was sent into exile at Harvard University, so alienated by my state's action that I never returned there to live.

Then, when I went to North Carolina to do research for my doctoral dissertation, I was not permitted to use the state archives until a separate room could be set aside for my exclusive use. So that the stack assistants, all of whom were white, would not have to serve me, I was given a key to the stacks and told that I could go in and collect the manuscripts and other materials as I needed them for my own use. That arrangement continued for about two weeks, at which time the white researchers protested that they were being discriminated against because they did not have the privilege that I had of access to the stacks. The stack privilege was taken from me on the day of the protest, but the segregation and the discrimination continued. I was denied the use of the search room where all of the white researchers worked and used the reference materials. Thus, the stack assistants were now required to serve me.

Then came the assault on segregation and discrimination in higher education, and ultimately in the public schools. The decisions of the United States Supreme Court in *Sipuel v. the Board of Regents* (1948), *Sweatt v. Painter* (1950), and *McLaurin v. Oklahoma State Regents* (1950) made it possible for Black aspirants to higher education to attend the public universities in their own states and enjoy the equal protection afforded by the Constitution. When I went to Howard University to teach in 1947, the only restaurants I could use while doing research at the Library of Congress were those in the Supreme Court building and the Methodist building. If I worked on weekends, when those two places of public accommodation were closed, I had to bring my own lunch or leave the area altogether if I wished to have a hot meal. Meanwhile, my white fellow researchers could go anywhere on Pennsylvania Avenue or the side streets where already the specialty eating establishments were springing up. Those of us who were Black and wished to pursue a life of the mind paid a high price, not only in time and energy wasted in being denied service by white restaurant owners, but also in emotional stress arising from the absence of constitutional protection in our quest for even a cup of coffee. It was the Supreme Court that opened the restaurants of this city to Blacks in *District of Columbia v. John R. Thompson Company* (1953). In the Civil Rights Act of 1964, and in the Supreme Court decisions upholding the constitutionality of that act, notably in *Heart of Atlanta Motel v. the United States* (1964), and *Katzenbach v. McClung* (1964), the right of Blacks to enjoy public accommodations was affirmed.

Members of the Committee, I come here today because I am deeply concerned about the future composition of the Court, knowing full well that what you do in this matter will greatly affect the future of our country. I will not demean this discussion by even taking notice of the claim advanced by some that the criticisms of Judge Bork are patently political. Surely one can differ with Judge Bork's philosophy, his remarkable activism in pressing for the acceptance of his views, or his opinions on the Circuit Court, without having to respond to the specious claims that those who oppose his nomination are politically motivated.

Nothing in Judge Bork's record suggests to me that had he been on the Supreme Court at an earlier date, he would have had the vision and courage to strike down a statute requiring the eviction of a Black family from a train for sitting in the so-called white coach; or the rejection of a Black student at a so-called white state university; or the refusal of a white restaurant owner to serve a Black patron. As a professor he took a dim view of the use of the commerce clause to protect the rights of individuals to move freely from one place to another; or to uphold their use of public accommodations. He said, "If Congress can dictate the selection of customers in a remote Georgia diner because the canned soup once crossed a state line, federalism — so far as it limits national power to control behavior through purported economic regulation — is dead."

In 1973, at the Senate Hearings on his nomination to serve as solicitor general, Professor Bork recanted those views, saying that Title II of the Civil Rights Act "has worked well . . . and were that to be proposed today I would support it." Views may change, of course, but history cannot be recanted. I am concerned that had Judge Bork been on the Court in 1964, before the statute had a chance to work well, he would have asserted that it was an unconstitutional exercise of the commerce clause, and it may never have become law. It is not comforting to discover that only in a confirmation hearing has the nominee relented on a matter so obviously desirable and constitutionally protected as the proposition that all persons shall have equal access to public accommodations. One wonders, for example, if Judge Bork continues to view as constitutional the proposed anti-busing bills of 1972 and 1973 which he supported and Congress rejected. One wonders if he would have supported this administration's ill-fated proposal to grant tax-exempt status for educational institutions that practice racial segregation and discrimination. One wonders if he continues to dismiss the efforts of those persons honestly seeking formulas for the resolution of the problem of admission of Blacks to certain areas of higher education from which they had been excluded for centuries.

These are some of my concerns. Perhaps the greatest concern is that the remarkable and historic strides that this country has made during the past thirty-five years in at least mitigating some of the cruder aspects of its problem of race, could become the victim of one who has rarely shown judicial restraint in this area. There is no indication — in his writings, his teachings, or his rulings — that this nominee has any deeply held commitment to the eradication of the problem of race or even of its mitigation. One searches his record in vain to find a civil rights advance that he supported from its inception. The landmark cases I cited earlier have done much to make this a tolerable, tolerant land in which persons of African descent can live. I shudder to think how Judge Bork would have ruled in any of them had he served on the Court at the time they were decided. We cannot afford the risk of having a person on the United States Supreme Court whose views make it clear that his decisions in this area would be inimical to the best interests of this nation and the world.

Thank you, Mr. Chairman.

I CAN'T FORGIVE HER, THE WAY SHE USED TO BEAT US*

Collected by J. Mason Brewer

I don't know anything 'cept what happened when I was a child. I know I was born in slavery, and I know they was awful mean. I was born in 1855 and the War started in '61. My white folks was awful bad and mean. I'm telling you what I know; they was mean; they beat us till the blood run down our legs. When we left here we was naked; my sister was the weaver and she was weaving some clothes for us, and old Mistress took that stuff off the loom and took it upstairs and hid it. We went away naked . . . You know chillen get into mischief, and they get whipped for it. I often told my mother time after time that I didn't blame old Mistress for whipping us, but she didn't need to kill us; she coulda just

---

*Reprinted from *American Negro Folklore*, J. Mason Brewer (Quadrangle Books, 1968).

whipped us. We didn't have on but one piece winter or summer, and she would pull it over our head and whip us till the blood run down, and we was dasn't to holler. I can't remember now like I can back yonder; but I can remember that just as plain as day. We stayed there a year after freedom 'cause we didn't have sense enough to know we was free. My mother took care of the chillen and washing and ironing, and she took me with her to wash socks and handkerchiefs. They used to keep her hired out 'cause she wouldn't let her (Mistress) whip her; so they hired her out and finally sold her. But she come back 'cause they said she only had two chillen and she was sound, and they found out that she had had fourteen chillen, and when she was a girl she had knocked her toe out of place, and she was a little cripple; so they had to take her back. You know if you sold stock and it wasn't sound like you said it was, you would have to take it back; so that's the way they did. I seen Mistress come in there with a bucket of hot water to throw on my mother, and mother grabbed the bucket and threw it on her, and the old woman hollered murder and all the chillen came running in with sticks and things; then the old woman said she wasn't mad, she was just happy in her soul. One of the boys took the stick he had and hit me a lick or two, but they wouldn't let him hurt me; and he wouldn't touch mother.

You know that old woman was mean. When she was dying she said she was all right, and I said to mother, "Yes, she is all right: all right for hell." Mother said I ought to forgive, but I can't forgive her, the way she used to beat us. Ain't no child what don't deserve a whipping. We'd eat green apples, eat dirt and things like that, and if she caught us we would hide it behind us, and if she asked what we had, we'd say "Nothing"; you see we done tole a lie right there and she would whip you. I'm telling you the truth; I can't lie 'cause I got to go before my God, and she's dead and can't speak for herself; but she beat me till the blood run down to my heels. Mother said when she was sold she had a baby in her arms, and her other boy next to the baby was standing by the fence crying. When she come back, she had me. I was her baby. My father was a Bailey, but mother and father separated before I was born. I was born in '55 and that was in slavery time. In '61 I was six years old, and that's when the War started. No, they didn't sell him; he and mother just got mad in a quarrel and separated. He tried to get her back and the white folks tried to get her to take him back, but she wouldn't do it, 'cause he drawed back to hit her with a chair, and he'd never done that before. He woulda hit her too if her brother hadn't been there and stopped him.

Mother was put on the block three times after that; but they couldn't sell her. They tried to bid her off for a dime, but nobody would give it. I don't know why they wouldn't but I just know nobody would. Why, in them days they would sell a baby from its mother and a mother from her baby, like cows and calves, and think no more of it.

No'm, we didn't have plenty to eat. The chillen never did get no meat. We had bean soup, cabbage soup, and milk, with mush or bread in it. The grown folks got a little meat 'cause they had to work, but we didn't. Once a man brought some old hog heads and pieces of fresh meat like that to old Mistress in a barrel, to make soap with, and the things was just floating on top; and she got mad 'cause the grown folks (slaves) wouldn't eat it. She give it to us chillen, and 'course we was glad to get it, 'cause it was meat, and we eat it till it made us sick, and they couldn't give us any more. Mr. ——— (the man who had given the meat) came by and found out what she had done, and he said, "I just brought that meat here 'cause I thought you might want it to make soap. I didn't know you was going to make nobody eat it. I wouldn't give it to my dogs." You know she was mean. When I heard she was dead I couldn't help but laugh, and I was grown then and had a child. She ought not to do me that way.

Marse Jack Barbee, he was so good to we chillen. He jerked her off of us many a time, and he'd say, "Plague take you, you trying to kill that little baby." If he found any of the old rawhides she'd use, he'd cut 'em up and take 'em out to the woodpile and burn 'em. Then she'd go to them old sprouts in the yard. Sometimes I'd rather it been the cowhide, 'cause sometimes the sprouts would have thorns on 'em.

My aunt, she'd slip meat skins through the crack to us chillen till that hole would get right greasy. She had a little hole in the floor that she could use; and we would go down to the orchard and broil them or cook 'em some way. We'd put the little ones in the henhouse, through the hole they left for the hens; and they'd come out with an apron full of eggs, and we'd take them out to the woods and cook 'em some way; and we would steal chickens too. Me and sister Lottie was the biggest ones in the bunch, and we was real little. The white chillen would help us eat 'em too, and they would go to the house and get salt, you know.

RECONSTRUCTION DAYS:
KU KLUX*

Collected by J. Mason Brewer

I know one time Miss Hendon inherits a thousand dollars from her pappy's 'state, and that night she goes with her sweetheart to the gate, and on her way back to the house she gits knocked in the head with a ax. She screams, and her two nigger servants, Jim and Sam, runs and saves her, but she am robbed.

Then she tells the folkses that Jim and Sam am the guilty parties, but her little sister swears that they ain't, so they gits out of it.

After that they finds out that it am five mens — Atwater, Edwards, Andrews, Davis, and Markham. The preacher comes down to where they am hanging to preach their funeral, and he stands there while lightning plays round the dead men's heads and the wind blows the trees, and he preaches such a sermon as I ain't never heard before . . .

There was some colored young men went to the schools they'd opened by the government. Some white woman said someone had stole something of hers, so they put them young men in jail. The Ku Klux went to the jail and took 'em out and killed 'em. That happened the second year after the war.

After the Ku Kluxes got so strong the colored men got together and made the complaint before the law. The governor told the law to give 'em the old guns in the commissary, what the Southern soldiers had used, so they issued the colored men old muskets and said protect themselves. They got together and organized the militia and had leaders like regular soldiers. They didn't meet 'cept when they heared the Ku Kluxes was coming to get some colored folks. Then they was ready for 'em. They'd hide in the cabins, and then's when they found out who a lot of them Ku Kluxes was, 'cause a lot of 'em was kilt. They wore long sheets and covered the

---

*Reprinted from *American Negro Folklore*, J. Mason Brewer (Quadrangle Books, 1968).

hosses with sheets so you couldn't recognize 'em. Men you thought was your friend was Ku Kluxes, and you'd deal with 'em in stores in the daytime, and at night they'd come out to your house and kill you. I never took part in none of the fights, but I heared the others talk 'bout them, but not where them Ku Klux could hear 'em.

One time they had twelve men in jail, 'cused of robbing white folks. All was white in jail but one, and he was colored. The Ku Kluxes went to the jailor's house and got the jail key and got them men out and carried 'em to the river bridge, in the middle. Then they knocked their brains out and threw 'em in the river . . .

A DEEPER LOOK AT AESOP

Abridged from the book *Blacks Before America III*
by Mark Hyman

Aesop, the Ethiopian, who was sold on an auction block in Asia Minor five centuries before Christ, created more than 300 fables, all of which have come down to us from 2,600 years ago. Although today many of them are said to have been written by other authors, the touch and style of Aesop remains evident. All have lessons for life. *The Goose and the Golden Egg*, for instance, teaches about greed. A man finds that his goose has laid a golden egg. Instead of waiting for more golden eggs on a daily basis, he kills the goose to get all of them at once. He opens her up, only to find no eggs.

Belling the Cat is better known to Americans as *Who's Going to Bell the Cat?* There was a group of mice who lived in stark fear of the cat in the house. After a very serious meeting, the mice decided that if a bell were put around the cat's neck, they would always know his whereabouts. The big question was: which one of the mice would put the bell around the cat's neck?

In Aesop's tale about *The Dog and The Shadow*, a dog with a piece of meat in his mouth walks across a narrow bridge. Looking down into the water, he sees his reflection. Thinking this is another dog with another piece of meat, he drops the meat he is carrying in his mouth to take the meat from the reflection in the water.

Many everyday expressions come from Aesop's fables. The

expression "sour grapes" from *The Fox and The Grapes* is a famous example. Coming to an arbor of juicy grapes, a thirsty fox jumps up to grab a bunch of grapes to quench his thirst, but he misses. Again he jumps and misses. After several failures, the fox walks away with his nose in the air, saying, "I'm sure they are sour!"

Aesop's fables such as *The Wolf in Sheep's Clothing, The Town Mouse and The Country Mouse*, and *The Hare and the Frogs* have been used to teach lessons in honesty, fear, reason and justice in a hundred or more languages and dialects. Aesop's tales spread into North Africa, where they were studied by the son of Roman General Severus. More than 200 of his fables were collected in the library of Alexandria in Egypt. During the Middle Ages, Aesop's fables became part of the intellectual world of Europe. Eventually the fables were used as the basis for reading and spelling books. And they are now part of modern folklore.

One of the most lasting of Aesop's fables, *The Fisher*, has strong political and historical overtones. It has been read, used, and enjoyed in many nations. A fisherman took his bagpipe to the river and played for hours, but no fish jumped from the river into his net. He put away the bagpipe and cast his net into the water. Soon he hauled in a net full of struggling fish. The fisherman played his bagpipe again and the fish began to dance. The message in this fable is clear: "When you are in a man's power, you must do as he bids you."

WADE IN THE WATER

Marian E. Barnes

Introductory Commentary

Although real names and places are not used, "Wade in the Water" is based on the lives of people who once lived. I learned their stories by talking with formerly enslaved persons during my childhood, and with elderly members of my family, and by consulting the library records of U.S. government-sponsored interviews with formerly enslaved people conducted by writers in the 1930s.

Perhaps because "Wade in the Water" is not a pretty story, its path to the public has been obstructed. Although written originally for *Talk That Talk*,[1] it was rejected by the editor. Subsequently taped to be broadcast during Black Heritage Month, the producer of the program for which it was intended refused to air the story, saying it made slavery seem too cruel. When a series of attempts to find a publisher failed, I decided to include "Wade in the Water" in a self-published anthology. Surprisingly, respected reviewers advised that it be excluded rather than risk alienating readers.

What underlies the resistance to presenting "Wade in the Water"? To say it makes slavery seem too cruel is not plausible since the story does not portray slavery to be nearly so cruel as it actually was. And readers should not be alienated by a depiction of life in the era of the American slavocracy unless the depiction conflicts with information, ideas, and ideals with which the reader is comfortable.

I believe that to be the case, having encountered Americans of every hue who accept the highly sanitized version of the American slavocracy generally put forth, i.e., *The institution of slavery, though misguided, evolved during that era because of the country's developmental needs, and the cultureless state of captured Africans.* Also: *Captives received civilizing benefits from exposure to Western culture that outweighed the loss of freedom and abuse of human rights.*

Believers of this myth are disturbed when it is pointed out that captured Africans came from a part of Africa where a successful smallpox vaccine was being used.[2] (Not until 1796 would Dr. Edward Jenner become the first Western physician to develop a similar vaccine.) They are further disquieted by evidence that ancestors of the captives possessed knowledge and technological skills in astronomy exceeding that of twentieth-century Western scientists;[3] and by evidence that much of the progress of modern civilization rests upon the inventions, discoveries, and spiritual leadership of the captives and their descendants.[4]

---

1. *Talk That Talk, An Anthology of African-American Storytelling*, eds. Linda Goss and Marian E. Barnes (Simon & Schuster, 1989).

2. *Before the Mayflower, A History of the Negro in America 1619–1964*, Lerone Bennett, Jr. (Johnson Publishing Co., 1964).

3. *The Sirius Mystery*, Robert K. G. Temple (St. Martin's Press, 1976).

4. Moral and spiritual leadership came from key abolitionists such as Frederick Douglass, Richard Allen, Absalom Jones and Sojourner Truth during the slavocracy in America. Dr. Martin Luther King, Jr., Dr. Ralph Abernathy, and

Such people are equally distressed facing the reality of slavery in America for which there is no historical parallel. *Never before nor since has the enslavement of a people included the systematic destruction of their history, culture, languages, communities, families, and personal self-esteem as implemented by Americans. The bestiality of members of the master class is also without precedent*: in the instruments and forms of torture devised; in enslaving their own children; in multiple incestuous unions with their children and grandchildren, whom they customarily enslaved or sold; in the attempt to legally dehumanize the enslaved population;[5] in barbaric lynchings that were still occurring almost daily long after freedom had been proclaimed.[6] "Newspapers advertised lynchings in advance. Crowds came from afar on chartered trains . . . Victims were roasted over slow fires and their bodies were mutilated."[7] In addition, bodies were often cannibalized.[8] People hoarded body parts as souvenirs,[9] and photographs of lynched, mutilated bodies were sold as picture postcards.[10] Well beyond the 1920s, lynchings were still being tallied. Yearly totals were publicized along with the Gross National Product and other national records.

Although "Wade in the Water" does not emphasize the most heinous aspects of the institution of slavery, its portrayal of life during those times is jarringly at odds with the popular concept of a nearly benign slavocracy, and for many Americans such a portrayal is unsettling. Historians have largely settled the problem by creating the widely accepted version of the era of slavery. Educators and students have followed suit by accepting that version without question.

---

other ministers of the Southern Christian Leadership Conference provided such leadership during the Civil Rights Revolution of the 1950s and 60s. In present-day society, the country's leading spokesman on the morality of America's foreign and domestic policies is the Rev. Jesse Jackson.

5. *U.S. Constitution,* Article 1, Section 2, Part 3.

6. *Before the Mayflower,* Lerone Bennett, Jr.; *The Killing of Claude Neal,* James R. McGovern (Baton Rouge: Louisiana State University Press).

7. *Before the Mayflower,* Lerone Bennett, Jr., 236.

8. *Ibid.; Slave Narratives,* South Carolina Narratives, Part 1, Vol. 1 (Scholarly Press. Inc.)

9. *Ibid.; 100 Years of Lynching,* Ralph Ginzburg (Black Classic Press, 1962); *The Killing of Claude Neal,* James R. McGovern.

10. *The Killing of Claude Neal,* James R. McGovern.

Aframericans deal with the concept of the American slavocracy in different ways, most of which reject reality. Some romanticize slavery and the "survival behavior" of that time.[11] Many do not want to remember their history. In my own family there was icy resistance to any attempt to probe the past. Most of the African-American young children and teenagers I have encountered in traveling across the country have been taught virtually nothing of their history by their families, community organizations, or schools. I meet young people who do not know what Dr. Martin Luther King, Jr., did, or who Malcolm X was, or what types of music African-Americans have given the world. And they generally know nothing about the enslavement of their ancestors.

Children of most ethnic groups are taught their special culture and history by their families and in community settings. The reason this custom is not widespread among Aframericans can, perhaps, be discerned from an expression made by many Afro-Americans during the television dramatization of *Roots*:[12] "I don't want to see what happened back then. It's too painful. We need to forget about all that!"

Nothing could be further from the truth. *We need to remember all of our history.*

The legacy of slavery imprints upon the life of every African-American from birth to death. Forgetting the past means living with the imprint and not knowing what caused it, nor how to counteract it or benefit from it as the need may be.

We need to remember.

An estimated one hundred million Africans were kidnapped from their homeland and sold into captivity,[13] and it is believed by many historians that of that number, more than thirty million were slaughtered or died of maltreatment or disease.

We need to give tongue to their every wound!

The American holocaust of enslaved Africans lasted nearly three hundred years. It is impossible to number the millions of

---

11. See "The Laugh that Meant Freedom," *Talk That Talk,* eds. Linda Goss and Marian E. Barnes (Simon & Schuster, 1989).

12. *Roots:* A televised, serialized dramatization based on novelist Alex Haley's story of his search for his roots in which he was able to document the capture and enslavement of an ancestor.

13. *The Journey of the Songhai People,* Robinson, Battle and Robinson (Farmer Press, Philadelphia, 1987).

men, women and children who were whipped, tortured, hanged, butchered and roasted during those centuries.

We need to remember.

The death-dealing afterglow of the holocaust in which we now live continues to claim lives daily, directly and indirectly.

We need to remember . . .
We need to remember . . .
We need to remember . . .

* * * * *

WADE IN THE WATER

Queenie was really scared! Mas'r Johnson had sent for her and she had found him here with Mas'r Josh Platt from the next plantation down the road. They were laughing and talking about a price for her like she wasn't even there! Mas'r Josh rubbed his thick, heavy, hairy hands all over her ten-year-old child's body just showing the first slight signs of coming womanhood. Queenie's frightened eyes stretched wide and filled with water.

"Ain' nothin' to her, John. The money you askin' fo' huh is way outta line."

"Look heah, boy, Ah didn' send fo' you; you come to me askin' 'bout huh."

"Ah know. But Ah kin see she's so little she cain't be much use to nobody roun' heah. It'll be years befo' she'll be any real use to you — and even then, she's built little, so she ain' nevah gonna be no strong worker.

"But you take me, Ah'm a single man, and Ah'm gonna need somebody to run my house fo' me again pretty soon. An' Ah'm thinkin' this un is good an' young, an' Ah kin train huh my way."

"Like you trained MayBelle a few yeahs back, huh? What's the mattah? MayBelle gittin' a little too old for your likin'?" Johnson's bawdy laughter filled the room.

" 'Taint that exackly. MayBelle ain' even twenty year ole yet, but seem like she's always feelin' poorly nowadays. She cain't do nothin' much no moh. She ain' got no strength — no life like she used to have. I figure it'll be all she kin do to help train a new one."

"Well, this un ain't but ten, and you squawkin' about the price. You ole hound dawg! For what you got in mind she'd be cheap at twice what Ah'm askin'."

Queenie's throat felt like it would burst. Tears were rolling down her agitated, chocolate-colored face.

"Get outta here, gal," Johnson shouted at her impersonally. "G'wan. GIT!"

Queenie bolted blindly from the room straight into the arms of a shadow that slipped off the wall and became the cook who hugged the child fiercely, then hurried her down the hall.

From the moment Queenie had been summoned from the vegetable patch, where she and her twin, Li'l King, were working, the intelligence system among the enslaved[14] people on the plantation had operated intensely and flawlessly as always. All over the South, behind vacant stares and blank, impassive faces of enslaved Black men and women (who built roads, constructed buildings, laid rails, hewed lumber, shined shoes, made beds, washed clothes, nursed babies, drove carriages, weeded gardens, picked cotton, tended children), were eyes and ears that missed nothing; and minds that keenly interpreted the words, behaviors, and thoughts of the white master class.

Now, throughout the silent Big House, invisible black ears had heard everything, and lips whispered the news to enslaved houseworkers who had not heard. Moments later a stout, short enslaved woman stepped onto the back porch of the Big House carrying a laundry basket filled with wet clothes. She was called Hap-Hat, shortened from "Happy Hattie," a name she had earned because of her constant lusty singing.

Walking toward the clothes lines, Hap-Hat felt the eyes of field hands boring into her. Veiled beneath sun hats, hidden behind corn stalks, "innocently" looking across the land, their eyes watched her, waiting for her message, waiting to be told what was happening to Queenie in the Big House.

Hap-Hat set her basket on the ground, withdrew a clothespin, and, pinning a shirt on the line, began to sing mournfully:

---

14. Because captured Africans and their descendants in America unceasingly resisted captivity and enslavement, the term "slave," which implies their acceptance of their condition, is not used in this narrative. Their refusal to consider themselves slaves is recorded in many ways, including the music they created:

> *Before I'd be a slave*
> *I'll be buried in my grave*
> *and go home to my Lord*
> *And be free!*

Without a father, without a mother
Without a sister, Lord, or a brother
What a mean world to live in
Lord, I got to live here, until I die!

Hap-Hat's song electrified the field hands. Mad Dog Platt was buying Queenie just as he had bought MayBelle! Poor MayBelle, pitiful now, broken, sick, and old before her time. It would be worse for Queenie. She was younger than MayBelle had been. And Hap-Hat's song had said "without a brother," which meant Platt wasn't buying King. Queenie was going to be separated from her twin!

Spontaneously the field hands began to moan their anguish in harmony, then to mournfully intersperse their moaning harmony with the sad refrain sung by Hap-Hat, venting their grief because tragedy was striking the child who belonged to all of them. The song and its sorrowful message traveled through the air from one field of workers to another, and from plantation to plantation, until virtually every captive in the county knew what was happening to Queenie.

The story of Queenie and her twin was well known to most of them. Their mother had died when they were born. Johnson, the plantation owner who had fathered them, had tried to sell the babies. Unable to do so, he had let them grow up in the quarters for the enslaved. No one had ever named the children. Cared for, loved, and waited on by all around, they were facetiously called "Li'l King" and "Li'l Queen," which evolved into "King" and "Queenie."

Inside the Big House, Queenie was crying. "He gon sell me, Cookie; he gon sell me sure!" she sobbed. "An' they ain't said nothin' about Li'l King. He gon sell jus' me!"

"You hush, Li'l Queen," the cook said. She wiped Queenie's face with her apron, then pulled her close. "It'll be all right. Don't you fret."

Queenie strained away from the cook's ample, smothering bosom to peer up into her face. "How kin it be all right? How kin it, Cookie? MayBelle ain't all right. Folks say it's his fault. Folks say . . ."

"I know what folks say! But that's not goin' to happen to you! Trust me, chile!"

"Ah cain't, Ah cain't, Ah cain't," Queenie wailed over and over as Cookie wiped her tears and rocked her in her arms. "Ain't NO-BODY kin help me!"

Just then, through the screened windows of the house, they heard the tortured, mournful song of the field hands and understood that they knew what had happened. A strong, vibrant voice rang out above the others in the field and changed the song. The new melody sang their present anguish and called up beautiful scenes of Africa that were memories for those recently captured, and tantalizing visions for others enslaved from birth in an alien land:

> *Sometimes I feel like a motherless child*
> *Sometimes I feel like a motherless child*
> *Sometimes I feel like a motherless child*
> *A long way from home*
> *A long way from home*
>
> *Sometimes I feel like a-moanin' down*
> *Sometimes I feel like a-moanin' down*
> *Sometimes I feel like a-moanin' down*
> *A long way from home*
> *A long way from home*

The song made the overseer uncomfortable. He was hated and feared by the captives, and he liked it that way. *That's why I get so much work out of their dumb, black hides,* he often told himself. Still, there were times when they made him feel uneasy, and this was one of those times.

"Ain' no cause for nobody to be moanin' roun' heah YET," he snarled, punctuating the threat with a resounding crack of the snakeskin whip he carried.

Instantly a lusty, powerful voice raised a rousing jubilee song:

> *Hallelujah! There's a meeting here tonight!*
> *Hallelujah! There's a meeting here tonight!*
> *I know you by your daily walk*
> *There's a meeting here tonight*
>
> *Get you ready! There's a meeting here tonight!*
> *Get you ready! There's a meeting here tonight!*
> *I know you by your daily walk*
> *There's a meeting here tonight*

All the hands joined in shouting the chant, improvising seemingly meaningless verses to what sounded like a nonsense song. The overseer's face relaxed into a twisted smile. *Fool niggers. Always singin' some "pretend" song 'bout something they wish they could have. Know they ain't allowed to have no meeting where they kin plot against white folks. But let them sing like fools. They work better that way.*

That night, recruited by the song, captives gathered at their usual meeting place. The spot was protected on one side by the river. The shore, encrusted with pebbles and rocks, made slippery, noisy footing for anyone approaching on horseback or foot except for those traveling the hidden path that led to it. To "catch" or muffle sounds made during the meeting, a massive cast-iron pot was placed upside down in the area. For further protection, lookouts were placed strategically and "invisible" vines strung across nearby paths to topple any rider who came too close.

The meeting was emotional, filled with grief and remorse for Queenie, "their child" facing a hideous fate, and for MayBelle, whom they had not been able to save. The group was overwhelmed by feelings of frustration at the surface powerlessness of their enslaved condition. Above all, they were determined that Queenie would not be next in a series of preadolescent enslaved girls — at least one of whom he had fathered — that Joshua Platt had ruined.

The primary responsibility for finding a way to save Queenie was given to the cook and Uncle Ezra. The oldest among them, he was widely respected for his wisdom and healing knowledge. Not only was he the doctor for captives on the Johnson plantation, his skill in curing physical ailments was sought after by people for miles around, Black and white, captives and the master class alike.

Within a week the sale of Queenie was finalized, and Platt arranged for her to be brought to his place in a wheeled cart. But when Queenie was sent for, the cook said the child was sick.

"What's the matter with her?" Johnson asked, surprised.

"She's got a high fever. Uncle Ezra and I have been doctorin' on her, but it doesn't seem to do no good so far."

"Well," he paused and cleared his throat, "Mas' Josh has bought her, so she gon have to go on over there and stay where he is, sick or well, don't make no difference. He'd be responsible for gettin' her well now."

"She can't be moved," the cook said. "I told you she has a high fever. You don't want to kill the child, do you?"

"Well, naw. Guess if she died, he'd want his money back. But jus' git huh on over there soon as you kin."

Meanwhile, behind the scenes, enslaved captives were feverishly plotting an escape to freedom for the twins. The plan was to prevent Queenie from being moved until Moses[15] came, then put her and King on the Underground Railroad[16] to freedom. But nobody knew exactly when Moses was due. Many said she was coming soon, but would it be soon enough? Could they keep the child out of Platt's hands until Moses arrived?

Days passed. Platt and Johnson pressed for information about Queenie daily. They were told there was no improvement; that the child was nearly comatose; that she was being treated by Uncle Ezra. When asked about her, the old man would shake his head as though dumbfounded. "Nevah saw nothin' like this in all my borned days. Nothin' I give her ain' helpin'."

A week had passed in this way when "Old Judas," as the captives called Johnson secretly, summoned the cook. "Listen heah," he said. "Pack that gal's things an' take huh ovah to Mastah Platt's today."

"But . . ."

"I don' wanna heah nothin' else." He raised his hands, palms pushing outward. "Ah don't care if she's sick or well, if she lives or dies. She has to go to her new mastah. She's *his* responsibility now. Ah don' want her dyin' heah on MAH han's — she goes today!"

"So that's it," the cook said to Uncle Ezra in the captives' sleeping quarters shortly afterward, her black eyes blazing angrily. "We can't stall any longer. We have to take her to Mad Dog Platt." Uncle Ezra was feeding Queenie, who ate listlessly and didn't seem to know they were there.

"Always knew it could happen," he said. "Hoped it wouldn't happen 'fore Moses got here."

"What you gon do?" the cook asked heavily. "She ain' gon be no MayBelle over there, Ezra, if I have to take care of it myself."

---

15. Moses: Code name for Harriet Tubman, an escaped captive who repeatedly led escaping captives to Northern antislavery states and Canada.

16. Name given the clandestine system by which escapees from enslavement traveled north.

"I know. I know." He stroked Queenie's hair. "But ain' no cause to do what I can't change yet. Not yet." He handed Cook the empty dish. "Like she is now wouldn't stop *him* none," he muttered. "I have to put her down further. Even then, how kin you know? You cain't never know 'bout a mad dog. Moses need to git here!"

Later, they wrapped a blanket around Queenie, now completely limp and unresponsive, and traveled by wagon to Platt House, where MayBelle arranged for the child to share her room in the Big House. "I'll be lookin' in on her every day," Uncle Ezra said, giving MayBelle two packages of measured portions of herb powders. "Mix one from this bag in her cornmeal mush every morning. You hear Moses is coming, don' give her no more o' this, start givin' her one from this other bag."

Their hearts heavy, Cook and Uncle Ezra climbed into the wagon and left. Inside the Platt mansion, MayBelle listened to the fading sounds of the horses' hooves and wagon wheels as she watched Queenie deep in sleep, her breathing heavy and labored. Slowly, she lifted Queenie's little-girl hand in her own hands, now rough, bony, and claw-like, and she remembered the first night she had spent in this house when her hands had been like Queenie's were now.

Memories began to wash over her: How the other captives had tried to help, even trying to keep her away from Platt. In the end, nothing anybody did could stop him. They had shown their love in countless ways, trying to comfort her tortured soul and body with soothing words and Bible quotations, with salves and ointments.

She remembered the times her juvenile body had conceived, swelled, and aborted babies it was unable to carry. Then last year it had seemed she would carry a baby full-term, and she had pleaded with Uncle Ezra. "Please, you got to help me! I can' have no baby for Platt to do it like he doin' me. And I don't want to kill it after it's here. Help me now!" Shortly afterward she had buried a still-born daughter. Since then, ill much of the time, her insides often feeling fiery, she had not gotten pregnant again although Platt's sexual abuse of her had not lessened.

When he told her one day that he was planning to get someone to help her run the house, her heart leaped wildly! She was surprised. She hadn't seen it coming. But she knew this meant someone else would replace her in Platt's bed. Someone else would have to stand his pawing, clawing, jawing all over her body! She had not cared who that would be. *She* would be free of the horror, and nothing else mattered.

Now tears were rolling down her face, splashing on her hands and Queenie's hand that she clutched, and the sorrow of her soul was for herself, and for Queenie.

She had been a little girl on the Johnson plantation when Queenie and Li'l King were born. Sometimes it had been her job to feed, diaper, and care for them while the grown-ups worked. For this child to replace her in the Platt mansion was unthinkable! "Never!" she sobbed, rocking her tense body. "Oh, never! *Never*!"

From that moment she guarded the child fiercely, managing to always have herself or someone else in the room with her. Platt ordered that the door be kept open so he could keep abreast of Queenie's condition. Angry, and afraid he had made a bad bargain, he peered through the bedroom door at Queenie, who was always asleep or stupefied. He plied MayBelle and Uncle Ezra with questions, and paced through the mansion.

The week after Queenie moved into Platt House, word came that Moses was coming to lead an escape from the area the night of the new moon. Every day the songs of captives singing in the fields spread the word:[17]

---

17. Many songs created by captives to be messages survive as spirituals, with their significance as message songs during the American slavocracy largely forgotten. For example, the following songs heralded an imminent escape:

> *Steal away, steal away, steal away to Jesus.*
> *Steal away, steal away home*
> *I ain't got long to stay here*
> . . .
>
> *Swing low sweet chariot*
> *Coming for to carry me home*
> *I looked over Jordan and what did I see*
>
> *Coming for to carry me home*
> *A band of angels coming after me*
> *Coming for to carry me home*
>
> *If you get there before I do*
> *Coming for to carry me home*
> *Tell all my friends I'm coming too*
> *Coming for to carry me home.*

The old man's a-coming for to carry you to freedom
Follow The Drinking Gourd[18]
Follow, follow, follow The Drinking Gourd

. . . . .

The gospel train is a-coming
Get on board little children
Get on board little children
Get on board little children
There's room for many a-more

. . . . .

I'm on my way to Canaan Land [19]
I'm on my way to Canaan Land
I'm on my way to Canaan Land
I'm on my way, praise God
I'm on my way

With the first alert that Moses was coming, the medicinal herbs being given Queenie were changed. "You just fine," Li'l Queen," MayBelle told her as she became more alert. "We keep you so Platt won't bother you, but you ain't never been in no danger. Uncle Ezra make sure you eat good, and I move your limbs around plenty every day. Moses comin' soon now, and we gettin' you ready to go No'th. But if anybody 'ceptin' us knows you is well," she warned sternly, "they might slip up an' let Platt get a-hold of it!"

Despite urging from Cook and Uncle Ezra, MayBelle was not among those planning to escape. "I'm not strong enough," she said. "I'd hold the others back."

Uncle Ezra also was not leaving. "Too ol', too ol'. These bones too old to make that journey now. Anyway," he added, "I got to stay here 'cause I'm teaching Smiley what I knows 'bout healin' so our folks here will have somebody kin help 'em after I'm gone."

The night of the new moon fell dark and silent with no moonlight to illuminate movement or shadows, no rain to make traveling difficult, no damp earth to preserve telltale tracks. In the morn-

---

18. Drinking Gourd: The name given the Little Dipper. Fleeing through unfamiliar terrain, fugitives looked in the sky for the North Star located in the Little Dipper, or Drinking Gourd, as a guide for traveling north.

19. "Canaan" was a code word for Canada.

ing after what seemed a perfectly normal night to the captors, captives were missing from every plantation in the area. The escape was not detected immediately. At the Johnson plantation the morning had seemed routine until horsemen from neighboring plantations raced onto the grounds, their animals lathering, and shouted that there had been an escape. "Any of your niggers missing?" they called to Johnson.

"Help me get a head count!" Johnson yelled. The riders rapidly scattered across the plantation, calling to the drivers in each field. "Count your niggers! Some of 'em escaped last night!" Johnson was relieved to find none of his hands missing and thought: *I know how to treat niggers, that's why none o' mine run away.* Nevertheless, in neighborly concern he joined the riders as they headed for Platt Place.

Joshua Platt had awakened that morning in an evil temper, viewing the young captive who shared his bed with disgust. Forcing whiskey on her all night had been useless, changing her from stiff, quick and scared to loose, stupid and scared as she was now, her huge, frightened eyes glued to his face. Platt planted a foot in the middle of the girl's body and shoved. Her slight form sailed off the bed and thudded to the floor. The impact burst the blisters on her buttocks made by the heat belt.[20] She pulled herself up painfully and stood crouching, arms clutching her body to dull the pain. Her dewy eyes searched Platt's face, not knowing if he meant for her to go, or if he was beginning another round of pleasure.

"Git!" he said, and watched her hobble out the door.

Later, unshaved, head pounding, eyes angry and red, he went to MayBelle's room to check on Queenie, as usual. He flung the door open and faced MayBelle standing between him and the girl's form on the bed behind her.

"How's that gal this mawnin'?" he shouted.

MayBelle looked over her shoulder toward the bed as though afraid his voice might wake the child.

"Ef she sleepin', she don' need no Gah damn body guard!" he bellowed. "She half dead, and you half dead stickin' ovah huh like a fuggin' buzzard all the time! Ah'm tiahed o' you hangin' in this room day an' night, doin' nothin' for yo' keep. Ah'd sell your nigger

---

20. A heated strip of metal banded across a mattress and anchored in fire pots on each side of a bed was used to force captive women to move their bodies during sexual intercourse.

hide down rivah ef Ah could fin' a fool would buy it!" He smashed the open door against the room wall and lumbered down the hall and out of the mansion.

Platt was mounted, surveying his fields, when the riders dashed onto his property with news of the escape: "None o' yo' niggers gone, is they?" For a brief moment his eyes were questioning, then his jaw slacked as if he had been struck. Spinning his horse around, he dug his spurs into the animal and galloped headlong toward Platt House, the party of puzzled plantation owners at his heels.

Something was wrong at Platt House; the certainty crackled through Platt's body like a bolt of lightning. He had known it, talking to MayBelle earlier, but his whiskey-dulled senses had failed to alert him. Now, with the pounding hooves of his horse singeing the earth and kicking up spurts of dirt beneath them, he remembered MayBelle's face that morning — expressionless as a mask. She had been waiting for him to open the door! And the door *had been closed defying his order that it be kept open!*

As the horse thundered up to the front porch, he lifted his eyes and saw MayBelle standing statue-still, watching him from her window. Flinging himself from the horse, he dashed into the house and tore up the stairs, John Johnson right behind. Inside the room he lurched past MayBelle, seated quietly, and ripped the cover from the form on the bed, exposing pillows and a bolster. With a hoarse roar he lifted MayBelle from her chair by the collar of her dress.

"Where is she?" he rasped, the words scarcely intelligible. "Where is she?"

"I don' know," MayBelle whispered. His fist struck her mouth and blood spurted on his hand. "Where is she? Where is she?" he roared again and again, smashing his fist into her face each time he repeated the question.

Then Johnson was pulling him away. "Come on, Josh. She ain' gon answer you. Let's go back to my place and talk to the twin. I took a head count of fiel' niggahs," he worried out loud, "wasn't thinkin' 'bout no chil'run an' house niggahs. But if that gal's gone . . ."

Sure enough, when the children on the Johnson plantation were counted, Li'l King was missing. Then it was quickly discovered that the cook and Hap-Hat were also gone. Johnson was enraged. "Let's git after 'em! They can't be gone far, takin' that sick gal!"

In addition to the local patrols, always on the lookout for escaping captives, Johnson, Platt, and the other owners formed an emergency posse, taking bloodhounds from each of their plantations. Dogs barking and yelping, nosing the ground and straining at their leashes, men shouting and cursing, horses galloping furiously, the riders took off, their dogs following the scents of the escapees.

Even before they left, the field hands began singing:

> *Wade in the water*
> *Wade in the water, children*
> *Wade in the water*
> *God's a-going to trouble the water*

The song was a message to the escaping captives: *They are chasing you with bloodhounds! Get away from the land and wade in water so the dogs will lose your scent!*

Nobody knew where the runaways were. But airborne from hands on one plantation to those on another, the refrain traveled northward, crossing the dividing lines of states. Somewhere along the way the fleeing captives heard the musical message and took to the water.

Afraid, tired, and hungry, they also learned from the melody how to recognize Underground Railroad supporters prepared to help them:

> *See those children dressed in white*
> *They must be the children of the Israelite*
> *Wade in the water, wade in the water children*
> *God's a-going to trouble the water* *

After four days the posse returned empty-handed, the owners livid. Accused of knowing about the planned escape, captives were whipped, already meager food rations were reduced, work hours — always grueling — were increased to compensate for the missing hands, and virtually nonexistent "privileges" were revoked.

---

* The color worn by supporters was special to each escapee and the song was changed accordingly:
> *See those children dressed in red*
> *They must be the children that Moses led*

Josh Platt went immediately to MayBelle's room. It was empty. In a howling rage he demanded information of one person after another. Nobody could tell him anything. "All right," he screamed, through foam-rimmed lips, eyes dancing madly, "Git them dawgs out agin! She cain't get far! Dumb, half-dead niggah bitch. Ah should-a sold huh ass yeahs ago!"

This time the dogs plunged forward, following a single trail that led to the river front not far from the house and a small neatly folded pile of MayBelle's clothes. The animals pounced into the pitiful lump of clothes. There was the sound of ripping fabric, scuffling, yipping. A brief moment of circling and nosing the ground, then they picked up the trail again, dashed headlong to the edge of the river, and stopped — baying, whining, circling. MayBelle's scent had disappeared.

Shrieking a stream of curses, Platt laid his whip about on animals and human beings alike. His subsequent questioning of captives proved futile. Who had seen MayBelle? Who had talked to her? Had anyone seen her talking to anyone else? No one admitted knowing anything.

The enslaved captives at Platt Place were not as sure of MayBelle's end as Platt seemed to be. In quiet whispers they questioned each other. *Had Maybelle taken off her clothes,* waded into the river, and drowned herself? Or had she left the clothes there as a decoy, put on other clothing, and made her *way north on her own?* No one knew the answers.

In the fields, workers began to chant in a woeful minor key:

> *Wade in the water*
> *Wade in the water, children*
> *Wade in the water*
> *God's a-going to trouble the w-a-a-ah-ter*

Meanwhile, on the next plantation, incensed by evasive answers and "bewildered" facial expressions, Johnson was lashing out at Uncle Ezra. "You' lying, boy! I know you' lying! You an' that cook was thick as thieves! An' ain't no way that gal could ha' been sick as you been sayin' she was. She couldn't ha' traveled outta heah with that bunch an' stayed in them woods four days 'thout bein' found. An' you know somethin' 'bout why them dogs couldn't pick up no scent from them niggah women that left heah. Ah b'lieve you give 'em somethin' to put in they shoes to th'ow the dogs off!

"Well, they may be gone, but you' heah, boy, an' you' gonna get the whippin' o' youah life! Jake! Jake! Get over heah!" He was calling the most savage among the drivers who beat the captives. But when Jake arrived, Johnson had a change of heart. "Naw, naw, naw!" he said, snatching the whip from Jake's hands. "I want Smiley to do it."

Smiley was a gentle soul. Strong and strapping, Johnson had bought him three years earlier, when he was twelve. He was an unusual boy, his skills with plants and animals as unfailing as his love for nature and people. Uncle Ezra had found in him a perfect understudy, and for three years he had been teacher, and father, and friend to the boy.

Now, at the whipping grounds, tears were streaming down Smiley's face. Johnson was set on making him whip the old man while the other captives watched. Uncle Ezra's body was swinging from a pulley on a cross-beam between two posts.[21] Following Johnson's orders, Jake had drawn Uncle Ezra's left foot up and tied it, toes down, to his right knee, making the left knee a "handle" with which to turn his body. At the resting level of the dangling right foot was the sharply pointed end of an oak stake or stob that had been hammered into the ground. The trussed position of the old man had stretched the skin of his back until it was shiny, making it easily cut by the whip.

"When that niggah start whirlin' round he gon put his foot on that stob to stop hisself," Johnson told the crowd, "and when he stop hisself one o' you other niggahs that's by that knee handle grab it and spin him round on that stake. An' if you don't, you gon git from my whip what Smiley is givin' him with this whip." With that he shoved Jake's whip into Smiley's hands. "You in charge now."

"Oh, please, Massa. Please," Smiley pleaded. "I cain't! I cain't!"

"You jes think you cain't, Smiley. I'm gon help you. Every time it looks to me like you thinkin' you cain't, Ah'm gon give you some help!" Johnson swooped his split-end whip down on Smiley's bare back and shoulders. The multiple ends of the whip

---

21. The punishment described was known as "the picket," "swinging from the gallows," or "swinging between heaven and earth." See: *Slave Life in Georgia: A Narrative of the Life, Sufferings and Escape of John Brown, A Fugitive Slave,* ed. F. N. Boney (Savannah Beehive Press, 1972).

snaked themselves around the boy's sweating skin, then slithered off reluctantly, leaving a split welt for each tongue of the whip.

"But why me, Massa? Why me? I don' wanna whip *nobody*!"

"You because I say you! You gon whip that niggah 'til *Ah* git tired! Ah'm gon make sure him an' you an' every niggah on this place knows Ah'm mastah heah! He ain't nevah gonna git outta his place an' think he gon outsmart me no more!"

"Oh, but Massa, I cain't! I *cain't*!"

"Don't tell me what you cain't do, boy! Start whippin' that niggah *now*! An' I don' wanna heah no mo' from you. If'n Ah do, I'll put you up there in his place, an' when I cut you down, you still gon have to whip him!" As he spoke he struck Smiley with his whip again and again until the boy's back was a crisscross mass of bleeding welts.

His face awash with tears, Smiley began the flogging. Coached by Johnson, he laid on five lashes from Jake's bull whip at one time, then waited a moment for Uncle Ezra to "come to and catch his breath," as Johnson ordered. At first the groans and shrieks of the old man could be heard over a mile away, but as the punishment went on they died into a scarcely audible moan. Several times he tried to steady his twirling, nauseated, pain-wracked body, placing his foot on the pointed stake. Immediately, by a touch of his whip, Johnson selected a captive to grasp Uncle Ezra's "knee handle" and spin his body around, driving the point of the stob into the sole, heel, or ball of his foot all the way to the bone!

When the torture had gone on for an hour and there were no sounds or signs of life from Uncle Ezra, Smiley appealed to Johnson again. "Please, Massa. He's done gone down. He can't feel nothin' now."

In answer, Johnson laid into Smiley with his whip. *"Ah'm* not tired yet. You jes' keep puttin' that whip to him. Ah'll let you know when Ah'm tired."

When at last Smiley was allowed to help cut Uncle Ezra down, the old man's back was a clump of lacerated flesh and blood, the flesh of his wrists had been gouged out by his bonds, and the sole of his foot had been pierced to the bone in three places. The oak wood was stained deep red from the blood that had streamed from his foot, and beneath the beam where he had hung was a pool of coagulated blood.

As Smiley carried Uncle Ezra to his quarters, Johnson called after him, "Don't you be forgettin' to wash his back and foot in salt water and red pepper. 'Do, ah'll have you swingin' an twistin' on that gallows next!"

* * * * *

Uncle Ezra tried to open his eyes and closed them quickly. The blurred, twirling walls of the room came swirling into him. Nausea swelled up from the pit of his stomach, and he was spinning, spinning, spinning. He did not know what had happened to him, or where he was, or how long he had been where he lay — an hour, two, a week, a month? He did not know that Smiley had bathed his body, which he could not feel or move, with soothing herbs and water. He did know that Smiley was with him. And he knew that Smiley was not smiling. He also heard the song being sung by captives nearby:

> *I am bound for the promised land*
> *I am bound for the promised land*
> *Oh, who will come and go with me*
> *I am bound for the promised land*

"Smiley," he whispered. "Smiley . . ."
Smiley put his ear to the old man's lips to catch the words. "You hear that singin'? . . . Nothuh train leavin' heah goin' No'th . . . Pl . . . Please . . . git on it . . . Please . . ."

SLAVERY TIME PARTY

Marian E. Barnes

Josiah, coachman, butler, and all around handyman on the Hugenot's South Carolina plantation, was quietly spreading the word. Field hands on the Jed Harris plantation outside Savannah, Georgia, had killed a wild hog, and they were pitching a big party tomorrow night. Josiah was going to drive the Hugenot coach to the party and take as many enslaved captives as the large, fancy coach would hold.

He chose his passengers very carefully. Nobody too big taking up too much coach space. Few, if any, captives with very black skin whose color might be seen and give them away if the coach motion moved the window curtains. Captives who could take turns to relieve him, driving the long miles to Georgia and back.

Whether they were going with Josiah or not, captives on the Hugenot plantation were excited. They bustled, secretly getting ready for the event, or helping those who were going to the party. Fine clothes inherited or surreptitiously "borrowed" from the Hugenot family were prepared, along with perfumes and cosmetics similarly obtained or made from flowers and herbs. Enslaved captives without a role to play were energized by the activity of the others and by a heady feeling brought on by the anticipation of outsmarting the master class once again.

The next evening, after the Hugenot family had been fed, pampered, and settled for the night, Josiah went to the carriage house where carriage and horses were waiting. As he had ordered, field horses were in the carriage traces, and the usual carriage horses were in their stable stalls. They would be fresh and rested when Hugenot saw them the next day, and there would be no troublesome questions to answer. Now the passengers slipped into the carriage, and they were off!

First they rode through familiar territory, and later over roads and through towns where the Hugenots and their carriage were not well known. In either case, with the carriage window curtains tightly closed, concealing the racial identity of the passengers, Josiah in his fine coachman's outfit drove with authority.

"Yeeow!!" he yelled, cracking his whip fiercely. *"Yeeow!* Get out of the way!" And lowly members of the master class on foot near this impressive sight quickly scrambled out of the way of the dashing hooves of horses and this regal carriage bearing wealthy, upper class whites — they thought.

The party was in a clearing far away from the Big House on the Harris plantation, the same area where captives enslaved there held forbidden church meetings. Huge, cast-iron washing pots were turned on end and positioned between the clearing and the Harris house to "catch the sound." Lookouts were stationed strategically to watch for vicious patrollers, always searching to catch captives in unauthorized places or activities and mete out bloody punishment. Booby traps were in place to protect partying captives from unwanted visitors.

When Josiah and his group arrived, the party was in high gear. Improvised tables were laden with food and drink of every description, much of which had been unknowingly provided by members of the master class for miles around. Game captured in the wild or "captured" from storehouses of the master class was roasting on spits over open fires. There was guitar playing, banjo playing, singing, dancing, games, and storytelling.

Josiah and the other captives partied long into the night before starting the long ride home from Georgia. They arrived as the first light of dawn began to streak the sky pink. The weary horses were released from the carriage traces, led immediately to the fields and hitched up for work. The exhausted travelers quickly changed into working clothes and started the day's chores.

Now they must work from "can to can't" — from the time there was enough daylight to be able to see until it became too dark to see anything. Although they were tired to the bone from traveling the long distance, and from dancing, singing, eating, playing and drinking too much, a long, hard day of grueling work as an enslaved captive stretched out before them.

However, they had beat the system and lived to tell about it, a most satisfying thought. They had been part of a party they would remember for life. And the memory of that evening and others like it would be passed down to following generations.

ENSLAVED

Former Captives Tell About Slavery

The following excerpts are from the Texas volume of Slave Narratives, *a folk history of slavery in the United States from interviews with former slaves (Scholarly Press, Inc., reprinted 1976, Library of Congress, Federal Writers' Project, 1936-38, Works Projects Administration for D.C., assembled for Library of Congress Projects).*

"I know I was borned in Morocco, in Africa, and was married and had three chillen befo' I was stoled from my husband. I don't know who it was stole me, but dey took me to France, to a place called Bordeaux, and drugs me with some coffee, and when I knows anything 'bout it, I's in de bottom of a boat with a whole lot of other niggers. It seem like we was in dat boat forever, but we comes to land, and I's put on de block and sold. I finds out afterwards from my white folks it was in New Orleans where dat block was, but I didn't know it den.

"We was all chained and dey strips all our clothes off and de folks what gwine buy us comes round and feels us all over. Iffen any de niggers don't want to take dere clothes off, de man gits a long, black whip and cuts dem up hard. I's sold to a planter what had a big plantation in Fayette County, right here in Texas, don't know no name 'cept Marse Jones.

"Marse Jones, he am awful good, but de overseer was de meanest man I ever knowed, a white man name Smith, what boasts 'bout how many niggers he done kilt. When Marse Jones seed me on de block, he say, 'Dat's a whale of a woman.' I's scairt and can't say nothin', 'cause I can't speak English. He buys some more slaves and dey chains us together and marches us near La Grange, in Texas. Marse Jones done gone on ahead and de overseer marches us.

"Dat was a awful time, 'cause us am all chained up and whatever one does, us all has to do. If one drinks out of de stream, we all drinks, and when one gits tired or sick, de rest has to drag and carry him. When us git to Texas, Marse Jones raise de debbil with dat white man what had us on de march. He git de doctor man and tell de cook to feed us and lets us rest up.

"After 'while, Marse Jones say to me, 'Silvia, am you married?' I tells him I got a man and three chillen back in de old country, but he don't understand my talk, and I has a man give to me. I don't bother with dat nigger's name much, he jes' Bob to me. But I fit [fought] him good and plenty till de overseer shakes a blacksnake whip over me."
Sylvia King

* * * * *

"My mama belong to old William Cleveland and old Polly Cleveland, and they was the meanest two white folks what ever lived, 'cause they was allus beatin' on their slaves . . . Old Polly, she was a Polly devil if there ever was one, and she whipped my little sister what was only nine months old and jes' a baby to death. She come and took the diaper offen my little sister and whipped till the blood jes' ran — jes' 'cause she cry like all babies do, and it kilt my sister. I never forgot that, but I got some even with that old Polly devil and it's this-a-way.

"You see, I's 'bout ten year old and I belongs to Miss Olivia, what was that old Polly's daughter, and one day old Polly devil comes to where Miss Olivia lives after she marries, and trys to give me a lick out in the yard, and I picks up a rock 'bout as big as half your fist and hits her right in the eye and busted the eyeball, and tells her that's for whippin' my baby sister to death. You could hear her holler for five miles, but Miss Olivia, when I tells her, says, 'Well, I guess Mama has larnt her lesson at last.' But that old Polly was mean like her husban', and I hopes they is both burnin' in torment now."   *Mary Armstrong*

* * * * *

"Us never got 'nough to eat, so us keeps stealin' stuff. Us has to."   *Sarah Ashley*

* * * * *

"All four my young massas go to de war . . . when Billy was wounded at Howard Gap in North Carolina and dey brung him home with he jaw split open, I so mad I could have kilt all de Yankees. I say I be happy iffen I could kill me jes' one Yankee. I hated dem 'cause dey hurt my white people. Billy was disfigure awful when he jaw split and he teeth all shine through he cheek."   *Lorenza Ezell*

* * * * *

"Massa never 'lowed us slaves go to church, but they have big holes in the fields they gits down in and prays. They done that way 'cause the white folks didn't want them to pray. They used to pray for freedom.

"When the white folks go off they writes on the meal and flour with they fingers. That the way they know if us steal meal. Sometime they take a stick and write in front of the door so if anybody go out they step on that writin' and massa know. That the way us larn how to write.

"Old massa didn't give 'em much to eat. When they comes in out of the field they goes work for other folks for something to eat."   *Ellen Butler*

* * * * *

"If some niggers was mean, they'd git it. Massa tied they hands to they feet and tied them to a tree and hit 'bout twenty-five licks with a rawhide belt. Hide and blood flew then. Next mornin' he'd turn them loose and they'd have to work all day without nothin' to eat. He had a cabin called jail for the nigger women, and chain them in with cornbread and one glass of water.

"One nigger run to the woods to be a jungle nigger, but massa cotched him with the dogs and took a hot iron and brands him. Then he put a bell on him in a wooden frame what slip over the shoulders and under the arms. He made that nigger wear the bell a year and took it off on Christmas for a present to him. It sho' made a good nigger out of him." ***Louis Cain***

* * * * *

"De way dey done at weddings dem days, you picks out a girl and tell your boss. If she was from another plantation, you had to git her boss's 'mission and den dey tells you to come up dat night and git hitched up. They says to de girl, 'You's love dis man?' Dey says to de man, 'You loves dis girl?' If you say you don't know, it's all off, but if you say yes, dey brings in de broom and holds it 'bout a foot off de floor and say to you to jump over. Den he says you's married. If either of you stumps you toe on de broom, dat mean you got trouble comin' 'tween you, so you sho' jumps high . . .

"I knowed a slave call Ben Bradley and he was sold on de auction block and his massa chained him hand and foot and started for Texas. Dey got to de Red River and was crossin' and de chains helt him down and he never came up." ***Jeff Calhoun***

* * * * *

". . . massa marry dem dis way: Dey goes in de parlor and each carry de broom. Dey lays de brooms on de floor and de woman put her broom front de man and he put he broom front de woman. Dey face one 'nother and step 'cross de brooms at de same time to each other and takes hold of hands and dat marry dem." ***William Davis***

* * * * *

"Massa use me for huntin' and use me for de gun rest. When him have de long shot, I bends over and puts de hands on de knees and massa puts his gun on my back for to git de good aim. What him kills, I runs and fetches and carries de game for him. I turns de squirrel for him and dat disaway: de squirrel allus go to udder side from de master and I walks 'round de tree and de squirrel see me and go to massa's side de tree and he gits de shot.

"All dat not so bad, but when he shoots de duck in de water and I has to fetch it out, dat give me worryment . . . I won't go in dat water till massa hit me some licks. I couldn't never git use to bein' de water dog for de ducks." *John Finnely*

* * * * *

"Iffen a nigger run away and dey cotch him, or does he come back 'cause he's hongry, I seed Uncle Jake stretch him out on de ground and tie he hands and feet to posts so he can't move none. Den he git de piece of iron what he call de "slut" and what is like a block of wood with little holes in it, and fill de holes up with tallow and put dat iron in de fire till de grease sizzlin' hot and hold it over de pore nigger's back and let dat hot grease drop on he hide. Den he take de bullwhip and whip up and down, and after all dat throw de pore nigger in de stockhouse and chain him up a couple days with nothin' to eat. My papa carry de grease scars on he back till he die . . . Papa was mighty good to mama and me and dat de only reason he ever come back from runnin' 'way, to see us. He knowed he'd git a whippin' but he come anyway. Dey never could cotch papa when he run 'way, 'cause he part Indian. Massa Charles even gits old Nigger Kelly what lives over to Sandy Point to track papa with he dogs, but papa wade in water and dey can't track him.

"Dey knows papa is de best tanner 'round dat part de country, so dey doesn't sell him off de place. I 'lect papa sayin' dere one place special where he hide, some German folks, de name Ebbling, I think. While he hides dere, he tans hides on de sly like and dey feeds him, and lots of mornin's when us open de cabin door on a shelf jus' 'bove is food for mama and me, and sometime store clothes. No one ain't see papa, but dere it is. One time he brung us dresses, and Uncle Big Jake heered 'bout it and he sho' mad 'cause he can't cotch papa, and he say to mama he gwine to whip her 'less she tell him where papa is. Mama say, 'Fore God, Uncle Jake, I don't know, 'cause I ain't seed him since he run 'way.' And jus' den papa come 'round de corner of de house. He save mama from de whippin' but papa got de hot grease dropped on him like I told you Uncle Big Jake did, and got put in de stockhouse with shackles on him, and kep' dere three days, and while he in dere, mama has de goin' down pains and my sister, Rachel, is born." *Sarah Ford*

* * * * *

"Let 'em ketch you with a gun or a piece of paper with writin' on it and he'd whip you like everything. Some of the slaves, if they ever did git a piece of paper, they would keep it and learn a few words . . . You would think they was going to kill you, he would whip you so if he caught you with a piece of paper."

Austin Grant

* * * * *

"My husban' said a family named Gullendin was mighty hard on their niggers. He said ole Missus Gullendin, she'd take a needle and stick it through one of the nigger women's lower lip and pin it to the bosom of her dress, and the woman would go 'round all day with her head drew down thataway and slobberin'. There was knots on the nigger's lip where the needle had been stuck in."

Auntie Thomas Johns

* * * * *

"I seed slaves sold, and they'd make them clean up good and grease their hands and face, so they'd look real fat, and sell them off. Of course, most the niggers didn't know their parents or what chillen was theirs. The white folks didn't want them to git 'tached to each other.

"Missie read some Bible to us every Sunday mornin' and taught us to do right and tell the truth. But some them niggers would go off without a pass and the patterrollers would beat them up scand'lous.

"The fun was on Saturday night when massa 'lowed us to dance. There was lots of banjo pickin' and tin pan beatin' and dancin', and everybody would talk 'bout when they lived in Africa and done what they wanted.

"I worked for massa 'bout four years after freedom 'cause he forced me to; said he couldn't 'ford to let me go. His place was near ruint, the fences burnt and the house would have been but it was rock. There was a battle fought near his place and I taken Missie to a hideout in the mountains to where her father was 'cause there was bullets flyin' everwhere.

"When the war was over, Massa come home and says, 'You son of a gun, you's sposed to be free, but you ain't, 'cause I ain't gwine give you freedom.' So, I goes on workin' for him till I gits the chance to steal a hoss from him. The woman I wanted to marry, Govie, she 'cides to come to Texas with me. Me and Govie we rides that hoss most a hundred miles, then we turned him a-loose and give him a scare back to his house, and come on foot the rest the way to Texas.

"All we had to eat was what we could beg, and sometimes we went three days without a bite to eat. Sometimes we'd pick a few berries. When we got cold, we'd crawl in a breshpile and hug up close together to keep warm. Once in awhile we'd come to a farmhouse and the man let us sleep on cottonseed in his barn, but they was far and few between 'cause they wasn't many houses in the country them days like now.

"When we gits to Texas we gits married, but all they was to our weddin' am we jus' 'grees to live together as man and wife. I settled on some land and we cut some trees and split them open and stood them on end with the tops together for our house. Then we deadened some trees and the land was ready to farm. There was some wild cattle and hawgs and that's the way we got our start, caught some of them and tamed them.

"I don't know as I 'spected nothin' from freedom, but they turned us out like a bunch of stray dogs, no homes, no clothin', no nothin', not 'nough food to last one meal. After we settles on that place, I never seed man or woman, 'cept Govie, for six years 'cause it was a long ways to anywhere. All we had to farm with was sharp sticks. We'd stick holes and plant corn and when it come up we'd punch up the dirt round it. We didn't plant cotten 'cause we couldn't eat that. I made bows and arrows to kill wild game with, and we never went to a store for nothin'. We made our clothes of animal skins."   ***Toby Jones***

* * * * *

"I sometimes wish I's back on the plantation. I's took good care of and massa am awful good . . . Not once does I know of de massa whippin', and him don't talk rough even."   ***Zek Brown***

* * * * *

"Old Marse bad. He beat us till we bleed. He rub salt and pepper in. One time I sweep de yard. Young miss come home from college. She slap my face. She want to beat me. Mama say to beat her, so dey did. She took de beatin' for me."

Agatha Babino

* * * * *

"He sends me for firewood and when I gits it loaded, de wheel hits a stump and de team jerks and dat breaks de whippletree. So he ties me to de stake and every half hour for four hours, dey lays ten lashes on my back. For de first couple hours de pain am awful . . . den I's stood so much pain I not feel so much . . . I lays in de bunk two days gittin' over dat whippin' . . . in de body, but not de heart. No, suh. I has dat in de heart till die day."

Andy Anderson

* * * * *

"When I'm 'bout seventeen, I marries a gal while master on drunk spell . . . He takes a big, long knife and cuts her head plumb off, and ties a great weight to her and makes me throw her in the river. Then he puts me in chains and every night he come give me a whippin' for a long time . . . Master helt me long years after the war. If anybody git after him, he told them I stay 'cause I wants to stay, but told me if I left, he'd kill him 'nother nigger.

". . . Master got kilt . . . I nearly starved to death befo' I'd leave New Orleans . . . Finally I gits up nerve to leave town, and stays the first night in white man's barn . . . Every time I hears something, I jumps up and master be standin' there, lookin' at me, but soon's I git up he'd leave. Next night I slep' out in a hay field, and master he git right top of a tree and start hollerin' at me . . . I gits back to town fast as my legs carry me.

"Then I gits locked up in jail. I don't know what for, never did know. One the men . . . takes me to the woods and gives me an ax. I cuts rails till I nearly falls, all with chain locked 'round feet so I couldn't run off. He turns me loose and I . . . starts roamin' 'gain like a stray dog. After long time I marries Feline Graham. Then I has a home . . . You know, the nigger was wild till the white man made what he has out of the nigger. He done ed'cate them real smart."

Frank Bell

* * * * *

"The rows was a mile long, and no matter how much grass was in them, if you leaves one sprig on your row, they beats you nearly to death."

Wes Brady

* * * * *

"Dere a old cullud man name George and he don't trouble nobody, but one night de white caps — dat what dey called —

comes to George's place. Now, George know of some folks what was whupped for no cause, so he prepare for dem white caps. When dey gits to he house, George am in de loft. He tell dem he done nothin' wrong and for dem to go 'way, or he kill dem. Dey say he gwine have a free sample of what he git if he do wrong, and one dem white cap starts up de ladder to git George, and George shoot him dead. 'Nother white cap starts shootin' through de ceilin'. He can't see George, but through de cracks George can see, and he shoots de second feller. So dey leaves and say dey come back. George runs to he old massa and he takes George to de law men. Never nothin' am done 'bout him killin' de white caps, 'cause dem white caps goes 'round 'busing niggers."

Charley Hurt

* * * * *

"My papa was strong. He never had a lick in his life. He helped the marster, but one day the marster says, 'Si, you got to have a whoppin', and my poppa says, 'I never had a whoppin' and you cain't whop me.' An the marster says, 'But I kin kill you,' an' he shot my poppa down. My mama tuk him in the cabin and put him on a pallet. He died.

". . . My mama had two white chillen by marster and they were sold as slaves . . . When women was with child they'd dig a hole in the groun' and put their stomach in the hole, and then beat 'em. They'd allus whop us." *Mother Anne Clark*

* * * * *

"My earliest recollection is the day my old boss presented me to his son, Joe, as his property. I was about five years old and my new master was only two." *Martin Jackson*

* * * * *

"Had to get out there fore it was light, hoe in hand. Boss man there with whip. When light enough to hoe, give order, 'Heads up!' Then lots of women fell dead over the hoe . . . When women fell dead, lie right there till night where body drop."

Uncle William Oliver

* * * * *

"Massa have overseer and overlooker. De overseer am in

charge of wo'k, and de overlooker am in charge of de cullud women. De overseer give all de whippin's. Sometimes when de nigger gits late, 'stead of comin' home and takin' de whippin' him goes to de caves of de river and stays and jus' comes in night time for food. When dey do dat, de dogs is put after dem and den it am de fight 'tween de nigger and de dawg . . . When dey whips for runnin' off, de nigger am tied down over a barrel and whipped ha'd, till dey draws blood, sometimes.

"Now I tell 'bout some good times. We is 'lowed to have parties and de dance . . . Sometimes dey have jiggin' contest and two niggers puts a glass of water on dere heads and den see who can dance de longes' without spillin' any water. Den we has log rollin . . . Sometimes a couple am 'lowed to git married, and dere am extry fixed for supper. Sometimes de overlooker don' let dem git married. I 'splains it dis way. He am used to father de chillun . . . Dem dat he picks, he overlooks, and not 'low dem to marry, or to go round with other nigger men. If dey do, it's whippin' sho'."

Fred Brown

The following excerpts are from Slave Narratives, South Carolina, *Volumes I and II.*

* * * * *

"A man once married his ma an' didn't know it. He was sell from her w'en 'bout eight years old. When he grow to a young man, slavery then was over, he met this woman he like' an' so they were married. They was married a month w'en one night they started to tell of their experiences an' how many times they was sold. The husban' tol' how he was sol' from his mother who liked him dearly. He tol' how his ma faint' w'en they took him away an' how his master then use to bran' his baby slaves at a year ol'. W'en he showed her the bran' she faint' 'cause she then realize' that she had married her son."

Henry Brown

* * * * *

"I was de youngest slave, so Missy Grace, dats Massa Joe's wife, keep me in de house most of de time, to cook and keep de house cleaned up. I milked de cow and worked in de garden too. My massa was good to all he slaves, but Missy Grace was mean to us. She whip us a heap of times when we ain't done nothing bad to be whip for. When she go to whip me, she tie my wrists together wid a rope and put that rope thru a big staple in de ceiling and draw me up off de floor and give me a hundred lashes. I think 'bout my old mammy heap of times now and how I's seen her whipped, wid de blood dripping off of her."   *Fannie Griffin*

* * * * *

"I wants to be in hebben wid all my white folks, just to wait on them, and love them and serve them, sorta lak I did in slavery time. Dat will be 'nough hebben for Adeline."
Adeline Johnson, alias Adeline Hall

* * * * *

"My old masser was as good and kind to me as he could be, so was my missus. My mother died when I was ten years old, and Missus was just like a mother to me all the time . . . Old Missus used to come to the house where I lived and teach me my alphabet . . . I . . . used to hitch-up the horse for him and go with him on his way to see a patient. Bless his heart, he let me take my Webster's blue back speller and my history with me when I would drive with him. I would study those books and Masser would tell me how to pronounce the hard words. That is the way I got my education. Master would tell Missus that Jimmie was a smart boy, that he had no father nor mother and that they must be good to him. They sure was. I never wanted for a thing. Sometimes on our drives Masser would tell me some Latin words, but I never did study Latin — just English . . . Missus would let me practice on her organ or her piano in the house. I got pretty good on these, so when I got to be a young man, I taught lessons on both the reed organ and the melodian, then on the piano."   *J. J. Murray*

* * * * *

"Christmas mornin' marster would call all de slaves to come to de Christmas tree . . . Don't tell me dat wasn't de next step to heaven to de slaves on our plantation. I sees and dreams 'bout them good old times, back yonder, to dis day."
Junius Quattlebaum

* * * * *

" 'Twas not 'til de year '66 dat we got 'liable info'mation and felt free to go where us pleased to go. Most of de niggers left, but Mammy stayed on and cooked for Dr. Sam and de white folks. Bad white folks comed and got bad niggers started. Soon things got wrong and de devil took a hand in de mess. Out of it come to de top, de carpet bag, de scalawags and then de Ku Klux. Night rider come by and drap something at your door and say: 'I'll just leave you something for dinner.' Then ride off in a gallop. When you open de sack, what you reckon in dere? Liable to be one thing, liable to be another. One time it was six nigger heads dat was left at de door. Was it at my house door? Oh, no! It was at de door of a nigger too active in politics.

". . . [I] Can read, but [I] can't write. Our slaves was told if ever they learned to write, they'd lose de hand or arm they wrote wid."

Robert Toatley

* * * * *

Uncle Bill said there was some humor at times when a slave was whipped. His hands and feet tied together, the slave would be laid across a rail fence, feet danglin' on one side and head on the other side; then the master would give the slave a push or shove and he would fall heavily on the ground on his head. Not being able to use his feet or his hands, the slave's efforts to catch himself before he hit the ground was something funny. "That was funny to us Niggers looking at it, but not funny to the Nigger tied up so."

Uncle Bill Young

JUNETEENTH, FIRST AFRICAN-AMERICAN HOLIDAY
Gift of Texas

Marian E. Barnes

"Juneteenth," the first African-American holiday, commemorates June 19, 1865, the day on which captives in the state of Texas first learned that slavery had ended, and they were free.

President Abraham Lincoln had abolished slavery in Southern states — where the federal government which he headed had no authority — by signing the Emancipation Proclamation on January 1, 1863. Interestingly, the president had also signed a measure which left the "Peculiar Institution" intact in states that bordered the South where the federal government did have power to act. Therefore, some four million people remained enslaved in these states until the military collapse of the Southern Confederacy in the spring of 1865.

The Emancipation Proclamation declared that all captives enslaved in Southern states were free as of January 1, 1863. Further, if any of these states did not free those people being held in bondage within its territory, the Union Army would come in, read the Emancipation Proclamation, and administer the process of releasing captives.

Many states maintained slavery until the Union Army took over, and captives in such states were freed on whatever day the army arrived. As a result, the day on which slavery ended and captives were emancipated differed in various states, sometimes by more than a year. Even so, people in these states usually adopted January 1, 1863, as Emancipation Day.

On June 19, 1865, two and a half years after the signing of the Emancipation Proclamation, a U.S. government ship sailed into the harbor at Galveston, Texas, bearing Gen. Gordon Granger. The general came ashore and read the Emancipation Proclamation, and Texas became the last state to end slavery. Since then, African-Americans of Texas have celebrated June 19 as "Juneteenth," Day of Emancipation.

Through the years, the custom has waxed and flourished by turn, sometimes surrounded by controversy. There are those who object to observing the Juneteenth holiday, saying it is based on a "paper freedom" which they contend has yet to become a reality. Still others have refused to participate, protesting that the custom commemorates a "gift of freedom" from Abraham Lincoln, and they insist freedom was not his to give or withhold. And there are those who look askance at the day which they interpret as an undeserved memorial to Abraham Lincoln, recalling Lincoln's statement in his letter to Horace Greeley written August 22, 1862: *"My paramount objective in this struggle is to save the Union, and is not either to save or to destroy slavery. If I could save the Union without freeing any slave, I would do it; and if I could do it by freeing all the slaves, I would do it; and if I could save it by freeing some and leaving others alone, I would also do that."*[1] At

---

1. *Dictionary of Quotations,* Bergen Evans (New York: Delacorte Press, 1968).

present Juneteenth celebrations are mushrooming around the country, fueled in part by former Texans who have moved to other states and imported the holiday, and in part by activists who are saying, "Let us all celebrate Juneteenth, not for the Emancipation Proclamation, whose true objective will forever remain in doubt, not for any power broker of the slave society, not for Abraham Lincoln, who never showed concern for the human rights of enslaved people, but for those long struggling, long suffering Abolitionists and Underground Railroad Freedom Fighters like Frederick Douglass, Harriet Tubman, Gabriel Prosser, and Denmark Vesey, who fought from day number one of slavery in this society to make Juneteenth a reality."

WE MET A LITTLE TRAGEDY ON A NAVASOTA PLANTATION

Excerpt from *I AM ANNIE MAE:*
The Personal Story of a Black Texas Woman
Collected and edited by Ruthe Winegarten

Five or six years after Mama moved to Dallas — she were married again, must have been 1922 — it was Depression time[1] — and we moved down to Navasota, on a plantation in Grimes County, where we met a little tragedy. Navasota, Grimes County, was just across the river from Brenham, Washington County. And Washington County was a free country, and Grimes County was slavery — well, that's what they say. Well, it was like slavery times, it was, it was. I worked in the fields down there. This old man had a big bell, and they rang the bell for them to unhook the mules and come to dinner, ring the bell for them to go back out at 1 o'clock; you know, that kind of stuff.

We had been back about seven or eight months, maybe not that long, when my stepdaddy Wilson said something out of line

---

1. In the early 1920s, American agriculture entered into a sharp and damaging depression. Prices of farm land and food fell, while almost all the costs of farming stayed the same or rose. At the same time, banks in the South and West cut back on credit issued to farmers. Thousands of tenant farmers, Black and white, were either out of work or not earning enough to buy the basic necessities. (Russell Lord, *The Wallaces of Iowa* (Boston: Houghton Mifflin, 1947), 169, 218-219).

that wasn't for Black people to say in that time. I never knew exactly what he said. Anyway, that evening when my stepdaddy put his mules up, Old Man Kirk, the overseer, he's dead now, called to him and said, "Now, Wilson, I know you didn't know what you were saying, but they're gonna come out here tonight and whup you up." He told my stepdaddy not to stay home that night. So my stepdaddy decided he wasn't going to take no whuppin. He laid down in the branch, and he say he seen two cars drive up with five mens, three mens driving in one car, two in another, and when he seen those mens drive by the house, he went berserk, he went half nuts. He was 'tween the house and the Brazos River. Went that way to the Brazos River. He knew where people left their boats, but he say he don't even remember getting there. He don't know how he got across that Brazos River. But he crossed that Brazos River.

Those white people come in our house, and they pushed my mama around, pushed her up against the wall; told her she better get that *nigger* back, and of course we were standing there trembling, me and my brother and sister, just like little leaves on the tree when the wind's going through it. When they left, my mama decided that she couldn't stay there, she was leaving. Sent my brother to Brenham, and Grandpa sent us some fare. So we got ready one day, and went to town, so we could catch that train going down to Hempstead from Navasota.

It run about 2 or 3 or 4 o'clock in the morning. We were sitting there at Miss Sissy's house, laughing and talking, playing, the children. About 10:30 or 11 o'clock at night, here come Mr. Bud Jones [2] and told my mama, "Come on out here."

She said, "I'm not going out there." And, of course, we all stood still when Mama spoke up, cause that's the only thing we had was Mama. He grabbed her, and pushed her out the door and off the porch, and she stumbled. And he pushed her on out the gate, an old gate, and when she got to the car, Old Man Morrett, he hauled off and slapped her three or four times, and throwed her in the front seat of the car. Then, at that time, we come running, me and my sister. My brother was gone. We jumped in the back seat,

---

2. Bud Jones was a Black man who was apparently forced to do the bidding of Old Man Morrett, a white man. Said Mrs. Hunt: "Whatever Morret say, Bud done. Old Man Morrett had Bud under some kind of spell or had something held over him. Now Bud Jones was his slave, some kind of slave."

and they had her in the front seat with them, and slapped her and asked her questions all the way to the Navasota River near the farm, going on back down toward our house.

And you know, Old Man Morrett whipped her, and Bud Jones holding her. My mama couldn't walk for 13 weeks. And they broke my arm. This old guy, this overseer Mr. Kirk, told Mama there was no doubt it was broke. I had to hold my arm in a sling like this two or three times a day, and then Mama'd change it, and it come down. Then I'd put it back up, then back down, so it wouldn't grow stiff. I have trouble with it now, always have. I understand that where you been broke once, arthritis is fall in those places. And Old Man Morrett broke my sister's nose with a pistol. Mama had to take paper and tear it up, and put it up her nose so the wind could go through it, and it could heal up. By being broken here and knocked apart, by them keeping it pressed open, it made it grow funny. I'm sorry I'm crying. That was the way. That is what happened long time ago. [3]

WARTIME TROLLEY

Marian E. Barnes

The following story recounts a ride on a Philadelphia trolley car in 1944, after National Guard troops had put down a city riot which erupted when a federal directive forced the city's transportation company to hire African-American operators on streetcars.

Anyone, anyone at all may be seen on Number 40 trolley car. Genuine royalty, enrolled at the University of Pennsylvania; shipyard laborers who never learned to write; Genivieve Duane, of Bryn Mawr and 20 hundred Locust Street; and Dave Jackson, of The Bottom,[1] who cleans sewers for a living.

---

3. Although there is no evidence that the attack on Annie Mae and her family was that of the Ku Klux Klan, the 1920s saw the KKK making a strong comeback in Texas. Their crimes of murder, rape, and arson were particularly numerous in Southeast Texas. In 1924 Ma Ferguson, the first woman ever elected governor, won office on an anti-Klan platform. Under her leadership the legislature passed an anti-mask bill, which finally crippled the Klan.

1. A Philadelphia neighborhood so named by inhabitants because of the low sequence of its numbered streets, as opposed to "The Top," with higher numbered streets. The name also came to relate to the economic state of the area.

Before sunrise one foggy morning in late August of 1944, Number 40 crawled out of the wharf section and Mathilda and Julie were the first passengers to board. Every morning at this time they returned, unkempt and disheveled, from a night along the river front. Mathilda was fat, platinum, and forty-six. Julie was bony, impossibly red-headed, and forty-eight. Huge blobs of paint masked their aging faces. A strong smell of liquor enveloped the conductor as they paid their fares and went back in the car.

At the next corner a happy drunk on his way back to The Bottom got on gleefully singing "Three Blind Mice." He sat behind the iron rail in the middle of the car, crossed his legs, and began to wave his hands in time with the tune as though he were conducting a symphony orchestra.

A few Defense Department workers boarded next, some going to work, some returning home. Then Charlie, the Irish conductor, remembered the joke he'd meant to tell Joe, the coal black motorman. It couldn't wait. He whisked away to the front. Anyone wanting to get off would ring the buzzer and he'd hear it.

But he didn't hear the buzzer. The irate Defense worker pushed it, and pushed it again. But the joke was a good one, and Charlie knew just how to tell it. The trolley whizzed past the crucial corner.

"HEY!"

"I'm sorry. I'm sorry." Charlie hot-footed it back to the conductor's booth.

"SORRY HELL!" yelled a minute, dark-skinned woman with a stentorian voice. "That was my stop! It hasn't been three weeks since you was killin' one 'nother 'bout driving these damn trolleys, and now you're so blame thick people have to ride past their stops while you keep each other company! You take colored people for a damn fool!"

"Ma'am?" The conductor was bewildered.

"I said: You take colored people for a damn fool! But you ain't so smart! I got your number every time!"

Charlie's perplexity was not mitigated by this series of remarks. "Honest, lady," he began, "I didn't mean . . ."

"Aw, shut up, and let me off before you pass **this** stop! I ought to report you."

When she got off, the drunk, who had stopped singing during the excitement, resumed his musical tale of three blind mice. Charlie went over and spoke to him.

"I ain' botherin' nobody. Jus' singin' a li'l song."

"Yeah, but you're singing too loud."

"All right. All right," he said cooperatively, then began to sing almost inaudibly, waving his hands and posturing like a concertmaster.

Just as Charlie turned away, a rock came crashing through one of the windows. "Wake up, you niggers and Jews! You sleep on the job all night!"

The drowsy, dozing passengers were jarred back to life. Tiny splinters of glass flew everywhere, and the trolley screeched to a stop. Charlie opened the door and looked out, but it was still dark, and he saw no one. "Was anyone hurt?" He grabbed his book and pencil.

There were a few very minor bruises and scratches, but the passengers refused to have their injuries recorded. Charlie was putting away his book, and Joe was about to resume driving, when a moan from the rear of the trolley stopped them. A plump, white-haired woman was clutching her heart. Both Joe and Charlie rushed to her side.

"What's the matter?"

"I yam hoit," she panted.

"HURT!"

"How?"

"Joost now — the rock —"

"The **rock**? The rock came through the front of the car, and you're in the back!"

"Yess, but you see, ven the car stopt fast, I vas shook up!"

There were derisive cries from the other passengers: "Fake!" "Somebody call an ambulance!" "She'll settle out of court for ten thousand!" But the lady was unabashed. Charlie must write up the injury and solicit the names of witnesses.

The trolley moved off to the accompaniment of "Three Blind Mice," which was once more gaining volume. People piled on at every stop now. When Mathilda and Julie got up to get off at 12th Street, they had to push and worm their way toward the door. Mathilda made better progress than Julie, who was forced to stop dead about three feet from the door.

"Hey, Tillie," she yelled coarsely, "give me a pull, will ya?" Mathilda reached behind her for the hand that Julie extended, and gave a yank that brought Julie spinning through the crowd; and sent a number of passengers sprawling on top of still other passengers who were sitting down. Not one of the upset passengers protested, however. The tough, seamed faces of Mathilda and Julie inspired humility.

"Make way for the lady with the baby! Y'all let this lady with the baby off at 13th," a gruff man's voice pleaded from the extreme front of the car. The impossible happened. In their sympathy for this unfortunate lady who must carry a baby through such a horde, people melted, into the seats, into each other, and formed a tiny aisle. Down this aisle an unshaved dwarf of a man appeared, walking with ease! Whenever a hip, or a leg, or an elbow appeared to block his path, he caused the erring member to melt away by renewing his roguish cry. "Let the lady through, please. Here comes the lady with the baby!"

"BROAD STREET! BROAD STREET NEXT!" Charlie shouted. This was the only stop that he ever called. And he called it loud and often. "BROAD STREET! CHANGE HERE FOR THE SUBWAY!" People jammed both doorways, those at the exit half jumping, half falling out; hordes at the front, some trying to enter, others trying to leave at the same instant. The unfortunates standing in the aisle were pushed, squeezed, and mashed unmercifully.

A pretty girl in tight-fitting slacks could hardly keep hold of the strap, and almost lost her lunch tin in the rush. A man who had been watching her a long time, and who was not so young as he used to be, was moved to give her his seat. She came when he beckoned. He slid out of his seat, accidentally stepping on the foot of an old lady standing over him. He was terribly sorry, and meant to say so; but just then the girl smiled at him by way of saying thank you. He lost consciousness of everything except that he must return the smile — almost lost consciousness, that is, for he touched the old lady's elbow in a vague, gentle gesture of apology.

"You hit me!" a prim, little woman said to the musical drunk.

And indeed with a wide, vigorous sweep of his hand to indicate the emphasis on the note for "blind," he had knocked her hat askew.

"Oh, oh!" He lifted the hat away from her adjusting fingers and clumsily began to adjust it himself. "I will do it," he said thickly. "I will do it."

The woman snatched her hat away, with a glare that sent her assistant far back into his corner, and for full half-a-minute killed the urge to sing "Three Blind Mice." Her vexation spread to the unsuspecting gentleman being crushed by the crowd against her other side. "If you want to go to bed," she said tersely, "I'll get up!"

Just then Joe turned the lights off inside the car. The sun was coming up.

"Get your hand out of my pocket!"

"You talkin' to ME?"

"Yeah, YOU!"

"I DIDN'T HAVE MY HAND IN YOUR POCKET!"

"Oh, yes you did! Yes you did! I saw you!"

"What the hell I'm gonna put my hand in your pocket for? I got money."

"I don't give a damn! Your hand was in my pocket!"

"I ain't takin' that off of nobody! Take it back, or I'll cut you four ways, long, wide, deep and re-pee-tidly!"

"You're takin' it off me! Your knife don't scare me none, brother. Bring it on! Bring it on!"

"Put 'em off! Put 'em off! I gotta get to work!" someone shouted.

"Yeah, put 'em off!"

Joe opened the doors, and several people pushed the belligerent gentlemen. They tumbled into the street, rolling over and over, fists flying; and Number 40 moved on.

At 26th Street the Marine Corps employees got off, leaving the trolley far less crowded. A huge, flawlessly neat man found that he could move away from the front doors. He walked into the car and caught a strap directly over a woman, who took one look at his broad, black face and hopped up. He contemplated her mildly, and slowly withdrew from his pocket a snowy white handkerchief. Then, with every eye upon him, he used the obviously new handkerchief to carefully wipe off the vacant seat. He worked with cool deliberation. No crevice or crack escaped him. When he had finished he reached over, flung the window wide, and pitched the handkerchief out. Then he seated himself with the complacency of a great, amiable cow. He chose not to join in the hearty laughter of his fellow travelers, or to gloat at the crab-red face of the woman who had watched him, unable to move.

Finally, it occurred to her that she would be happier out of sight of this man. She moved angrily away. As luck would have it, a dusty gentleman boarded the trolley at the next corner, made his way back, and inadvertently brushed against the humiliated woman. He paused, obviously to apologize, but the pinched, revolted look on her face arrested him. He came to a halt, grabbed a strap, and leaned close to her ear. "Ef you don' like it," he whispered, "git on off!" He continued almost inaudibly. "They runs taxi service twenny fo' hours a day for the likes of you, so you kin be nice an' comf'table on yo' chauffeur's day off!"

Now that the sun was high, "Three Blind Mice" gained unbearable volume. Charlie was forced to admonish the singer once again. "You're annoying everybody. If you don't stop, I'll have to put you off."

"Don' put me off." The man's eyes got watery. "I won' sing loud no more." He subsided meekly. But for all his good intentions, the song grew loud of itself. He just couldn't help it. Louder and louder, louder and louder. His hands beat the air. It was such a joy to sing! Then he saw Charlie coming again.

"All right, Bud. Let's go."

"No. No. No. 'Sall right. I'll sing quiet."

"No. I'm sorry. You said that before. Here's your carfare. You have to get off."

At once the man began to cry. "I didn't bother nobody," he whined.

"You're about to run us all crazy with that song!"

"I wasn' botherin' a soul. Jus' singin' a li'l song, tha's all," he pleaded. Charlie put his arm beneath the man's shoulders and half guided, half carried him to the door.

"The Lord is gonna get you! It would be better for a mill stone to be hung roun' your neck. I didn' do nothin'. The Lord will fix you for this."

Once in the street, the drunken tears increased. Charlie led him gently out of the street and onto the sidewalk, then returned to the car.

"Oh, the Lord will fix you. He will fix you. I didn' do nothin', an' you put me off. 'Sall right. 'Sall right. Gawd sees everything."

Number 40 rolled away, leaving the erstwhile passenger standing on the corner. However, for full half a block the man could be heard crying brokenly, his sobbing words wafting through the open windows of the trolley:

"Oh, the Lord is gonna get you — YOU SON OF A BITCH!"

The bright rays of the sun had dispelled the last vestige of fog when Number 40 droned along the last blocks of its route. Joe heaved a relieved sigh as the final passenger alighted.

"The war has everybody's nerves on edge. That's why there's so much excitement on these trolleys."

"It's worse since the war, all right," Charlie answered. "But I don't know. You always could see a lot on 40."

"All of life, I guess," Joe said. "All of life — all at once."

GONE WITH THE WIND:
JESSIE MAE HICKS REMEMBERS TIMES PAST

Jessie Mae Hicks
As told to Marian E. Barnes

She is in her seventies, but you would never know it. Small and full of life, Jessie Mae Hicks is the founder of Hicks Beauty School in San Antonio, Texas, from where she has taught hundreds of people to earn a living. Through the years, she has combined her highly successful business activities with a dedicated effort to improve the world around her. During the civil rights revolution, she traveled the country as an activist. Since then, she frequently honors requests that she return to cities where she once demonstrated for civil rights and tell audiences about life as it used to be.

Perhaps her most vivid memories are of marching with Dr. Martin Luther King, Jr., in 1965 in Selma, Alabama, protesting for the right of African-American citizens to vote. "Dr. King would walk up and down beside the marchers," she recalled. "He would say, 'I want all of you men to walk on the outside lines. Mothers, please stay on the inside lines, keep the children with you, and hold the younger children by the hand. We're nearing a small town now, and I don't know what may happen.'

"We went to the office of Gov. George Wallace," she said. "When we got there we were told, 'The governor is drinking a pop and eating a sandwich. He can't see you now.'" Nevertheless, Ms. Hicks added, such rebuffs failed to put down the protest, or stop the improvements the marchers were demanding.

Audiences learn from the vivacious Ms. Hicks about life in Texas before the civil rights struggle. "You couldn't wear a big hat like you're wearing now," she said to a man in an Austin outdoor audience. "If a Black man wore a big hat, or fancy boots, or an expensive tie into the city, he got beat up. Black people had to ride in the back of the buses, and use separate toilets. Sometimes there weren't any toilets for Black people. And if you wanted a drink of water, you had to find a water fountain marked 'colored.' Once a Black man got caught drinking water from a 'white' water fountain and they knocked his head into the fountain and broke his nose."

Remembering life sixty-four years ago in Grapeland, Texas, her hometown, Ms. Hicks described a racially segregated one-room schoolhouse she attended. "Every day we had morning devotions. There was a line drawn on the ground in the schoolyard playground to separate males and females; and we had one Black teacher who taught all of the students from first grade to eighth grade. Children brought a lunch bucket to school carrying a meal; usually there was a layer of syrup on the bottom, then a biscuit, a layer of fat meat, and a potato on top," she said.

In Grapeland, many people made a living by planting cotton. Ms. Hicks has pleasant memories of cows that gave "sweet milk," from which families churned butter and made buttermilk and clabbermilk; and of Christmas time, when children hung their stockings by the fireplace on Christmas Eve for Santa Claus to fill when he came down the chimney. On Christmas morning, they woke to find their stockings bulging with apples and oranges, a bit of candy, decorated pine cones, and, sometimes, a handmade toy.

Ms. Hicks recalls that Juneteenth was a gala, two-day celebration that started on June 18. Festivities included overnight guests, dinner "spreads" on the ground after church, and hog killings, where children lined up to help "draw the liver out" of the animal, make a fire, and broil the liver. *Good eating!* Since there was no refrigeration, she said parents would bring ice and bury it in the ground overnight. On Juneteenth, it would be dug up and used to cool drinks and make ice cream for the Juneteenth celebration.

"A child's life was very different from today," Ms. Hicks said. Among the chores for children: gather eggs; feed the younger children; slop the hogs (with dishwater); fill the oil lamps; trim the lamp wick; clean the lamp chimney; sweep the yard; remove the ashes from fireplaces and woodstoves. Also, when a family had guests for a meal, it was the job of the children, using a large tree branch, to fan flies away from the food on the table while the guests ate.

Children wore clothes made from bags in which stores sold flour, sugar, chicken feed, and so on. Parents used water they had poured on ashes to bleach printing off the sacks, then used the cloth to make towels and sheets and clothes that they decorated with fancy stitches, ribbons, and embroidery.

Boys wore "stove pipe" pants and knickers until they were almost grown. Girls wore long dresses and skirts, or fancy, balloon-type bloomers that extended beneath the hemline of shorter dresses. Both boys and girls wore "high top" shoes that laced up over the ankles. They were called "bilikings." Much later, girls began to wear anklets that covered the ankles and allowed part of the bare legs to show. People called them "whoopie socks."

Women made beautiful quilts back then, Ms. Hicks recalled. They used every scrap of cloth they could find — old sheets and towels, and clothing that had gone into holes. Nothing was ever thrown away. When women visited each other, they would sit and talk and work on the housewife's quilt together.

When there was a death in the family, women wore black for a year. The second year after the death they went into what was called "second mourning" and wore dark colors. By the beginning of the third year, they could start wearing lighter colors, but sometimes by then someone else had died and they had to start wearing black all over again. Men wore black arm bands when they were in mourning. Strips of black cloth were stitched around the upper part of the sleeves of the arms of their suits to make the bands. Eventually, men began to wear only one arm band. They wore it on the left arm because it was nearer the heart.

Ms. Hicks remembers the time the whole country was doing jigsaw puzzles. Some puzzles were beautiful pictures, so large they almost covered the dining room table. When company came to a house, they would go straight to the dining room table, sit down, and everyone had fun working on a puzzle together. They also enjoyed putting a puzzle together as a family. "Sometimes it took days to find a special puzzle piece," she said. "At other times, there was a piece that kept fooling us. It almost fit a million places, but in the end, it didn't even belong to that puzzle! When we finally finished, we would look at our perfect picture, proud of what we had done, then we would break it up and start all over again, or start another puzzle."

According to Ms. Hicks, store-bought toothbrushes were not

part of those times. Teeth were brushed with a "tooth brush" made from a special tree branch. "Chewing gum" was the peeled stem of the sweet gum tree. There were no dentists in Grapeland. A tooth was pulled by tying one end of a string around the ailing tooth and the other around the knob of an open door, then slamming the door shut! The antidote for insect bites was an application of snuff retrieved by an older person from its cache between lower lip and gum, and used to make a snuff "seam" around the bite of the insect. Facial tissues were unheard of in the community. Privileged people and industrious adults used fancy, cloth handkerchiefs that they bought or made. The poorer underclass and children used "snot rags."

Kotex did not exist in those days. Women used rags — parts of sheets, or undershirts, and so on — during their period, or "time-of-the-month' or "courses." Those were some of the names used for the menstrual cycle. When your period was over, you washed the rags in cold water so the stain would not set, and then you boiled them clean. They were dried in out-of-the-way-places, and each person kept hers in a separate bundle and hid them away until it was time for her menstrual period again.

There was no strained and bottled baby food to be purchased in stores in those years. Mothers chewed food for their babies, regardless of the bad shape of a mother's teeth. And nursing mothers nursed each other's babies.

On Sunday evenings, recalled Ms. Hicks, women sat on the "gary" or "garret" — it's called a porch nowadays — and combed and wrapped their daughters' hair into styles that might last for a week or more. They parted the hair into little squares, and circled each section of hair from scalp to end with strong thread. They made creative, artistic patterns and designs on the scalp, and beautiful hair styles. This way of wrapping hair was passed down from life in Africa.

Obviously feeling nostalgia for bygone times, Ms. Hicks said, "I was born in the Mount Zion rural community of Grapeland, Texas, so far out that when older people would hear trains rumbling in the distance they would say it was going to rain! There was family unity then that we do not have today. In those days we had family prayers all the time. And when one person would finish praying, another would begin by saying, 'Let us continue in prayer.' We don't have family prayers anymore. Families don't sit down around a table and eat together anymore either." Reminiscing about the years in Grapeland when mealtimes meant happy, healthy families seated around tables filled with plates and platters of hearty, country food and there was laughter, and caring, and sharing, she said sadly, "At dinner time nowadays you won't hear anyone say to somebody across the table, 'Pass the biscuits, please.' Those times are no more."

OF FAMILIES AND LOVE

GRANNIE JUS' COME!

Ana Sisnett

I's Tuesday afternoon! Grannie always come!
I's Tuesday after lunch! Grannie soon come!
Look over there, see! Grannie bus come!

She 'ave on new shoes Mommie give to her:
    "Dey fit me foot comfortable an nice y'see!"
She 'ave on the new dress Auntie sen' for her:
    "Come from States, it pretty, no missis?!"
She 'ave on 'er glasses, dey 'ave gol' rim:
    "Protec' me highs* from too much wind!"
She 'ave on 'er everyday wide brim blue straw hat:
    "For sun beat hot, hot, hot, no good for headtop."
She 'ave on 'er everyday two-strap blue purse. It 'ave
    *"busfare, kerchief, glasscase, plus peppermint candy
      and melcoche** for three."* Grannie say, *"You mus' share."*

I's Tuesday afternoon an' Grannie jus' come!

Come Grannie Come, si' dung right 'ere,
come tek a lickle*** res' for a while.
Pu' dung yu purse an' tek off yu hat.
Tek off yu glasses, pu' dem in de case.
Tek off yu shoes and pretty new dress.
Put Daddy slippers on an Mommy house dress.
Yu want some water? Yu want some tea?
Grannie say, *"Tanks me luv, yu sweet, no sugar!
But please fa some juice . . . and vanilla wafer? Two!"*

I's Tuesday after lunch an' Grannie jus' come!

Oh Grannie, Ah say, yu smell so good! She say:
    "A lickle talcum powder 'ere an' ere, tank yu me luv!"
Oh Grannie, Ah say, yu skin so soft! She say:
    "Lickle Pond's cream, rose water is all, but tank yu me luv!"
Oh Grannie, Ah say, yu hair so white! She say:
    "A good washin' an' blue rinse, yu like it? Tank yu me luv!"

---

  *eyes
  **peppermint stick candy
  ***little

Oh Grannie, Ah say, Ah luv yu so much! She say:
   "From Ah first set eyes 'pon yu, Ah luv yu plenty, plenty me luv!"

I's Tuesday afternoon an' *my* Grannie jus' come!

COMBING GRANDMA'S HAIR

Dorothy Charles Banks

Can I comb your long,
heavy hair, Grandma?
Can I dress it up with
seventy ribbons,
letting them hang
loosely down your
long, long neck,
so strong, so sweetly brown?
Can I braid your silver hair
in tiny stems of cornrow
love like you still do mine
when your aging fingers
feel healthy and agile
with speed?

Can I comb your long
heavy hair, Grandma?
Like you did my mama's
when she was a little
girl sitting snugly between
your soft brown knees,
feeling love ooze like
raw maple syrup as your
nimble fingers created
new words for her to sing?

Can I comb your long,
silver hair, Grandma?
And create new words
and songs for my daughters
to sing when their fingers
feel loose, nimble and quick?

WHAT IS A GRANDFATHER?
Christine Wright

He's the path to the river on a sunny day,
A baiter of hooks, new games to play;

He's the fun and games at the park,
Strong hands to hold when you're scared of the dark.

He's the storyteller of all time
With his wise and knowing eyes.
With all this and more, it comes as no surprise
That Grandpas are needed by every boy and girl;
He's the most special person in this whole world.

WARM THOUGHTS
Farhana Qazi

Grandfather falls asleep in the chair,
wrapped in his armor —
the store bought quilts.
'Don't like it,'
he says,
'hurts my body,
interrupts my thoughts.'
He refers to the cold and the violent wind
that sweeps by him
until it reaches a dead end.
We help grandfather out of his chair
and into his bed.
'I can think now,'
he says,
'good, warm, solid thoughts.'
He falls asleep
with heavy words resting on his lips.

FOR ANNA MAE
Rebecca Sims

In a small town in Ohio
on an even smaller street,
in an even smaller,

whitewashed old house,
spirits dance.
In the dim light,
surrounded by dark
wallpaper and wood,
reflected in the rainbow-glass
on the sideboard,
ghosts waltz.

Ivory lace
and eggshell porcelain
are on the table,
while miles away
my great-grandmother
dies.
This is her house.

MOTHER

April Parra

My head wears your hair
    as you did when you were young.
My face is your face
    but I have my father's eyes.
I can wear your clothes,
    and sometimes you borrow mine.
We look good in the same colors
    and our tastes are similar.
Sometimes this works against us:
    I did not inherit my father's easy agreement,
I received your stubbornness.
Us two, we could be the Great Wall,
    we can be so unchanging.
We butt heads like goats
    or a type of prehistoric dinosaur.
Maybe we are dinosaurs:
    little plastic figures with scales
and sharp teeth.
    You'd be the Tyrannosaurus
and I'd be some quiet herbivore
    until our stubbornness kicked in.

> Then we'd be Boneheads again
> crashing and crashing
> in some grassy prehistoric plain.

TO JOAN, MY LOVING DAUGHTER

Marian E. Barnes

It seems just a whispered prayer ago that I held you in my arms on the first day of your life knowing all days before had only been prelude to this moment. How quickly they came and went, the years of infant cuddling, watching the wonder in your darting eyes as I showed you things: the sky, clouds, a man, a moving car; of coach-pushing while you explored the air with tiny fingers, learning about the weather; of holding your hand while you toddled, making friends with people and animals; and calming your young fears of an antique light fixture and one strange-looking tree.

Now I see myself jumping, at your request, to pick tree leaves for us to examine. I relive the wrenching, bittersweet memory of your first day at school; the fun we had skating, picnicking, and traveling together; the endless rounds of ballet and piano lessons and programs, girl scouting, camp outings, choir singing. I recall sad days we shared after the deaths of loved ones, and during family strife; and growing-pains squabbles we had when you were thirteen, often about your cluttered bedroom; and how you always won the battle by vigorously enumerating socially prevalent disastrous behaviors of which you were not guilty; and how I would subside, thinking I was blessed indeed that you kept a chaotic room! Then, very suddenly, you were graduating from high school, your girlhood behind you.

When did it happen? I remember the first time you moved inside my body, your first smile, your first word, your first tooth, your first step. But I do not know when you first blossomed into womanhood. One instant you were a little girl, the next, a young woman, and though I had strained to capture the moments of change, they had eluded me!

Now you stand on the threshold of marriage, about to take an irreversible step into God's plan for complete womanhood and the family. How proud I am of you! Although I have served in several professions, traveled the world, and through the miracle of electronics touched millions of lives, having you as a daughter is the experience beside which all others fade. You have blessed my life with love, wonder, beauty, understanding, and happy laughter.

Now, as you walk into tomorrow, I delight in the inner beauty of your womanhood. I joy in the love, wisdom, and honor you will bring to your husband, your children, and your home. I glory in the strength and purpose that springs from your life, touches others, and enriches the world around you!

GRANDMOTHER'S ROOM

Joan Barnes Stewart

There is a worn spot in the rug beside my grandmother's bed where she has said her prayers for almost two decades. Each dawn and evening she has knelt there to pray and to praise the God who had sustained her and her loved ones down through the years. An antique chandelier, with four of its crystals missing, disperses dim, yellow light, shining with the memory of glories now past. On the floor by the dresser, the bronze statuette of a once majestic Great Dane is now only a tired ornament fallen on its side but still at attention. And there is an old, beautiful needlepoint stool, its vibrant colors now muted by time; forest green interrupted by patterns in the palest pinks, stitched so long ago.

So many memories of so many things in Grandmother's room. A rocking chair with a broken arm fixed up just right with Grandpapa's homemade all-purpose glue. The biggest, softest bed in the world was in there. *Her bed.* To lie in it would have been like dying and going to Glory. To get caught lying in it would have been an entirely different matter. Well, actually, the dying part would have probably been the same!

Grandmother had a big, oriental rug in her room. Rich navy blue and deep crimson and white danced all over the floor, weaving an intricate and exotic pattern. And every morning in Grandmother's room the radio would call for sinners and backsliders to repent, to get their sins blotted out, to get right with The Lord, to be made whiter than snow. Big, white, lace curtains framed a picture window with a third-story view of oak trees and row houses. Warm, dark cherry mahogany antique furniture. All of this was in Grandmother's room.

Then there was Grandmother herself. A grand lady she was indeed. Her skin was smooth and black. She didn't have wrinkles, and she didn't have a lot of gray hair. She just looked a bit tired and a bit worn. Her eyes, though once piercing, were now dim and nearly useless. Her vision was limited to the times when The Lord would lift the veil that clouded her eyes and allow her enough light to notice the knees of anyone foolish or brave enough to wear a short skirt in her presence. Her laughter and her voice were soft and low. But, mind now child, she could cut you with her words; leave you bleeding right there all over that fine oriental rug, worn spot not withstanding! But you knew she loved you so much. So it was O.K. You could even laugh a bit while you licked your wounds.

There was something special about Grandmother's room. The love that was in her heart filled that room to overflowing. The room is gone now. It exists only in memory. But the love from there lives, grows, and goes on forever.

THE CRUMB SNATCHERS

Jawara

Essie waited impatiently for me to finish my chores. We wanted to go to the movies. "Hurry up, Jan! I gotta ask Grandmom if I can go."

My stomach churned. "She may not want you to go with me."

"Girl, don't mind Grandmom. She's like that with everybody." *No, she's not,* I thought as I slowly followed her.

"Grandmom, can I go to the movies?" Essie shouted. I stood nervously in the vestibule, pulling up my socks, patting my hair.

I could hear Miss Mattie's footsteps. "Sure, Baby, who you goin-?" The footsteps halted and Miss Mattie stared at me with distaste. "Oh! One of Berniece's crumb snatchers. Sit on that piano stool and don't move; don't want you droppin' no roaches in my furniture," she mumbled. Essie looked at me in distress as tears welled in my eyes. Humiliated, I avoided her comforting hands and bolted from the house.

Later, I heard Mom calling, "Circletime!" so the family would form a circle on the floor where she would tell stories diverting attention from our growling stomachs. If the electricity had been shut off, we heard stories; if the ice cream truck was nearby,

Cousin Betty would start a noisy game like tug-of-war, drowning out the tantalizing music of the truck as we pulled and screamed until we fell exhausted.

"Circletime!" Mom called again and opened the door expecting to find us all waiting. Instead, she found me huddled in a corner. Her eyes widened in sudden fear.

"It's nothing, Ma. Miss Mattie was just talking about us." She gathered me in her arms. *Oh, it felt so good!*

"Baby, we're poor, and we're a big family. Some folks think that makes us less than them. You just have to learn not to hear them. We are fine people."

Cousin Betty and the younger children came in. She shot Mom a questioning look. Mom yelled, "Circletime!"

As the candles flickered, Mom told stories of great African kings, and stories of proud people, passed down to her by her father. She ended with a song. And quietly the older children carried the younger ones up to bed. In the distance I heard the ice cream truck. Mom and I smiled. Crumb snatchers? Maybe. But crumb snatchers growing up with love.

DEPRESSION LOVE

Marian E. Barnes

We had warm apple pie for dessert one evening during the Great Depression. The shape of plump, sliced apples pushed against a shiny, dappled tan pie crust with fork prints all around the edge, and small knife slits in the middle. Pretty! A rare treat, and the whole family wondered, without asking, how my mother had been able to make it.

She had baked it, sliced it carefully into eight equal portions, and then served a piece to my dad, and one to each of us seven children around the table. It was a wonderful pie! Halfway through my slice I looked at my mother to share the joy of eating it. *She wasn't eating pie!*

"Mother," I asked, "why don't you have any pie?"

"I don't care for any," she said quietly.

I finished my pie, still enjoying it, but my little girl's mind was grappling with an unanswerable question. *How was it possible to bake such a marvelous pie and "not care for any" — even a taste — when everyone else in the family was happily enjoying it?*

The question followed me through the years. Now, some sixty years later, I can still see that pie, and recall the feel of that evening. I still hear myself asking my mother why she wasn't eating pie. I see her dark, serious eyes steadily looking at me, hear her quiet voice saying, "I don't care for any." But there is no little girl's mind grappling with a question that it cannot answer. Now, I know the answer.

Now, I know what love is.

THE WOOD BOWL

Marian E. Barnes
Based on a Folk Tale

I remember when it was springtime in my life. Morning. A long time ago. Mama and Grandma always called me "Pretty Girl," and hugged me tight-tight, and played "This Little Piggy" with my toes. I remember the first time Mama showed me a flower and let me touch it, and smell it . . . And the day Grandma took me on the porch and let me look up at the clouds and see the rain, and let it fall on my fingers, and splash on my face. And I remember Papa throwing me in the air, and Mama screaming, "Don't let her fall, Charles!" And I remember birthdays and Easter, and Christmas, and Mama and Grandma cooking in the kitchen, and good smells, and singing, and laughing, and Grandma's beautiful china and glasses and silver shining on the table. I loved Grandma's dishes! Sometimes she'd tell me stories about how Grandpa had bought them for her when she was a bride, and how she gave them to Mama when she married Papa, and how one day Mama would give them to me when I married.

And when I got married, Mama gave all Grandma's dishes and glasses and silver to me. "She wanted you to have them," Mama said. You could say that was the summer of my life then. The middle of the day, with lots of things goin' on, and hard work, and happiness. John and I prayed hard, and worked all the time to send the children to school, and give them special classes too. We wanted them to go further in life than we did. They did, too. People say Janet and both my boys got real fine jobs. And there was plenty of love in our house. On holidays Mama and I would be in the kitchen cooking together. We'd set a pretty table with my

Grandma's dishes; and Mama would tell my Janet that when she got married, those dishes would be hers.

And that's the way it happened. I gave Janet Grandma's dishes when she married Rob. I hated to give them up, in a way. They were really a part of me. But it was like a family tradition, and I knew Mama and Grandma would want me to pass them on to Janet. So I did. John died not long after that; and it seems like I could never get over it. It was hard when Grandma left, and Papa, and Mama. But John . . . Seemed like the light started fading in my life. There wasn't much to laugh about anymore. Janet and the boys were married and gone from the house. I couldn't see like I used to, or hear good, or get about well. I remember thinking, this is the fall of my life, the twilight years; and feeling shadows gathering round me.

Then Janet said, "Mom, come live with Robert and me." I was so glad! I would be the Grandma in her home like my Grandma had been. I would tell my grandchildren stories; teach them things; hug them tight-tight, and play "This Little Piggy." Janet and I would cook together in the kitchen and fill the house with delicious smells, and set a pretty table with my Grandma's china and glasses and silver.

I don't know what is wrong. I know I am in the winter of my life. Night is falling fast. I get so confused! I try to walk straight, but I stumble and fall. I try to eat careful, but I spill food on myself and on the table, and on the floor. My hands, they tremble so! One day I almost dropped Grandma's gold-rimmed crystal glass on a china plate. Grandma used to give me warm cookies on it. Janet caught the glass, and it didn't break the plate; but since then, she sets my place at the table with a wood bowl and a plastic glass; and she spreads a napkin under the bowl so I won't soil the linen tablecloth I gave her.

I'm sitting here at the table now by myself, trying to eat from my bowl. I eat so slow they always leave me here to finish eating alone. I understand why they give me this wood bowl. I understand . . . But food from this bowl never tastes right; and water from this plastic glass tastes kinda bitter. It doesn't matter. It's getting hard for me to eat or drink anything at all. When they set the table and I see my grandma's pretty dishes, I remember the happy times when we used them, me and the children, Mama and

Grandma. We all loved Grandma. She made me happy. We used to run to her for cookies and stories and hugs.

My grandchildren don't come to me for anything. Janet and I don't cook in the kitchen together. And I never ever see my sons or their children. Some of them look like me, they say. But I don't know. I haven't seen them. Janet's children say "Hi, Grandma," as they run by. I think of them at night. But then I have sad dreams. I wake up crying, and I don't know why I'm crying. And then the first thing I always see in my mind is this wood bowl. Does the bowl make me cry? Is that why I'm crying now? Tears are falling on my hands — so stiff and rough and knotty they can scarcely hold the bowl. They used to be so soft and pretty. Pretty hands, "Pretty Girl." Why do I feel so sad? Because of this bowl? I don't know why I feel so sad . . . so sad . . . Mama . . . Papa . . . Grandma . . . I wish you were here to tell me a story in the dark, and call me "Pretty Girl," and hug me tight-tight . . . "This little piggy went . . ."

* * * * *

Janet found her mother's lifeless body slumped across the table, the wooden bowl askew, the plastic glass toppled.

"I wish you children could have known your grandmother when she was younger," she told her son and daughter as they helped pack her mother's belongings to be given away. "She was a very happy person — fun to be with. It was really hard for me to see her like she was when you knew her. But Grandma's gone to be with The Lord now. He has taken her to a better place."

Now the box was ready to be closed, filled with old-fashioned under garments, dresses, jewelry, and faded aprons. Only the wooden bowl remained to be packed. Janet was walking toward the box with the bowl when her daughter rushed across the room and took it from her hands. "Oh, no, Mom, don't pack the bowl," she exclaimed. "I'm going to need that for you."

URBAN LIFE AND DEPRESSION YEARS: THOUGHTS OF NORTH PHILADELPHIA

Marian E. Barnes

Sundays were special when I was growing up in North Philadelphia. Everybody dressed up — "dressed to kill," we used to call it. The day began with the Wings Over Jordon Choir, The Southernaires, The Norfolk Four, and other African-American quartets on the radio. Sunday mornings had a savory smell. The tantalizing perfume of hot rolls baked in my aunt's oven permeated the neighborhood, and people came from far and near to buy them for ten cents a dozen. She also sold pies, which she made every day, baked in muffin tins and priced three cents each. Sometimes I delivered pies to customers, no tasting permitted. Once, tasting without permission, I scorched my tongue trying to consume the evidence before getting caught, and to this day, there are blackened taste bumps on my tongue as a reminder!

On Sundays we went to church in a house on 25th Street where Brother J. Alphonso Josephs taught us music and poetry, biology and history. We learned from him that "down in Zulu land" our African forebears were writing their history when most of the rest of the world were living in caves. So when public schoolteachers told me I was from an unimportant, unintelligent, non-contributing race of people, and I shouldn't expect much of myself, I knew better.

In North Philadelphia, the neighbor with the whitest steps was the envy of the whole street. Our neighborhood sparkled with white, marble steps, scrubbed until they gleamed like precious jewels. Customarily you scrubbed your steps and the steps of the house that joined yours, using plenty of Old Dutch Cleanser and Bon Ami. When you swept your pavement, you swept the pavements of the houses on each side of yours. However, when one neighbor began sweeping, most of the others came out and we all swept together. Then someone would open a fire hydrant for a general street wash-down, which often ended with the children playing water games in the gushing water as a substitute for a neighborhood swimming pool. I seldom played because I hated feeling debris in the water running over my feet.

There was a tavern on our corner secretly dubbed "the sanctified beer garden" because the clientele was dignified, quiet, and sober. It was the only business in the area owned by African-Americans. Caucasians controlled the neighborhood economy. Afro-Americans flocked into their stores by thousands, buying at marked-up prices recorded by a storekeeper on his credit "book." Virtually no African-American business could survive the destructive economic pressures employed against it by white merchants, which included their organized refusal to patronize wholesalers who traded with a Black American businessperson.

I remember pushcart peddlers and horse-and-wagon hucksters; gas street lights; picnics at Smith's Playground; boat rides to Red Bank, New Jersey; summer at Camp; local talent shows where children named "Baby" this or that sang and tap danced their way to popularity. I remember "sneaking" to stage shows (my parents said they were sinful) to see people who became famous later, like Billie Holiday, Lena Horne, Moms Mabley, Red Foxx, Billy Eckstein and Cab Calloway. In those days there were street gangs called "The Top," "The Bottom," and "The Forty Thieves," but there was practically no killing among them, and drug abuse seemed to be only a problem of show business people.

I remember riding the open-air trolley to Woodside Park; three-cent ice cream cones, and Jewish pickles, soft pretzels, and big shiny apples for a nickel. I remember chewing roofers' tar because it would make my teeth white, eating sour grass that made me sick, and not pointing to hearses or crepes hung on doors where someone died because my finger would rot off. I remember jumping double dutch, and playing jacks, and being the best at dodge ball.

I remember folks talking about "the depression," furniture of evicted families lining the streets; poor people searching dumps for foods discarded by markets; people applying for public assistance being told to go home and finish the last morsel of food in the house before returning to apply for help; nasty, insulting, arrogant, overbearing visitors from Public Welfare offices who had been taken off Public Welfare and given the job of visiting the homes of others still unemployed; Halloweens without razor blades or poisons in the treats given children, and without vicious "tricks" played on adults; Halloween parades down Ridge Avenue; houses that looked so much alike that my Mom once mistook the house next door for ours, went inside and scolded a child whom she mistook for one of hers for still scrubbing the floor my mother thought she had left her scrubbing when she left the house earlier!

I remember sitting on my steps on a summer Sunday night while broadcasts from two local churches filled the air with song. "Will There be Any Stars in my Crown?" one church was asking musically, as the other sang vigorously, "No, Not One!" Even then, I knew that tired joke about two congregations singing those songs, so listening gave me a chuckle as the memory still does.

North Philadelphia years ago was filled with love and laughter, heartache, headache, struggle, defeat and victory, and exceptional people. In many important ways it remains the same today.

THE LETTER

Marian E. Barnes

"Write a letter to Angie," my mother said. I was ten years old and idle, and Mother always found chores for an idle child. Now, as she worked about the kitchen, she dictated a letter to her sister in South Carolina, and I sat at the table carefully writing down every word she said. I put a three-cent stamp on the letter and took it to a mailbox on a street corner where a boy in knickers was yelling, "Extra! Extra! Read all about it!"

I didn't have a nickel to buy one of the papers under his arm. However, the last time I had read a story considered so important an extra newspaper had been printed to publish it, the story had consisted of one short paragraph with scarcely more information than the newspaper headline. So I mailed the letter and went home with little concern for what I was missing in the newspaper.

In almost no time, my aunt's reply to my mother's letter arrived.

"Read Angie's letter to me," my mother said. And as she continued her work, I sat down at the kitchen table and started reading her sister's letter. Until this day, I can only remember the first line of that letter. In fact, I'm not sure we ever read the rest of it!

"Dear Essie," I read cheerfully, with no premonition of the explosion I was about to set off. "You must not call me 'Angie.' You must call me 'Sister Angie.'"

"WHAT?" Whatever my mother was holding crashed to the floor. Startled, I looked up to see her eyes sharp, and stretched in disbelief.

"You called her *Angie?*"

"Well, yes —"

"Oh, child!"

"You said 'Write a letter to Angie,' and I wrote: 'Dear Angie.' You always call her Angie."

"I don't call *her* 'Angie.' I call her *'Sister* Angie.' She's older than I am!"

85

My mother was more distressed than I had ever seen her. Now a letter had to be written apologizing for the affront:

Dear Sister Angie:

I am very sorry that Marian called you "Angie" in my letter. The child wrote the letter for me, and she did not understand. I didn't read the letter before she mailed it, so I didn't realize what she had done. I hope you will understand and forgive the mistake . . .

Although I suffered a great deal of guilt and emotional trauma because I had made a colossal social error that got my mother in trouble with her sister, the time came when I looked upon the incident as a cultural blessing. The experience was a doorway that allowed me a glimpse of ancient culture that I would never have had without it. It has also helped me to understand many of the cultural formalities that dominate life as an African-American even though they are virtually nonexistent in the larger society. For example, in most African and Afro-American social or business settings, I have found it is highly inappropriate to attempt to interact with people on a "first name" basis without their permission — which is seldom easily obtained. In fact, I have friends with whom I went to junior high school who have let me know they now wish me to address them formally.

For a while, as a staff member of an African-American hospital, I sometimes attended hospital meetings hosted by prominent Caucasians. During these meetings, the hosts typically introduced themselves by their given names, and immediately spoke on a "first name" basis with everyone present, a basis I'm sure they assumed we had long been on with each other. Well, they were wrong. During the two years I worked there, first names were never used — except during such meetings. Pressured by the prestige of the visiting hosts and the knowledge that they thought we used first names with one another, while guest hosts were around we did so. And when they left, we went back to calling each other "Ms. 'This' " and "Dr. 'That.' "

I always smiled and remembered the letter.

LOVE AND RESPECT BEAT A BLOODY PADDLE
Marian E. Barnes

I was horrified, shrinking from a huge, wooden paddle spattered with dried blood that a teacher was trying to give me.

"Here. This is what you use on them," he said.

"How on earth are you able to get away with beating children with that paddle?" I wanted to know.

"Oh, kids don't tell," he grinned.

"Well, I am *not* going to use that paddle," I said emphatically. And there was probably no mistaking the way I felt about the fact that others had used it. The word spread fast, and in a few moments the principal arrived to lecture me diplomatically.

"As you have been told, we have this class of Special Education students that is completely out of control. When they are in their classroom, they make so much noise classes can't be held in the rooms near them. But they don't usually stay in the room. They run through the hallways, and out in the yard and in the street. Their regular teacher has had a nervous breakdown brought on by their behavior, and she will not be back this semester. Since that happened, these kids have been making a game of seeing how quickly they can get rid of every substitute teacher sent to replace her.

"Now, you've got to be firm. And don't take anything from them, or they'll run over you. They need rigid discipline and absolute authority. Most of the substitute teachers have only lasted one or two days. We had one man who was controlling them a little better than the others, but the school secretary said we should send for you."

I listened to all this with growing wonder. Until this day, I cannot understand why anyone thought of me. The appalling teaching approach he was requesting sounded like the job description for a policeman. I was anything but a disciplinarian or authoritarian along the lines he was describing, and I told him so.

Right before my eyes the principal "lost his cool," crumpled, and began to whine. *"Oooooooh! I should have kept that man!"*

"Well, yes, you should have," I agreed. "However, I am here now, and although I am not going to be a disciplinarian, I ask that you support my approach to the class until you can get the man back again."

"I should have kept that man!" he groaned, and it was doubtful that he had heard what I asked him to do.

When I entered the classroom, students interrupted the mini-riot in progress and scrambled into their seats. They quietly looked me over. I knew I would be allowed about one minute of this scrutiny before someone threw a rock or a sandwich, or did whatever they did to begin to sabotage a new instructor. Once that happened, it would simply be a matter of time until I joined the army of defeated, departed "subs." A very short time.

I looked the students over as well, and except for an especially calculating look in their eyes, they seemed no different from junior high school students I was teaching throughout the Philadelphia school system.

I turned, wrote my name on the chalkboard, quietly repeated it for them, and said, "I am your new substitute teacher. I know what you have been doing with the teachers that were here before me. However, you can get rid of me much faster than you did any of the others because there is something inside each of you that tells you what is right and you can start listening to that, or I will be out of here."

After that, we discussed appropriate behavior. The students made their own rules for class conduct, which proved to be stricter than those I would have made for them. They also established penalties for infractions of rules. These were very fair, and very rigid. As their teacher, I gave them permission to leave the room whenever they felt it was necessary so long as I was informed in advance. They tried me out on this to begin with, to see if I really meant it. After they found I lived up to the bargain, students seldom left the room.

Once the students began to behave properly, I pursued a curriculum that allowed them to discuss love, to write poems and stories about love, to work on projects based on feelings of concern and caring for others. They were given assignments that permitted them to show love to each other and to other people in their lives. The lesson plans allowed me to demonstrate love for them as well. Also, I never missed an opportunity to praise a student for work well done, or for a worthy effort. And I went out of my way to show each of them respect, affection, and love at one time or another.

The results were remarkable. The students bloomed like thirsty flowers after a warm, spring rain. They were caring and affectionate and cooperative in sessions they had with me and in their classes and interactions with other faculty members.

"How did you do it?" other teachers asked me time and again.

"I didn't do anything," I would say. "The students did it all themselves." And I would explain that the emphasis in the classroom was on love and respect.

"Come to my room. *My* class needs you now!" was also said to me.

One day toward the end of the semester the principal came to visit, all smiles, his "cool" completely intact again. "You," he said, "have made a believer out of me! And if ever you should need a letter of reference, I'll be glad to write one for you."

On the last day of the semester I went to the administrative office, where the chief clerk handed me papers to sign and smiled.

"I *told* them to send for you," she said, smugly.

"Why?" I asked. "I would never have sent for me. Why did you?"

"I just knew," she said. And that is all she would say.

So I will never know what she knew, or how she knew it. Even so, in the end I came to be glad I was called into the situation. If this had not happened, no doubt I never would have seen respect and love work miracles after a bloody paddle had struck out.

FOR YOUTHFUL MINDS

Born to a world crazed by godless lusts and ills and power
With challenges to set aright accepted by too few
Your strengths can make a difference, my children of this hour
With confidence unbridled, I pass the torch to you

Marian E. Barnes

EAGLES

Leon C. Anderson, Jr.

Who is he that pens an eagle?
There're so few eagles
in this land
The eagle, it seems to me,
such a beautiful sight to see,
should not be restrained
by selfish man

Therefore, if within yourself
there resides an eagle
who sits not precisely
where he wishes to be
then remove the locks
from your mental cage
and SET YOUR EAGLE FREE.

THE RIDE

Leon C. Anderson, Jr.

I once leapt the San Jacinto River
on a Red Schwinn Bicycle . . . I did
pedalling down the Old Rock Road
when I was just a kid
Starting out at Walker's Funeral Home
gaining speed as I passed Mrs. Bluett
faster past the Civic League Park
I'd reach the river...I knew I'd do it
faster still...on down the hill
and across the Old Gully Bridge
around the curves, building up nerves
for that moment I'd reach the ridge
Up! . . . Up! . . . Up! . . . out across the muddy water
then landing softly on the other side
wished I'd had my three chums there
to watch me take that ride
Yes-sir-ree they should'a been there
they could've told all about the kid
when I leapt the San Jacinto River
on a Red Schwinn Bike . . . I did . . . *I did!*

PROGRESS . . . OR ODE TO A CYNIC

Jonathan Sheppard

Humans think they're geniuses
so sure about their smarts
They're so technological with plastic coated hearts
With microchips for minds and computer tapes for souls
they're running down their batteries
to reach their spaced-out goals.

Children sold in bottles now
on supermarket shelves.
Simulated chromosomes make simulated cells
Bodies artificially prolonging useless lives
of corrugated husbands and factory outlet wives.

Radio activity runs rampant in the air.
All the cats and dogs have died
but robots couldn't care.
The world has finally ended
and all the signs of life have gone.
But three cheers for the human race
the idiots live on!

TO MARTIN

Maj. Gen. John F. Phillips

- To one whose dream still beckons all
- I pray to God we heed the call

- Your love and forgiveness waned not a day
- Your divine inspiration still shows us the way

- The laws of injustice you fought with pride
- Though insults and dogs abounded from all sides
- Yet you marched in dignity, never losing stride

- America, you "challenged" to cure her ills
- For some, less moral, 'twas too bitter a pill

- They taunted and hunted you with grimaced eyes
- And cowardly shot you, but your dream never died

- In death as in life you rally the call
- For universal brotherhood — God loves us all

- We have slipped and hedged on living The Dream:
- The young brother on drugs doesn't know what it means

- The "crack" born child, so innocent it seems
- Is sentenced at birth, never knowing The Dream

- The violence of youth, which kills and demeans
- They too have lost sight of your "Glorious Dream"

- We all need The Dream, less our ills grow deeper
- And shirk not our role as "My Brother's Keeper"

- Remind America that "justice" be done
- For her to be great — We must live as one

- Martin, you suffered for your fellow man
- And though not seen, we feel your hand

- For us, you paid the ultimate price
- You fought the battle and gave your life

- You left quite clear the freedom mission
- We'll stay the course and keep the vision

- Steadfastly we'll march to the mountain top
- We must not tarry, we will not stop

- And when at last the journey's done
- You'll smile down and say, "We did overcome"

Maj. Gen. John F. Phillips is commander of the Joint Logistics Systems Center, Wright–Patterson Air Force Base, Ohio. He is responsible for managing the design, development, implementation and maintenance of an integrated Department of Defense Corporate logistics process system, and facilitating development of improved business practices.

Born September 3, 1942, in Neches, Texas, the general is a senior pilot with over 3,000 flying hours. From December 1978 until the fall of the Shah of Iran, he was a logistics systems analyst at Doshan Tappeh Air Base, Iran. General Phillips remained in Iran until the expulsion of Khomeini in February 1979. His numerous military awards and decorations include the Legion of Merit, Meritorious Service Medal with two oak leaf clusters, Air Force Commendation Medal with oak leaf cluster, and Republic of Vietnam Gallantry Cross with Palm.

DORIS ("DORIE") MILLER: PEARL HARBOR HERO

Marian E. Barnes

December 7, 1941. USS *West Virginia* was pitching and rolling in the calm waters of Pearl Harbor in the early hours of a clear, beautiful, lazy Sunday. Below the main deck, Navy enlisted man Doris Miller was methodically collecting laundry, so accustomed to the motion of the ship in the water that he was unaware of it. His body was steady, his footsteps firm and sure.

His was not a challenging job. Miller *knew* he was capable of far more than the job required, far more than he was ever permitted to do. However, Doris Miller, often called "Dorie" Miller, was an African-American, and the U. S. Navy enlisted African-Americans as cooks, stewards, or waiters, and nothing else. So, like millions of Black Americans of his time, in order to survive he had to submit to doing less than he knew he could, and being less in the eyes of the world than he knew he was.

Suddenly, with no warning, the calm of the Sunday routine was shattered. Something was happening! But what? *Explosive noises. Bombs? Loud cries; guttural sounds; rushing footsteps; more explosions!* Miller dashed up ship ladders to the main deck into a scene that would replay in his mind time and again during the remainder of his short life.

Ship sirens wailed, cutting across the blaring voice on the loud speaker: "Man your battle stations! Man your battle stations!" Overhead the sky was specked with Japanese fighter planes, circling, diving, and bombing the American ships in the harbor! On deck, the captain of the *West Virginia* lay mortally wounded, and beside an anti-aircraft gun lay the body of a gunner who had been killed. Miller pulled the captain to safety. Then he sprinted to the dead sailor's unmanned gun, thinking, *I can do it! I know I can!*

He had never been trained to use the weapon, but he was certain he knew what should be done. Japanese fighter planes were raining bombs on the ships. Taking his time, Doris Miller aimed carefully at an aircraft, then at another, and another. Firing calmly, deliberately, and with precision, he brought down four Zero Fighter Planes before the order came to abandon ship!

Though Miller was cited for bravery and decorated with the Silver Star on May 7, 1942, this recognition of his courage was not followed by a promotion or a transfer to more appropriate duty. Instead, he was sent to Harlem to drum up support for U.S. War Bonds, after which he was assigned to the USS *Liscome Bay* as a steward.

The USS *Liscome Bay* went down in the Pacific Ocean on November 25, 1943. There were no survivors. One year later, Doris Miller was presumed dead by the U.S. Navy. He was issued the Purple Heart and other honors posthumously.

Quiet, soft-spoken, and intelligent, Doris Miller was named after the midwife who attended his birth. It was a name he enjoyed having during his brief life. It is a name the world remembers with love, pride, and gratitude.

* * * * *

Everyone thinks that the future is in astrophysics and computer engineering, but the perfect future is Earth's own past: the first man that thought and learned to use his own hands — the tribe of subsistent nomads that traveled the plains of the world. These people did not pollute the world; they did not change its state of balance. Old world man found his niche in the environment of Earth. **Sean Erickson**

MORNING DEW DROP

Jimmy Stanley

You are like a dew drop
on a mid-spring morn.
I admire you from afar
watching you glisten in the sun.

I know not where you go,
but I know that no matter
how many days pass,
I could never bring myself to
violate your beauty.

WHITE PAWN

Jennifer Hansen

Empty and alone
Cold and numb
Waiting for what is to come.
Feeling like a pawn without control

In this game we call life.
Who controls our destiny?
Certainly not your or me.
What is to become of us?
Why are we here?
Secluded in this shell of an existence
With only myself to feel.
Rubbery and smooth
Like a water balloon.
Pliable but concrete.
Hurling through infinity,
Aware that one day it will end somewhere
Or maybe not.
Black and white checkers
Stretching out of my reach,
No longer a balloon
But ivory again.
Hard to the touch
With smooth lines
Rolling off the table and falling. . .

IN SPITE OF MYSELF

Kyisha Diefenbach

The sun
is coming up over the horizon
The sky
a soft pink, yet blazing red
I'm running
I know there is danger
yet I cannot stop.
A cliff,
I know it is there, but my feet won't stop!
Running toward it, I scream,
but still I run.
The edge of the cliff,
I stop.
Standing on beautiful soft green grass,
I hear my name.
Turning to see who is calling me,

I see myself, yelling,
"Stop, Stop, Don't jump!"
I laugh, then turn.
In spite of myself, I laughingly
leap off the cliff,
into the air.
Soaring, I am a white feather drifting
Slowly to the ground,
leaving myself weeping on the cliff.
I wake up, holding my breath,
crying and gripping my bed.

A CHANCE FOR THE FIRE DEPARTMENT

Christina Mullins

You are like a burning theatre
Holding a crowd inside

Your fire rages high,
yet not many people get out.

No matter how much they scream
your outside seems calm and peaceful.

You will burn
until you and your people crumble.
Your chance to summon the fire department
will be gone,
and only the silent ashes will remain.

SONG OF MYSELF: A REQUIEM

Colly Patton

I depreciate myself, and cry for myself,
And what you see is not reality,
For every mask I don is unknown to you.

I strain and hide my true self.
I strain and hide my discomfort about observing
a life falling apart.

> My pen, my pad, both made for no real reason,
> Born on this paper is obfuscation and misinterpretation,
> false conclusions.

I, but sixteen years old, in ill mental health, begin,
Hoping for an end to come soon.
> I am the poet of reality and I am the poet of pain,
> The pleasures of heaven are unknown to me and the pains
> of Hell are too much to bear,
> The first I have surrendered, the latter I have concealed,
> until now.

MAMA, WHAT DON'T WHITE BOYS HAVE?

Cedar Sexton

Mama, I know they have all the advantages
but Mama,
What don't white boys have?
They don't have sense
They got power, they got money
They even got judges trained to say
Innocent
Mama, what don't white boys have?
Mama eyebetcha they don't have no love
I guess that's why they gotta have
everything else
Mama, I think it's sad what white boys don't have.

* * * * *

The pale cloud swells
With full-bellied
delight
Waiting
Anticipating
the Perfect Moment
to begin.

Forever
it seems
before a
single
drop
pierces the
delicate skin
of the cloud
tearing it open
and giving birth
to a
Rainstorm

Christina Mayne

ANSWERS AND QUESTIONS
Diego Prange

They say oil and water don't mix,
but what about oil and blood?
And what about blood and sand?

They say that if we don't learn from history
we are doomed to repeat it.
So have we learned anything?
Or are we lemmings,
jumping off another cliff
into the abyss?

They say flags are sacred
and men (and now women) can kill
and be killed to protect them
and the idea they symbolize.
So how many men?
How many flags?
And which flag is it this time?
Is it old glory and the almighty union,
the cross and almighty God,
or is it the almighty dollar?

JUST ANOTHER SOLDIER
Michelle Dion

Some say feminism died when women got the vote,
but it didn't.
It didn't die until Sally died.
She was shot in the stomach; they couldn't save her.
War was falling around her
like one of those oriental dressing partitions.
It all had happened so suddenly.
She had forgotten why she was there
in the middle
of the large battle field, a canvas
spread upon the ground to collect the bodies.
And there Sally lay
perfume mixed with blood,

uttering last prayers.
Like I said, when they found her
they were too late; they couldn't do anything.

A notice was sent to the family.
They cried.
Her husband carried the flag from her coffin
under his arm
as he walked away.
Just something else to remember her by,
she was his soldier.

The press came to take pictures
lugging their equipment up the knoll.
Sally was another one of those "firsts."

It was another story they were covering for the 6 o'clock show.

MERRY GO ROUND

Trice Ijeoma*

Some people like to play hockey, baseball and basketball.
But I like to participate in my own way, I like to ride the
Merry go Round, Merry go Round on the horses that go
up and down.
My boyfriend said I ride the horses like a cowgirl in the
rodeo.
Merry go round, Merry go round.
My mama said "Girl lets go to another ride."
Merry go round, Merry go round.
I am getting dizzier and dizzier, everytime I go around.
But I am not getting off.
Merry go round, Merry go round.
I am having so much fun, but I really have to go. Fooled
you!
Merry go round, Merry go round.
This time I'm really going to get off. But it has been fun.
I Love the Merry go Round, Merry go Round, Merry go Round.

*Trice Ijeoma wrote this poem as a second-grade student at St. Andrew's School in Austin, Texas. Merry Go Round was inspired by a song.

ROUND AND ROUND

Amanda Johnson

How do I love thee?
Let me count the ways
Thy strong and sculptured body,
Lean and taut beneath me.
Thy graceful curves,
Arching under the strain.
Thy tantalizing muscles,
flexing sensuously
As you carry me away.
The music plays
We go round and round in
rhythm to it,
Stopping only when I am
Too dizzy to continue.
You are my one true love . . .
    My carousel horse.

SCHOOL PLAY AUDITION

Doris Barnes Polk

"Please see me after class today"
My English teacher stated
"Quote Shylock's speech," she said to me
I smiled, and was elated

How well did I know Shylock's speech
And proved it on my test
Down to the punctuation marks
Mine *must* have been *the best*

"To bait withal," I softly said
And then my courage grew
My voice was loud and stronger now
For Shylock's speech I *knew*

She stopped me quite abruptly
With a "You may go now, Dear"
So caught up was I in my speech
I almost didn't hear

I walked out of the room that day
Frustrated and defeated
She didn't want me for the play —
She thought that I had cheated

TONKA TRUCK

Will Angst

The blue Tonka truck rolled across the cold linoleum floor. Its hard, plastic windshield was cracked from countless collisions with kitchen counters. The children played carelessly, though just a room away the constant bickering continued. The two were accustomed to this sound. They were hearing the words, but not really listening.

Suddenly, the door flew open, and with it came Dad saying, "If I'm so damn bad, why don't you get a divorce?"

The truck rolled to a halt, forgotten for the moment. The kids hadn't heard their parents go to this extreme before. "Okay!" Mom shot back as she sprang out of the room after him with her pink flowered bathrobe fluttering behind her.

Dad charged out the front door with his wife and small children trying to keep up.

The last words they heard him say before he jumped in his pale blue Chevy Impala were, "Next time you see me will be in court."

The truck was abandoned for the day. The kids went to their rooms, not wanting to break the strange silence that had settled over the house.

VOICES

Marian E. Barnes
Inspired by an Oral Tale as told by Saundia Coleman

Life was sweet and simple until the school years came, and then Pat began to hear voices. Crying out, arguing, pitted against each other, battling for control of Pat's mind and life. All the while, as we shall see, an invisible presence was also there, always silent, never calling attention to itself.

"Listen to your parents," the first voice said. "They want what is best for you. They are experienced. They know about life and living. Follow their advice and base your life on old, established values for living a good life that have proved themselves and been passed down to us by the best minds of other generations."

"Don't listen to your parents," the second voice countered. "Your parents are old, they've had their lives, they don't know anything about the world today. You'd be a fool to let your parents or some long dead philosopher dictate values for you to live by. Anyway, if you listen to your parents, your friends will laugh at you, and you'll be an outsider. Your friends understand what's really going down these days. Listen to them."

Pat thought the second voice was "hip," and exactly right.

In time, the first voice spoke again. "Get a good education, Pat. Study hard, work with your teachers, and educate yourself. An education will enrich your life and provide a solid foundation for whatever you choose to do later on."

But Voice Number Two disagreed. "An education? For what? A diploma? That's nothing but a piece of paper to hang on the wall, and that's all you'll get from head-tripping with a bunch of teachers who don't know *beans* about real life! You could teach them a thing or two. Anyway, you're smart enough to learn all you need to know now without trying, and catch up with whatever you miss just before college — or after you get there. Time enough to 'hit the books' then. You're too young to tie yourself down studying now. You should be having fun and enjoying yourself."

Pat smiled, and agreed.

After awhile, the first voice spoke again. "Pat, choose your friends carefully. They be can be uplifting and help you toward high goals, or they can be a destructive force dragging you down into self-destructive behavior. Make decisions for yourself based on what is best for you. Teach yourself not to think or behave as part of a crowd in ways that do not benefit you or anyone else."

"That's crazy talk!" the second voice sneered. "The definition of a 'nerd' if I ever heard one. And you know how everybody treats them! You want to be with the 'in' crowd, an *insider*, always 'in the know,' not an *outsider* that everybody laughs at or ignores."

"That's true," Pat said. "That's really true."

It was some time later that Voice Number One began to plead with Pat. "Don't let quick money tempt you to become a law breaker, Pat. Stay within the law. Get an honest job, and earn an honest living. No, it won't be quick or easy. And you won't earn huge sums of fast money. But you'll have enough to live on, and with time, you will earn more. Living this way, you can be proud of who you are and what you do, and others will be proud of you. Breaking the law never pays. *Never!* You seldom keep the money you earn. You become somebody decent people don't want to be around. Your activities destroy many lives, including your own. And perhaps worse than destroying your life, you become someone you do not like. And in the end, you'll have to pay for your crimes with part of your life, or all of it."

"Ha! Ha! Ha! Ha! Ha! Ha!" The second voice was laughing shrilly. "What a truckload of garbage! You won't keep the money you make? Decent people won't want you around? *HA!* The president of this country, and every 'big wig' in it — *they* are the biggest outlaws. Little guys couldn't operate outside the law overnight without the big shots that make it possible. And you better believe they keep all the money they make — and half of what *you* make, if you're dumb enough to get a two-bit job where you're taxed to death! As for people not wanting them around, everybody wants to be seen with them. They get their boots licked by the fanciest people in the world because they are *big*. Compare what the president is saying in the White House to what street gang members are saying on the corner, and it's the very same thing. Only street gangs are talking about local, neighborhood turf, and the president is talking about countries around the world. Gang members get squashed, but the president is too big to tackle, so everybody kisses up to him.

"It will be the same for you when you're making big bucks from drugs, gambling, prostitution, automobiles, or whatever you get into. The very best the world has to offer will be yours. Clothes, cars, jewels, lovers, houses, and land. You'll be respected and admired by everybody, including the police. In fact, you will *own* the police. If you're big enough, they will never touch you. That's the secret, Pat. Be so big that nobody can touch you!"

Pat thought about the two lifestyles and decided the one offered by Voice Number Two was the smart way to go. And indeed, much of what Voice Number Two predicted came true. Pat became wealthy, admired, respected, feared, and untouchable for many years. Until one day when Pat's protective network cracked, then split, bringing the illegal empire it had taken so long to build to a crashing end.

Pat was incarcerated, and in prison there was time to think, time to remember the voices heard over the years, time to consider the choices and decisions that had been made. And then Pat faced the truth: *I have been wrong. I listened to the wrong voice. I made the wrong choices. Voice Number One was right. I hate the person I have become, destroying lives and communities. Nobody really loves me. People show me respect out of hate and fear! But I can change, and I will. I will! I will! I will start over again and make the right choices. I will live a different life. I will be a different person. I will! I will!*

Then the presence that had remained unseen and silent through the years leaped up, and thundered, "NO, YOU WILL NOT, FOR I WILL *KILL* YOU!"

Now it began to swirl and swell. And swell. And swell. Just as it seemed it would smother Pat's struggling, flailing body and burst the walls of the room, it began to shrink rapidly, getting smaller, ever smaller; gathering itself at last *into* Pat, bringing slivers of pain that waxed and waned.

Heart slowing; eyes clouding; limbs trembling; breath choking. Pat wanted to scream the questions that burned, but the words came in hoarse, halting gasps through drying, stiffening lips:

"Who are you?" Pat whispered as life slipped away. "Why are you killing me? What is your name?"

The answer resounded, reverberating endlessly through the fleeting moments of Pat's ebbing life.

"MY NAME IS *T I M E ! !*"

A KNIFE IN HIS HANDS:
THE STORY OF DR. BENJAMIN CARSON

Marian E. Barnes

Once, using a camping knife, he tried to stab a boy. Today, using a surgeon's knife, he renders brilliant human service.

What is it like to be an African-American youth in a big city, to narrowly escape the pervasive death traps claiming Black males, then become world famous for human service in your early thirties? Dr. Benjamin Carson, director of neurosurgery for Johns Hopkins Children's Center, knows the answer. At thirty-five, Dr. Carson led a surgical team in separating Siamese twins joined at the skull and sharing major blood systems in the brain. At an even younger age, he successfully operated on the brain of a baby still in its mother's womb. Now forty, boyish, soft-spoken, and sometimes called "Gentle Ben," when he describes his teenage days on the streets of Detroit it is difficult to conceive of him as being the same person.

"I had a pathological temper," he said. "It was out of control. When I perceived that someone had infringed upon my rights, I took pains to be sure that person suffered as a result. Whatever was available — rock, hammer, bottle, knife — I would go after them with it. One day I tried to stab another teenager with a camping knife. He had on a large metal belt buckle, and it broke the knife.

"It struck me then that if he hadn't had that belt buckle on, I would be on my way to jail or reform school, and he would be on his way to a hospital, or dead.

"I went and sat in the bathroom on the edge of the bathtub for several hours, and I thought about my temper. I prayed to the Lord to take my temper away."

There can be no doubt that the anger that raged inside Ben Carson as a teenager was, at least in part, his response to an educational system that at times excoriated him because of his race. For example, as an eighth-grade student in a predominantly white junior high school, he earned a prize as the best student in his class. Instead of being proud of Ben's achievement, his Caucasian instructor was furious.

"That teacher blasted the rest of the class for letting me be Number One. Obviously, they weren't working hard enough if a Black kid was Number One. I'll never forget that," he said quietly.

The death-dealing social quicksand of the inner city nearly claimed young Carson again in high school as his friends tried to influence his life decisions. "I started listening to my friends," he remembered. "They were into all kinds of alcohol and drugs. It was ridiculous, but I started listening to them. I wanted to be part of the crowd."

His mother, however, was constantly pleading with him to step away from the crowd; to recognize that he was on a path of self-destruction; to use his brilliant mind to raise his falling academic grades and work for a bright future life.

It took an entire year, but Ben finally listened to his mother and began to study again. His mother, a divorcée, who worked two and three jobs to keep her family stable, was determined to convince Ben and his older brother that they could build special lives for themselves, no matter who, or what, was against them.

"We got lots of negative messages in society, but my mother just put an end to those kinds of thoughts quickly. You might say she brainwashed us into believing that we could do anything," he said.

Armed with this belief, Carson won a scholarship to Yale University. He would later hold two of the medical profession's most prestigious awards in surgery. Even so, his matriculation at Yale was not free of problems. In the beginning, he almost flunked his science courses. Recognizing that high school science classes had not adequately prepared him to cope as a Yale science student, he said, "I realized I had to do a substantial rearrangement in the way I studied and become an in-depth learner. But I did, and rectified the problem. I just have never, under any circumstances, thought of giving up on anything I do.

"The big difference between people who succeed and people who don't is not that the ones who are successful don't have barriers and obstacles. Everybody has barriers and obstacles. If you look at them as containing fences that don't allow you to advance, then you're going to be a failure. If you look at them as hurdles that strengthen you each time you go over one, then you're going to be a success."

The young doctor's method of mastering hurdles worked well for him when he began to study accounts of surgical procedure to separate Siamese twins joined at the head. The surgical record was dismal. It seemed to Dr. Carson that massive loss of blood during the operation was a major problem. *If I were ever the surgeon in such a case, I would stop the babies' circulation beforehand, lower their body temperatures, and then operate,* he thought, though he doubted that he would ever have such a case.

A scant three weeks later, a German doctor arrived at Johns Hopkins Hospital with records of Benjamin and Patrick Binder, Siamese twins born in West Germany. Their mother had been unable to bring herself to agree to sacrifice either child to save the life of the other. However, no surgeon in Europe knew of any other way to separate the boys. Dr. Benjamin Carson was consulted.

"I went up and looked at the films and said, 'Yeah, I can do this,' " he recalled, his gentle voice reflecting confidence and energy. With Dr. Carson in a leading capacity, a seventy-person team performed the separation surgery using techniques Carson had developed. The operation took twenty-two hours, but when it was over, Patrick and Benjamin Binder were two separate, healthy, intact babies.

"I guess I would have been afraid if I didn't have so much faith in God," Dr. Carson observed. "I never have the feeling He's going to let me get into something He can't get me out of."

A deeply religious man, Ben Carson believes his talents are a gift from God. He does not smoke, drink, or eat meat. The father of three children, he is married to the girl he fell in love with in college.

Is his religious faith at odds with a hospital environment? "It's not fashionable by any stretch of the imagination," he says. "But it's what I believe, and I don't have any qualms about telling people." He also has no qualms about speaking out to young people throughout the country, many of whom are much like he was not long ago. His message to youth groups never varies.

"I tell them to take responsibility for their lives. I tell them that education gives them independence and an ability to control their own lives. That message has got to get across to our young people!"

Perhaps nobody is better suited to get that message across than Dr. Carson, who changed himself from a teenager on the streets, holding a knife aimed to kill, into a physician on the world stage, using a knife to bring healing, health, and life into the world around him.

EAST MEETS WEST

Marian E. Barnes

"What the *hell* kind of name is Kwame?" Tyrone spat the words at the hated newcomer to Washington Junior High. It would have made any red-blooded Black dude fight, but the chump didn't make a move. His face went "flat" all of a sudden, like somebody had turned off a light behind it, but he just *looked* at Tyrone from eyes that weren't saying anything. When he finally spoke, Tyrone could barely hear him.

"It's an African name," he said. "It means 'Saturday's child.' I was born on Saturday."

"You Af'ican?" Tyrone sneered. "That how come you wear them Af'ican *dresses* like a *girl?*" The silence between them was electric. Tyrone was poised to spring. But again Kwame answered in a voice that was low and measured. "Actually I was born here. But my family lived in Africa most of my life. My father works for the state department." Without warning, Kwame turned and strode away.

Tyrone took one startled, lurching step after him and stopped short. He was "Tyrone the Terrible" Jackson — "*Mister T.*" He was not going to go running down the hall after some *niggah* in a dress! The whole school walked like he walked, talked like he talked, laughed at what he said was funny. He would make that wimp fight on his own terms.

Tyrone's eyes narrowed as he watched Kwame striding down the hall. He didn't walk like a Black dude with a little hop-and-roll step and a hand flip now and then; he didn't talk like a Black dude with all those fancy words and some kind of "almost-accent," and he certainly did not *act* like a Black dude, buttering up the teachers talking about school work, getting high grades and working to make them higher. Everything about him made Tyrone mad, but worst of all — the really *scary* thing — some of the guys were beginning to act different when Kwame was around. They weren't quite imitating Kwame, but they weren't acting just like "Mister T" as they always had before. And sometimes when "*Mister T*" was talking, they were only *half* listening. He could tell. Part of their attention was still on *him.*

We got to fight, he thought. *I've gotta beat that mothuh or he'll be the big Mister 'round here, and I'll just be a "has-been" that nobody wants to know!*

"What's the matter, T? Is something wrong?" It was Denise, his "main squeeze." Well, she wasn't his girlfriend yet, but he was working on it. All the guys knew she was strictly off-limits.

"Hi, Niecy," he said, forcing his attention away from Kwame. "It's that damn African. He gets on my *last* nerve — my *reserve* nerve!"

"How come you always picking with him, T? He seems nice to me. He never bothers anybody."

Tyrone didn't like for her to defend him. "He bothers me," he snorted. "Believe it, girl. He bothers me."

The next day Tyrone walked into his social studies class while

Miss Denby was taking the roll. He was late, as usual, but she decided to ignore it. The principal frowned on teachers who wrote too many pink slips.

Tyrone slammed the door so hard that the room and windows vibrated. He whipped out a paper hat shaped like the African okpu Kwame wore, squashed it on his head and headed for his seat, taking exaggerated pitch-and-roll steps, sweeping his right hand in huge semicircles. The class was yowling, laughing, out of control.

"Dig Mister T, y'all."

"He strollin' big time!"

Miss Denby smashed her yardstick down on her desk repeatedly, screeching, "I want order in this room! Order! *Order!*" This increased the fun and the chaos.

"Get in your seat and take that hat off at once!" Miss Denby shrieked, slapping her desk with the yardstick with each word.

"How come you ain't making *him* take *his* hat off?"

"Take that hat off this instant or you are going to the discipline office if I have to call and have them get you out of here!"

Tyrone snatched the paper hat off his head and pointed it at Kwame. "What about *him?* He wears a hat near 'bout every day and you don't never say nothin' to him!"

"That's cultural," the teacher said.

"Well, hell, he ain't the only one in this class that's got culture."

"You watch your language in this classroom!"

"That's *my* culture! And it's damn sure the only way my culture ever gets heard in this class. We study 'bout the Romans and the Greeks and the Chinese and every damn body in the world but us!"

A chorus of voices rose to support Tyrone.

"That's right, Miss Denby."

"That don't make no kind of sense!"

"This is supposed to be a social studies class and we studying about everybody else but ourself."

"All right, let's have some order here." Miss Denby was trembling. "This class has a planned curriculum. We can't study whatever we feel like studying."

"Yeah, but it ain't only in this class. I been in school all my life, and they don't never allow us to study about us."

"Why is that? Must be some reason."

"It's racism. You know why it is. They don't want you to know nothin' good about yourself."

"Yeah. They teach you they did you a favor to bring you over here as a slave. That's supposed to be good."

"Well, bad or good, that's all the social studies *we* ever get. Ain't that right, Miss Denby?"

Miss Denby was frazzled. The class was no longer in an uproar, but there was a threatening undertow of anger and she didn't know how to cope with it. Unable to answer the students' accusations, she found herself feeling guilty without knowing why. If there was racism in the school course plans, she certainly was not responsible. It occurred to her that the students were showing more interest in this discussion than they had in any lesson of the course, and she decided to take advantage of it.

"I'd like to follow up on what Tyrone was saying. What do you mean when you say profanity is cultural, Tyrone?" she asked.

"I mean that's the way we talk. We always talk that way. It don't mean nothing. That's our culture. Black folks talk different from white folks. We talk loud. We curse a lot. And we talk poetic. We got our own language. We call it 'Our Spectacular Vernacular.' If white folks talked that way and we didn't, they'd be writing books saying we haven't *evolved* into the poetic stage yet! But because we do it and they don't, they try to ignore it or make fun of it."

"All of us don't talk alike, T," Denise said. "Don't even try it! The only poetry you hear in my house will be from a book. And we don't use profanity. As for 'talking loud and drawing a crowd' — the loud mouths are so *loud* they *sound* like the majority! But look around when you're on the bus, at a ballgame, in school, or *wherever*, and for every Black person cursing and being loud, there'll be twenty-five just the opposite. Being rude, crude, lewd and loud may be *your* culture, but it's not mine!"

Tyrone laughed. Her flashing eyes and fiery answer made her seem prettier than ever. "I don't know how you can say that, Niecy."

"What do you mean, you don't know how I can say it? I can say it because it's true!"

"I'll tell you what I think is going on," Kwame said. The laughter died on Tyrone's lips and his eyes went cold. Kwame took no notice. "The way I see it," he continued, "three kinds of heritage affect our culture, *African heritage, slave heritage*, and *the heri-*

tage of captivity. As captives in this country we had to do lots of things just to survive — loud talking, for example. We were *forced* to yell. Whatever we said had to be loud enough so it could be heard in the Big House even if we were in the field. That way whites could be sure we weren't plotting against them.

"We also had to laugh all the time, even when we felt like crying. We had to laugh so they would think we were happy and not sell us downriver. Some of our people acted slappy-happy or feeble-minded so their so-called owners would feel comfortable around them and not sell them away from their families.

"As for cursing and acting vulgar, the master class encouraged our people to behave that way *with each other* because . . ." Kwame pressed back a different finger of his left hand to number each point. "Number one, it made them feel superior to us; number two, it made them feel justified in enslaving us; and number three, it served as proof of what they were saying — that we were three-fifths of a human being, 'talking cattle' with child-like minds and no morals.

"As their captives, we had to do all of these things just to survive. Sometimes to survive economically today our people do the same kinds of things. That's the *heritage of captivity*. But when we allow self-destructive, inferior, survival behavior forced on us during slavery to become an internal part of who we are, I call that *slave heritage*. All of us don't accept it as our culture and try to glorify it, but I think *slave heritage* is a problem for all African-Americans in one way or another.

"In addition to the *heritage of captivity* and *slave heritage, African heritage* is a very important part of our culture. We've been taught to disrespect it, but that part of our culture comes from our history before we came to this country, from Africa and the great civilizations that Africa was first to give the world." Kwame finished speaking and the class was still.

Suddenly, thudding drum beats and a guttural chant shattered the moment. "UG-BUH! UG-BUH! Af'ica! Af'ica!" Everybody looked toward Tyrone, who was bending down, chanting and pounding the underside of his desk top. "UG-BUH! UG-BUH! Af'ica! Af'ica!"

"All right, Tyrone, that's it!" Miss Denby snapped. "You're out of here!" She marched to the pink slip pad on her desk while Tyrone protested.

"That wasn't me, Miss Denby! I was tying my sneaks! It wasn't me!"

Later, as he left the discipline office and headed for the lunchroom, Tyrone was furious. The class had let him down, and Kwame was to blame! First, he had spouted off like he was the damn teacher, then nobody had tried to help Tyrone put him in his place. He had depended on the students to join him as they always had before. With everybody chanting and drumming, old Denby could not have picked on him.

Instead, Denby had fingered him and given him another pink slip. One more slip and he'd get suspended again. Well, what the hell... He crumpled the pink slip and pitched it basketball fashion into a hall trash can several yards away as China Man, Sweet Wille-Jo, and Treetop joined him.

"Not bad, man!"

"Yeah, you gon be the next basketball millionaire!"

"Move over, Doctor J!"

"How come you mothuhs let me take the fall in Denby's class?"

"Everything went down so fast, it was over before we knew what happened," Treetop said as they walked into the cafeteria. The lunchroom was seething with noisy students, but Tyrone saw only two people. His eyes were drawn like magnets to the spot where Kwame and Denise sat smiling and talking and eating, as though they were alone in the world.

Propelled by his hatred of Kwame, Tyrone charged across the room, shoving students from his path. "What you doin' with *my* girl, niggah?"

Kwame stood up and Niecy jumped between the boys. "What's the matter with you, T? I'm *not* your girl! Where do you get off saying that? You acting like a fool!"

"FIGHT! FIGHT! FIGHT! FIGHT!" Students raised the fight chant, stamped in time with it and crowded around.

"Look, Tyrone, I don't want to hurt you," Kwame said.

"Hurt me? Hurt me?" Tyrone snarled. They were circling each other. Denise was between them, trying to prevent Tyrone from hitting Kwame, who apparently did not want to fight.

"That dress you wearing ain't enough to hide in? You got to hide behind a real girl too?"

"FIGHT! FIGHT! FIGHT! FIGHT!"

"Kwame gon fight Mister T."

"Have mercy!"

"He don't want to fight."

"I don't blame him. He ain't no fool."

All of a sudden Tyrone pushed Denise out of the way and swung mightily at Kwame. The blow never landed. Instead, he found himself enveloped in Kwame's garment, smothering, his face completely covered, his head gripped in a vise-like head-hold, his arms and legs entangled and flailing. Breath was oozing from his body and he was losing consciousness when Kwame released him and stood back.

Tyrone could not understand what was happening. Angry tears filled his eyes, and he jumped at Kwame. Even as he did, he was aware that he had lost his usual cool, deliberate fighting style, that he was being clumsy and frantic and fighting like a girl. Or *trying* to fight like one, for again although he had jumped, he didn't land on Kwame. Rather, he felt Kwame's foot in his chest, excruciating pain, and once more he was tangled up in Kwame's robe, his head clamped in a sickening vise.

His eyesight was getting blurred, and the voices around him were fading away. Still he heard his buddies laughing and heard what they were saying.

"Well, whaddayou know? The great Mister T done met his match at last!"

"The bigger they come, the harder they fall."

"He sure falling *hard*!"

"Ain't he now!"

"Tell me about it."

"He's crying! He's fighting like a *girl.*"

They were all laughing now. It wasn't fading laughter anymore; it was loud, raucous, piercing. The sound softened, faded, stopped.

The world went black.

He awoke on a cot in the nurse's office and looked straight into a pair of eyes. Kwame was leaning over him.

"You okay?"

Tyrone groaned and shut his paining eyes again. His neck hurt, his head hurt, his chest hurt, his limbs ached.

"What you doing here?"

"I was afraid I really hurt you. I tried not to, but it's hard to control. I was worried about you."

"Then you the only one in the school that is." Tyrone laughed dryly. It swelled the pain in his throat and head. He stopped laughing. "You the new Mister Big in this school now." To his surprise he felt relieved. "These dudes 'round here don't like me. Never did. They was just scared of me 'cause I could beat all of them together if I had to. Now that you beat me, they're glad; and they'll be looking at you as 'Number One.' "

"That's ridiculous," Kwame scoffed. "I've got plans for my life, and they do not include being 'Number One' at Washington Junior High — at least not in fisticuffs. Scholastically, maybe."

"What's the use of being Number One scholastically? It takes more money than any of us got to go to college. And you may graduate 'Number One' from Washington, but if there's a scholarship or a job out there, you won't get it. They'll give it to the white dude who graduates 'Number 199' from Hallahan — or the white dropout from Hallahan." Tyrone spoke wearily.

"If that happens, I'll make my own job. I'll send myself to school, or do whatever else I want to do. I've always planned to be my own boss sooner or later, one way or another. If it comes sooner rather than later, so be it."

Tyrone forced himself to open his eyes and study Kwame's face. *You some kind of off-the-wall dude*, he thought. But Kwame's words had shown him another way of looking at life.

"What kind of fighting was that, some kind of new karate?" he said.

"Not at all. I used African martial arts — two forms of it. I can teach you if you like. If you have to fight unexpectedly, this buba robe I'm wearing can be used as a weapon, as you now know. The kick to the chest was a form of martial arts called dambe. We wear special garb for that. But it can also be used when you're wearing ordinary pants."

That day was the beginning of a friendship between Kwame and Tyrone that eventually affected the whole school. The boys learned from each other. Kwame found that wearing jeans was fun and relaxing. Tyrone discovered a feeling of dignity and elegance in wearing African robes, and tremendous pride in knowing his African heritage.

Kwame learned that Black English was more than broken English, indeed a most "spectacular vernacular," colorful and witty, poetic, metaphoric, continuously contributing language to standard English.

Even though Kwame refused to accept the combative role he had won from Tyrone, students at Washington looked up to him and followed his lead. Because he continued to respect and befriend Tyrone, others did the same. It became the "in" thing at school to wear African garb. The African martial arts lessons he gave Tyrone soon mushroomed into a highly popular after-school class in the gym. And for the first time in the memory of anyone at Washington, the student body was enthusiastic about classwork, homework, and outstanding grades.

On Graduation Day, to ear-splitting applause, class president Kwame Carter strode to the podium resplendent in colorful, flowing kente cloth and a regal African robe. "As many of you know, I lived most of my life in Africa, although I was born in the United States," he said.

"Until I came to Washington Junior High School, I thought of myself as an African. And most of you who are now my friends considered yourselves Americans. Although we called ourselves African-Americans, each of us was honoring only part of a great heritage. But living in this country brought me face to face with the history of my people in America, and the culture we have developed here. Also, my presence here made many of you aware of your African roots. It took us awhile, but we finally understood that we are Africans *and* Americans and that recognizing, understanding, and honoring both parts of our history and culture makes us whole and healthy, and beautiful."

I LIKE SPIDERS

Ada DeBlanc Simond
As told to Marian E. Barnes

I like spiders. They are survivors, they are self-sufficient, and you never find them standing around waiting for someone to give them something. They make what they need for themselves. I am not afraid of spiders. I have learned to identify the black widow spider that is supposed to be fatal if she bites a person. But I am not afraid of the ordinary spiders that you see sometimes. I never feel as if I need to kill them.

I identify with a spider because he is a survivor, providing for himself and taking what is available to make what is needed. He knows how to supply his need for water. Remember the song: "The eensy, weensy spider crawled up the water spout . . ." The spider makes a home near the source of water.

A spider is always weaving. When he sees a place where he plans to stay, he builds a house for himself. While he is building his house, he builds a place to trap his food. He probably also stores his food in the web he weaves.

The fluid the spider uses to make his web, weave his house, and weave his trap comes out of him. He is using from within himself to make the things he needs for life. He's not looking for somebody else to come along to provide something for him. Human beings can learn a valuable lesson on taking what is available and making what you need just by watching a spider.

HOW A HORSE SPOKE TO ME

Marian E. Barnes

One clear, hot day I found myself in the country standing under a brutal, broiling sun beside a horse whose face was covered with flies. She was not a sleek racing mare with rippling muscles. She was a "Farmer Brown" type horse, her muddy-white-colored hide splattered with a zillion blue freckles that were hard to distinguish from the swarming flies.

My city upbringing had left me with no understanding of animals. And I was more than a little afraid of this horse, but I knew she had to be miserable. And though there was nothing I could do about the sun beating down on her, something could be done about the flies festering on the profile of her face next to me. So, very cautiously, I began to fan the flies away while I wondered what had attracted them to her face. Perspiration? Something she had passed through that had left a residue?

All at once, the horse turned her huge head toward me, nearly knocking me down. I jumped away. Scared. Then I realized the horse was showing me that the other side of her face, which I could not see before, was also covered with flies. She was asking me to brush them away too!

And, so I did.

That was a moment to be treasured. We were two creatures existing on different planes of life, but we had bridged the gap and communicated as friends. And each of us had enhanced the life of the other.

LET'S LAUGH!

Most short-short stories and poems in this section, and many in the entire anthology, were written by fourteen- and fifteen-year-old Austin Independent School District students. However, contributors vary from a six-year-old in first grade, through seventeen-year-old high school seniors, and include all ethnic groups. Their poetry speaks to universal life experiences and to cultural situations shared by all U.S. citizens. The majority of these student writers attend the Liberal Arts Academy of Johnston High School. Special thanks is due to their instructors Carol Hovland and David Meischen for assistance in selecting and coordinating contributions.

A republican is an elephant?
To believe this thing, I simply can't
A donkey is a democrat?
Now who could ever think of that?
If you think left or you think right,
to be called a name's just not polite.
Did Dukakis have a card?
 Is Dan Quayle a dumb retard?
Gary Hart and Donna Rice:
did they rallly 'do it' twice?

Take politics seri'sly, who really could?
Such trash belongs in Hollywood.
Michelle Wilkinson

LANGSTON HUGHES AND JESSE B. SEMPLE: THE MAKING OF A FOLK HERO

John Henrik Clarke

The character Jesse B. Semple was born quite by accident, according to his creator Langston Hughes. Jesse B. Semple was first introduced in a column that Hughes was writing for the *Chicago Defender* during the Second World War. Semple is an urban folk hero and a philosopher whose appearance in our literature was long overdue. From his evening vantage point in a Harlem bar, Semple observed the world of the Afro-American and judged it as wisely as he judged himself. His comments on that world, and his own daily troubles, have made him a permanent and very important part of Afro-American literature.

Langston Hughes has stated that much of the material for the books on Semple was derived from actual conversations overheard in bars and on the corners of the largest urban Black community in the world, reflecting not the Harlem of the intellectual and the professional but that of the ordinary "man in the street" — the basic Harlemite who may not always know the answers to the questions that trouble mankind but who has enough good sense to often laugh to keep from crying.

Semple is a latter-day Aesop whose fables are as entertaining as they are meaningfully true. He is a man, like most men, in revolt against the world around him and those circumstances that are forever blocking the paths of his ambition. Semple is a dreamer and an optimist who is always willing to give the world a second chance. In his own earthy approach to American race problems, he says more in a few sentences than some Ph.D. authorities have said in a small mountain of books.

In the following quote, the problem is put in a capsule: "Now, the way I understand it," said Semple one Monday evening when the bar was nearly empty and the juke box silent, "it's been written down a long time ago that all men are borned equal and everybody is entitled to life and liberty while pursuing happiness, so I do not see why it has to be resolved all over again."

In this brief statement, Jesse B. Semple has told us what the so-called race problem and the problem of democracy in America are all about — they are about a broken promise, a resolution that has been ignored. Then, he makes you pause to wonder: Was the promise of democracy really made to the Afro-Americans? When the millions of Americans make their daily pledge of allegiance to the flag and end by saying, "liberty and justice for all," do they see the Afro-Americans as a part of all that? If so, why are they a problem?

The character Jesse B. Semple is a kind of proletarian everyman. The urban ghetto is his window on the world.

In explaining the creation of the character Jesse B. Semple, Langston Hughes has said: "Semple, as a character, originated during the war. His first words came directly out of the mouth of a young man who lived just down the block from me. One night I ran into him in a neighborhood bar and he said, 'Come on back to the booth and meet my girl friend.' I did, and he treated me to a beer. Not knowing much about the young man, I asked where he worked. He said, 'In a war plant.'

"I said, 'What do you make?'

"He said, 'Cranks.'

"I said, 'What kind of cranks?'

"He said, 'Oh, man, I don't know what kind of cranks.'

"I said, 'Well, do they crank cars, tanks, buses, planes or what?'

"He said, 'I don't know what them cranks crank.'

"Whereupon his girl friend, a little put out at this ignorance of his job, said, 'You've been working there long enough. Looks like by now you ought to know what them cranks crank.'

" 'Aw, woman,' he said, 'you know white folks don't tell colored folks what cranks crank.' "

That was the beginning of Semple. Langston Hughes said that he had long since lost track of his friend in the Harlem bar who helped give birth to Semple. But out of the mystery as to what the cranks of the world crank – to whom they belong and why – the character Semple evolved, wondering and laughing at the numerous problems of white folks, colored folks, and just folks, including himself. Sometimes, as the old blues say, Semple might be "laughing to keep from crying."

In the more than twenty-five years that the character Jesse B. Semple appeared in newspapers, magazine articles, and in two stage plays, he made comments on every aspect of Afro-American life. Of the many stories about Semple, my personal favorite is "Banquet in Honor," taken from the first book of his adventures, *Simple Speaks His Mind*.[1] The story is obviously about the shameful neglect of Dr. W. E. B. DuBois by a Black bourgeoisie class who only remembered him when they wanted to exploit his name and reputation to raise funds.

In the many books about Jesse B. Semple, Langston Hughes has made this talkative Harlem bar-hopper a major figure in American literature. With warmth, good humor and good sense, he has looked beyond the problems of colored folks – and just plain folks – at the problems of the world. The best thing that can be said about the character Jesse B. Semple is that he will probably outlive the circumstances of his creation.

WILLI AND JOE JOE AND THE PAMPER DIAPER

Temujin the Storyteller

This is a West Indian story because me like West Indian stories.

Now, me got two friends, Willi and Joe Joe, and them love to go fish.

One day Willi, him go to Joe Joe's house and him say, "Joe Joe, you go fish?"

Joe Joe say, "Man, me can't go. Me got to watch the baby."

"Bring the baby!"

"Man, me can't bring the baby."

"Why can't you bring the baby?"

"The baby only do a few things: him eat, him sleep, him cry, him mess up diaper. Man, me wash dirty diaper all day long."

---

1. See note on spelling of Semple, p. xii.

"You ain't never hear of them Pamper diaper?"

"Pamper diaper? Pamper diaper? What kind of diaper is that?"

"Oh, man, it a wonderful thing. You put it on the baby . . . the baby mess it up, and you throw it away."

"Throw it away? Throw it away? Where me get something like that?"

"You got to go down to Kingston — any grocery store, them got Pamper diapers."

Three days later, Willi go back and knock on Joe Joe's door.

"Joe Joe, you go fish?"

"Man, me been waiting for you for three days. Me got them Pamper diaper and them a fine, fine thing."

"You got one on the baby now?"

"Yah. Boy, go show Uncle Willi them Pamper diaper."

The baby walk out — Pamper diaper drag along the ground.

Willi look and shake he head and say, "Man, you got to change that thing."

Joe Joe say, "No. Me read the box, it say good for twenty-five pounds. Ain't but ten pounds in there now."

"GOODIE TWO SHOES"
Good Deed Makes a Barefoot Lady

Marian E. Barnes

The cross-country bus came to a stop. A lady sitting across the aisle from me made her way to the front and got off. It was the dead of night, and everyone else on the bus seemed to be asleep except the driver and the plump lady sitting behind me. On the floor beneath the seat the passenger had left, I saw a pair of sandals. "Too bad," I told the plump lady, "she left her shoes under the seat."

"Oh, what a shame!" the plump lady said. "You should give them to her."

"It's too late. She's gone now."

"No. She's right outside in that car. Someone came to pick her up."

Indeed, someone was loading luggage in the trunk of a car beside the bus. Still, I didn't want to leave my warm, comfortable seat to follow someone into the cold night with a pair of sandals.

Anyway, the activity outside the car was slowing down. "They're almost ready to drive away now. I could never catch her," I said.

"The driver could catch her. Give them to the driver," the plump lady commanded with a smile. I was out of excuses. But I still didn't want to move. The sandals were probably an old pair of "kick-abouts" that the passenger had relaxed in while riding, that she really didn't care about, I thought. Anyway, if the plump lady was anxious to have the slippers returned, why didn't she do it, instead of pressuring me? Looking at her closely, I saw that her body spilled from her seat and covered most of the seat next to her. I doubted if she could move as quickly as seemed necessary, or if she could bend down in the narrow aisle to retrieve the shoes. With her eyes, she was imploring me to act. Feeling guilty about hesitating, I stooped, picked up the slippers, and gave them to the bus driver. He ran with them and hailed the car just as it was pulling away. On the bus, we heard the lady thank him heartily for bringing the shoes.

Pleased that I had done a good deed, thanks largely to the plump lady, who seemed equally pleased, I settled down for the last leg of my journey and went to sleep.

My eyes flew open about sixty miles down the road when I heard someone saying desperately, "Where are my shoes?" A lady who had been asleep on the seat behind the passenger who left the bus was frantically feeling around on the floor and peering under her seat. "My shoes! My shoes! I can't find my shoes!" I was wide awake and on my feet, a sickish feeling of fear and anticipation gripping my entrails. This couldn't really be happening.

"Did you have a pair of wooden sandals?" I asked weakly, already knowing the answer.

"Yes. And they're gone; I don't see them anywhere!" Now, she was practically crawling along the floor in her search. I looked at the plump lady, and she looked at me. I couldn't find my tongue. The plump lady spoke up.

"That lady what was sitting in front of you took your shoes when she got off the bus," she said clearly.

"She WHAT? Oh, my God! Oh, my God!" She was wailing.

"What's wrong? You do have another pair of shoes, don't you?" I asked, a trace of panic in the question.

"No. I don't. That was the only pair I had!" I looked at her bare legs and feet, and tried to imagine her walking on the ice-cold cement. No wonder she was wailing. The plump lady's eyes were boring into mine. The barefoot lady was continuing to call an unanswering God, and I was feeling increasingly guilty, not knowing what to do.

"What size shoe do you wear?" I asked.

"Size eight. Oh, my God! How could she? How could she take my shoes?"

"That's a shame," the plump lady muttered. "Now, you know that other woman knew she didn't leave no shoes on this bus. How could she take them from the driver? Some people is terrible!"

I was wearing a pair of "slip-slops" for comfort while riding the bus. I decided I'd just have to wear them the rest of the time I would be away from home. I took my best shoes from my luggage, handed them to the barefoot lady, and said, "Take these."

"They're too large," she said between moans, as she tried them on. "I'll just have to do without shoes. But that is very nice of you," she added, between groans.

"Well, I was mixed up in it," I said vaguely. (That was as close as I could come to saying, 'I gave your shoes away' — I'm such a coward!) Fortunately for me, the barefoot lady was too agitated to want an explanation.

"Yes. That sure is nice of you," the plump lady said. "You don't have nothing to worry about. You done your part, honey. You sure did!" She was trying to console me but not very successfully. Indeed, I had done more than my part, which is what caused the problem!

The bus driver announced our arrival at my destination and I got off, guilt-ridden and tormented by visions of what would happen on the bus after I left. Call it ESP, woman's intuition, or whatever you like, but I know as surely as I know I'm alive that I was scarcely out of sight when the plump lady leaned toward the barefoot lady and whispered, "Honey, I couldn't tell you before, but that lady that just got off gave your shoes away!"

That's what she said, all right. And that was my just reward for my "Goodie-Two-Shoes-good deed" that changed a peacefully sleeping passenger into a harried barefoot lady.

POOR SONNY BOY DIED IN VAIN

Marian E. Barnes

Sonny Boy was a chicken. Not any kind of old barnyard chicken, understand — in fact, I don't think Sonny Boy ever saw a barnyard in his life. Sonny Boy was a pet. The Elderberry family got him from a guy who came through the neighborhood selling baby chicks for Easter one year. The other chicks he sold all died, but Sonny Boy just kept growing, and strutting around the house and backyard and on the pavement out front. He was everywhere! We all thought he was a member of the Elderberry family, along with Mr. and Mrs. Elderberry and their daughter Wanita.

Sonny Boy knew his name. He came when he was called; and he played games with Wanita and the rest of us. Everybody on Bailey Street knew Sonny Boy, and we shared food with him, a little rice here, and a little corn there, or potatoes or candy. Anyways, Sonny Boy got fat, and that was saying something! It was Depression time and food was scarce. People in our neighborhood didn't have much to eat themselves. Still, everybody loved Sonny Boy, so everybody fed him a little bit, and he got very fat and very sassy.

One night Sonny Boy got to crowin' and wouldn't stop. It shocked the neighborhood. Well, hells bells! He was such a people bird, nobody figured he could crow! He was mighty mixed up about it, though, 'cause a rooster's supposed to crow for daybreak, but Sonny Boy started crowin' 'round midnight. And a hour later he was still crowin' to beat the band, and wasn't no stoppin' in sight — or maybe I should say "in sound."

Anyways, by 'n by Mr. Elderberry come to his back door in his bathrobe. I peeped through my window and seed him tying his bathrobe belt and yelling at Sonny Boy in the backyard, really bawling him out!

"What's the matter with you?" he hollered. "Shut up and stop that crowin' this minute! You *dumb* chicken. Roosters crow in the morning, not all night long, waking up the whole bloody neighborhood. Fool! You crow one more time — I dare you! I'll come back out here and wring your neck! You hear me? Stupid bird! I dare you to crow again!"

Just when I was thinking Mr. Elderberry was gonna be keeping the neighborhood awake by hollering just as long as Sonny Boy had kept us awake crowin', he went inside and slammed the back door. Then I giggled all over myself 'bout Mr. Elderberry talking to Sonny Boy like he was a real person and could understand all that stuff he said, and then daring him to crow again. I figured Sonny Boy didn't understand a word of all that talk, and the way he had been crowin', I expected him to take Mr. Elderberry's dare as soon as he slammed the door. I thought to myself he was just a bird that wanted to crow, an' he was gonna crow! And I wondered what Mr. Elderberry would do then.

So I'm lying there waiting for Sonny Boy to start crowin' again, and the whole neighborhood is waiting with me, I know. Well, I'm here to tell you, that bird fooled me and a lot of other folks. He didn't crow n'er 'nother time that night! He didn't crow at dawn neither. And, matter of fact, far as I know, he never ever crowed again at all. He just went right back to being a person bird, playing games with us, and answering to his name, and being fat and sassy.

One Sunday, Mrs. Elderberry had a headache, and she wasn't in the car when Mr. Elderberry and Wanita came to pick his Sunday school class members up for church. He taught Sunday school, and every Sunday he gave all the Bailey Street kids in his class a ride to church. Then he used to invite all of us to eat dinner at his house after church. Everybody on Bailey Street had the same flat-tasting government food the Welfare gave out. But Mrs. Elderberry had a way with a spoon, and we all looked forward to eating at her house on Sundays. She used to take that Welfare hash and serve it in the shape of a fish, a turtle, a crab, or anything else she thought about. She would season the hash so it would have the taste of whatever it looked like. Then she'd season some of that flour or yellow cornmeal the Welfare gave out, roll the hash in it, make whatever shape she wanted, and deep fry the shaped pieces in that Welfare lard. You talk about something tastin' **good** — you had it!

Anyways, this particular Sunday after church, the Elderberry house smelled like fried chicken, and we couldn't wait to sit down to the table. Sure enough, when she brought the meat to the table on a large platter, it was piled up with chicken drum sticks and wings and thighs and breasts. I even saw what looked like a neck, and the part some folks call "the parson's nose," or "the last part that goes over the fence." It was so brown and pretty it looked like a picture in a magazine, and my mouth started to water.

"Elvira, you have outdone yourself," Mr. Elderberry said when she handed him the platter so he could put meat on everybody's plate like he always did. Then he stuck a fork in one of the drumsticks. Everybody was really watching him, wanting him to hurry up, and we saw this real funny look come on his face when he put the fork in the meat. He sort of stopped, like he didn't know what to do, and he was looking at his wife with this real strange look in his eyes. Wanita stopped looking at him and looked at her mother; then she started looking all around the table, and saying, "Where's Sonny Boy? Where is Sonny Boy?"

Usually, whenever Sonny Boy heard his name, he came to whoever was saying it if he was anywhere around. But this time he didn't show, so Wanita started calling him. "Sonny Boy! Sonny Boy!" And she was sounding scared and excited, but he still didn't come. Mr. and Mrs. Elderberry were still staring at each other across the table, and the rest of us were looking from one of them to the other, and then at Wanita, and then at each other because we were all getting this awful feeling, but we didn't know what to do. Then Wanita pointed to the pile of chicken on the platter and said, "Dear Mother" — She always called her mother that — "Is this Sonny Boy?"

Mrs. Elderberry didn't answer. She just looked real confused and unhappy. Wanita started crying, and her father, still looking at his wife, said in this real deep voice, "*Elvir-raah!*"

"Well, I bought Sonny Boy and those other chicks so we could have some decent meals when they were grown." You could tell she was begging us to understand what she had done, and agree that it was all right. "The others died, so we can't eat them. But it doesn't make sense for us to keep Sonny Boy walking around all over the place while we eat this nasty Welfare hash day after day!"

She was crying real soft now, and Wanita was crying loud, and the rest of us kids around the table were staring at that platter of chicken and sniffling, and crying, or trying to keep from crying, and wondering how in the world she could have done that to Sonny Boy. Then Mr. Elderberry cleared his throat real hard, pushed the drumstick off the fork he was holding back onto the platter, and excused himself from the table without eating anything. Wanita jumped up from the table and ran upstairs, then the rest of us excused ourselves and went home without eating. When we left, Mrs. Elderberry was clearing the table off — everything but Sonny Boy, who was still piled on the platter. It looked like she didn't know what to do with him.

To this day, I don't know what happened to the remains of Sonny Boy. Wanita won't talk about it. Nobody could eat him, not even Mrs. Elderberry, I know that. But I still wonder what she did with him. Nothing they could have done seems right to me. I hate to think of Sonny Boy being put in the trash or garbage, or fed to other animals, or other people. I don't think the Elderberrys really would have done any of that. It doesn't seem like they should have buried him either. He had been fried in Welfare lard, for goodness sakes! It would be crazy to bury a fried chicken, even if it was Sonny Boy!

Anyways, I guess I'll never know. And maybe that's best. Ever since that awful day, whenever I meet Mrs. Elderberry, it's hard for me to treat her like she hasn't killed somebody. If I knew what she did with Sonny Boy's body, it would be even harder.

HOW A HOE BECAME A 'HO' AND TURNED INTO A RAKE

Or How They Changed My Stories and Gave Me Other Surprises!

Marian E. Barnes

Here I was in Oklahoma trying to tell a great story to a gymnasium overflowing with fourth- and fifth-graders, and it's like struggling barefoot up an icy hill! I know why. I really do. But I don't want to believe it. To tell you the truth, I *cannot* believe it.

I've told this story for years in urban areas of the East Coast, and if thousands of those streetwise young minds had heard the story, and played the roles of its characters with never an untoward word or snicker, it was not possible that children in this off-the-beaten-path, semirural spot would be more gross — was it?

So I keep on struggling up this hill, trying to pretend nothing is happening, and all the while it keeps right on happening, bringing to life a hilarious nightmare. Hilarious, maybe; but also more dreadfully embarrassing than I could have imagined.

All right, I suppose I could have imagined it might happen — even, in hindsight, *should* have anticipated the incident, especially in the urban East. But the sad point is, I did not see it coming. The result was, I had to make changes in the way I tell the folktale "Kalulu and his Money Farm," *after* my storytelling encounter with Oklahoma's "li'l darlin's," that I would have made before telling the story the very first time if my mind had been working in tandem with my North Philadelphia roots.

To understand what happened, you need to know that in the story I was telling, Kalulu, the hare, a popular show-off character in Bantu African folktales, boasts to his chief that he can grow money. He "blows" the money the chief gives him to grow; then, empty-handed, stalls him three harvest-times by saying, "Money is a slow-growing crop." Finally, the chief asks a series of animals to go with Kalulu to see what's happening on his money farm; but Kalulu tricks each animal into running away and leaving him alone until the chief sends the tortoise, who is known to be smart. First, Kalulu tells tortoise they will have to sleep at the money farm that night and he has forgotten his pillow, so he must go back home and get it. But wise tortoise says there's no need for that because he has brought a pillow in his satchel which Kalulu may use. Kalulu then says that he has also forgotten to bring his hoe, and asks tortoise to wait while he returns to the house for his hoe. However, again tortoise has anticipated Kalulu and says that will not be necessary either because he has brought a short-handled hoe along which Kalulu may use.

By this time, two of Oklahoma's future generation, on stage playing the roles of Kalulu and tortoise with my assistance, were having a terrible time saying their lines. Their classmates, who knew the story line from having heard it when Kalulu tricked the first animals sent to follow him, began to titter when Kalulu said he was going home to get a pillow because he planned to spend the night at the farm. The small boy playing the role of the tortoise was then supposed to pull a pillow from the satchel he held, hand it to the boy playing Kalulu and say, "I brought a pillow, Kalulu. You can use mine."

Instead, he shoved the pillow toward Kalulu, and fixed *me* with a waxy stare. "I brought a pillow, Kalulu. You can use mine," I prompted him twice.

"You can use mine," he muttered finally, still gazing at me, inspiring a flurry of surreptitious giggles from his buddies in the audience.

At this point, Kalulu was supposed to announce that he had also forgotten to bring his hoe along and ask the tortoise to wait while he went back home for it. But, no. "Kalulu" was as silent as the grave, looking from me — prompting him through clenched teeth — to the waxy-faced tortoise, to the floor, struggling painfully, but unsuccessfully, to control his contorting face; and all the while giggling from the audience was becoming less and less subdued.

Here I should explain to the uninitiated what streetwise readers know already: In Black English (the Spectacular Vernacular), the word for a lady of the evening is spelled "who' " but pronounced exactly the same way as the farm tool Kalulu "forgot."

To the everlasting credit of the boy playing the role of Kalulu, he was trying his very best to cooperate, to ignore his snickering classmates and say his lines without laughing. He just could not do it. "Say, 'I forgot to bring my hoe,' " I prompted him again and again. Whereupon he would look at me, stretch his eyes, and open his mouth, but nothing would come out!

I appreciated the fact that this child was trying to help me out, trying not to laugh, but by this time, I had a different problem. I was trying not to cry! *They were "trashing" my beautiful story.*

"Say, 'I've got to go back home and get my hoe,' " I kept saying desperately, but the result was always the wide-eyed, silent same. Then, without warning, "Kalulu" started to squeal. *"Eeeouch! Eeoowww!! Eeeeeooooooowww!!!"*

Poor fellow! In the intense, emotional upheaval of the moment I had obviously "lost it." Because he appeared unable to utter the words I knew he was trying to say, at some point I had grabbed him by the neck and started trying to squeeze the words out of him! I was wearing a massive ring on my right thumb which was digging into the flesh of his neck. I was squeezing harder and harder, and he squealed louder and louder, until I finally "came to."

I remember feeling just awful for the child, and thinking, *My goodness! I hope I haven't hurt him. This ring could really cut him badly.* "I'm sorry," I said. "I'm really sorry!" The audience used this as an excuse for an honest belly laugh, supposedly related to my extra-story difficulties. At that instant, I gave up on "Kalulu" completely as I finally understood. That line was never going to come out of this child's mouth. So I abandoned him abruptly and hopefully turned to the tortoise once again.

"You don't have to go home for your hoe, Kalulu. I brought a hoe with me, and you can use mine," I prompted him rather too loudly out of total frustration and fear that once more friend tortoise was going to be waxy-eyed and silent. And he was. So I prompted him again, and again, and again. (For some reason, it was really hard for me to "throw in the towel.") By this time, of course, sneaky giggles, snickers, and titters had turned into healthy guffaws as on and on I went!

Well, I finally got up that icy hill. But ever since that day, when I tell "Kalulu and his Money Farm," Kalulu says he is going to spend the night at the farm. He also says he has forgotten to bring his pillow and must go home for it. But he does not say he has forgotten to bring his hoe with him. He now says he has forgotten to bring his rake. Once I made it a shovel. But then I decided to stick with "rake" because, like "hoe," it has two meanings.

Change-making incidents are not always so multifaceted and full of action. Once I pointed to the first hand that went up when I asked for volunteers to play the part of a frog. To my dismay, the hand I thought belonged to a ten-year-old really belonged to a rosy, dimpled-cheeked little fellow who tumbled from his mother's lap and toddled up the aisle. This child was three to four years old — "*max.*" A baby! I had always been careful to select older children as volunteers. What on earth was I to do?

I found out fast enough. All I had to do was let him "do his thing." To begin with, he had a bass drum voice, hoarse, deep, and resonant — the best "frog's voice" I have ever heard. And whatever that little boy was told to do, he did it. And did it *well!* Since that marvelous day, when I choose volunteers, I don't consider age.

The story he was in, "How Frog Lost his Tail," is an unfailing source of unexpected laughs and groans: Because the forest animals scorn and ridicule Frog for not having a tail, he is given a tail by the Skygod along with a job guarding the magic well that never goes dry. When other wells go dry and animals come to Frog's well, he repays their former unkindness by refusing to let them drink. The animals tell Skygod, who punishes Frog for being unforgiving by removing his tail for all time.

Children playing the animal roles sometimes stray from the story line quite appropriately, making the presentation their special version of an ancient tale. Sometimes young actors improvise statements that would change the story inappropriately, but usually a gentle suggestion along the plot line will nudge the young person in the right direction. But there are also those "no-nudge-possible" times when all that is left for storyteller and audience is a building-shaking laugh or groan.

Such a laugh comes to mind recalling the day the animals elected the bear to go tell Skygod that they were dying of thirst because Frog would not let them drink from the magic well. Draped in his black "bear skin cloth," a seven-year-old "bear" approached Skygod and said clearly, "I am here to represent the other animals. They want me to tell you they are dying because Frog won't let them drink water from his well. *Me, myself, I drink water from the river!*"

Laugh? I thought I'd die! The father of this clear-thinking "bear" was in the audience, actually rolling on the floor with laughter at the brilliant stage presence of his son. Since then, when I tell the story, I dry up all wells, rivers, brooks, creeks, lakes, oceans and rain!

Once, I needed a handkerchief for a "Skygod" who had taken very seriously his task of making smoke pour from his nostrils! Then there was the time that a Skygod overruled the story plot and would not budge. Bedecked in royal African kente cloth, rich purple, and a paper crown of gold and "jewels," he listened with a stony, sour face as a committee of animals reported Frog's abominable behavior.

"Well, what do you want me to do about it?" the Skygod snarled.

Put off by the gruff, unfriendly attitude of the Skygod, the confused "animals" began to grouse and chatter.

At this point, I suggested that the problem would probably be solved if the Skygod took away Frog's new tail. Here "Skygod" folded his well-developed arms across his ample chest, glared at the "animals" around him, and said, "NAW!"

"But, he was really *mean* to all the animals," I nudged.

"*So* — I don't blame him! I'd ha' done the same thing!"

"But . . . but we're all going to die, if you don't do something," the animals objected, and I was reenforcing their complaints.

"That's just too bad! How about what y'all did to him? You don't remember that now, do ya? Well, *I* remember it. And I'm not taking away his tail, *and that's that!*"

And so it was. Skygod "sat out" the rest of the story in tight-lipped, folded arm, scowling splendor while I finished telling the tale the way ancient storytellers had passed it down.

Once I picked a youngster to play the part of a character in a story although he hadn't volunteered. I'm not sure why I chose him. He was very near, very still, and his sad eyes were watching me from somewhere deep inside himself. I reached toward him and said, "I'd like for you to come up here with me and be the main character in the story." He was so startled that he jumped, then sat staring at me in disbelief.

Later, a parent who was in the audience told me the boy's teacher had also jumped when I called on him, then gasped, *"Oh, no! HE can't do that!"*

I'm glad I didn't hear what the teacher said. It would have influenced me. As it was, I invited the boy to come up a second time. When he realized I really meant what I said, he slowly made his way from his seat and joined me on stage.

At the beginning, he stood silent and immobile no matter what I told him to say or do. But I kept the story moving smoothly by saying the lines and performing the actions myself; and the next time he was to perform, I would tell him what to do again.

Gradually, he began to say his lines and do as he was told. His speech and actions, slow, soft, and halting at first, were delivered with more skill and confidence as the story unfolded. By the time the tale ended, the youngster was playing the role, and now and then he showed flickers of special life. I was impressed! If the story had lasted longer – who can say? James Earl Jones, move over?

What I *can* say is that a young man of whom little was ever asked, and from whom virtually nothing was ever expected, surprised his teachers that day with the ability he showed on stage. Most likely he will never forget his moment in the limelight, which may become an inspiration for him. To enhance his memory and aid his inspiration, he will have a photograph of himself on the school stage which appeared on the front page of the local newspaper the next day.

The teachers in that school will also remember that storytelling presentation for a while. "I watched you select students to act out parts in the story from everywhere in the audience," one of them said to me. "Yet every kid on stage, except one, was a Special Education student. It was like someone was guiding your hand!"

I agreed this was strange. But I hoped the excellent story-play they put on helped their teachers realize how much these students had to give, if only they were asked, if only they were expected to perform well.

My very favorite storytelling audience "revolution" happened in the heart of urban North Philadelphia at a school where students noted for boisterous energy and lack of intellectual pursuits successfully challenged the moral of an ancient fable. And based on their analysis of the tale, I was forced to change the ending for all time.

The story tells of a battle between winged creatures and land animals. Because Jackal was a coward, General Lion gave him the noncombatant position of umpire, ordering him to stand on an anthill and hold his thick tail high in the air as long as the land animals were winning. The winged creatures were winning the battle, and the animals started to run away. But Jackal cheated and kept his tail in the air. Seeing the tail still high, Lion ordered the animals to return because they were winning. The land animals returned and began to win. But Honey Guide, an observant bird, told General Eagle what had happened. General Eagle sent the bee to sting Jackal's tail. Jackal yelped in pain, dropped his tail, and ran. The land animals saw their victory signal fall, thought they were losing the battle, and turned and fled. The story ends with the moral: It only proves that cowards and cheats never win!

No sooner had I finished telling the story when an obviously agitated fifth-grader raised his hand in the air and nearly shook it off, seeking permission to speak.

"I disagree!" he fumed. "I disagree! I say if you're fighting and you're losing, *fight on anyway. You might win in the end!*"

Now a girl entered the fray. "That's exactly right!" she snapped. "And why was the jackal more of a coward and a cheat for not dropping his tail, than the eagle and the bee for stinging the jackal's tail and making it drop?"

I could not counter either of the points these young people made. To me, they seemed at least as valid as the original moral of the story, perhaps a tad more valid. So from that day on, whenever I tell "The Battle of the Animals," I give two endings — one based on the book and the other based on that classroom confrontation.

Way to go, North Philadelphia! Way to go!! *Once again you have done me proud!*

LESSONS

Marian E. Barnes

The Special Education classroom was crammed with teenage boys, and I was their substitute teacher. There were no lesson plans, or educational objectives for this class. The school considered these young men mentally slow, basically "uneducable," so I could teach whatever I liked, or not teach at all, so long as the students were kept quiet and orderly.

My experience in the schools for which I was substitute teaching had made me an extremely "hard sell" on believing students were mentally slow and "uneducable." In many of the same schools years before, teachers had frequently taken one look at my face, concluded I was mentally slow and "uneducable," and treated me accordingly. Most present-day Black male students I encountered in Special Education programs, in my opinion, were normal and brighter than normal boys who had been failed by their families, and by schools that did not understand their needs nor how to teach them. The schools solved their dilemma by herding these young men into Special Education programs where they were held and miseducated until they were old enough to be released into society.

While it wasn't possible to repair the educational damage that had left most of them virtually illiterate in their teens, I spent the time teaching them things that would make life easier for them; things they could have learned years before. How to tell time, how to read maps, Black history. Periodically, there was a free period in which everyone could do what he wished from possibilities provided inside the room.

One afternoon, one of the boys asked me to play checkers with him during a free period. I agreed, expecting the game to be a "snap" — no game at all. And I was absolutely right. The game was over before it began. I'd just been wrong about who the winner would be.

That young man wiped me out so fast it was undignified! It left me stunned. *Me!* The "champeen" checker player among the children in my family. And I'd held my own among the best players on Page Street. True, that had been some time ago; there was probably a little rust around the edges. But I still expected to win. To be beaten mercilessly in three or four moves was unforgivable. I couldn't forgive myself or my opponent.

We had played a game that was won or lost on a player's ability to best an opponent in thinking strategically and quickly; in planning ahead and in anticipating the other player's strategy. My opponent was a Special Education student considered mentally slow, and *I was his teacher, for crying out loud.* For him to beat me so unceremoniously at a mind-game like checkers was totally inappropriate.

As I wrestled with these thoughts, the student looked across the table, read my countenance, and understood instantly. "Oh," he sighed sympathetically. "Would you like to play again?" I couldn't seem to find my "teacher's voice," so I didn't answer. I just sat there. If I hadn't been the teacher, I'd say I was pouting. But I was the teacher, so I won't say that.

Now, the winner gripped the edge of the table and leaned forward, all sympathy gone from his voice and demeanor. "I'll play you again if you want. *But you will never win!* Do you want to play again?"

I knew he was right. But if I did not make the mistake of playing another game with him, it would be easier to repair my "teacher" image. So, I said, "No!" Not in my "teacher's voice," but in the "little girl" voice I would have had twenty-five years earlier if my non-checker-playing sister who didn't know how to put a crown on a king had all of a sudden vanquished me at checkers in three moves.

This had been an excellent lesson. *Perfect.* The kind of lesson you find yourself remembering long after it ends; the type lesson you use as a model for others. It could not have been structured more simply.

The second-grade class was seated in a semicircle around me, and each of us was to share with the class a personal experience. The objective was to give the youngsters an opportunity to develop verbal skills, and there was no "right" or "wrong." Talk about quality time! One after the other each child contributed a gem to a brilliant necklace of storytelling that sparkled with colors and pictures and words and action and information.

For the second part of the lesson, each person was to tell the class what she or he had learned from listening to the others. I had been first to speak for part one, and I also started off part two. It was pleasant to recount for the children many of the things I had learned from them, from a unique way to sharpen knives to special ways of making friends, and myriad things in between.

When I had finished, it was time for the first student speaker to follow suit. I turned to the first child seated immediately to my left in the horseshoe arrangement before me, and smiled as a signal for him to begin.

What happened next is indelibly stamped on my mind. With every eye in the classroom on him, the youngster threw his head in the air, took a deep breath, expanded his chest, and said proudly, *"I learned that I am a young man!"*

My mouth fell open in surprise. What was he talking about? Nobody had told a story that could have taught him that. The proverbial pin dropping on that classroom floor would have clattered as students and teacher stared at this boy swelled up with pride at the wonderful lesson he had learned.

I was just about to say "No — " when a light bulb went on inside my head and I understood what had happened, for which I will be forever thankful. To have questioned his answer would have dulled the glow of a shining moment in his life.

Instead, I said, "That is very nice!" comprehending at last that my way of addressing this boy and other boys in the class as "young man" had made a greater impression upon him than all the stories he had heard from over thirty students and his teacher. It did not matter that it was not part of the lesson plan. He had been taught a lesson he would always remember.

A long time before, I noticed that referring to children in "human" terms upgraded their concepts of themselves and uplifted their responses to my contacts with them. To refer to students as "kids" seemed to give them license to behave irresponsibly — and they took it. But when I addressed young people as boys, girls, students, youngsters, young men, young women, or young ladies, they behaved less like irresponsible "kids" and more like youthful human beings. That simple communications rule seemed to elevate young people I encountered in their own eyes. The way they behaved as a result of that made my job easier, so I latched on to the custom and never let go!

I thought of all this as I looked at that seven-year-old young man with his proud eyes shining, his chest puffed up, his head held high. *"I learned that I am a young man!"* he had said. The lesson he had learned was not the lesson I had consciously taught, but he was happy he had learned it, and so was I.

Once upon a not-so-long-ago time, I referred to an African-American boy as a "boy," and he "jumped salty" on the spot.

"You called me a *boy!*" he shouted.

Actually, I had slipped up. If I had been thinking, I would not have used that word for a Black youth so soon to become a man because I understand how its use infuriates African-American men, historically called "boys" as a racist rejection of their manhood. This, however, was in truth a junior high school *boy* to whom I had spoken.

I understood his anger on behalf of Black manhood. Still I was not prepared to grovel, apologize, and explain my mistake to this young man before the classroom of students who were present.

So I very quietly said, "Yes, I did. Would you rather that I call you a 'kid'?"

One long searching look into my face and a moment more processing what he saw. Then he spoke. "Oh, *NO!*" he said, vigorously shaking his head from side to side, and his hands also — as if to ward off the offending word. "No. No. No, indeed!"

That ended the exchange except for the feeling of mutual respect that engulfed us both.

The boy had surprised me. I don't know what I expected him to say or do. But he had fully understood my reasons for using the term "boy," and my prejudice against the prevalently used word "kid" without one word of explanation. In so doing, he reinforced my realization that bright, sharp minds abound among inner city youths. It was a lesson that I was continually relearning as a teacher of the urban young.

Most of the class was out of control. With their regular teacher away, students were indulging themselves in "substitute fever," pretending to fight each other, pitching make-believe "balls" made of wads of paper into the waste basket, yelling from the windows to their friends in the street below.

Following my policy as a substitute teacher, I was near the entrance to the classroom involved with those students who wanted to have a lesson. There were only a few of us, and it was difficult to communicate and maintain continuity above the racket the other students were making. However, we managed to follow the outline I had prepared for a social studies discussion, to make ourselves heard despite the uproar, and to voice divergent opinions on a number of important and interesting issues.

Suddenly, as a member of our group was making a telling point, one of the students shouting out the window to friends below darted away from the window into our group and began to argue against the point the student was making.

"You just be quiet," I said, more than annoyed. "Don't interrupt. You have spent your time racing around this classroom, yelling out of windows, paying absolutely no attention to the lesson, and you have no idea what is going on here."

"That's not true! I know everything you said. *Everything.* Ask me anything you want about the lesson. Anything."

I was absolutely sure this particularly obstreperous young man could not have followed the lesson. After all, those of us trying to concentrate on the discussion had found it difficult to follow because of the noise coming from him and others like him. So I asked him a simple question, certain he would not know the answer. But he did. Thinking he had "lucked out," I asked a more difficult question, then another harder yet, and still another. I fired question after question at that young man, and he answered each promptly, decisively, correctly. There could be no doubt about it — he had been following the lesson closely. I was flabbergasted. Mouth open. How many other students had done the same thing — *were still doing the same thing even as we spoke?*

At this point, he decided to enlighten me.

"You see, I am going to be a minister one day." He was clear-eyed, articulate, and purposeful. You could almost see and hear him taking his text! "But I am only twelve years old now. I'm still in my playing years. However, when I become a minister, I intend to be the very best. That means that even now, while I'm very young, I cannot afford to miss anything of value that happens in a classroom."

In retrospect, many reactions were possible at that moment. I might have felt a bit intimidated, foolish, or embarrassed. I felt none of those things then; nor have I felt them since. I might have felt, albeit grudgingly, pride in this child, and hope for what he would bring to the future. Those feelings did come later. But not then, my friend. Not then. Then I was infuriated, and nothing else! And I told him so.

"I am angrier with you than I would have been if you had been ignoring the lesson!" I snapped, glaring at him.

And do you know what that young rascal did? He grinned. Have you ever seen someone grin with his entire body? Well, that is what he did. He reached down inside himself, fetched that grin from the bottom of his soul, brought it up, and flashed it about until it enveloped the entire group.

Well, I am here to tell you — trust me on this — he was grinning all by himself!

UNSUNG LIFESTYLES

VASELINE

Evelyn Martin-Anderson

No ash
God in heaven
No ash
Got to get that ash away
From around mouths
knees, elbows, ankles
No ash please
Warts perhaps
Even pimples
But heaven forbid
No ash.

Take two fingers of vaseline
Rub it between two hands
And smooth it over little brown faces
Especially around the mouth.
Away goes the ash.

Take another two fingers of vaseline
Rub it between two hands
And knead it into those frail coconut colored arms
Away goes the ash
Then the legs
Away goes the ash

Smooth it away
Knead it away
Until the little brown figure is
A glistening mask of protection
From the ash.

BLACK MAN

Marian E. Barnes

Black Man
First man
Strong, Spirited, Spiritual
SURVIVOR . . .

Beleaguered, beset, belittled
Envied, hated, *feared*
TARGETED . . .
Because
Fired in life's fiercest furnace
At your best
YOU ARE PURE GOLD

FIFTY MEN OF COLOR WHO CHANGED THE WORLD

Marian E. Barnes

AESOP
"The Ethiopian" — world's greatest creator of fables
   RICHARD ALLEN
      Founder, African Methodist Episcopal Church
         CODY ANDERSON
            Broadcast entrepreneur
               CRISPUS ATTUCKS
                  First person to die for American independence
DANIEL BARNES
Husband-father-family provider-evangelist-counselor of ministers
           LUDWIG VAN BEETHOVEN*
           Composer
               TONY BROWN
               Broadcast journalist
                   SIDDHARTHA GAUTAMA BUDDHA
                   Founder of Buddhism
                     GEORGE WASHINGTON CARVER
                     Gentle savior of southern agriculture
JOHN HENRIK CLARKE
    World renowned historian-folklorist-author-educator
              SAMUEL TAYLOR COLERIDGE
               Composer
BILL COSBY
    Husband-father-family provider-comedian-philanthropist

---

*For information on Beethoven's complexion, see Thayer's *Life of Beethoven* (Princeton University Press, 1967), 72; J. A. Rogers, *Sex and Race* (St. Petersburg, FL: Helga M. Rogers, 1972), 306–309.

BENJAMIN O. DAVIS
General, U.S. Army
MARTIN DELANEY
Ethnologist–physician–explorer–scientist
MARTIN DE PORRES
Roman Catholic Church saint
NATHANIEL DETT
Composer
FREDERICK DOUGLASS
Abolitionist
W. E. B. DU BOIS
Author–historian–scholar–civil rights leader
ALEXANDRE DUMAS
Novelist
JAMES CHARLES EVERS
Civil rights activist
MEDGAR EVERS
Civil rights martyr
ARTHUR HUFF FAUSET
Scholar–folklorist–author–educator
JOHN HOPE FRANKLIN
Historian–author–educator
MARCUS GARVEY
Founder, Universal Negro Improvement Association
HENRY LOUIS GATES, JR.
Scholar–author–editor–literary editor
ABRAM HANNIBAL
Military commander
JOSEPH HAYDEN*
Composer
MATTHEW HENSON
Explorer
MARTIN LUTHER KING, JR.
Martyred world civil rights leader
BOB LAW
Broadcaster–educator–community activist
MICKEY LELAND
American Statesman

---

*For information on Joseph Hayden's appearance and ethnic background, see J. A. Rogers, *Sex and Race*, 307.

    C. ERIC LINCOLN
    Historian-religionist-educator-author
    TOUSSAINT L'OVERTURE
    Military strategist
     NELSON MANDELA
     South African leader
      THURGOOD MARSHALL
      Supreme Court Justice
   GARRETT A. MORGAN
  Invented the traffic light and the gas mask
     ADAM CLAYTON POWELL
    U.S. congressional leader
     GABRIEL PROSSER
     Antebellum insurrectionist
      ALEXANDER PUSHKIN
      Russian Poet

PAUL ROBESON
Singer-athlete-social pioneer
  EDWARD ROBINSON
   Historian-educator-lecturer-singer
   J. A. ROGERS
    Historian-ethnologist-scholar-author
    KING SOLOMON
    Biblical philosopher of surpassing wisdom
LEON H. SULLIVAN
Founder of international educational and human rights programs
  NAT TURNER
   Antebellum revolt leader
   DESMOND TUTU
   South African archbishop, Church of England
BOOKER T. WASHINGTON
Founder, Tuskegee Institute
     DANIEL HALE WILLIAMS
     First successful heart surgeon
   CARTER G. WOODSON
   Founder, Association for the Study of Negro Life and History
MALCOLM X
Martyred world-stage Muslim minister

     * * * * *

BLACK WOMAN

Marian E. Barnes

Mother of the world
loving, giving, laughing
Soft . . .

Keeper of the race
Knowing, guiding, surviving
Steel!

Showing . . .
Children of her womb
Godliness, human service, respect
Shaping the African soul and spirit

Molding . . .
Children of the master class
Manners, gentility, hospitality
Building Southern culture

Teaching . . .
Students in her classrooms
Heritage, history, pride, confidence
Planting seeds of leadership

Black woman . . .
*Pride of the race
Pillar of the nation*

FIFTY WOMEN OF COLOR WHO CHANGED THE WORLD

Marian E. Barnes

SADIE T. M. ALEXANDER, J.D.
    Trailblazer for women, African-Americans, and attorneys
MAYA ANGELOU
    Author-scholar-poet-actress-composer
JOSEPHINE BAKER
    International entertainer
E. C. BARNES
    Wife-homemaker-mother-educator-entrepreneur-
      righteous warrior

IDA WELLS BARNETT
  Anti-lynching crusader–writer–lecturer
MARY MCLEOD BETHUNE
  Founder of Bethune Cookman College
HATTIE BRISCOE
  Pioneer attorney for African-Americans,
  women and social progress
MADELINE CARTWRIGHT
  Educator
SHIRLEY CHISHOLM
  Congresswoman–ran for nomination as presidential candidate
CLEOPATRA
  African queen
BESSIE COLEMAN
  Internationally licensed aviator
MARVA COLLINS
  Educator
CAMILLE COSBY
  Wife-homemaker-mother-record album producer-
  philanathropist
ANGELA DAVIS
  Educator–civil rights revolution activist
SADIE EIKERENKOETTER
  Proud–stalwart–inspirational family and civic example
MERLIE EVANS
  Congressional candidate
LENORA FULANI
  Presidential candidate
CHARLAYNE HUNTER GAULT
  Television journalist
FANNIE LOU HAMER
  Civil rights revolution activist
ANITA HILL
  Educator–lightning rod for women's rights advocacy
BILLIE HOLIDAY
  Legendary singer
ZORA NEAL HURSTON
  Folklorist–anthropologist–novelist
JUDITH JAMISON
  Dancer

MARY CHURCH TERRELL
  Delta Sigma Theta and NAACP leader-women's
    rights champion
SOJOURNER TRUTH
  Abolitionist
HARRIET TUBMAN
  Underground Railroad conductor-Union troops
      assistant-nurse
MADAM C. J. WALKER
  Millionaire businesswoman
FRANCES CRESS WELSING
  Physician-author-educator-lecturer-social causes motivator
        PHILLIS WHEATLEY
          Internationally famed poet
MARY LOU WILLIAMS
  Legendary singer-educator
        MERZIE WILSON
            Historian-homemaker-poet-businesswoman
BARBARA YOUNGE
  Educator-Zeta Phi Beta Sorority and social causes activist

* * * * *

Black women
    yes Black women are always
    runnin'
I mean check it out.
    They run from catchers
    who want to put them on slave ships.
    Who want to enslave them.
    They swim, run from the jaws
    of the shark of the sea.
    They run from the auction blocks
    so not to be sold away from
    their loved ones
They run
    from the master class
    who forcefully violate them
    in the name of rape
    creating the mulatto class.

MAE JEMISON, M.D.
Astronaut, National Aeronautics and Space Administration
EUNICE JOHNSON
International promoter of fashions
BARBARA JORDAN
Congresswoman-educator-orator
FLORENCE GRIFFITH JOYNER
Track star, winner of four Olympic medals
EARTHA KITT
Socially and culturally aware actress-singer
WILLIE L. McNEAR
Motivating force in family and community
EMILY MORGAN
Fabled "Yellow Rose of Texas"-tricked General Santa Anna into losing San Jacinto Battle, leading to the addition of Texas and nine other states to the U.S.
VASHTI TURLEY MURPHY
Founder of Delta Sigma Theta Sorority
NEFERTITI
African queen
ELEANOR HOLMES NORTON
Attorney-educator-human and civil rights spokeswoman
ROSA PARKS
Sparked the civil rights revolution
AMELIA PLATTS BOYNTON ROBINSON
Key organizer of 1965 Selma, Alabama, Voter's Protest March
WILMA RUDOLPH
Discarded leg braces to become Gold Medal Olympic track star
THE QUEEN OF SHEBA
Arabian queen
ADA DE BLANC SIMOND
Historian-educator-journalist-storyteller
BARBARA SIZEMORE
Educator
JUANITA KIDD STOUT
Pennsylvania Supreme Court Justice
GRACE SULLIVAN
Educator

They run
> from the plantation, to get
> away from the terror of life.
> To get to freedom, to find
> their lost loved ones.

They run
> to save the children and
> sometimes their men from
> the horrors of slavery.

Black women always runnin'.
They run
> from pain
> disrespect
> and death.

Times have not changed.
> 'Cause our women are still runnin'.
> Still runnin' from the white boy.
> Runnin' from sexism, chauvinism.
> Runnin' from the back of the bus
> to the front.
> From bombed churches
> and Ku Klux nites.
> Runnin' from the bottom of the
> heap of human dignity.
> Runnin' from selfish, childlike
> Black men.
> Runnin' from their own children.

This is not a happy poem, but a poem to make
> you think.

We as a Black nation must STOP you from
> runnin', and allow you to rest.

Alli Aweusi

NEGRO

Alli Aweusi

A
NEGRO
IS
LIKE
AN

OREO
COOKIE
BLACK
ON
THE
OUTSIDE
WITH
WHITE
SANDWICHED
IN.

Note: "NEGRO" was first read by the author to a gathering of some 15,000 activists and civil rights leaders on the campus of Howard University in 1968. Many believe the poem originated the terms "oreo" and "oreo cookie," Black English names for a Black person with Caucasian values. Aweusi notes that other ethnic groups have since coined similar terms: "Apple" — Native American; "banana" — Asian; "coconut" — Hispanic.

CREATIVITY

Dottie Curry

They wouldn't let me join their art club —
Said I wasn't no artist
I guess I ain't
I been too busy creating
I create babies
I create safe space
I create a way out of no way
I been too busy
to sing
or write
or draw
much less dance

AMERICA'S BLACK HOLOCAUST MUSEUM FOUNDED BY NEAR-LYNCH VICTIM, JAMES CAMERON

Marian E. Barnes

America's Black Holocaust Museum was founded in Milwaukee, Wisconsin, by a man who was once nearly lynched. In 1930, sixteen-year-old James Cameron and two friends were accused of murder and rape in Marion, Indiana. Over 10,000 people stormed the jail, lynched his friends, then returned for him. Ignoring his plea of innocence, Cameron said, "they grabbed me and beat me all the way down the steps, all the way to the courthouse lawn. Then they put the rope around my neck."

Taken to the area where the limp, dead bodies of his friends hung on a tree, a rope was knotted around his neck and tightened until he lost consciousness. Miraculously, Cameron escaped being lynched. He is the author of *A Time of Terror*, which documents the story.

Inspired by a visit to the Jewish Holocaust collection in Jerusalem, he established the only museum in America that focuses on African-Americans as the victims of lynchings by other Americans. "The Black people in our country need a reminder of the atrocities committed upon our race," he said, "a memorial so that the world can never forget what has happened to us. *Within two years after the Civil War ended, over 50,000 people, mostly freed Blacks, were lynched by the Ku Klux Klan.*"

America's Black Holocaust Museum contains thousands of items, photographs, and literature related to lynchings. Part of the exhibit highlights accomplishments of Afro-Americans.

Thoughtful visitors to the museum gain rare insight into the holocaust perpetrated upon Africans in America: *enslaved in perpetuity for nearly three centuries; stripped of their families, language, land, religion, culture and history; countless millions tortured and killed.*

In remembering America's holocaust, Cameron never belittles the pain of the Jewish people, insisting that when one race suffers, *all* humanity suffers. He adds that America's treatment of Blacks and Native Americans has been disgusting and shameful, as was the treatment of Jews by the German Nazis. "My purpose for the erection of **America's Black Holocaust Museum** is to shame society into a compliance with the rules and regulations of decent human conduct as set forth in the United States Constitution," he explains.

Unfortunately, the museum, which has suffered financial shortages since its inception, is presently in desperate need of funding. At times Cameron has had to draw from his Social Security to make ends meet. He has appealed to well-wishers for monetary assistance, donations of museum equipment, and information of any kind relating to racist atrocities committed upon Black ethnic groups.

BLACK AMERICAN COWBOYS AND COWGIRLS

Marian E. Barnes

When the Civil War ended, over 5,000 African-American cowboys and cowgirls rode the range, joined round-ups, and served with ranch crews during the cattleman era of the West. While the numbers can never be verified, it has been widely reported that for every four cowboys, one was Black or Mexican.[1] It has also been estimated that about one of every three cowboys was Black. Lured by thoughts of the open range, regular wages, and starting new lives, their contributions were vital to the taming of the West.

Research indicates that the word "cowboy" originated on the U.S. East Coast as a name for the African-American males largely responsible for working with cattle. The term traveled to the West and was initially detested by cow hands, who accepted the name only after it had been glamorized by literature, film, and folklore.

After the war, hundreds of thousands of cattle, including longhorns, were running free in Texas. Cowboys like Henry Beckwourth, called "the Coyote" and "the mountain man," rode the plains searching for these dangerous nomads, which they hogtied and branded. There was no market for beef in Texas, so they organized trail drives north. In addition to herding cattle, these cowboys, their successors and predecessors joined the cavalry, established businesses, and became forces on both sides of the law.

Among the most flamboyant of the Aframerican cowboys was Bill Pickett. Many historians of the American West credit him with originating bulldogging – a way of riding beside a steer, grabbing it by its horns, jumping from one's horse and throwing the steer. "Bronco busting," taming wild horses or mustangs, was a feat at which an African-American cowboy named Bob Lemmons excelled by making wild mustangs believe he was one of them!

Some Black cowboys were badmen. Cherokee Bill, for example. At least one town, according to some records, "in the inter-

---

1. Based on consultation with Art Burton, author of *Black, Red, and Deadly* (Eakin Press, 1991), and oral historian Morris Richardson of West Columbia, Texas. Both trace the fancy dress of modern cowboys to dressing customs of early Mexican cowboys.

est of preserving the lives of its citizens," passed an ordinance making it a misdemeanor for anyone to molest him when he was abroad within its limits.[2] Cherokee Bill thus was allowed to freely ride from crime to crime and — lover that he was — from woman to woman. Sentenced to hang at last, he walked quietly to the gallows on March 17, 1896.

Hundreds of tickets had been given out. People without tickets climbed fences and trees. His mother was in the crowd, which he viewed calmly before saying, "Look at all the people. Something must be going to happen." After obeying a request that he stand over the trap door that would be sprung to hang him, he was asked if he had any last words. His reply: "No. I came here to die, not to make a speech."[3]

Another such cowboy was Nat Love, also known as "Deadwood Dick," who wrote his own story, *The Life and Adventures of Nat Love: Better Known in Kattle Country as "Deadwood Dick" — by Himself*.[4] Black Mary (also known as "Stagecoach Mary"; see *Mary Fields* in supplement, "African American Inventions Get Us Through the Day"), Bill Pickett, Jim Beckwourth, Cherokee Bill, Deadwood Dick, Bose Ikard, Bob Lemmons, and "Bronco Sam" were a few of the thousands of Black Americans of the Old West who helped to shape an exciting chapter of American history.

HOSPITAL CORPSMAN BATTLEFIELD HERO

Marian E. Barnes

Whenever the Navy awards two medals to the same man, behind the formal citation language is a story, a big story — warm, real, moving. Such is the story of Jeffery Lynn Cogborn, a hospital corpsman second class, with the United States Navy during the undeclared war between the U.S. and Korea.

The only African-American in his battalion, the Alabama-born youth earned Bronze Star medals twice in seven days for heroic achievement while serving with a Marine infantry company in

---

2. *The Negro Cowboys,* Philip Durham and Everett L. Jones (Curtis Brown, Ltd., 1965), 174.
3. *Ibid.,* 175.
4. *Ibid.,* 192.

Korea. He was a member of the famous "Lost Battalion," which was cut off for days from the outside world in the North Korean hills. For forty-eight hours he was reported dead after running straight into enemy fire. And once, while lying on the ground, Jeff Cogborn threw a grenade that destroyed an enemy machine-gunner, saving his own life and the lives of six companions.

Jeffery Cogborn's story of bravery began the afternoon of September 15, 1950, at Inchon, on Invasion Day. After nearly a week at sea, the Marines hit the beach. Bullets sang around the amphtrack, sang over it, *in* like flies around a garbage pail. Jeff dived to the ground and lay still for a moment, looking around to get his bearings. There was heavy mortar shelling, scattered machine-gun fire, and every tree, every bush, every chimney had a sniper. It was raining hard, and the air was clogged with smoke. To his right, naval gun fire had crumbled a giant sea wall. In front of him, napalm bombs dropped by Marine flyers had left the beach a flaming inferno.

They took their first objective at 8:00 that night. Miraculously, Jeff's outfit, the First Platoon, suffered no casualties. After that, the advance was fairly rapid, fairly steady. The cry of fallen men calling "Corpsman!" became a familiar summons to Jeff as he cared for the wounded.

On the second day after they landed, Jeff was in the rear guard, a squad of seven men. They were walking across a rice paddy some distance behind the main body when, without warning, a machine gun opened on them from the rear. They dropped to the ground and found themselves behind a small mound of dirt, separated from the main body, which was now being machine-gunned from the front.

It was certain death if they dared move. Well aware of how securely he had them pinned down, the gunner began to aim over their heads at the main body.

No one said a word. They lay there, as close to the ground as they could get — scared. Jeff's heart was beating so hard it jarred his body. He fingered the hand grenade in his pocket. He had never fired one before, but he knew how they said it was done. Pulling the pin out, he waited, then stood up quickly, heaved it — and *missed!* The surprised gunner stopped shooting a moment, then trained his gun on them.

Bullets were chopping into the ground all around. Jeff had

another grenade, but what good was it now? He couldn't stand up again, that was certain. He had muffed his chance! If he could only throw it as he was now, full-length on the ground . . . It didn't seem possible. It would be the second grenade he had thrown in his life, and if he had missed before with his target in full view — a machine gun set up in the window of a small hut — how could he hope to hit what he couldn't see?

His hands were clammy and his throat dry. Briefly, he glanced at the others. This was their last chance for life. His damp palm closed around the grenade. He had to *remember* where that window was.

Stiffly, his body flattened against the earth. He lobbed the grenade where he thought the window should be. A wild yell, a thundering explosion. This time he hadn't missed.

"We can't stay here. We've got to join the others," he said. They were all huddled together, frightened, knowing that Jeff was right, but watching the gun in front waiting to chop them down.

"If I go, will you follow me?" Jeff asked tensely. Nobody answered. He turned and ran zig-zagging across the rice paddy. He made it. Another man followed him, then another, and another.

The next day they were dug in on Hill 123, waiting for orders. In so short a time the greenhorns weren't green anymore. They had dug their foxholes about ten yards apart. The men were tired and grimy, and suffering miserably from the white-hot heat. The sound of rifle fire came from a long way off.

Suddenly, something moved in the valley below them. Jeff craned his neck above the foxhole. "See something?" Turner asked in his Virginia drawl. "I should have known things were too peaceful." Somehow Jeff and this Caucasian boy from the South always dug in together.

"Over there," Jeff nodded his head toward half a dozen North Koreans in the valley just as someone opened fire on them. Then others were firing as the enemy ran for protection. It was a welcome diversion from the heat, and mud, and blistering feet. It happened so quickly, only two of the North Koreans were dropped. The others took cover quickly and fired cautiously, most of their shots going wild. Then someone opened up a machine gun.

"*Knucklehead!*" Jeff spat.

"They specifically told us, no machine guns!" Turner was incredulous. " 'No machine guns unless it's absolutely necessary.

They'll give your position away.' And some *jerk* —" Whatever else he might have said was drowned in the thunder of answering machine-gun fire from the next hill. Deadly accurate mortar-shelling followed. The cry of "Corpsman!" seemed to come from all directions at once. Jeff answered it instinctively, administered aid efficiently, automatically.

He was on one knee fixing a bandage when a mortar shell landed a few yards away, directly in the center of a group of men. Jeff was thrown to the ground. For a moment everything spun around, then faded away.

"Corpsman! Corpsman!"

The cry yanked him back. Stumbling to his feet, eyes glazed, he saw inert bodies of men all around him. Long ago they had radioed behind the lines, explaining their position and asking for more medical supplies, for stretcher bearers. But help had not come.

"Corpsman!" It was Tisen. Jeff reached him and dropped to his knees. He had been hit in the head, just outside the corner of the left eye. But before Jeff touched him, his eyes fell on Marks, too badly injured to call. His jaw bone had been rammed out of his mouth, and his teeth bent under his tongue. Jeff put a bandage inside Marks' mouth and immobilized the jaw, trying not to be jarred by the persistent calls for help as he worked.

"Oh, Lord, why doesn't help come?" he found himself pleading as he turned to bandage Tisen. He went from one to the other — blood plasma, bandages, morphine — and still no help. He looked at Marks. The kid needed a doctor badly. Lifting him, he started down the hill. The Aid Station was a mile and a half behind the lines, but he made it, shielding the wounded boy while zig-zagging to avoid enemy fire.

At the Aid Station, he quickly recruited ten men and, without stopping to rest, led them back, zig-zagging, hitting the dirt, running, crawling to avoid being hit. They all made it.

It was for organizing this party of stretcher-bearers and safely conducting them through enemy fire that Jeffery Cogborn received his first citation.

They left Hill 123, now officially named "Shrapnel Hill" because of the terrible drama enacted there, and began the long march to Seoul through mud, rain, and heat.

On September 25, the assault of Seoul began. Early that morning, the company moved into a residential section. There was dangerous sniper fire, rough house-to-house fighting.

During a lull in the fighting, a scouting party was sent ahead. They never got out of sight. From somewhere a machine gun cut down two of the men. The third man took cover.

"Corpsman!" Jeff recognized Kusky's voice. The machine gun was between him and Kusky, and to answer that call he would have to cross its direct line of fire. But the instant he heard Kusky calling, he sprang up without thinking and began running hard toward the sound of his voice.

"Corpsman!" That would be Tortirello. *This is where they get me,* Jeff thought. But he reached Kusky's side unharmed. Never before in combat had he had a premonition of death, but this time he felt that his number was up.

He bent over Kusky, who had been shot in the arm. Bullets tore through his clothing, ripping off his medical kit. It rolled down the hill, and he rolled after it. By the time he got back, Kusky had been shot twice more, once in each hip. He dressed Kusky's wounds, but for Tortirello's leg he needed a Tomlin splint, which he didn't have. It hadn't been like this in Corpsman school. You always had everything you needed there. His eye fell on Tortirello's rifle. With it he improvised a splint, using bayonet and all. There was blood plasma to be given, but in the excitement he had lost the two-way needle. That hadn't happened in school either. What was wrong with him, thinking crazy thoughts like that? He dumped the water in the plasma and began shaking them together.

Afterwards he turned his thoughts to getting away from there. That gunner couldn't keep missing. He made covert signs to the boys in the street below, pointing out the position of the gun, but to no avail. Finally, in desperation, the premonition of disaster heavy upon him, he stood up to his full height and pointed to the building that housed the machine gun. Half a minute later the gun had been blasted to bits, and he was surprised to find himself still alive.

When disaster finally did strike Jeff, he had no premonition whatsoever. Later on in the day, the First Platoon became lost from the company and walked into an ambush. When they had fought their way out, they were sobered by the number of casualties. Joe Henderson, the platoon comedian from Philadelphia, was their first dead; and they had lost Lieutenant Eyers.

The next evening, September 26, Seoul was declared a liberated city.

A few days later, South Korean Marines and United Nations troops stood security guard in and around Seoul for the return of Syngman Rhee, accompanied by General MacArthur. Thus, Jeff got his first glimpse of the legendary general.

Later, his company moved out of Seoul and set up on dreary, battle-wrecked Hill Number 224. For six days nothing happened, but earlier a Marine outfit had been overrun in this spot, and the boys were nervous. If a mouse moved, it attracted rifle fire. They hand-grenaded the wind in a bush; machine-gunned harmless panda bears and deer.

On October 6, they were ordered back to Inchon for a rest. There Jeff had his first shower since the Inchon invasion three weeks before. They camped just outside a large, bomb-wrecked factory. During the day, they washed their clothes and bodies, ate hot food regularly for a change, wrote letters to the folks "Stateside." At night, they sat around a big outdoor fire. To Jeff it seemed like heaven. They told jokes, talked about their girls back home. Davis, a little fellow called "Turtle-eyes," was the life of the fireside party. Still they were conscious of the missing ones: Kusky with his perpetual argument, Henderson with his natural comedy. Tisen, Marks, Lieutenant Eyers, and so many others.

Jeff encountered little or no racial friction. Occasionally, a lanky Floridian would feel impelled to declare his love for the colored people, especially those who used to work on his dad's farm. "If that's all you've got to say, shut up," Jeff would interrupt dispassionately.

"That's a right good idea." Turner's drawl would draw a round laugh and close the incident.

One week of lounging, hot baths, and hot food. Then on October 14 they boarded a landing ship for tanks, destination unknown. After twelve dreary days at sea, they landed at Wonsan and moved up into the mountains of Majoni to relieve South Korean troops. Their purpose there was to take prisoners and to maintain a road block of a mountain pass. They stood off two "Banzai" attacks and suffered no casualties, but each combat patrol that ventured forth was ambushed. It was here that they became for a time "The Lost Battalion" because, in the heart of the North Korean hills, surrounded by 37,000 enemy troops, they lost touch with the outside world. They held the road block until they regained contact and were relieved by the army.

The first taste of the bitter Korean winter came the morning the truck convoy wound its way out of the hills of Majoni. It was nine degrees below zero, and it took most of the day to travel from Majoni to Wonsan, some thirty-five miles. When they arrived they were cold and hungry. That night and the following day, the platoon stayed in an old monastery. Afterward, they moved up near Hamhung, where they remained a week, and ate Thanksgiving dinner out of aluminum mess kits. Here Jeff was decorated for the first time, and by Colonel "Chesty" Puller himself.

Then the company moved far north to Hagaru-ri on a snowbound plateau, frozen too solid to allow digging in. It was twenty-seven degrees below zero most of the time, often colder.

A perimeter defense was set up, and Bouncing-Betty land mines provided adequate protection against repeated Banzai attacks, but they were surrounded by enemy troops. Alerted all that night, the men huddled half-frozen in cramped positions, awaiting the inevitable "H-Hour." In the morning, when Jeff tried to stand up, he keeled over.

"What's the matter, kid?" Turner was right beside him.

"My foot!" Jeff gasped. "My foot! Good Lord, my *foot!*" He was crying, the tears freezing on his face.

"Here, let me get those shoes off." Gentle as a woman, Turner removed the heavy army boots. Then he opened his coat and tucked both of Jeff's nearly frozen feet in his bosom.

"Don't cry, Jeff. Don't! You'll be all right. Just don't cry." It frightened Turner to see Jeff crying. Somehow they had all come to think of him as the one thing stable and invulnerable in a world gone haywire.

Gradually, the warmth from Turner's body began to penetrate into Jeff's feet. The bursting sensation was replaced by heavy pulsing. Eventually, he was able to limp around.

The night of November 28, the dreaded assault came. They fought back gamely, but every man knew the frigid, inaccessible plateau was an ice-locked death trap. And now it was being sprung.

There came a hiatus, momentary and strange in the midst of battle. Then a mortar shell landed less than ten feet away from Jeff. To him it seemed the explosion was inside his head. He jumped up, and before anyone could stop him, headed straight into enemy fire. It was the last time anyone saw him for forty-eight hours.

Rumor reported him both captured and dead. But two nights later, he turned up at an Aid Station behind the lines, feverishly brandishing a .45 with which he threatened to shoot anyone who came near him. His clothing was disheveled, his eyes bloodshot. He screamed wildly of the battalion's having been surrounded, the lines broken through. It took several men to subdue him and administer a sedative. When he awakened the next morning, he could not remember anything beyond the explosion.

"You have a concussion," the doctor told him. "We could hospitalize you over here, then send you back to join your buddies. Would you like that?"

"Yes, sir, I would."

"I thought you would." He finished what he was writing and looked up. "You've had enough, son. You're going home."

On his birthday, the first of December, Jeff was evacuated. Upon his release from hospitalization in the Philadelphia Naval Hospital, he was decorated for the second time, and meritoriously advanced to Hospital Corpsman Second Class.

Following his second decoration, Hospital Corpsman Jeffery Lynn Cogborn was assigned to the dry cleaning plant of the Philadelphia Naval Base. It was his duty to press military uniforms.

MY DAY AS A MIGRANT FARM WORKER

Marian E. Barnes

He was *really* drunk. Rubbery limbs, slack jaw, glazed eyes, oblivious to everything, including the raw wind that flapped his worn pants and the holes in his overcoat. "Well," somebody murmured, "he's feeling no pain." So *that's* what that expression means, I thought. Not somebody roaring drunk for the "fun" of it, but somebody drunk beyond feeling his pain and misery.

But if the brother was feeling no pain, most of the rest of us on the corner of Ninth and Jefferson in Philadelphia were feeling plenty of it as we waited for a farm labor transport bus to take us to New Jersey to pick tomatoes. It was a raw, damp, fall morning, long before sunrise. Waiting was tiresome and cold. Someone had a fire going. It didn't help. A vendor was selling hot coffee. Several people had been drinking something stronger.

It was 1977. Most of us were jobless, struggling to survive in a hostile economy. There were young fathers, middle-age mothers, teenage girls with their ten-year-old brothers, grandfathers almost seventy, great-grandmothers nearly eighty, Purple Heart veterans in the prime years of life. All were Black, with one exception, a young woman who told me she had been reared on a farm and that she usually earned sixty dollars a day picking tomatoes. I was glad to hear it. It made me sure I'd make at least half that much.

I tried to board the first bus which arrived at 4:30 A.M. "No women! We're picking peaches," the driver said. As other buses arrived, some drivers refused to accept children, or took only their "regular" workers.

Workers were selective too. Many passed up offers to board numerous buses, waiting for a preferred bus to arrive. Most people told me to wait for "Horace." He was a minister; he had "good" tomatoes; his bus was best. But several buses had refused me already, and Horace had refused me the day before. I was anxious, and afraid that for the third day I'd be left standing on the corner with the disappointed "rejects" as the last bus pulled away. So when Mary came and agreed to take me, I boarded her bus in spite of the "you'll be sorry" looks from those who had told me not to go with Mary because she had "bad" tomatoes.

I sat beside a portly, dignified gentleman who appeared to be in his seventies. He said this was his first time as a farm worker. Mary was a "together" lady, born to command. Wearing a wide straw hat over plaited hair, and spotless white pants, she selected her workers carefully, drove the bus, bossed activities in the tomato fields. Members of her family acted as a team to help her conduct the various operations, including a food-stand.

"Everybody out!" Mary shouted. It was just about dawn. The bus had stopped on a road surrounded by waist-high grass. I didn't see any tomatoes, and I wondered why we were getting out. I followed the group to the far end of a huge, soggy field where everyone dropped the plastic bags they all seemed to be carrying. I put my purse down.

"I want red-ripes — full baskets!" Mary thundered. While I was trying to understand, people darted by me, scrambling to snatch stacks of wood baskets lying on the ground, establishing claims with Mary to pick from certain rows of tomatoes, which I couldn't even see. I looked intently and finally saw that tomatoes were growing among the grass and weeds.

By the time I reached the spot Mary assigned me, the distance of half a city block, the high, wet grass had soaked my clothes, and the muddy ground was pulling my shoes apart at the seams, nearly sucking them off my feet.

Working in the soggy shoes and wet clothes was miserable. Also, there were "tricks of the trade" I didn't know. Why else were others lining up full baskets at the ends of their rows while I struggled to fill one? And when I finally filled it, there was Mary, taking tomatoes from it because they were not ripe enough, or another member of her team saying, "Your basket isn't full."

I learned much: A filled basket had to be watched until it was counted, because someone else might claim it. It was easy to get lost in the fields because there were no man-made landmarks. I learned that the omnipresent plastic bags held lunches, and containers of water, which workers drank instead of the water provided for them in a huge container exposed to the open air. Some people used the bags to smuggle produce away from the fields for home tables, or to be sold for a little extra money.

Each of the 5/8 bushel baskets I was scuffling to fill seemed to hold a ton. My anticipation of my earnings was diving on a rollercoaster. Several workers were singing an old spiritual. I wanted to join in, but I sensed that concentrating on the words and timing of the song would slow down my struggle to fill baskets.

And my struggle was already being slowed by clumsy fingers, by mud-logged shoes that were coming apart and falling off my feet as I walked, by aching limbs and stiffening joints. Still, I kept on struggling, but there was no song on my lips.

By noon the sun had burned the chill from the air and dried my clothes. Soon I was hot and thirsty. Afraid to chance the water, I considered buying a soda for forty cents. It seemed a fair price. Then I realized that was the sum I earned for picking two baskets of tomatoes, and the price seemed outrageous. Nothing was worth two baskets of tomatoes! But the hard work and scorching sun were making me sick. My head felt light. Nausea welled from the pit of my stomach. I had to stop.

I walked to the food stand at the edge of the field, bought a ginger ale, and sat under a tree beside the road. Other workers were there eating lunches bought from the food stand. Some had hot platters and soft drinks equal in price to what we earned for picking over twelve baskets of tomatoes. I wondered how much of their earnings would be used to pay for their food.

"I found four full baskets that didn't belong to nobody!" A small, leathery man said gleefully, "and I told Mary they were mine!" Earlier a tearful young woman had told me four baskets of her tomatoes had "disappeared" before Mary counted them. Now I pointed this girl out to the man who had apparently "found" them. He ignored me.

The man sitting next to him took a sudden interest in me, however. He observed me closely for a time, saying nothing. Then a faint air of disapproval crept into his expression.

"What are you doing here?" he asked.

"The same thing you are doing here," I snapped.

"But you could be a clerk or something."

"Maybe I could. And maybe I couldn't. It's not that easy. Maybe you could be something else."

He stared at me without speaking, and his expression changed. I had earned his respect by fighting back. Half-smiling now, through narrowed eyes, he said, "You don't have to go in the fields. You can make twenty dollars a day just for being here. Plenty of them do."

"*What?*" But now he was cautious. Somehow I had made him afraid to speak. He pressed his lips together, his smile replaced by a knowing look. "What do you mean? How can I make twenty dollars just by being here?" I prodded him. He pursed his lips tightly. Only his eyes answered.

With some difficulty, because of the absence of landmarks, I found my way back to where I had been working. The tomato field looked like a blanket of high grass and weeds, and it was nearly impossible to identify a particular spot. Looking around, I realized that I was one person in what could have been a slavery-time plantation scene. Wide sun hats, colorful bandannas, Black bodies bending and lifting, Black hands picking produce, Black voices talking, calling, singing spirituals.

The soda and the rest had refreshed me. As I started working again, I set a new goal for myself. I knew now that it wasn't realistic to expect to make thirty dollars for the days work. I was being paid only twenty cents for each 5/8 bushel basket I picked; and I had to be selective and choose only tomatoes that were red-ripe. The work was strenuous, and my body was tired and aching. Production was very slow. I made up my mind that I wanted to earn at least five dollars for the day's work.

If I worked steadily, without stopping again, I might make the new goal, which somehow was linked in my mind with my self-respect. Never mind, for the moment, the cost of transportation to and from my home to the point where the bus to the farm took on and discharged passengers; never mind that the mud had totally destroyed the pair of shoes I was wearing, or that I could probably not use the other clothes I was wearing again; never mind how much I must spend for lunch. My pride would be saved if at the end of the day I could say I had made five dollars.

The sun felt good now, and I started to sing. Suddenly, the song was interrupted by a howl of rage. Screeching at the top of her voice, a woman was rushing toward me and a man working not far from me. "Get away from her, or I'll cut you a new ass hole!" she shouted.

She was racing in my direction. My jaw dropped, and my eyes popped in confused amazement as I realized she was enraged about me!

Not until this moment had I seen her or the man. "Every time a new woman comes to these fields you set out to get her! I see you sniffing behind her. Well, you'll shit another way when I get through cutting your ass!"

I looked at the man. He seemed embarrassed, but not afraid. He didn't move. The woman was streaking across the ground, and she meant business. I moved quickly out of her path, to the end of the row.

As the woman's shrieked curses and threats of impromptu surgery filled the air, I remembered my conversation with the man who had challenged me earlier.

I had not come here to be the "other woman" in a love triangle, or to earn twenty dollars for doing nothing, but quite obviously there was more going on around me than picking tomatoes. And if I didn't keep my wits about me, I could find myself a victim of circumstances I didn't understand.

Toward the end of the day the farmers came to the fields. They collected the baskets of tomatoes and dumped them into huge cargo trucks. Their white skins reddened by the sun, they shouted orders, most of which Mary relayed to us. Once again I was overcome with the similarity to a slavery-time plantation. "Mary, clean that mess up from the other side of the road where them people ate lunch. That ain't my property over there," one of the farmers bellowed.

"All right," Mary answered. She gritted her teeth and violently kicked a stone out of her path. "I hate for anyone to holler at me," she hissed softly, "and I don't leave my dirt for nobody to clean!"

After all the tomatoes had been loaded on a truck, and the grounds cleaned on both sides of the road, we were driven to a private picnic grove several miles away. While some workers bought food and alcoholic beverages from nearby stores, Mary set a cash box on a picnic table and began to pay off. She tallied each worker's pay based on the number of baskets he or she had picked, minus the cost of any food purchased. After deducting forty cents for the ginger ale I had purchased, she handed me five dollars.

My limbs were aching and beginning to stiffen as I walked to accept it. But I had made my goal! I earned more than many others. Two men were paid about twenty dollars; and a few people earned between five and ten dollars. But it seemed to me that most workers made less. The old gentleman who sat beside me on the bus that morning earned two dollars and twenty cents. His gentle, sensitive face was expressionless as he quietly put the money in his pocket. Nobody seemed bitter. A youthful husband and father was paid four dollars eighty cents, while he smiled and talked about his family. A Korean veteran, still carrying a bullet from the war in his body, earned five dollars. He bought a large pickle which substantially reduced his earnings, and told us that store owners in areas such as this often raised the prices charged newly paid farm hands.

I wasn't bitter for myself. Bone-tired, bleary-eyed, and aching all over, my day as a farm hand had been a journalistic adventure I might never have to repeat.

But this was a way of life for the Korean veteran, the young father, the old women and old men. How did they live? It was worse than slavery in some ways. Then you were not paid. But you also did not have to buy food or clothes or pay rent. Now, most of these people left their homes at 4:00 A.M. and returned at 8:30 in the evening. Between these hours they slaved for the few pennies they earned, which was not enough to provide food for their families.

I was bitter for the wounded Korean veteran who had gone to fight someone else's war, and returned to become a slave for five dollars a day; and for the young man who must provide for his family with four dollars and eighty cents; and for the old man struggling to maintain his dignity with two dollars and twenty cents pay.

Some people couldn't bear to watch the television dramatization of the Alex Haley novel *Roots*. They said it hurt too much to watch what our ancestors went through. Others said that things are different now, and it does no good to look back. These folks should spend a day with migrant farm laborers and learn what some of our brothers and sisters are going through now — to see how little difference there is between slavery and "freedom" for some of us.

I've enshrined the money I earned as a farm hand. Hard times have come, and gone, and come again since then, but I don't ever plan to spend that five-dollar bill.

PRESIDENT JOHNSON'S GIFT TO ME

Marian E. Barnes

June 29, 1967. President Lyndon Baines Johnson was coming to Philadelphia, and I was going to cover the story. Being a television reporter for the ABC network affiliate station in the city over the past two years had brought many rewards. I had interviewed statesmen, heads of state, world church leaders, presidential cabinet members, even the vice-president. But never before had I been given a presidential assignment. I was excited.

The president was coming to see the Operations Industrialization Center (OIC) Program in operation, and to sign a Teacher Corps bill. Founded by Rev. Leon Sullivan in an old, dilapidated jail in the heart of a poor African-American area, OIC skills centers had given job skills, pride, and hope to poor people in Philadelphia; and now such centers were being opened in other countries. Today President Johnson would sign a bill that would enlarge the Teacher Corps and help OIC.

The wheels of the presidential plane touched down in Philadelphia at 9:25 A.M. Before 10:00, Reverend Sullivan was guiding the president through the OIC skills center at the old, renovated jail house to see classes being taught in telecommunications, restaurant training, tooling, sheet metal work, dressmaking, drafting, electronic assembly, and chemistry.

A multitude of people waited outside to greet the president as he left, and he walked among them shaking hands. Less than half an hour later he was speaking at OIC's administrative center, where hundreds of people had gathered, including reporters from every news agency in Philadelphia and surrounding areas. I was seated on the first row of the audience. It was hot, and TV cameras and their lights added to the heat. Still-camera flash bulbs popped continually.

Unfazed, the president spoke enthusiastically: "I have seen this place this morning myself . . . the jail that Rev. Sullivan wanted because, as he said: 'It is the most dank, most dismal place in town, a symbol of tragedy. If I could transform that building, I could transform men.'" President Johnson also said, "I have seen so many things that were right here this morning that I wish everyone in America could not only see them, but emulate them and follow them."

When he finished speaking, Mr. Johnson stepped to a table and signed the Teacher Corps bill, using several pens, as Reverend Sullivan looked on. He then gave one of the pens to Reverend Sullivan, and each of the other pens to someone important to the success of the OIC program. Then he introduced Mrs. Johnson and the Honorable Sargent Shriver, who were with him, and the party proceeded to leave.

The president was greeting each reporter that he passed with a handshake. I was about the fifth reporter on the row, and I was anticipating my turn with pleasure. I had never shaken the hand of an American president. When he reached me, he smiled warmly and shook my hand. Standing there looking at me, his smile broadened. Then, to my surprise, he interrupted the handshake and said, "I would like to give you something. I don't have any more pens, but I would like you to have one of the boxes that the pens came in." After saying that, he walked back to the signing table, picked up the pen boxes, returned and gave one to me, and one to each of the reporters that he greeted after me until all the boxes were gone.

The pen box that President Johnson gave me bears his signature and the presidential seal in blue on a glossy, white lid, covering a gilted gold bottom that is slowly turning silver as it ages. Inside the box, on a layer of cream-colored satin that was probably white when I received the box, there are two ink cartridges, refills for the missing pens. They are packaged in cellophane, once clear and pliable, now smoke-colored and brittle. There is also a typewritten statement on a yellowing slip of paper that reads: "One of the pens used by the President on June 29, 1967, on approving H.

R. 10943, An Act to amend and extend Title V of the Higher Education Act of 1965."

Sometime after President Johnson returned to Washington, Reverend Sullivan was informed that Mr. Johnson considered his visit to OIC one of his "best days" in his term as president of the United States.[1]

June 29, 1967, most certainly was one of my "best days" as a television reporter. On that day, the president of the United States of America made me feel special.

SCENES FROM THE LIFE OF MALCOLM X, MARTYRED MUSLIM LEADER

Marian E. Barnes

"The most important thing that we can learn to do today is to think for ourselves." [*]

Coming from the lips of fiery, controversial Malcolm X, the words were powerful. They took on a life of their own. His audience of teenagers listened, mesmerized as Malcolm's spellbinding voice continued, *"It's good to keep wide-open ears and listen to what everybody else has to say, but when you come to make a decision, you have to weigh all of what you've heard on its own, and place it where it belongs, and come to a decision for yourself; you'll never regret it. But if you form the habit of taking what someone else says about a thing without checking it out for yourself, you'll find that other people will have you hating your friends and loving your enemies. This is one of the things that our people are beginning to learn today — that it is very important to think out a situation for yourself. If you don't do it, you'll always be maneuvered into a situation where you are never fighting your actual enemies, where you will find yourself fighting your own self."*

---

[1]. *Build Brother Build,* Leon H. Sullivan (Philadelphia: Macrae Smith Company, 1969).

[*] Quotations are from a speech given by Malcolm X, December 31, 1964, at the Hotel Theresa. He was speaking to thirty-seven teenagers from McComb, Mississippi. Their visit to New York was sponsored by the Student Nonviolent Coordinating Committee as a reward for youth who had been outstanding in the civil rights struggle of their area.

Born Malcolm Little in Omaha, Nebraska, Malcolm moved with his mother to Detroit, Michigan, after has father was murdered by whites in 1931. When he was sixteen, he dropped out of school. Later, he moved to New York — alone — and became a part of the street crime scene. Variously known as "Red," "Detroit Red," and "Big Red" because of his height and sandy hair, before he was twenty-one Malcolm was imprisoned for burglary.

He was incarcerated at the Charleston, Massachusetts, state prison from 1946 to 1952. When he reentered society, it was as a staunch follower of Islam and of The Honorable Elijah Muhammad, leader of the largest Muslim movement in America. Now he was Malcolm X, having adopted "X" as a surname as many African-American Muslims did. The "X" dramatized the loss of knowledge of true surnames that occurred when enslaved ancestors were forbidden to use their real names.

After Malcolm X had become a minister functioning in the community, the Honorable Elijah Muhammad, national leader of the Islamic movement to which Malcolm X belonged, assigned him to leadership of Mosque Number Seven in Harlem. Very shortly, Mosque Number Seven was the most prominent mosque in the movement. Malcolm X, now often called "The Big X," was national spokesman for the movement. And Malcolm's voice became the voice of Islam for millions of Americans who heard his strong, strident, intelligent orations through the media, or in person.

Malcolm X was suspended as minister of Mosque Number Seven in 1963. He then formed the Organization of Afro-American unity and traveled the nation preaching Black pride, Black manhood, and economic independence. He visited Africa and returned to the West with a greater understanding of international and interracial kinship. On February 21, 1965, Malcolm X was assassinated in New York City's Audubon Ballroom under circumstances that remain unclarified.

EXILED FROM SOUTH AFRICA, MY HOME

Joseph Mwalimu[*]
As told to Marian E. Barnes

Ten years ago I sat praying in an airplane as it glided into the skies above South Africa. Below us, Johannesburg police had arrived. *They wanted me!*

South Africa is my beloved homeland. I was born there, as were my ancestors since history began. But I had told stories and written plays describing my life as a Black African in my country, and for this, white authorities who controlled the government had branded me "subversive."

In South Africa, storytellers who speak or write against the government can be imprisoned for ninety days with no court hearing and no visitors. The ninety-first day you can be rearrested, and this can be repeated endlessly. Time and again I was seized and incarcerated — for stories told, or plays I wrote, for forgetting the body-pass that indigenous Africans must carry.

Prisons for Black South Africans are the worst in the world! I was crammed along with fifteen other men into a poorly ventilated space about fifteen by eighteen feet. We had no provisions for bathing, and an uncovered bucket was our toilet. South Africa's cornmeal is stored in huge tanks, and meal that clings to the sides and gets rotten is fed to pigs and Black South African prisoners. We had to dig worms out of it before we ate it. If guards caught us sleeping, they beat us. We had to sleep listening for their keys, and when we heard them jingling, even in the middle of the night, we had to jump up and stand at attention. We were also tortured physically. Guards attached electric wires to our testicles, and to our ears, then they turned the electric current on. Sometimes, while they were doing this, they wore canvas bags over their heads so they could not be recognized. Since I have been gone, I have heard that guards now use pliers to break the teeth of Black prisoners, and to pull their fingernails off!

After my last prison term, friends arranged for me to enter the United States as a student. However, police received an anonymous tip that I was going to produce one of my plays in America. They came to the airport and attempted to stop my plane. The plane I was on was airborne when they arrived, but they still could have forced it to return. I will never know what happened, but whatever the reason, police did not intercept the flight.

I have been living in exile since 1977, but I will return to my homeland after the revolution which will erupt in South Africa at any time. Meanwhile, I hope everyone will boycott television shows like the one I saw which called Nelson and Winnie Mandela terrorists. They are our leaders. I am also disturbed by storytellers who say, "Leave politics out of storytelling." Our living condition *is* politics!

I have lectured in Denmark and Sweden, in Norway, England, the U.S., and Canada. Everywhere I go, all over the world, I see the same pain, and hear the same cry of oppressed Black people.

Art for art's sake is not for us!

Joseph Mwalimu is a pseudonym

I MUST SPEAK OUT!

Deborah L. Orr-Ogunro

I cannot be silent while they beat
my brothers down in the street
and try to suffocate their souls

I cannot sit by silent and watch
while they beat my brothers down
telling my brothers they are not
human and they only understand pain

My brothers and sisters became violent
fighting, burning and rioting
Deep down inside they are hurting
They do not have the knowledge to break
the cycle

If I sit by silent and watch
my brothers being beat down and say nothing
Next they will disgrace my father
Silence my mother
Use my sister

If I am silent and say nothing, I will always
be afraid, watching, waiting, and wondering
When will they come after me

THE DEATH OF A KIKUYU

Marian E. Barnes in collaboration with Dr. Wacira Gethaiga,
Kikuyu Consultant

Maina was dying, and he knew it. He was old, the eldest of the elders in his village. One by one his children, followed by their children, had come and bowed before him. He had placed a feeble hand on each head and in a voice scarcely above a whisper pronounced a special blessing on each life. Now his wife, her brother, and Maina's dearest and oldest friends were quietly moving about the small, round, mud-walled house. This house, with its roof of thatch, had been Maina's home for many years. These same friends had helped him build the house when he and his wife were beginning their life together. Now they were helping her prepare to take him to a dying hut. After they had taken him there and left him to his fate, they would return to this house and carry out purification rituals necessary to cleanse the home of evil spirits that had caused Maina to sicken and die.

Maina knew the rituals well. He had performed them countless times for dear friends who were about to join the ancestors. And now it was his time. He watched through dim, filmy eyes as the men in the room prepared a litter on which they would carry him to the death hut. The eyes of memory replaced his failing vision, and he saw his wife clearly. Her steps slowed with age, she was preparing his favorite meal. He saw her gnarled hands placing a pot over the three standing stones in the fireplace; he saw her precious face blurred by puffs of steam from the pot.

The men bore him gently to the death hut where the litter on which they carried him became his bed. They surrounded him with things that had been important in his life: his favorite walking stick and fly whisk and magic charms; his spear and shield; the small stool on which Maina, who was the village praise singer, had sat to tell stories and sing the praise songs of his people. There was food for him to eat and water for him to drink, enough also to satisfy the hunger and thirst of the evil spirits that were killing him. For it was always possible that the spirits might change their minds and decide to let him live. If they did, it was good to have food for them inside the death hut; otherwise, they might become angry again and kill Maina after all.

The men built a stone-rimmed fire in the middle of the room, banked firewood against the wall, which Maina could use to keep the fire going, and helped his wife place pots of food within his reach. Then one by one the men approached Maina, whispered a blessing, and left the building. His wife was the last to leave. He felt her trembling hands on his body, and her wet face against his; he felt her shudder, heard her sob, "Maina . . . Maina . . . oh, Maina." Then she was gone; and Maina was alone with his memories of his life, and thoughts of joining the ancestors.

This was the second time in Maina's long life that he had been taken to a death hut. The first time, struck down by a raging fever, he had known nothing until the stinging slap of a hyena's paw raking across his face had jarred him back to consciousness. He had awakened to a sea of hyenas' eyes boring into him. With all of his strength he had roared, reached for the heavy walking stick left for his protection, and chopped and slashed it fiercely at the sharp white teeth and piercing eyes of hyenas swimming all around him.

The hyenas had turned and run away, whooping and laughing like old women gossiping at the well. However, they had lurked nearby watching and waiting. Watching for signs that he was dead; waiting to come in then and devour his corpse, flesh, muscle, hair, and bone.

He had known he was in a death hut built by his family and friends especially for his dying. They had left food which he could eat and weapons with which he could defend himself. They had built a fire to frighten preying animals away. Then his loved ones had left him in the house to live if he could eat the food, tend the fire, use the weapons; to die if he could not.

A death hut, as far away from the family dwelling as possible, was necessary to protect the home and family from evil spirits. If Maina should die, as they believed he would, the sinister powers responsible for his death would remain in this hut to which no one planned to return. For they believed that illness and death came only through witchcraft or evil spirits, and that these forces would also harm anyone in a house in which a person, especially an elder, had died. If an elder died at home, it was necessary to burn the homestead down and move to new ground.

On that day long ago when the fire had gone out in the death hut and hyenas had come, Maina had crawled to the rock-rimmed fireplace and rekindled the flames. He had been able to keep the fire burning, to drink some water, to eat a little food. The next day, surprised that wisps of smoke were still coming from the death hut, his family returned. They had taken him home and nursed him back to health. The ancestors were not ready for him yet! Certain there was work they still had for him to do, he had resumed his life with vigor, dutifully and willingly doing whatever it seemed the ancestors wanted him to do. He had lived a good life, guiding the way toward strength and purpose, happiness and love in the lives of many of his people. Now, once again, Maina was in a death hut waiting for his life to end. This time he knew that he would die.

Maina did not expect another miracle, nor did he want one. He was not afraid of dying. Life had been long and fruitful, and he welcomed the coming end. Death would bring communion with the elders, rest, reunion with many of his age-mates. Age-mates? How many had gone through the circumcision with him that season? How many of them were still living? He could think of only one, Kamau.

Maina's thoughts turned to Kamau, son of Kiama. He must have been bewitched by that wife of his. Ten years ago Kamau had returned his wife to her parents' home because she was barren. Soon after her departure, Kamau became sick with a never-get-warm affliction which made him shiver anytime he left his compound regardless of the weather outside. He had taken to his bed. It was a fate worse than death . . . Maina trembled at the memory.

Why dwell on such morbid thoughts? His mind wandered to the night before his initiation. Once again he saw all of the initiates acting out their childish fantasies without fear of reprimand because they were about to break with childhood forever. On this night, even the older women joined the festivities and especially enjoyed taunting the big boys with mock sexual advances. They danced sensuously as if to suggest what awaited the boys after they became men. However, even under these conditions, everybody drunk with merriment and lust, the boys knew it was forbidden to carry out any physical advances, especially with circumcised women. Though everyone believed a boy could not father children before he was circumcised, it was still taboo for an uncircumcised boy to have intercourse with a circumcised woman. Maina recalled that aroused desire in the boys had only increased their determination to go through with the ordeal awaiting them at daybreak.

Becoming a man, or woman, is the beginning of knowledge among our people, Maina thought, remembering the excitement of his initiation ceremonies that had started at dawn with a swim in Honia River (the River of Life).

Now the memories unfolded inside his film-clouded eyes like motion pictures on a theater screen. There was the *murwithia* (the circumciser), with his quick, sure strokes delivered without anesthesia. And then the *PAIN*. Oh, the *PAIN!* It had started at the core of his being with a screaming sensation of sound that swelled as the pain increased, both bursting outward against the edges of his body until it seemed his body would explode! Eyes squeezed shut, he had endured the flaming red sound-pain consuming his body without flinching as required; and so had all his age-mates, earning the ulalation of the women for their bravery. Then the father of each proud initiate had wrapped his son in new sheepskins and taken him deep into the forest to the hidden healing house, which also served as an academy. His teachers were leaders of the community who instructed the boys in Kikuyu traditions, a function Maina would perform many times later in life.

Such pleasant memories! The young men had gained strength and learned. While they healed and learned, they ate several bulls and rams, for each father had contributed at least one bull and one ram. The boys had stayed in the forest until they had consumed all the gifts. By then their well-oiled bodies were shining and rippled with muscles. The initiates were taught how to slaughter cows and goats, which specific cuts of meat belonged to the elders, the age-group, women and children, and methods of preparing each. They learned which herbs and roots were used for seasoning, and which were good for healing various diseases.

The academy also prepared Maina and his age-mates for their duties as the next generation of warriors. They had learned how to defend themselves, and how to use their weapons in battle to protect the family and community. They also learned that until the majority of them were married and had children, it was their duty to defend the Kikuyus from attacks by outsiders. They learned how to approach women, how to talk with them, when and how to have sex, taboos and stigmas associated with their actions, their roles and responsibilities as husbands and fathers. They had learned the gentle art of verbal defense in a manner that reduced personal confrontation. They had learned the many secrets of the Kikuyu, which none but those initiated as they would ever know.

Maina heard the howling of the hyenas outside, but he ignored them. He was reliving those years when he and his age-mates emerged from the forest to rejoin their families, as grown men.

Immediately he had noticed his new status: everyone treated him with respect; the women related to him as a potential lover; the young boys and girls responded immediately to his requests;

and, surprisingly, no one expected him to look after the livestock. This was now the job of the younger boys in the community.

During his absence, the women had completed plastering and decorating the man's hut that he had constructed before initiation. Now he and his age-mates had a place to socialize, away from his mother's hut. Life was merry, full of dancing and getting to know the girls of his age. The young women, too, had gone through circumcision and training as thorough as that which he and his friends had received.

The following few years were interrupted sporadically by forays into encampments of neighboring Masai people for livestock and women. The older Masai women were usually ransomed for more livestock. The warriors had to be alert, for the Masai also sometimes attacked the Kikuyu. Casualties were usually not high, for neither side sought subjugation or enslavement of the other, but simply a redistribution of resources.

Maina's bravery in these encounters was recognized time and time again and was well rewarded with livestock. Together with what his father had willed him, he was able to amass enough bridewealth for his first wife and start a family before any of his age-mates.

Yes, Maina reflected, *those were great times. Our young people became warriors and fought against Masai and the Wakamba and any other group that had designs on our land. We prospered and I saw my children and grandchildren become proud Kikuyus. But alas, how things have changed!*

Suddenly, Maina's pleasant reverie turned bitter as he remembered the first white strangers who had come to Kikuyu land. They came as beggars. They looked like death — all white like the evil spirits from the ashes from a homestead of a witchcraft practitioner. They looked so helpless!

The outsiders who were with them said that these ugly-looking beings were human beings from a far-off land. They meant no harm. All they wanted was a place to build a shrine for their god. In time, their god would help them to return to their homes and they would leave peacefully. They seemed so lost . . .

The Kikuyus did not know what to do. After his eldest son took a wife, Maina had become a member of the council of elders. He was one of the decision-makers. Now, in hindsight, too late to do any good, he wished he and the other elders had had the foresight to deny the strangers a place in their midst.

He had listened attentively to arguments for and against granting these creatures a place to build an altar for their god. Those opposed pointed out that these strangers were not like the Masai of Wakamba.

They asked, "What kind of a god is this who needs a shrine built by man?" The strangers looked evil. One should be careful not to give shelter to a snake which might turn around and bite him.

Maina found himself siding with those who felt that these strangers might become a problem to The People later on. He had a nagging feeling that something was not right with these strangers. Many questions went through his mind: What kind of people were they? Where did they come from? How far? How did they get here? And most disturbing, how did they get these outsiders to speak for them? In the end, someone reminded the elders that long ago, when Ngai (the only God of The Kikuyu) helped Gikuyu and Mumbi (the first parents) establish The People, He brought strangers to them.

It was comforting for Maina to remember the story: A long time ago, Ngai created Gikuyu and Mumbi and gave the land where the Kikuyus reside to them and their posterity. Gikuyu and Mumbi were the first people and there were no others. They were blessed with nine daughters and no sons. Gikuyu and Mumbi had named all the plants, animals, and their daughters. Ngai did not demand any worship from Gikuyu and Mumbi other than that they should live in harmony. He was like an elder whose children had grown and were free to make their own decisions. However, whenever they ran into an insoluble problem, they consulted Ngai in a manner that He had taught Gikuyu.

Gikuyu's daughters were maturing and he did not know what to do. He brought his concerns to Ngai, who gave him specific directives on what He wanted done. After Gikuyu had done Ngai's bidding, along came nine handsome young men whom his family warmly welcomed. He gave his daughters to them in marriage. This was the beginning of The People. Ngai's direct communication with The People ended when Gikuyu died after a long, long life.

After Gikuyu's passing, Ngai had used prophets and seers to warn The People that strange creatures, who moved like snakes, would invade the land. The People must be ready and guard against the invaders. But these creatures, though ugly, did not look like snakes!

"What if Ngai," went the argument, "is testing us to see if we have forgotten his generosity? Don't we teach our young that they must always be kind and welcoming to strangers? It is not as if these strangers are asking to be adopted into our community. All they want is a place to build. We do have some land that separates us from the Masai that we can share. If we have need of that land, we will ask them to move to another place. They may already be gone before anyone knows they were here."

This moderate view won unanimous approval, and the strangers were allowed to stay. Maina had lived long enough to see those ugly, scrawny, poor beggars not only build their shrine but multiply and become a problem to all The People. Not long after they were given permission to stay, they started encouraging The People to go to them to learn some strange magic that they called reading and writing. Soon Kikuyu children were flocking from all over the country to attend what was called "school."

Many of Maina's age-mates went to work for the strangers, and it was not long before they started talking about strange spirits and gods. They said the stranger's god was powerful and must be the only god. A few of them started dressing in the clothing of the strangers and went from compound to compound, talking nonsense about people living in what they called sin, saying that anyone who does not believe in the new gods will go to some place called "hell." The majority of The People dismissed these carriers of doom and destruction as mad men. But they persisted.

A conversation that Maina had with one of these confused people intruded on his thoughts:

"Maina, I come to you in the name of the Lord," he had said.

"What do you mean in the name of the Lord?" Maina had asked. "I didn't know that Kikuyu people had a lord. The Kikuyu People are governed by a democratic council of the elders. They do not have a 'lord' or 'ruler'."

"I know, Maina, but this is not that kind of a ruler, but God, the Creator."

"I know of only Ngai, the God of Gikuyu and Mumbi, and you should too," Maina had retorted.

"It is the wish of the strangers' God that all people believe in

Him and give up all their other Gods and only worship Him," the man said.

The conversation became difficult. Maina was becoming very agitated, especially when this man, who didn't even have a homestead of his own, started saying that having more than one wife was against God's will, and that all the ceremonies The People participated in were vulgar and . . . and . . .

Maina somehow managed to remain in control and invited the man to leave before something bad happened. From that moment on, Maina knew that the life of The People would never be the same. He tried to learn as much as possible about the strangers. He continued to warn people that it was a great mistake to let these strangers come in their midst.

Alas, it was of no use! The strangers were becoming too strong. They had called in others like them who took more and more land, beyond what had been given to them initially. These newcomers came with long sticks that spat fire and killed people as if by magic. If one of the strangers was killed, they retaliated by killing ten innocent people — man, woman, or child.

The people who went among the strangers and agreed to take the new gods were given new names that sounded strange. They began to be sent among The People with orders from the strangers. The strangers became like a dragon demanding human sacrifices and promising awful devastation unless he was satisfied.

The strangers built stockades. If they gave an order which was disobeyed they would come and take whatever number of cattle they wanted and put them in stockades until The People complied. Soon the animals were no longer returned but wantonly slaughtered or shipped out using a long, snake-like conveyor on metal rails. Once they were gone, they were gone.

Later the strangers built large houses they called jails. Now, if they demanded that people go build a road, for example, and were refused, they sent their lackeys in to do their bidding, and the recalcitrants were locked up like animals until they complied.

Maina had witnessed these things. Unlike many of his comrades, he was spared the worst indignities, partly due to his distance from the strangers, and partly because of his standing in the community as an elder. It was the young warriors who were most humiliated.

The strangers had also introduced small, round metal disks they called money. They gave these to people who worked for them as compensation for their services. The strangers soon required that all children sent to their school must pay for their schooling with these metal pieces. The only way to get the metal pieces was to work for the strangers or exchange your livestock for money.

If it was not one thing it was another! As their numbers increased, so did their demands for more land. They pushed owners from ancestral homesteads, imprisoned those who refused to move, and burned their houses and crops. Their long killing sticks got fancier and deadlier. The demands of these strangers were unending. The Kikuyu People had invited a plague among themselves and now it was destroying them! It seemed that no amount of sacrificing to Ngai would rid The People of this pestilence.

Converts of these strangers were quick to point out that the strangers' god was greater. Hadn't he helped these strangers rise from nothing to total control of the whole country? Had they not seen how their god helped them with killing sticks and snakes on rails that kept on increasing their number? What more proof did anyone need that Ngai was dead and they must now give reverance to the new god?

The fire that had burned brightly earlier was little more than embers now, and Maina was growing weaker. His heart was fluttering like a dying bird; his breath came in rasping, labored gasps. Yet, wrapped in thoughts of the destructive powers of the strangers, Maina could feel his anger rising. He was afraid for the survival of his people. He moaned, agonizing that his great-grandchildren would never know the mysteries of The Kikuyu People, never know their honored way of life.

Now the strangers were demanding that The People stop circumcising female children! What did they know about the meaning of Kikuyu life, about customs passed down for hundreds and hundreds of years, ever since Ngai created Gikuyu and Mumbi? They were strangers. *Strangers*! They had no right to interfere, change, insult and destroy! Some of The People were refusing to have their daughters circumcised and initiated in the old ways; they were sending their girls to the strangers' schools. They must have been given bad medicine, Maina thought, if they believed these girls could be women in the ways of the Kikuyu.

At first The People had rejected the converts and made fun of them, but the converts persisted because they were encouraged to resist by the strangers. Their daughters and sons were given employment by the strangers so they did not have to return to the community and withstand ridicule. These uninitiated girls had to marry people from distant lands in the beginning; and there were rumors that some had even been taken to wife by the strangers. But then some local young men attending the schools of the strangers agreed to marry these girls. What was the world coming to?

It was good that he was here in the death hut, Maina thought. He could no longer bear to see the deterioration of his people. The pain of living and realizing the depths to which The People had been reduced was worse than death.

The fire was completely out now: the memories it had lighted were gone. Without its color and warmth and life, the hut was cold and ugly. The howls of the hyenas were nearer. They would come soon, perhaps sooner than death. Maina did not want to feel their paws raking his skin, their breath on his face, their teeth tearing his flesh. Painfully he rolled his body from the litter, then inched himself the few paces to the door and lay against it. The hyenas would have to push their way in, and by the time they did, he would be with the ancestors.

The ancestors? What would they say when he joined them? Had he served them well at all times? Where had Ngai been all this time when The People needed him?

Where was Ngai?

Maina used the ancient knowledge to clear his mind of this evil thought which threatened to trouble his final moments on earth. In its place he visualized a man who would rise from The People. He would use the strangers' power against them.

He would have the knowledge of the strangers and the secrets of The Kikuyu People, and he would bring The People to their senses. He would instill pride in them for their traditions and move them to fight to regain their lost heritage.

The thoughts were calming; the room was slipping away. He did not see that the ashes in the fire ring were white. He did not know that the room was cold. He felt peaceful and serene. In the distance he heard the hyenas. Hadn't they been closer earlier? Now they seemed far away. They did not disturb his peace; ever so faintly he could hear them from afar, whooping and laughing like old women gossiping at the well . . .

Glossary

Honia River: River of Life.
Irua (not used in story): Rite of passage, or circumcision ceremony which marked the transition between childhood and adulthood among the Kikuyu people.
Kikuyu: The largest national group in the east African nation of Kenya, numbering more than fifteen million people.
Murwithia: Circumcision surgeon. (A male murwithia operates on boys; a female murwithia operates on girls.)
outsiders: Africans other than Kikuyus.
strangers: Caucasians from Western civilizations.
ulalation (also ululation): To howl, hoot, shout excitedly on festive occasions like births, weddings, dances, and circumcision ceremonies.

AFRICAN-AMERICAN CONTRIBUTIONS GET US THROUGH THE DAY

Marian E. Barnes

The creative genius of the African-American mind that gave the world civilization did not die or disappear among Africans captured, enslaved in the West, and renamed "negroes." The constant target of intellectual, psychological, and physical brutality, African captives nevertheless continued to invent, discover, develop, create, devise, and improvise. Their prolific inventions, their progressive philosophies and ideas, and their spirituality[1] helped lift the society holding them captive to heights it had never reached without them.

Systematically programmed for a life of servitude at a level of semibestiality, African captives were denied all rights to develop themselves within the society that enslaved them. They customarily were forbidden to pursue personal study, formal education, or cultural enrichment. And every effort was expended to erase from the mind of captive and captor alike all memories of the marvelous heritage the captives possessed.

The full truth can never be known as to the number and types of inventions and other social contributions through which enslaved Africans and later, African-Americans, enriched America. Pre-Civil War legislation mandated that invention patents not be

---

1. See *Language and the African-American*, in Commentaries section.

given to enslaved persons. The inventions of free persons of African descent were also often refused acceptance once the racial identity of the inventor became known. The law made expropriation of inventions of Black inventors by members of the master class virtually mandatory. It also assured there would be no historical record of inventions of enslaved persons. As a result, oral history in the Black community contends, countless inventions of Black men and women during the slavery era were credited to white members of the master class. The cotton gin is universally cited as an example of such an invention.

Oral historians also hold, although less widely, that the sewing machine was the invention of a Black man; and that paved roads were introduced to America by a Black Jamaican who paved the access roads to a home he had built for himself in Florida.

In the arena of social service contributions by Black Americans, oral historians present a fascinating litany of information. For instance, such chroniclers assert that the first group health insurance plan to operate in America was organized by African-American ministers Richard Allen and Absolom Jones through the Free African Society, a beneficial mutual aid society which the two founded in Philadelphia in 1787.

Among other customs reputedly originated by African-Americans are night games and All Star Games in baseball. These popular features of modern baseball are said to have been established by the Negro National League and the Negro American League during the days when professional baseball teams were racially segregated.

The lifting of racially restrictive patent laws and social customs did not eliminate problems of racism surrounding the contributions of Afro-Americans. Jackie Robinson, signed by the Brooklyn Dodgers as the first African-American member of a major league baseball team, became the constant object of racially abusive practices. Garret A. Morgan, inventor of the gas mask, initially found virtually no interest in his invention, though it would eventually save many lives during World War I. After Morgan used his "gas inhalator" to rescue men trapped in a tunnel below Lake Erie, orders for the device poured in from fire companies across the nation. But when it became known that Morgan was an African-American, many orders were canceled. In the South, Morgan had to employ a Caucasian to demonstrate his invention.

While the experiences of Jackie Robinson and Garrett Morgan occurred some time ago, there are golf courses throughout America today on which African-Americans are not permitted to play. Ironically, this means that George Grant, the Aframerican man who invented the golf-tee, would be barred from those courses!

America has come a long way since the era of enslaving captive Africans, but clearly at least an equal amount of progress is needed for the country to reach the point where racism against African-Americans has been eradicated from the culture, and the magnificent social contribution of this race is freely recognized and honored. There is something tragically amiss when every elementary school student in America knows the false story of George Washington and the cherry tree, but these students and most holders of doctorates do not know the name of Crispus Attucks, the African-American who was the first American to give his life so that the United States would be a free country.

Despite the lack of records for innumerable inventions and social contributions, *verifiable* African-American contributions number in the thousands. Inventions range from simple household conveniences and office devices to complex business machinery and vital mechanical technology. Some are as well known as the potato chip of Hyram S. Thomas, a Saratoga chef; the ice cream of Augustus Jackson, a Philadelphia confectioner called "the man who invented ice cream" (1832); the golf-tee of George F. Grant; the mop-holder of Thomas W. Stewart; and the player pianos of J. H. and S. L. Dickinson.[2] Others are the major achievements of such men as Elijah McCoy (the automatic lubricator);[3] Granville T. Woods (the synchronous multiplex railway telegraph); Jan Matzeliger (the shoe last machine); John Standard (the refrigerator); Alexander Miles (elevator); Charles Drew (blood plasma and the blood bank); and T. S. Wheatcraft (coin-operated vending machine with weighing, bagging, and heating mechanism).

There can be little doubt that several times during every hour

---

[2]. *Afro USA—A Reference Work on the Black Experience,* eds. Harry A. Ploski, Ph.D. and Ernest Kaiser (New York: Bellwether Publishing Co., 1971).

[3]. McCoy's lubricator was immediately imitated by other inventors. Not wanting to be duped into purchasing an imitation of McCoy's product, suspicious buyers asked "Is this the real McCoy?" so often that the expression eventually enriched the English language. "The real McCoy" came to be the measure of authenticity for any item.

of every day contributions made by African-Americans enrich the lives of every American citizen, probably of every world citizen. African-American contributions truly get us through the day. It also cannot be denied that the contributions of this racial group have played a major role in America's rise to world leadership.

Note: "African-American Contributions Get Us Through the Day," a supplement listing some contributions made by African-Americans, is available from the publisher.

COMMENTARIES

THE WAY IT IS:
African Words and Creative Expressions in English

Dr. Margaret Wade-Lewis

Margaret Wade-Lewis earned a Ph.D. in linguistics from New York University in 1988. She is assistant professor of linguistics and literature at the State University of New York, College at New Paltz, where she also chairs the Department of Black Studies. She teaches courses on African-American literature, Creole languages, and Black English. Among her research interests are the study of African-American contributions to American English, and the contributions of Black linguists to the field of linguistics.

As quiet as it's kept, ever since Lorenzo Turner documented 4,000 African words in Gullah in 1949 (the Creole language of the Sea Island, the Carolinas, and Georgia), a small, persistent band of researchers has been locating more and more of them in American English (Dalby, 1972; Vass, 1979; Wade-Lewis, 1988). Some are more concentrated among Black speakers, and others are so widely used in the American population and the English-speaking world that most people do not suspect their origins at all. Dictionaries ascribe some of them to non-African languages and list others as "origins unknown."

They fall into many categories, the principal ones being:

1. animal names;
2. plants and food items;
3. names for types of persons;
4. names of events;
5. names of body parts and functions;
6. musical terms, instruments, and dances;
7. religious terms; and
8. verbs of action.

Many are used casually as slang and colloquialisms. Others have become standard terms. Some are more popular among African-Americans than among Euro-Americans, or have a different range of connotation for the two groups. Among the terms used casually are the following.

1. *biddy* — from Kongo /bi di bi di/, meaning "a bird" (Turner, 1949: 63, 191) and Tshiluba /bi di bi di/, meaning "a small yellow bird" (Dalgish, 1982: 24). In the Southern United States, it means "baby chick." Elsewhere in American English, "biddy" is slang for a small older woman or a "fine" young "chick" (woman).

2. *boo boo* — from Hausa /buː₁ bu₃/,[1] meaning "an ulceration of the mouth"; and KiKongo /bu₁ bu₁/, "to be lame" (Turner, 1949: 68–69). American dictionaries generally ascribe the origins of "boo boo" to baby talk.

3. *bozo* — from Tshiluba /-bo za/, meaning "a stumble bum, one who smashes over things in passing" (Vass, 1979: 106). In English Bozo has become the name of a clown, who "bumbles" and commits funny and silly acts, or is a term to describe someone, especially male, who is clumsy or inept.

4. *bug* — from Mandingo /-ba ga/, is an agentive suffix meaning "a person who," as in "He is a real *jitter bug*." In English a "bug" is "an enthusiast" (Dalby, 1972: 178), or someone who has a passion for a particular hobby. Note *shutter bug,* a person who has photography as a hobby or takes many photographs.

5. *chick* — In casual speech, a woman is sometimes called a *chick*. The context may be flattering or disparaging. In Wolof, however, /ji gĕn/ is a standard term for woman (Dalby, 1972: 179). Often in English, a "chick" is an "attractive, pert, lively, hip girl or woman" (Wentworth and Flexner, 1967: 98). Perhaps *chick,* meaning "small bird," converged with the casual term meaning "young woman," because both an attractive young woman and a proud bird strut when they walk. Metaphorically they are both "young, tender and juicy" (see *Oxford English Dictionary,* 1933: 336).

6. *chinchy* — often slang for "stingy" and "small." A person may be *chinchy* or *a chinch.* The term derives from Ewe /ti ti/, which means "tiny" (Holm and Shilling, 1982: 41). It may also be the source of *cinch* as in "It's a *cinch,*" referring to some task which is "small" or easy to accomplish (see also *American Heritage Dictionary,* 1976: 234, 242).

7. *funky* — In English *funky* is both casual and slang with both positive and negative connotations. It can refer to "a terrible body

---

1. The tone markings are as follows: the lowered 3 means low-level tone; 2 means midlevel tone; and 1 means high-level tone.

odor," or the smell of anything, such as food, which has spoiled. On the other hand, it is positive when it refers to music from the Afro-centric continuum, particularly, "an earthy, pulsating quality with an uninhibited mix of jazz, rock, rhythm and blues, calypso, and country music... with soul music overtones" (*American Heritage Dictionary,* 1976: 833).

Another set of positive connotations refers to a style of self-expression which is characterized by originality, trendiness, or unconventionality, as in *funky clothes,* or outlandish, tongue-in-cheek humor *a la* Moms Mabley, Red Foxx, Richard Pryor, or Eddie Murphy. In KiKongo /lu fu ki/ is literally "bad body odor" (Thompson, 1984: 104–105). However, like its English descendant, the term can be positive or negative. For example, it is often utilized in KiKongo to praise persons for integrity in art, for having "worked out" to achieve their aims. It is connected to the concept of body odor in that physical exertion is identified with positive energy. The KiKongo expression *Yati, nkwa lu-fuki! Ve miela miami ikwenda baki* is literally translated as, "Like there is a really funky person! My soul advances toward him to receive his blessing." The "smell of a hardworking elder carries luck" (Thompson, 1984: 104–105).

8. *jive* – In Wolof, /jĕv/ and /jĕw/ are used as both nouns and verbs. As verbs they mean "to talk about someone" in his or her absence, especially "in a disparaging way." As nouns they are "misleading talk" (Dalby, 1972: 182). English *jive* has widened to include additional noun connotations including: (a) fast swing music, especially from the period 1938–1945; and (b) sex and sexual intercourse. There are additional verb connotations: (a) to talk in a jazzy rhythm and up-to-date slang; (b) to play or dance to *jive* music, or to play the music adroitly; (c) to joke or tell untruths (called *jivin'*), or to *jive* around with friends (talk and banter casually); or (d) to show off on an instrument while playing "cool" music (Wentworth and Flexner, 1967: 293). An object which is worthless, a person who is irresponsible or unserious, or a performance which is disappointing, may also be described as *jive*.

9. *ninny* – In Mende, /ni ni jä / is "breast water" or "water of the breast" (Westermann and Bryan, 1952: 43). In Mandingo /ni nĭ/ means "female breast" (Turner, 1974:199). In the Southern United States it refers to the breasts of a woman, the breast milk, and a baby young enough to suckle from the breast in its major connota-

tions (note *ninny jugs, ninny milk,* and *ninny baby*). The term has frequently been assumed to be a derivative of the Spanish term for "child," or a derivative of Portuguese *pequenino.* However, since there is good source evidence in African languages, it is entirely possible that Spanish and Portuguese borrowed the terms from the African languages rather than the reverse. For example, Mende has a parallel term which means "water of the eye" (tears). Semantically, *ninny* in English represents both synedoche and widening since it can also refer to the entire body. For example, a *ninny* is: (a) a small child who clings to its parents, especially its mother; (b) a child of any size who whines or cries too freely; or (c) an adult who complains regularly or is considered a simpleton or fool.

10. *sassy* — Mandingo /sa si/ is a verb meaning "to treat contemptuously, to ridicule" (Turner, 1974: 201). In American English it has become principally an adjective meaning "impudent" (*American Heritage,* 1976: 1153). It is also a Black expression in the Bahamas meaning "to talk impertinently" (Holm and Shilling, 1982: 176). In the United States *sassy* is a pejorative term used to describe children who "talk back" to parents and other adults in a disrespectful manner. On the other hand, it has positive connotations when it refers to older people, especially women, who are vibrant beyond their chronological years, as in "She is still fat and *sassy."*

The above terms are for the most part standard terms in the languages of their origins.

Among the standard terms from African languages which have also become standard in English are the following. Those which are animal names probably came into English after those animals were sighted in Africa by Europeans and captured for use in zoos in the western hemisphere.

11. *jamboree* — In Wolof a /jäm/ is a "slave," and a /jäm bōor/ is a "freed man." Hence, a *jamboree* is "a celebration of emancipated slaves" (Dalby, 1972: 181). The concept also appears as "a number of related African words referring to social gatherings, singing, etc.," among them Bambara /ja ma/ "an assembly, company"; Mandingo /ja ma/ "many"; and Twi /Jam/ "to condone with, express sorrow, grief or sympathy at the death of someone's relation" (Cassidy and Le Page, 1967: 243). The term has widened in

English to mean a large, joyous celebration. It is probably the source of the verb *to jam*, and the noun compound *jam session*, both associated with African-American parties, good times, dancing, and impromptu musical performances by a group or ensemble. In general American culture, the term has become so popular that it is the incorporated name of the Boy Scouts' annual national talent event, The Boy Scouts *Jamboree*. It is also often the name of country western musical events and large dance parties (see *American Heritage*, 1976: 700).

12. *chigger* — appears in a number of African languages. Turner recorded Mandinka (ji ga/; Wolof /Ji ga/; Yoruba /Ji ga/; Hausa /ji ga/₁; Ewe /Ji₃ ga/₁; Vai /ji ka/₃; and Mandingo /ji ke/ (1974: 195). In each African language it is an insect. In Wolof it means "insect"; in Ewe it is "a sand flea"; and in the other languages it is a "jigger," a type of mite. The English version is unchanged, that is, a "small tropical flea or mite, the female of which burrows under the skin and causes irritation and sores" (*American Heritage*, 1975: 233).

13. *chimpanzee* — The *chimpanzee* is native to the southern areas of Africa. In Kimbundu it is /ki pen se/ and in KiKongo it is /m pen jé/ (Maia, 1961: 114). Semantically, *chimpanzee* is unchanged in English. It is an African ape *(Anthropopithecur* or *Pan troglodytes)* bearing the closest resemblance to man of any of the anthropoids *(American Heritage*, 1976: 234). The term is neutral in connotation and standard in register except when it is used derisively to refer to a particular man as "a chimp."

14. *cola* — One of the most internationally popular soft drinks appears in Mandingo as /ko lo/, and in Temne as /ko la/ (*American Heritage*, 1976: 726). It has variants in other African languages (*Oxford English Dictionary*, 1933: 606). *Kola* is (a) either of two African trees, *Cola nitida* or *Cola minata*, bearing nuts used in the manufacture of beverages and medicine; or (b) the nut of the tree (*American Heritage*, 1976: 726). The term was introduced early in Brazil and the West Indies. The modern English term *cola* forms part of the trade name of any carbonated drink with the flavor of *kola*. Its most famous version is the brand name, *Coca Cola*. There are, of course, others. Among the rival drinks is the "un-*cola*."

15. *gumbo* — This popular food item is most associated with Southern United States culture, but is well-known across the United States. The Campbell's Soup company makes Chicken *Gumbo*, for

example. The original term means "okra" in a number of African languages. Among them are Tshiluba /tshĭn gôm bô/, and Umbundu /ot shĭn gom bo/ (Turner, 1974: 194).

16. *jumbo* — in English, an adjective used to describe anything larger than average, such as *jumbo shrimp, jumbo goobers,* or a *jumbo jet.* In at least three African languages, *jumbo* is a noun meaning "elephant." These are Kimbundu and KiKongo /ng zam ba/ and Umbundu /o jam ba/ (Turner, 1974: 195). The term was popularized in the United States after 1883, when P. T. Barnum bought Jumbo, an African elephant, and "the largest Elephant on record, from London's Royal Zoo. In America the animal quickly caught the public imagination and became the first major attraction of the Barnum Circus" (Wentworth and Flexner, 1967: 289). Speakers of American English seldom use the noun connotation except as a proper name. It may be used derisively as the name of an obese person.

17. *impala* — A number of terms from African languages have become proper nouns (note *kola*), a symbol that they are as standard as terms can become. *Impala* is one of them. It is "an antelope *(Aepuceros melampus)* of the open parts of South Africa, three feet tall, dark red fading to clear white, with spreading lyrate horns in the male." It appears in Sechwana and Zulu as /pha la/ and /m pa la/ (*Funk and Wagnall's,* 1963: 1775-1776). This antelope is known for its speed, which is perhaps why an American car by Chevrolet is named for it. One connecting link is that the animal and the car both move rapidly and have sleek lines.

18. *tot* — *Tot* and *toddler* are both colloquial terms in American English for small children. Their origin appears to be /-to to/, a widely distributed Bantu root meaning "small child." For example, in KiKongo and LoNkundo /ki to to/ is "baby" and /m to to/ is "child" (Welmers, 1973: 173, 177). In KiSwahili / m to to/ is "child" and /wa to to/ is "children." The term has widened greatly in that toddler is not only "a small child who has learned to walk but not yet perfectly" and "a size of clothing for children between the ages of about one to three" (*American Heritage,* 1976: 1350), it had also resulted in the infinitive "to toddle" and the gerund and adjective "toddling," used to describe the walking style of small children and elderly adults. *Toto* itself has been immortalized in American English as the name of small pets, the most famous of which is

Dorothy's dog in *The Wizard of Oz,* and in the recent African-American adaptation, *The Wiz.*

19. *yam* — Among the best-known food items from Africa is the *yam,* also called "sweet potato" in the United States. It appears in a number of languages, among them Mende /jam bi/, meaning "the wild yam." There are also Twi /ô ja mu/, "yam not taken out with the first crop"; Twi /a jam kau de/, "a large edible tuber or root"; and at least six other variants from other African languages (Turner, 1974: 204). The term refers to the tropical vine of the genue *Dioscorea,* which has edible tuberous roots. The root of the vine is used for food. In most English dialects *yam* and *sweet potato* are variants. However, the African tuber is larger, less sweet, and usually utilized as a vegetable rather than a dessert.

Some of the most popular terms in American English originated as verbs in African languages. In English some have remained as verbs while others have widened to include a noun context, or have become nouns, losing their meaning as verbs.

20. *bandy* — a colloquial term in English, meaning "to toss, throw or strike back and forth," "to give and take words or blows," "to discuss in a casual or frivolous manner" (*American Heritage,* 1976: 104). The term appears in a number of African languages; for example, KiTuba /ku ban da/, "to pull, attract" (Swift and Zola, 1963: 422); KiKongo /ban da/, meaning "to make a choice, to make fast, to climb"; Wolof /ban ka/ and Hausa /ban ke/, both meaning "to collide"; and KiKongo and Kimbundu /ban za/, meaning "to think" (Turner, 1974: 59-60). The term can be concrete or abstract. If one "*bandies* ideas about" the term is abstract.

21. *boogie* — The probable source of this term is Hausa, /bu ga/- (/bu gi/), and Mandingo, /bu gô/, both meaning "to beat," including "to beat drums." In Sierra Leone Krio /bo gi/ - (/bo gi/)/ is "to dance" (Dalby, 1972: 178). Each context refers to vigorous physical actions. In American English it is primarily a noun associated with African-American culture. *Boogie* occurs in its most frequent context with *woogie* as the name of a type of jazz piano music with eight beats to a bar, "characterized by a repeated rhythmic and melodic pattern in the base" (Wentworth and Flexner, 1967: 53; *American Heritage,* 1976: 151). Besides the *boogie woogie* music and its related dance, there are some less frequently used connotations in both the Caribbean and the United States. For ex-

ample, among young people, *boogie* can also mean to "engage in sexual intercourse," "to party," "to enjoy one's self thoroughly," and "to go out dancing" (See Holm and Shilling, 1982: 24).

22. *dig* — The Wolof verbs /deg/ and /de ga/ are standard terms meaning "to understand," "to appreciate" (Dalby, 1972: 179). The English connotation is about the same with perhaps some widening. The term may have converged with the English verb *to dig*, meaning "to excavate" (*American Heritage*, 1976: 368; Dalby, 1972: 179).

23. *jazz* — undoubtedly the most famous of the verbs from African languages in English. The most likely source of the English term is /jis/ and Temne /jas/, both meaning "lively and energetic to an extreme degree" (Dalby, 1972: 181). Other correspondences are Mandingo /ja si/, "to become abnormal or out-of-character" in either direction. i.e., "to become diminished" or "to become diminished" or "to become exaggerated, excessive." The term can also be used to describe "excessive or lessened love-making," and other changes in way of life (Dalby, 1972: 181).

While the African language uses of the term are as verbs, the major American English context is as a noun. *Jazz* is the original African-American improvisational instrumental music with "a strong but flexible rhythmic understructure, solos and improvisations on basic melody and chord patterns, and a highly sophisticated harmonic idiom" (Wentworth and Flexner, 1967: 286–287; *American Heritage*, 1976: 702). The noun form for the music most likely developed when African-American musicians moved from rural areas to the cities and created "city blues" or *jazz* as a result of imposing African rhythmic and chordal structures on Western instruments such as the piano and saxophone.

24. *jitter* — The probable source of *jitter* is the Mandingo stative verb /ji tô/, meaning "frightened, cowardly," from /ji/ "to be afraid" (Dalby, 1971: 182). In English it has numerous noun and verb contexts, the most popular associated with the dance the *jitter bug*, which is done rapidly. There is also the verb *to jitter*, meaning "to tremble, shake," "to be nervous and uneasy." The noun *jitters* refers to "nervousness, fear, cowardice" (Dalby, 1972: 182).

25. *juke* — Before the collision of Africa and America, there were no *juke boxes, juke joints,* or *juke houses.* The term most likely originated from Wolof /Jug/, "to lead a disorderly life, to miscon-

duct one's self"; and Bambara /Ju gu/ "wicked, violent, a naughty person" (Turner, 1974: 195). Thus, the *juke box* is a highly decorated box which plays music louder than the home stereo. It may be decorated with flashing lights and shiny metallic strips (Wentworth and Flexner, 1967: 298; *American Heritage,* 1976: 709). In some connotations, the term has become more positive. For example, one past feature of the Home Box Office channel was *Video Jukebox,* a short segment showcasing popular vocal and dance videos.

26. *joggle* — One of America's most popular individual physical activities is *jogging.* The best source of the term is Wolof /jô gal/ and /j$\overline{oo}$ gal/, meaning "to rise" and to "cause to rise." Among the Gullah people there is the *joggle board,* on which one bounces up and down for exercise and fun (Turner, 1974: 195). In at least one connotation, the term is abstract. That is, sometimes a person may have to *jog* his or her memory to recall a detail.

27. *tote* — *Tote* is found in many African languages, always related to carrying items. For example, there are KiKongo /to ta/; Kimbundu and Umbundu /tu ta/; and forms in Mende and Ewe. The Mende form is a noun meaning a person "who carries a message." In KiKongo it means "to pick up"; in Ewe it is to "lift a load from one's head without help." The Kimbundu and Umbundu forms mean "to carry" (Turner, 1974: 203). In the Southern United States, *tote* is still used interchangeably with "to carry." Beyond the South, many persons know *tote* in the noun compound *tote bag,* and as a proper noun, the brand name *Totes* (a line of umbrellas, scarves, and overshoes to offer protection from the rain; their distinguishing characteristic is that they are compact enough to *tote* around when they are not in use).

This list is only a sample of the terms with African origins which have come into English from as many as thirty different African languages.

On another level, African-Americans have continued to recreate English through a process described by Marian Barnes (1990). Clarence Major and others call this process "revolutionary." It is both creative and rebellious. Through it African-Americans demonstrate aspects of the retained African world view while exercising control over the language they speak (1970: 9–13). Stephen Henderson calls the process a tradition of "linguistic elegance," through which African-Americans say "things beautifully even when they are ugly things" (1972: 33).

Some examples are evident in the following processes:

(1). Translations of African phrases such as "Gimme some skin" / "slap me five" (Mandingo, "i golo don m bolo," literally "put your skin in my hand," from "the laying on of hands ceremony" symbolizing the idea that "I am part of you and you are part of me.") (See Smitherman, 1977: 45.)

(2). English terms used as coded dialect in a wide range of connotations, some being the opposite of the English definitions. In the case of the terms which follow, the Black English version is highly positive. Among the terms are: *mean, bad, wicked, terrible, smoking, chilled, stupid, fresh, sassy, insane, heavy, hard, blood* and *rap*.

(3). Existential phrases which speak to the Black condition and are "saturated" in the Black experience, such as "Keep the faith, baby" (from Adam Clayton Powell), and its ironic opposite, "Keep the baby, Faith" (from someone else); "nitty gritty," "straighten up and fly right," "my man," "my woman," "too much," "goin through changes," "doin it to death," "gittin down," "tell the truth," and "I hear yuh."

(And that's the God's truth!)

For further information on the topic, see the bibliography which follows.

Bibliography

Barnes, Marian. 1990. *Talk That Talk and Walk That Walk: African Roots of Storytelling.* (Audiotape); available from M. Barnes, P.O. Box 143262, Austin, TX 78723-4825.

Baugh, John. 1983. *Black Street Speech: Its History, Structure and Survival.* Austin: University of Texas Press.

Dalby, David. 1972. "The African Element in American English," Thomas Kochman, ed. *Rappin' and Stylin' Out: Communication in Urban Black America.* Urbana: University of Illinois Press. 170-186.

Dalgish, Gerard D. 1982. *A Dictionary of Africanisms: Contributions of Sub-Saharan Africa to the English Language.* Westport, CT: Greenwood Press.

Funk, Isaac K. 1959. *Funk and Wagnall's New Standard Dictionary of the English Language.* New York: Funk and Wagnall's.

Henderson, Stephen, ed. 1973. *Understanding the New Black Poetry.* New York: William Morrow.

Maia, P. António da Silva. 1961. *Dicionário (Complementar) Português-Kimbundu-KiKongo.* Cucujães: Tipografia das Missões.

Major, Clarence. 1970. *Dictionary of Afro-American Slang*. New York: International Publishers.
Morris, William, ed. 1976. *American Heritage Dictionary*. New College Edition. Boston: Houghton-Mifflin Company.
Oxford English Dictionary. 1933. Oxford: Clarendon Press.
Smitherman, Geneva. 1977. *Talkin and Testifyin: The Language of Black America*. Boston: Houghton-Mifflin.
Swift, L. B., and E. W. A. Zola. 1963. *KiTuba: Basic Course*. Washington, D.C.: Foreign Service Institute.
Thompson, Robert Farris. 1983. *Flash of the Spirit: African and Afro-American Art and Philosophy*. New York: Vintage Books.
Turner, Lorenzo. 1949. *Africanisms in the Gullah Dialect*. Chicago: University of Chicago Press (Reprinted by Ann Arbor: University of Michigan Press, 1974).
Vass, Winifred K. 1979. *The Bantu-Speaking Heritage of the United States*. Los Angeles: Center for Afro-American Studies, University of California, Los Angeles.
Wade-Lewis, Margaret. 1988. *The African Substratum in American English*. Ph.D. dissertation. New York: New York University.
Welmers, William E. 1973. *African Language Structures*. Berkeley: University of California Press.
Wentworth, Harold, and Stuart Berg Flexner. 1967. *Dictionary of American Slang*. New York: Thomas Y. Crowell.

LANGUAGE AND THE AFRICAN-AMERICAN

Marian E. Barnes

Nearly four centuries ago, our African ancestors were captured, transported to the Western world, enslaved, and forbidden to speak their own languages or practice their own culture on pain of annihilation. Nevertheless, early Africans in America found ways of continuing much of their culture in full view of their unsuspecting captors. For example, many people believe the famed Southern hospitality, gentility, and manners are forms of African culture passed down by children of the master class, received by them from enslaved African captives by whom they were reared. Forbidden to hold meetings, send code messages on the talking drum, or speak African languages, the enslaved population countered by meeting secretly, sending coded messages with tap-dancing feet and body-slapping "ham-bone" rhythms, singing code songs, and speaking coded English.

Enslaved Africans were inundated by their captors with negative language, a formidable, insidious psychological weapon designed to control the thinking of captives, destroy their self-esteem and warp their value systems. Newly enslaved Africans were not permitted to mingle with the established enslaved population. Housed in separated compounds, they were put through individualized "breaking-in" periods that might last three years, or however long it took to mentally and spiritually "break-in" the captured person.

Negative language permeated every crevice of life in the American slavocracy, renamed captives, redefined cultural heritage, circumscribed the future. Through changing a word, *Africans* with proud memories of their land and of ancient cultures were changed into *"negroes"* or *"niggers"* with no ties to the development of any land or culture, legally defined as three-fifths of a human being and considered a form of chattel, or talking cattle. By changing a word, *captives* who had been overpowered, captured and enslaved, and who continually struggled for their freedom, became instead "slaves," the chattel of an owner, held in bondage, servile and quiescent in servitude.

In the terminology of negative language, there were no African *nations*. Though nations or national groups might number in the millions and employ sophisticated governing systems, they were still called African *"tribes."* There were never citizens of African countries; there were, instead, African *"natives."* African males captured and living in America never reached manhood; they were eternally called *"boys."*

Negative language — the language of oppression, of subjugation, of racism — continues to thrive, adapting itself to current situations, and influencing the thoughts, concepts and beliefs of the total society including Africans and African-Americans. Of some 124 synonyms and figures of speech characterizing the color black in the English language, 123 are negative.[1] Angel food cake is white, devil's food cake is black; a black heart is evil, as is a black witch; a white witch, however, is good; a white lie is innocent, often helpful; a black lie is evil, wicked, and sinful. Negative concepts of the color black are unending, and the crossover to negative characterizations of Black people is inevitable and inescapable.

---

1. *Black Rhapsody, Building a Strong Foundation Through Corrective History. Dr. Ed Robinson "Live."* Long-playing album produced by Ed and Harriette Robinson, Philadelphia, PA. Copyright 1970.

The language of racism is extremely resistant to change. For example, long after the term "negro" had fallen into popular disfavor, denounced by African-Americans who declared themselves "Black and beautiful," it remained prevalent in literature, newspapers, and broadcasts. When negative wordsmiths finally made a change, it was restricted to lip service that left the language of racism intact. "Black" referring to race was written "black" as in the following newspaper excerpt: "Irish, Jewish, Italian, Korean and black residents attended the meeting." Asked why "black" is not capitalized as the proper noun equivalent of other ethnic terms, one is told the word is being used as an adjective. When analyzed, the implication is equal in racism and insensitivity to the term "negro" that it is replacing. In fact, because "negro" — the word for "black" in Spanish — had begun to be written "Negro" in recent years in response to decades of protest from African-Americans, the change to "black" can be considered a step backward.

Since the era of the slavocracy, attempts by the dominant society to deprecate and eradicate African and African-American culture, including language, have continued, as have methods of evading and overcoming such attempts.

It is interesting that while few will question the power of the centuries-old oral tradition of Old World cultures, or the literary merit of timeless, inspirational Eastern writings such as the Bible and the Qur'an, recognition of the language genius of descendants of these ancient oral historians and scribes is virtually nonexistent.

New words and phrases, distinctive for their creativity and color, are constantly flowing into standard English from the "Black English" spoken by many African-Americans. New language "spills over" into standard English from:

1. The African-American's natural facility with words, including a poetic speech pattern replete with repartee, raps, alliteration, rhyme, metaphor, understatement for effect, etc.
2. Coded language, designed and created by African-Americans for their exclusive use. (In an apparent attempt to compensate for lost, original languages, as the general population learns code words, African-Americans coin and substitute new terminology.)
3. Standard English words and expressions to which African-Americans give nontraditional meanings and applications.

A review of international human rights campaigns reveals that most are spin-off applications of philosophies and methodologies developed by African-Americans in their struggle for justice. (Rights for women, homosexuals, the elderly, the handicapped, and children come to mind.) "We Shall Overcome," theme song of the Civil Rights Revolution spearheaded by African-Americans in the fifties and sixties, has become the Freedom Song of the world. Inspired by its victory-foretelling philosophy that spells out methods of implementation, oppressed people in countries all around the world striving to right many types of human injustice now sing the song in their own languages, and apply its philosophy in their own ways.

While less significant than systematic creation of philosophy and language, broken English is also a component of Black English. Passed down from Africans captured, brought to America, and forced to speak English, nongrammatical speech is naturally acquired by some African-Americans, and adopted by others. It is customarily used at intimate ethnic gatherings by uneducated and super-educated alike.

The monumental contributions of African-Americans to world philosophy and language arts generally are unrecognized, dismissed as "sloganeering," or even denied. The history of the word "copacetic" (often given variant spellings) demonstrates this point.

At the peak of his popularity, tap dancer Bill Bojangles Robinson would frequently say, "Everything is copacetic!" Widely interviewed about this word that reporters could not find in their dictionaries, he explained repeatedly how he had coined the word as a baby; also that it meant things were superfine. For quite a while Americans imitated Robinson, and "Everything is copacetic!" reverberated around the country. However, although obituaries for Robinson in the *New York Sun* and *The New York Times* credited him with originating the word, no dictionary consulted for this word mentioned his name.[2]

"Origin unknown" appeared in virtually all word-reference-sources reviewed, many of which offered an array of "probable" origins totally unrelated to the African-American experience. Included in the definition given by *Random House Dictionary*,[3] for example: "of obscure origin; popular attributions of the word to

---

2. *New York Sun* and *New York Times,* November 26, 1949.
3. *Random House Dictionary of English* (New York: Random House, 1970).

Louisiana, French, Italian, Hebrew, etc. *Lack of supporting evidence."* (Italics mine.)

Writing in *A Second Browser's Dictionary*,[4] author John Ciardi says Bill Bojangles Robinson made "copasetic" *(sic)* his personal catchword and claims, "The form and meaning are inseparable from Hebrew." Searching for a line of transmission from Hebrew to Black English, he says, "I can find none." He, nevertheless, constructs an elaborate fantasy in which the Hebrew term *kol ba seder* (all in order) is used repeatedly by an imaginary Jewish "shopkeeper or pawnbroker" whose African-American customers adapt and alter the expression. He does not explain why Jewish customers, friends, and relatives of this fabricated merchant remained unaffected and uninvolved in the preservation of the term!

The path from contribution to denial is seldom so clear and provable as in the foregoing example, played out within the memory span of millions of people still living. Memories, however, have small credibility when they contradict the "authority" of dictionaries and similar reference works. Thus, with impunity, language "experts" erroneously equate Black English with broken English, stigmatize its speakers, and label such speech an impediment of which African-Americans must rid themselves if they would succeed, acknowledging none of the group's remarkable language skills.

To counteract the crippling, negative images that surround their purported lack of language ability, even before they begin school, African-American children should be taught in their homes, extended families, and communities that, like their ancestors before them, language is one of their strongest assets. They need to learn that although they belong to a small cultural group that is no more than a tiny fleck on the total body of humanity, *wherever they go in the world, they will always find some part of their language in use,* previously exported on the wings of creative expressions, inimitable music, or profound philosophy that embraces all cultures. Our children should be made to understand that in order to function acceptably in the business world, it is necessary for them to master standard English; and they should be challenged to enlist traditional language powers to master it well!

---

4. *A Second Browser's Dictionary and Native's Guide to the Unknown American Language,* 1st ed. (New York: Harper and Row, 1983).

At the same time our children must learn that it is vital that they develop ancestrally inherited powers of thinking and creativity such as those that have fueled the influx of language and philosophy from Black English into standard English; they must also be inspired to become creators of new language and philosophy to serve society's present needs.

Unfortunately, this is not happening. Most children who speak Black English enter American school systems with no previous instruction about their culture. Once in school, they quickly learn that their language is all "wrong," and, by implication, that the people they learned it from are unintelligent. This combines with a confluence of other social streams of negative "information" about their appearance, intellectual capacity, historical significance, etc., to inflate the poor self-concept that plagues African-Americans as a group.

Further, since the dominant society controls and restricts the ability to formally excel in all areas, including language, by demanding its own symbols of credibility such as educational degrees, official position, and social approval, the excellence of many African-Americans flourishes in negative areas where few restrictions interfere with its expression. As a result, creativity can be prevalent in verbal abuse of each other, profanity and obscenity among some African-American school-age children, and others.

On the other hand, the preoccupation some African-Americans have with achieving recognized accomplishments within institutionalized American systems can contribute to slowing or stopping the natural creativity flowing from the African-American community into the larger society. Ironically, Africans and African-Americans have historically made their greatest impacts upon the world using only their own cultural systems and traditions. In fact, the language, music, and philosophy of African-Americans have traveled around the world *in spite of* America's exclusive institutionalized systems!

Depending upon the educational systems of the dominant society to develop the language skills of African-Americans has not been successful in the past; it will not succeed in the future. Clearly, African-Americans must assume responsibility for teaching African-American children in homes and communities. Spiritual development, experiential learning, storytelling — these and other traditional African ways of learning and growth must be reclaimed and emphasized if our children are to reach traditional heights of spiritual, cultural, and technological excellence.

NOTES ON THE PSYCHOLOGICAL USE OF LANGUAGE AS A TOOL OF OPPRESSION

Marian E. Barnes

The psychological use of language as a tool to oppress one race or group and elevate another has not been restricted to any time, place, or people. Historically practiced in diverse places and circumstances, it remains a pervasive fact of life today. Implementation of such language against Africans enslaved in America and their descendants has been brutal, vicious, heavy-handed, relentless. On the world scene, however, similar language is often so subtle and indirect as to be unrecognizable. Either system effectively influences and controls the concepts, thoughts, feelings, and behaviors of most people who consistently use or hear the language.

The goal of oppressive language may vary from establishing the social level of one group above another, to the total elimination of one group by another.

To brutalize, kill, or enslave another human being is problematical, however, if that individual is an African, Asian, or European with a home, family, culture, and country. Therefore, the language that seeks to control, oppress, and subjugate always dehumanizes its victims. Africans become "niggers," "spooks," or "jungle bunnies"; Asians become "slant-eyes," "chinks," or "geeks"; Europeans become "honkies," "white devils," or "white trash." Eventually, users of such names and phrases come to believe these terms accurately reflect an inferior species of life whose culture is nonexistent or worthless. Further, that to degrade or destroy such substandard creatures and their culture is to make a contribution to the overall good of society.

Wherever groups of people struggle for power or identity, oppressive language specific to the situation evolves. The random sampling of oppressive language that follows relates primarily to the Black experience:

black:	word used to identify the Black ethnic group or culture (Black is a proper noun that identifies the race and culture of Africans and African-Americans whose skin color varies from black to white. The word is the grammatical equivalent of the name for any other racial group.)
boy:	word used for Black adult males
buck:	same as above
coon:	word used to identify an African or African-American
darky:	same as above
mammy:	name used for Black woman (Children of Black women were compelled to use this term rather than "Mother" during the American slavocracy.)
Master:	title African captives were forced to use in addressing their captors and other members of the master class during the slavery era
Middle East:	Eurocentric term that ignores the names and geographic locations of countries in north Africa and southwest Asia and defines them in terms of their geographical relationship to Europe
minority:	word used to define Africans and African-Americans
Mistress:	title African captives were compelled to use in addressing female members of the master class during slavery in America
native:	word used for indigenous citizens of African countries
negro:	same as "nigger" below
negress:	same as "nigger" below
nigger:	name contrived to replace the name "African" (the word destroys the spoken bond with Africa — its land, culture, and history — and downgrades the human status of the person thus addressed or categorized)
pappy:	children of Black men were compelled to use this term in addressing their fathers during the slavery era in America

pickaninny:	name used for a Black child
slave:	word imposed upon African captives and their descendants to disavow their status as captives
Third World:[1]	term is usually applied to "First World" countries (areas where civilization began)
tribe:[2]	word used for nations and national groups in Africa
witch doctor:	term used for indigenous practitioners of medicine in Black countries, even when the healing knowledge and skills of such practitioners surpass that of Western physicians

BLACK ENGLISH EXPRESSIONS
(Excerpt from a work in progress)

Marian E. Barnes

The informally obtained expressions that follow are offered as examples of Black English because I have heard them used frequently in the Aframerican community during my lifetime, or because they were suggested by seasoned speakers of Black English. Some are self-explanatory; others defy accurate explanation; still others have become part of standard English or been adapted from it and need little or no explanation. A thoroughly researched collection of Black English-language expressions is in progress.

The author is especially indebted to assistants who helped compile and edit the collection. They include Doris Barnes Polk of Philadelphia, for input into the Church Expressions division; and Zeta Phi Beta, Beta Delta Zeta Chapter sorors Barbara Younge, who proposed that work be done in this area, and Peggy Gilmore, who

---

1. No user of this term whom the editor was able to question could identify the first two worlds or explain the basis for the numbering system.

2. Most dictionaries note "tribe" as a synonym for "nation." In modern usage, however, the word "tribe" bears a connotation of primitive culture, and is used, virtually without exception, for people of color. Size of the land mass occupied, sophistication of culture, or numbers of people in a group appear to have no bearing. (The Kikuyu people, a national group in Kenya, are considered a "tribe" though they number some fifteen million and occupy much of Kenya's nearly 225,000 square miles. Twenty-nine thousand people in Monaco, occupying less than 70,000 square miles, and 750 people in Vatican City, occupying less than 109 acres, are considered "nations.")

contributed to this chapter. Thanks also to Joan Barnes Stewart, of Austin, Texas, for significant contributions to the collection and able editorial assistance.

a big hat / a big mahoff: an important person

a bird without feet: a playboy / playgirl (one who flies around and never lands)

A bold heart ever did fetch luck halfway.

a fair one: a fight

A chip can't fall too far from the block.

a ham-I-done: nothing; worthless ("It wasn't worth a ham-I-done.")

A hand full of "Gi' me," and a mouth full of "Much obliged." criticism leveled at those who expect or readily accept charity

A heap see, but a few know. Many people observe, but few understand.

A liar is not to be believed, although they do tell the truth sometimes.

A little tells what a great deal means. Small implications foreshadow the full story.

a South Street umbrella: Philadelphia term for a newspaper used as a shield against the rain

A whistling woman and a crowing hen will both come to no good end.

A windy March is lucky – let it blow.

a zero brother / sister: a worthless Black man / woman

Ain't that nothin'? This expression gives another dimension to "Isn't that something?" in standard English.

Aunt Hagar's daughter/ son: a Black person

After 'while, chocolate chile! Goodbye; frequent response to "See ya later, alligator."

After 'while, crocodile!	Goodbye; frequent reply to "See ya alligator."
as quiet as it is kept:	precedes a reference to a little known fact, or to the speaker's little known opinion.
attitude (also, 'tude):	Total self-absorption, self-motivation, and single-minded determination are key characteristics of a person with an "attitude."
Aw, shuh now!	an expletive that usually expresses high approval
bad:	great; smashing
beating around the bush:	failing to make a desired point, or to make the point quickly
beau:	extreme; maximum degree; also, beautiful/handsome (derivative of French word "beaucoup")
beaucoup:	plentiful (from French)
Beauty is only skin deep, but ugly is to the bone.	
behind:	because of ("I brought the dog in the house *behind* the rain.")
bent all out of shape:	upset
Bip-Bap, Georgia:	name given any far outlying area of Georgia, or any Southern state
Bite your tongue!	
Black is evil[1] *white and yalluh, low down* *Look heah, honey* *Ain't you glad you' brown?*	
Black don't crack.	refers to physical durability of members of the Black race; may also refer to their emotional stability

---

1. "Evil" in Black English means "bad tempered."

The blacker the berry, the sweeter the juice.	an endearing affirmation of Black skin
blind in one eye, and can't see out the other:	a reference to poor insight
book:	leave
boss:	excellent
bread:	money
brother / soul brother:	a Black male
brown-skinned service:	said by or of a Black person who renders a gratuitous service
Buckra:	Caucasian
bussin':	head wagging, hip swinging, "in-your-face" arguing
C.P. Time:	"Colored People's Time" (late)
called myself:	to believe mistakenly ("I called myself doing a good deed.")
calling hogs:	snoring
can to can't:	to work from the moment daylight permits sight until it becomes too dark to see.
can't cha don't cha:	careless, tacky, haphazardly done
cat (also **kitty**):	man
Check it out!	
Choose your enemy carefully, you will look like him one day.	
cool - chill - chill out - chilly:	relates to being calm, collected, sophisticated under stress
chump:	insignificant; a "jerk"; also, a city bus
club member / member:	an African-American
comin' out the kink:	said of someone given to substandard achieving who begins to perform at an acceptable level
copacetic / copesetic, (various spellings):	fine, excellent; glowing perfection; A-O.K.

crack up:	laugh
cracker:	pejorative term for a white person
cuda:	turtle
cuffy / cuffie:	an uncouth person
cumberfoot:	clumsy
cut out:	leave
cut off:	turn off
cut on:	turn on
cut loose:	break off/away, move freely without restrictions
cutting you loose:	severing a relationship
cutting the fool:	capering; clowning
decent:	excellent
did me (her/him) dirty:	behaved in an unprincipled or immoral way toward me (her/him)
dime:	squeal; ten-dollar bill
Do your own thing.	express your personal talents freely, disregarding pressures to conform
Do, what?	an exclamation made by a person surprised by what has just been said
Don't even try it!	verbal thrust to prevent a person from making a self-favoring point in a conversational exchange

*Down not the man that is down
   today, nor rejoice in his sorrow
For this old world is a funny old
   world, and you may be down tomorrow.*

the dozens / playing the dozens:	A word game in which insults are traded about family members of the players. The objective is to take the worst an opponent can offer without breaking, then deliver a greater insult than you received. In times past, insulting a person's mother was "off-limits." However, there are now players who stress

strong insults of mothers as a special test of stamina. Many people believe "The Dozens" prepares participants to cope with social rebuffs and assaults from the dominant society inherent in the lifestyle of African-Americans.

dragnasty / drag-nasty: a despicable person

dry long so: in a matter-of-fact way; apropos of nothing

dude: man

dusties: vintage musical recordings

eagle day: pay day

The eagle flies on Friday. Pay day is Friday.

each and every: This term, heard only in the Black community by the author for many years, is now increasingly being used by speakers of standard English.

Eat black eyed peas and greens on New Year's Day to have money all year long. Peas will bring you coins; greens bring dollars.

emptying sacks: The custom of telling persons who have offended you what they did wrong; sometimes accommodated in church settings on New Year's Eve.

Every knock is a boost. Every blow intending harm thrusts one ahead.

Every shut eye ain't 'sleep, and every "goodbye" ain't gone.

every which way/ every which-a-way: in every possible direction or way

evil: bad tempered; mean

Experience is the best teacher, although the fees are high.

*Experience teaches a dear school,
  but fools will learn in no other.*

Far out!

flutterby: butterfly

fly: as an adjective, "fly" means "very nice"; as a noun, it means "an unattractive suitor who will not go away"

friend boy: used in some areas of the country to distinguish a friend who is a boy from a boyfriend

friend girl: used is some areas to distinguish a girl who is a friend from a girlfriend.

from jump street: from the beginning

from the git / from the git-go: from the beginning

Further distance, better friends.

gaming: interacting falsely or dishonestly; playing head games

"Gettin' dark! Gettin' dark!": Word game. Played when an African American who is not wearing a watch is asked, "What time is it?" The reply is given as the fingers of one hand stroke the bare wrist above the other.

giffy: damp (After I worked out my clothes were giffy.)

Goodness, gracious, piece of life! baby-talk phrase; said to young babies

gray boys: white boys

greasin': eating

The hawk is howling! The hawk is out! Mister Hawkins is in town! Such phrases refer to wind so cold there is no standard English term for it.

heavy: smart

He/she don't take no tea for the fever! said of a bold, aggressive person who acts without fear of consequences

He/She/It has got it goin' on!	statement of praise or approval
He / she has the mojo and the say-so.	He/she has final authority.
He/she goes for bad.	He/she is a pugnacious, aggressive, fearless person.
He is a "Honey-do."	He is "hen pecked" (constantly responding to "Honey do this" and "Honey do that").
He / she is not wrapped too tight.	He / she is not too bright.
down on the farm with / visiting Uncle Ben:	in prison
high muckty mucks:	prominent socialites
hincty:	snooty
His / her bread ain't done.	He / she is not very bright.
hog:	Cadillac car
hoppergrass:	grasshopper
honky / honkey / honkie:	disparaging name for a white person
hummer:	an unanticipated reaction
I can see as far into the rock as another man can pick!	a bragging phrase
I clean forgot.	I completely forgot.
I don't play that!	A forceful rejection of a proposed or attempted activity.
I don't say this for no harm, but —	introduction to a harmful verbal blast (a signal to duck)
I know tha's / that's right!	
I laugh and grin, but I don't play!	a "back off" warning
I only have to do two things: die, and stay Black.	
If it wasn't for bad luck, I wouldn't have no luck at all!	

If you are not a part of the solution, you are a part of the problem!	challenge statement of the 1950s–60s civil rights struggle
If you're white, you're all right *If you're yellow, you're mellow* *If you're brown, you can hang around* *If you're black, **get back!***	
If you follow signs, signs will follow you.	
I'm looking for a higher bush and sweeter berries!	I'm looking for someone or something better.
It "bees" that way sometimes.	That's life.
from jump street:	from the beginning
It ain't no thang (or no biggie).	It is not important.
It's snowing down south!	Your slip is hanging!
It takes an entire village to raise a child.	
Keep gettin' up!	
Keep on keeping on!	
knee baby:	the second youngest child in a family
Lazy folks work the hardest.	
Like the farmer say to the potatah, I'll plant ya now and dig ya latah.	goodbye phrase
lolligagging:	wasting time with light-hearted chatter or behavior
Luck say: open your mouth and shut your eyes.	
Mama:	Used by African-American men as a flirtatious appellation. Used in Africa by indigenous Africans as a term of affection and respect for older women.

man: This appellation used frequently by African-American males addressing each other was begun when African-American men were customarily called "boy" by members of the dominant society.
Miss Anne: an Anglo female
Miss Thing: a flip, affectionate reference to a friend or acquaintance
mother wit: innate intelligence
More hurry, less speed.
much him up: flatter him
Mr. Charlie / Charlie / Chuck: Caucasian male
my main man: my best male friend
my main squeeze: the person of primary romantic interest
nanny: feces
Never pass by your first luck.
nice-nasty: someone who combines lofty principles with filthy behavior, or vice versa
No fool, no fun.
No news is good news.
Not worth the time of day.
obahutty: much love
Ofay / 'faye: Caucasian (pig Latin for the word " foe")
Ofey: Caucasian; transposition of the syllables of "feo," the Spanish word for "ugly."
on the greezy board/ greasy board: in a vulnerable position for being ousted from a position or situation
oreo: Black person who lives by a Caucasian value system; someone said to be "Black outside and white in-

Out o' sight!

passing: side." The term is derived from a chocolate wafer sandwich cookie that has vanilla filling.

This term describes a person of African descent and Caucasian appearance who breaks connections with the Black community and "passes" for white.

Poor as Job's turkey.

profiling; also, **styling:**   posturing behavior; conducting oneself with the objective of being observed by others

"Psyche!!"   Said when one person has successfully played a "head game" on another.

pushing up the daisies: dead ("By then, I'll be 'pushing up the daisies' twenty at a time!")

Put a handle on my/her/his name.   a request that a title be included with the name of the person addressed: (Mr., Dr., Aunt., etc.). Often said to younger people by those who adhere to African cultural standards.

put your hands together: clap

'que: barbecue

rap/ rapp/ rhap: to communicate; a derivative of "rapport"

Rise and shine!   Wake up call. Often used to awaken children for the day.

root doctor/man/woman: person believed to be skilled in curing with herbs

See ya later, alligator!   goodbye

Sent for you yesterday, here you come today!

Sho 'nuff!

show out:	show off
signifying:	"put-down" implications, statements, or verbal essays marked by indirect references, body motion, and sarcasm
sister / soul sister:	a Black female
somethin' else; som'pn else:	refers to a reality that differs from what is usual or expected
soul:	the essence of being Black; spiritual depth
Spectacular Vernacular:	Black English

The Lord doesn't love ugly,
  and don't care much about pretty!

The luck's in the Lord,
  and the devil's in the people.

The Man:	the white man; often used in statements that reflect control: "I've got to meet The Man in the morning." (I have to go to work in the morning.) The term was probably coined as a sarcastic rebuttal to the use of "boy" as an appellation for Black men.

The tongue is steel, but a closed mouth is a shield.

The truth is not to be known at all times.

There is more than one way to skin a cat.

This is the day I long have sought,
  and mourned because I found it not.

throw down / th'o down:	expression originally meaning "to fight," which now also means "to party"
to crack one's face up:	to smile
to jump bad:	to become angry and strongly confront opponents or potential opponents
to jump salty:	to become angry

to sit on the stool of do nothing:	to be idle
to the max:	to the maximum; to the extreme
tongue lashing:	a verbal thrashing
tote:	carry
tomming:	behaving in a self-demeaning way to gain favor with a member of the larger society; Uncle Tom behavior (see "Uncle Tom," below)

Tough times don't last, tough people do.

trifling:	used as an adjective to describe a person, "trifling" means to be spiritually depraved and decadent; to be nasty. (Standard English speakers, beware!)
trim:	sexual intercourse
Uncle Tom:	a Black person who places the interests of Caucasians above his or her own best interests; adopts a Caucasian value system
wanna-be / want-ta-be:	someone assiduously aspiring to be something else; a person struggling to improve her or his position and or image
wasted:	intoxicated

White folks are "how" folks, Black folks are "what" folks.

Who he when he home?!	Who does he think he is?
whosonever:	whosoever

What goes around, comes around.

what the Lord is pleased with:	the truth (I'm telling you what the Lord is pleased with!)
what's going down — what went down:	what is happening, or what has happened; the facts of a situation

When an elder dies,
  a library burns to the ground.

where one is
  "coming from":   thought or motivation for behavior

White folks "dress," and
  Black folks "dress up."
Also: White folks "dress down,"
  and Black folks "dress up."

who':   whore

wolfing / selling wolf   a loud, jovial word game of boast-
  tickets: ing, self-advocacy, and overstate-
                                   ment largely engaged in by young
                                   men

Young folks think old folks to be fools;
  *old folks **know** young folks to be fools.*

Your mouth's not afraid of
anything but hot hominy!
(added for worse offenders):

Give it a blow,
and you'll try that!   You speak without thinking.

Your tongue is loose   You talk too much!
  on both ends!

Church Expressions:

And when at last we stick our swords in
  the golden sands of time . . .   prayer phrase

Father, save these children who seem to be so contented
  in their sins.   family prayer phrase

Bless me, the least among all.   prayer phrase

Can't nobody do me like Jesus!   testimony phrase

Do, Jeesus!

Get on The Way, or
  get out of The Way.   pulpit exhortation to grow spiritu-
                                     ally or cease being a hindrance to
                                     others

God is a good god!   testimony phrase

Grant us traveling mercy /mercies / and journeying grace.	traveling prayer
He may not come when you want Him, but He's right on time.	testimony phrase
He woke me up this morning, and started me on my way.	testimony phrase
It ain't the ball, honey, it's after the ball is over!	a minister's explanation of his objection to dancing
Lead us from one good degree of grace to another.	prayer phrase
Lord, I come to Thee, knee bent and body bowed.	prayer phrase
"Mother, I don't believe in hell." "That don't put the fire out!"	Spiritual guidance in a family kitchen
on:	Many people will say this word before a day or week, but only when speaking in church settings (on today, on yesterday, on next week).
Prop me up on every leaning side.	prayer phrase
Remember all those we are duty bound to pray for.	prayer phrase
Rev. "stepped on toes" this morning!	The minister's sermon attacked transgressions of which some congregation members were guilty.
Sin is not in the short dress, it's in the short dresser.	sermon phrase
Sometimes the devil wears silk stockings!	sermon phrase
Strengthen us where we are weak, and build us up where we are torn down.	prayer phrase
Thank you, Jesus!	
Thankful we are clothed in our right minds, and have the activity of our limbs.	prayer phrase
Thankful we live in a cool world, a Bible land, and a gospel country.	prayer phrase
This joy I have, the world didn't give it to me and the world can't take it away.	testimony phrase

Teach me to pray and
   teach me what to pray for.   prayer phrase

We ask you to go before us like a guiding light,
   and behind us like a protecting angel.   prayer phrase

When time has failed us and we can no
   longer stay, give us a home where we can
   better praise you in that world that
   never ends.   prayer phrase

Greek Organization Expressions:

brothers:	fraternity brothers
frat:	a fraternity brother
crossing the burning sands:	the process of pledging
dean of pledges:	fraternity or sorority member in charge of pledgees
Eatin' that Delta Dust!	phrase that describes a rejected suitor of a member of Delta Sigma Theta Sorority
going over:	transition point at which one is upgraded from the pledgee category and becomes a full member of a Greek letter organization
the line:	the group of individuals pledging an organization at the same time
line brothers / sisters:	organization members who are, or were, in the same pledge line
line name:	a nickname by which a pledgee is addressed
microwave brothers:	members who join a fraternity through modern procedures without stringent entrance rituals endured by those who joined earlier
on line:	pledgees
sands:	organization members of the same pledge line
soror:	a sorority sister

the yard: the campus of a college where there are Black Greek organizations

Note: *Readers who would like to submit Black English expressions and related information to be considered for inclusion in a comprehensive work are invited to forward such material to: BLACK EXPRESSIONS, P.O. BOX 14-3262, AUSTIN, TX 78714-3262.*

NEWSPAPER COLUMNS AND LETTERS REVISITED

The newspaper columns and editorial letters that follow were written by me for a number of publications over a period of years. The columns appeared in Philadelphia newspapers; the letters were written to papers in Philadelphia and Austin, Texas. I elected to publish them in this volume because most of the subject matter remains relevant to the 1990s. In some instances, though the writing presents a point of view I once held, time has brought increased understanding of a situation and its underlying philosophy and causes, and I would not write the same column or letter today. Because some of the people mentioned or addressed may have experienced similar growth, I have eliminated their names rather than risk associating them with ideas and behavior they may no longer fully support.

Marian E. Barnes

MINISTER FARRAKHAN CHALLENGES BLACK MEN, DEFENDS BLACK WOMEN

But I See Room for Improvement

Looking around me there were about two or three males for every female present in an audience recently where Minister Louis Farrakhan was telling African-American men about themselves. The minister spared no punches. He blasted "brothers" for advocating polygamy while being unable to care for one wife. He called on men to live up to spiritual and life style standards demanded of them in the Holy Bible and the Holy Qur'an. He also said Black women who seem harsh in their attitude toward Black men are merely trying to challenge the Afro-American man to rise up and become what he is capable of becoming.

Well, I'll tell you, it felt good to be a woman in that audience! (Unusual in these days where the fight for women's rights and feelings of frustration and anger often dominate gatherings where female concerns are addressed.) Still, a gnawing uneasiness begged my attention. I refused to entertain it at the time, afraid it would take the edge off my joy. But later, I faced the unhappy fact that despite the truth of all Minister Farrakhan had said, we African-American women must accept primary responsibility for some weaknesses of our men.

In the course of a lifetime, Black men largely learn their values and behavior from the Black women who give birth to them, rear them, teach them, and marry them. Black men who respect and appreciate businesses and activities of other racial groups, but "bad-mouth" every such venture belonging to, or operated by Black Americans, all too often are simply regurgitating what they learned at "Mother's Knee." (Translation: They were taught to believe in their own inferiority.) Black men who are trifling in marriage, educational or work situations usually were failed first by mothers who took pride in their maleness, but did not teach them strong principles and values, then by wives, sweethearts, and female friends who continued the pattern by glorifying in their maleness while tolerating, even coddling their weaknesses. Black men who put-down the beauty of Black women and admire the beauty of women of other races are usually adhering to ideas imparted to them by mothers and sisters who taught them that straight hair is "good" and frizzy hair is "bad"; also, that narrow facial features and white skin are "pretty," but highly developed facial features and black skin are "ugly." In this regard, Black women are unique. To my knowledge, no other race of women rears its males to admire, respect and esteem the women of other ethnic groups above themselves — in effect, teaching their sons to look down them!

I'm glad Minister Farrakhan is challenging Afro-American men to get off their knees and stand tall. Black men also obviously appreciate his efforts for they flock to hear him. I was especially grateful for the lesson he delivered on how our women should be respected and loved by our men. We Black women can do much to assist Minister Farrakhan deliver this lesson, in fact, to eradicate the need for such a lesson at all, by admiring and respecting ourselves, and teaching our sons to do the same!

March 1979

WHO NEEDS RICHARD PRYOR?

Ever so often my radio assaults my ears with a stream of vulgarities from Richard Pryor designed to entice people who hear them to attend a Pryor performance. An announcer's voice tells us slyly that obscenities have been deleted from the cuts used on radio, then promises (clearly as a reward) that those who personally attend Pryor's show will hear him spew uncut, uncensored, undiluted, unmitigated obscenities.

Richard Pryor is not a funny man. I see him as a "sick" symbol of our "sick" society, capitalizing on low thinking, a dirty mouth, and a twisted view of life. But we live in a time when it is popular and considered sexy, smart, cute, funny and talented to be crude, vulgar, and filthy. Pryor, who has no equal in these, thrives and makes millions projecting his "talents" to the delight of mass audiences who come away praising "the genius of Richard Pryor!"

The "entertainer" is particularly offensive in his routines about church people. Pryor's church-related tales leave me with the impression that everyone concerned is hypocritical, lecherous, and unprincipled. The basis for the laughs he draws is the dirt in his characters — most of whom are portrayed as stupid — and the dirt Pryor throws on them.

Some of the most comical experiences I have ever lived through have been connected with the church. So I know a wealth of genuinely funny church stories exist based on church life as it really is. But in real life church humor, people are not immoral, prideless, hypocritical or dumb, as Pryor's joke folks are. Unlike the preposterous plots contrived by Pryor as props to project the filth he spews, true circumstances surrounding humorous incidents about church are realistic. Also unlike Pryor's jokes, real life situations are rib-cracking, side-splitting-funny. Yet everybody involved stands tall in the story, worthy of the highest respect of anyone hearing it. For example, in a future column I'll share the story of a real-life drunk who literally turned a real-life church out. But throughout the incident, nobody, including the drunk, behaved in a way that was vulgar, or immoral, or stupid.

In a recent column, I objected to network TV comedies about African-Americans because *all* of them are staged insults to Afro-American culture. "Entertainers" like Richard Pryor are a worse affront than these TV comedies. Everyone knows they are written by Caucasians and enacted by performers who need a job, and therefore may not be authentic. But Richard Pryor is an African-American — presumably he understands his race and its culture. Richard Pryor is rich — when he puts his race down, it cannot be because he needs a job. So Richard Pryor's performance has credibility for many of the millions of people he "entertains." The fact that everyone involved in his jokes, including Pryor, acts like a typical n——r is a delight to many of these people because it is what they want to believe, and to them, the entire routine is very, very "funny." And to them, this "comedian" is well worth the millions of dollars he is paid.

Who needs Richard Pryor?

Author's note: Shortly after this column was published, Richard Pryor announced his intention to eliminate from his routines much of the offensive behavior to which the column objected.

November 1977

MONSTER CHILDREN "UNREAL" HORROR STORY

I have an idea for a horror story in which the children of a community turn into rude, ill-bred, ignorant monsters suffering from a contagious, terminal illness called "progressive monsterism." The older the children grow, the worse they become. By the time they are teenagers they are *wild*! Eventually the disease will kill the children and the entire community culturally and physically.

People waste precious time and problem-saving energy debating the origin of monsterism. Some say it was spawned by modern society. Others insist progressive monsterism is the result of the community environment. Still others say the disease is inherent in the people themselves. There are also those who contend monsterism was first introduced into the community many years ago by monsters who enslaved the ancestors of the present community residents.

Such arguments are futile. The problem is not how the disease began, but how to cure it. The parents try to cure their children with prescriptions of expensive clothes and other possessions. It doesn't help. Instead, these often become an outward symptom of the inner sickness. Then parents start to blame other people for their monster children. "It's your fault," they tell the teachers. "You should teach them." But the children, by school age, have become virtually unteachable. (How do you teach enraged hyenas?) "We can't teach them," the teachers say. "Let us beat them."

"Yes, yes. Beat them," some parents say.

"No, no. Don't beat them," others protest. And while they take time out for a senseless squabble, the disease grows worse. The squabble is senseless because the parents only have to visit the schools to see that many teachers, who are suffering from progressive monsterism themselves, have long been beating the children. Physically, with yardsticks, slaps, pinches, hair-pullings, arm-twistings, and knee-jams under the buttocks of a child hard enough to cause permanent internal injuries without leaving a visible mark. And they beat the children psychologically — into blind submission to imposed authority, into acceptance of themselves as inferior to it.

This does not help. The children learn to duck as much of the physical punishment as possible, and to stoically accept what they cannot escape. They learn to believe in the inevitability and enmity of imposed authority, and in their own inferiority to it and virtually everything else. They also learn to hate the authority, and to hate themselves.

Their language is putrid; their rage and hostility omnipresent.

They deface, destroy, or appropriate property belonging to the authority or to each other. They organize to oppress and control each other, their "turf," their neighborhoods, their families. They rampage with fists, with knives, with guns. They wound. They maim. They kill. Everyone is afraid of them, especially their parents.

"It's your fault," parents tell police. "You should treat them like criminals. Crack their heads. Jail them. Kill them. Anything at all; just take them off our streets so we can be safe." The police do their best, but it doesn't help. Even if police could jail or kill all the children, parents keep giving birth to more babies, so the problem continues to increase.

Finally, the "social scientists" suggest a solution to the problem: Eliminate the birth of babies that become monster children. (You see, the babies are born normal. They get the monster disease when parents fail to teach them basic values as infants and toddlers, and later, relinquish or delegate their parental responsibilities in this area to others — teachers, preachers, police, monster children.)

Anyway, the social programmers get busy and provide birth control pills, abortions, vasectomies, and hysterectomies for adults in the community — free. It costs the government millions of dollars to prevent the births of many babies who would turn into monsters. But it helps. By the time the social planners have been at work several years, tens of thousands fewer babies are being born in the community, and tens of thousands fewer monster children are entering the community's schools.

There are a few complaints. The zeal of the social programmers sometimes results in hysterectomies being performed on teenage girls without the girls being told what is being done to them. Some people in the community object to that. A few others wonder why all the government-provided free help to eliminate babies is concentrated almost exclusively in their community, even though other communities have higher birthrates. A few people, such as educators, begin to be uneasy because their jobs are linked to the birthrate which is declining, and their future employment is in jeopardy.But mostly the community is pleased. It does not seem to occur to anyone that ultimately the survival of the community depends upon the survival of its people in educated numbers; that by eliminating their babies, they are eliminating themselves; that perhaps the cure for monsterism is not elimination, but education of the babies by their parents from birth, persistent training in basic values, ethics, morals, and behavior. Consistent involvement of parents in all phases of the lives of their babies and children, providing guidance, counsel, companionship and formal education in the pre-school years, and an ongoing involvement with the child and her/his educators after schooling begins.

No. The parents are delighted. At last something is working. Only it's slow. Although tens of thousands of babies have been eliminated, the monster children still number in the hundreds of thousands. So teachers beat them more than teach them. Police beat, jail, and kill the monster children. And their terrified parents buy guns and barricade themselves in their homes to protect themselves from their children while they wait for the social planners program to become totally successful and completely eliminate the monster children and the community.

As I said, I thought about writing a horror story about a community of parents living in fear of destruction from their monster children. But I decided against it. The idea is too far-fetched. There has to be a germ of plausibility in a good horror story. Instead of writing a story about monster children taking over their own parents and community, perhaps I'll write about a more believable horror — a life-threatening invasion of the community by a non-human life species, such as monster ants, or bees, or birds.

November 1977

REVERSE RACISM:
NEW PROBLEM IN THE NEW SOUTH

During my childhood, Afro-American families lived in the shadow of the Ku Klux Klan. Newspapers kept a tally of publicized lynchings and they numbered in the thousands. Traveling through the South was an ordeal for Blacks. Afro-Americans traveling on trains and buses were compelled to use segregated waiting rooms, drinking fountains, toilet facilities, and seating areas on vehicles. Black motorists were not permitted to use public rest rooms, or roadside restaurants. I was introduced to this form of racism on the first return trip my family made to our Southern home town when I was a small child.

Once as a young adult in Memphis, Tennessee, a sailor tried to incite riders on a crowded bus to attack me, because I sat in the front section. And, once in the New Orleans Airport restaurant a grimy short-order cook roared at me, "Get out of here, and go to the back window where the niggers get their food!"

Today, there is a new South. I ride where I like on public vehicles. There are no signs restricting my liberty, and I am seldom called "nigger." You would think these things indicate a new racial tranquility in the South that travelers could observe. Not so. On a recent trip to North Carolina, I saw many incidents with racist over-tones, and a weird "role reversal" in racism that I found highly disturbing.

For example, waiting to change buses in the Richmond bus station, I saw a white man, about forty years old, mopping the floor. A young Black woman, perhaps twenty, stopped to watch him, then said, "Mop that floor, boy." Carefully keeping his eyes on the floor, the man continued to work. She walked a few steps away, turned and barked at him again. "I said, mop that floor, boy!" She stood, seeming to want an answer which never came.

On the bus I boarded for Durham, N.C., nearly all the passengers were Afro-Americans. People in the back were drinking, including one white passenger. He, however, wanted to go to sleep. The tipsy Afro-Americans were loud and boisterous. The sleepy drunk asked them to be quiet, and a quarrel followed, with much foul language and many racial slurs. Finally a Black man dared the sleepy man to come to the back seat, saying he had a "piece" and would "blow his head away." The passenger rose and stumbled toward the back.

Like many other passengers, I was silently "steaming." Like them, I had been quiet while the man who complained was told repeatedly he was the only one annoyed by the rowdy behavior. Now, I told myself, no matter what happened, I wasn't going to sound off against a gun-toting drunk. Then I turned around and sounded off.

I told the "gunman" and his friends they were annoying more than one person and that they could be heard all over the bus. A lady behind me cautiously mumbled agreement, but the crowd in the rear pretended not to hear me. I rose in my seat and said it again — louder. Again they ignored me. Suddenly I came to my senses, faced forward, and was quiet, grateful that I had been ignored. Staggering back to his seat, the white man muttered, "Ahm gettin' offa this bus the next stop, and ah don' never wanna ride with none o' you people no more!"

In the bus station at Durham, I met a Southern Afro-American woman, well into her middle years. I told her about the incident in Richmond, and asked what she thought it meant. Did she think the young woman might have been joking?

"No. She wasn't joking," she said. "I see a lot of that down here. My own daughter tells me that when she sees one of them mopping, she says to the person, 'You must do a better job. Get that spot you missed right there.'" The woman's face was sad as she continued. "I don't approve of it. I enjoy seeing them do that kind of work. But I would never say a word. I think behaving like that doesn't show much dignity."

She put it well. There was a lack of dignity in the behavior of the young woman in Richmond, and a lack of dignity in the carousing on the back of the bus going to Durham. People died to equalize the situation between the races. Equal treatment should inspire us to behave with more dignity than our oppressed foreparents could. Incidents such as those I've described are sad evidence that some people are behaving with less.

February 1978

WHITE ANGEL LEARNS HER PROUD BLACK HISTORY
And I Feel Sad

"She's *a white n——r,* that's what she is, *a white n——r!*" Angel was shrieking, her midnight-color eyes ablaze, black, wavy hair whipping about her pretty cream-colored face as she tried to fling herself out of a door where her supervisor stood barring the way.

"Get out of my way! I quit! I won't work with her. She's *a white n——r! A white n——r!*" She screeched the phrase over and over again, trying frantically to get past the supervisor.

"Angel, watch what you're saying. Be careful," the supervisor whispered desperately. She was pleading with Angel to stop the *n——r* talk because I was sitting in the room.

"I don't care! I don't care! That's what she is, *a white n——r!* And do you know what *a white n——r* is? No offense to you," she shouted in the direction of my desk where I sat shuffling papers I couldn't see. *"A white n——r is somebody who looks good outside, but inside . . ."* now she was spitting her words out, the syllables like so many bullets, "in-side is *nothing!* In-side is **nothing!** Get out of my way! I'm quitting! I hate her! I won't work with a *white n——r!"*

Eventually the supervisor convinced Angel that she would only be hurting herself if she quit her job. Also that she would not have to work with the white co-worker whom she hated so much that she thought of her as being Black inside which obviously to her was humanity's lowest level.

Later, tear-streaked face washed, hair freshly combed, a cigarette in hand, Angel apologized to me. "What I said just now was no offense to you." I was working with my back toward her at a desk directly in front of hers. I didn't answer.

She tried again. I kept on shuffling papers and said nothing. I mean, what could I say? There was no appropriate answer. Anyway, I was only working in the office temporarily, sent there by a Temporary Employment Office where I had enrolled because I couldn't find a regular job. These agencies send people out to work for businesses that need help for a limited time. The pay isn't fabulous, but it helps with rent. The jobs aren't permanent, but when one job ends, there is usually another to replace it.

The job in Angel's office had been a pretty good one to begin with. The two of us shared an office. She was young, barely twenty, and grossly overworked. I had been hired to relieve some of the pressure on her, but in fact, Angel seemed to get more relief from shouting curses at the top of her voice in her native southern European tongue.

After the racial incident, however, things went downhill. Angel was civil and withdrawn. Her hot temper seldom flared. I sensed that my presence made her uncomfortable. Then one day I was moved into another office. Later, my agency representative phoned asking me to report to another company the next day because my present position was being terminated that afternoon, several days earlier than anticipated.

I went to Angel's office to bid her goodbye and left a note on her desk. I invited her to respond if she liked. This is what I wrote:

Dear Angel:
I was silent when you apologized to me for your remark

about a white "n——r" because I am so very proud of being an Afro-American that I can't deal with people who don't understand that. I was also very sad that you showed no pride in your African blood. Because of interaction among Black Africans and Nordic Europeans across the Mediterranean, many Africans on the north coast of Africa no longer are the same ebony black of Africans further south, and southern Europeans from Italy, Greece, Spain, etc. are no longer the pale white of Caucasians further north.

Whenever you slur an African because of his race, you slur yourself. This society has taught you to recognize only one-half of yourself, and to hate your ancestors who gave you much of your coloring, your looks, and your temperament.

You have much of which to be proud. Your African ancestors gave the world all the basics of our present civilization — math, sciences, religion. (Jesus was of the Tribe of Judah, the same tribe as the late Ethiopian, Emperor Haile Selassie. Members of their ethnic group, a non-European race of people, typically have brown skin and woolly hair.)

Your Caucasian ancestors such as Heroditus and Plato went to Africa, studied the civilizations, their basic knowledge, culture and philosophies and brought these back to the West. Sometimes they shipped the entire contents of repositories and libraries. In some cases, what could not be taken away was burned and destroyed, which is why most significant African artifacts from the Rosetta Stone to the Star of Sierre Leone are now in the West.

I hope you will learn more about your ancestors like Aesop, a Black African of ancient history, and about your modern Afro-American relatives and our discoveries and inventions which help make our civilization what it is today, like the traffic light, the self-lubricating engine, the coin-operated vending machine, the shoe-last machine, the automatic elevator, and blood plasma.

Angel, be proud!

I had barely returned to my desk when Angel was standing over me, eyes flashing. She spat out my name, and it startled me. I answered and waited, half-way fearing an explosion of her fiery temper. But there were no fireworks. "You're staying!" she blurted out.

"No. I'm supposed to leave today," I said slowly, not understanding.

"No, you're staying until Friday because I asked someone to

let you stay." A wave of emotion washed over me. Her eyes softened, and she quickly turned away.

"Thank you, Angel," I said to her fast retreating back.

Until our paths crossed, Angel had lived in a Caucasian world with little reason to think of the non-white world except in terms of the negative images with which we are all bombarded. Because of the constant propaganda against Africa and Africans, even some Afro-Americans resent being reminded of their African ancestry. In asking me to stay longer on that job, Angel was trying to tell me she understood what I had tried to teach her. And she was trying to show me love.

I would have liked to let her know I understood what she was feeling, and that I thought she had done a beautiful thing. I would have liked to show her love, but I didn't know how. I think I seemed aloof and reserved. Instead, all the while I kept feeling choked up inside as if I wanted to cry, although I didn't know why. I had learned something about Angel, and, quite unexpectedly, something about myself.

I like what I learned about Angel.

June 1978

RACIST INSULTS PLEASE A LISTENING AUDIENCE

The voice of an Afro-American man came from my radio, strong, strident, ringing with conviction. "We Blacks can't compete! We shouldn't be in schools with white students! First, they tried to teach me algebra, and I couldn't learn that. Then they tried to teach me trigonometry, and that was *worse.* Now, *they're trying to teach me the metric system!"*

The voice reached a fever pitch. "We Blacks should be in our own schools where we wouldn't have to try to compete with white people, or learn these things they're learning. We don't need that knowledge!"

I waited anxiously for someone to disagree with what had been said. Instead, other program participants supported the statements, and listeners phoned the show praising the program.

I was left wondering why the racist statements made by African-Americans on the show had drawn praise from other Afro-

Americans when undoubtedly the same statements broadcast by members of the Ku Klux Klan would have provoked a storm of protest from the Black community.

A RACIST INSULT IS A RACIST INSULT NO MATTER FROM WHOM IT COMES, OR FOR WHAT CAUSE.

The radio program participants backed up their statements with "reasons" as old as those first invented for enslaving captured Africans, and as new as tomorrow's news stories telling why the American Nazi Party says Afro-Americans can't compete, can't learn, don't need certain kinds of knowledge, and should be sent to segregated schools structured to deal with incompetent mentalities.

Such muddled thinking is equally racist whether it is promoted by bigoted whites or brain-washed Blacks. It is also equally preposterous. For example, since algebra was given to the world by Black Arabs like Ahmes, who lived in 1650 B.C., to suggest that over 3,000 years later their descendants cannot comprehend what the minds of their ancestors created is insane.

It is true, however, that some studies indicate that human energy used to solve math problems is the same energy used to fight the psychological battle for survival every Black student must wage in this society; and as a result, some African-American students begin a math problem with much of the energy needed to solve it previously drained away.

High school algebra was a terrible ordeal for me. Among a handful of African-American students in the school, I was regarded as a thing apart; advised repeatedly to drop the Academic Course for something "more suitable," such as a General Achievement Curriculum (designed for non-achievers); and, despite an above average I.Q., I was told I was mentally incapable of passing a mathematics course.

Whenever I tried to study algebra, I couldn't get past my memory that the teacher had said I was incapable, my fear that the teacher was right, my feeling of hate for the subject, my fear that I would fail the course, and countless other distracting thoughts and emotions that destroyed my ability to concentrate on the math problem at hand.

I did fail the course. At that point, it might have been comforting to allow myself to believe I had failed because "We Blacks cannot do algebra." But knowing those students who did well in the course, I strongly believed I could do anything intellectually that they could do.

Later, under different circumstances, I took two algebra courses, just to prove something to myself. I passed them with average grades. For the math courses I took in college, my grades were above average, although I continued to doubt myself and fear and hate the subject.

I'm glad I didn't take the "turn off and drop out" attitude promoted on the radio show because civilization passes over such people. Suppose, for instance, these people establish a school that does not teach the metric system. How will its students fare in a few years when the world will be using the metric system for measuring?

As unfortunate as it is that some African-Americans have come to believe racist propaganda promoting the intellectual inferiority of Afro-Americans, it is even more unfortunate that people with these convictions want company. So one never hears one of them say, "I have been conditioned to think I cannot compete . . . learn . . . achieve, and I now believe that is true." One hears instead, *"We Blacks cannot . . . "* do this, that, or the other.

African-Americans who advocate the intellectual inferiority of Blacks usually offer traditionally racist explanations: "We Blacks are different . . . think differently . . . are culturally inferior . . ." Sometimes, however, they say, "We Blacks cannot compete in this society because we are culturally (or intellectually) *superior.*" Try making sense of that!

Making sense of nonsense has a low priority with me. I prefer to remind Afro-Americans that people who cannot compete are incompetent. I would also rather challenge them to look to our glorious history, and to the achievements of present-day Afro-Americans for abundant evidence that we are a supremely competent race of people. Additionally, broadcasts such as this one, palmed off on the Afro-American community as a community service which, in fact, are a disservice to our race, should be examined thoroughly and rejected. When naive listeners fail to do so, sophisticated organizations should take on the responsibility. Further, I'm calling on African-Americans to recognize a racist insult and reject it whether it comes from an avowed racist whiter than a klansman's robe, or from a "soul brother" three shades blacker than a brand new Ford!

October 1978

"UNCLE TOMAHAWK" — "APPLE"
Sad Moment in a Sad Life

"Sure they call me an 'Apple,' red outside and white inside. But I just keep on preaching the word of our Lord and Savior, Jesus Christ, and I'm winning some of them over." He was a Christian missionary, speaking at a church meeting about his work among his own people on an Indian Reservation. Seated beside his Caucasian wife, he spoke of himself as an "Indian," never as an "Original American" or "Native American," terms preferred by many of his more revolutionary-minded kinsmen. His jet black "Indian" hair stood stiff on end in a two-inch crew cut, tipping a face that was smooth, round, plump, and beaming.

In essence, he was telling us that through his missionary service he was advocating that his people reject their own culture to improve themselves. The audience liked what he was saying, and conveyed confidence that church funds used to keep this missionary among the Indians was money well spent. The only African-American in a sea of Caucasians, I didn't want to "rock the boat," so I fixed a smile on my face and tried to look non-militant.

The missionary said that as a boy he had watched his father kicked down a hill by a white man. The man had told his father to dig a hole to bury a "dead man." Not realizing that "dead man" was a construction term meaning "foundation post," his father had dug a grave for a corpse. When he saw the grave, the white man had been so angry he had kicked the missionary's father again and again, rolling his body down a hill with the force of his kicks. The missionary said he had watched helplessly, feeling every kick of the man's foot on his father's body.

"That happened because my dad wasn't educated," the missionary told us. "I made up my mind right then I would learn to do everything a white man can do, and it would never happen to me!"

As I listened, my smile kept slipping out of place. I was still reluctant to seem militant, but I found I could not remain silent in the midst of the unquestioning, unwavering audience approval. Remembering my psychology classes, I lifted the corners of my mouth and asked in a "non-blaming" way what it was doing to the feeling of self worth of the people he was trying to help if they were being taught to believe their own culture was inferior, and should be rejected for that of another race.

"Oh, they're always saying something," he replied. "They say, 'We don't have horses anymore. The white man took them all away.' I tell them. 'You've got more horses than you've ever had. Just look under the hood of a car, you've got 106 horse power!' I tell them, 'You've got to walk in another man's shoes to understand him.' That's an old Indian saying. And I have put on the white man's shoes." Pulling up his trouser-legs, he held his feet out in front of him displaying a pair of high-heeled, pointed-toed cowboy boots on his feet. "They pinched and hurt at first, but I got used to it!"

Later, unbidden, he came to me and explained that he had married a white woman only because there were no unmarried girls of his own race in his age category when he wanted to marry. He showed me a picture of his daughter and asked if I didn't agree with him that she appeared to be more Indian than Caucasian. It seemed to be very important to him that I agree, so I said I could see some Indian characteristics about her. Still, he realized I didn't think she looked like an Indian, and it made him sad.

For a long moment we sat together in sad silence. His thoughts were his own. I was remembering how he had looked a few moments earlier, seated before the audience, his plump body, evidence that he had adopted the white man's diet and indoor living habits instead of the culture of his Original American ancestors; his crew-cut hair testifying to his preference for a white man's hairstyle over that of his forefathers; his legs stuck straight out before him, with pudgy feet crammed into narrow, high-heeled, ill-fitting cowboy boots. And I was remembering how he had summed up his life in a simple statement: "I have put on the white man's shoes. They pinched and hurt at first, but I got used to it."

November 1978

PHILLY'S AFRAMERICAN YOUTH HAVE PEACEFUL, CIVILIZED HALLOWEEN WHILE YOUNG WHITE HOODLUMS RAMPAGE IN SUBURBS AND CITY

I am tremendously proud of the way African-American teenagers and younger children conducted themselves throughout the Halloween nightmare. Chalk Night, Soap Night, Mischief Night and

Halloween were one big "treat" after another because our teenagers and younger children did not terrorize their neighbors with mean "tricks." I can't speak for children in all Aframerican neighborhoods. I am speaking for what happened in Mt. Airy where I live, and in areas I frequent, such as North Philadelphia.

Along with hundreds of others, my car was on the street every night. Nobody put a mark on it. Nobody slashed my tires, or painted my house. I neither saw nor heard of vicious "tricks" being played. In fact, I saw only one car with soaped windows during the entire season.

Since I traveled to Phoenixville daily, I could compare what happened here with what was happening in that suburban town and others near it. The "Middle America" appearance of these towns is clean, spacious, well cared for — pretty. But people who live in these areas told me youngsters in their communities made Halloween a living horror story for them. In some neighborhoods, tires were slashed on every automobile on the street. Mailboxes were uprooted, the "f——" word was painted on property. After the "mad-dog" violence, the same young people who were responsible rang doorbells of those they had harmed, and with knowing grins said, "Trick, or Treat!"

"They look at you and give you that sly grin because they know you know what they've done to you," one housewife told me. "But you'd *better* give them a treat when they ask for it, or they'll do something worse!"

Phoenixville police officers verified that some children in the community commit crimes against their neighbors and call them "tricks." They also spoke of adults who poison the "treats" they prepare for youngsters who come to their doors on Halloween. (Last year one suburban man poisoned wrapped candy with a hypodermic needle for Halloween "trick-or-treaters," and his own children were killed when they ate it by mistake.)

My only brush with hateful Halloween behavior occurred when raw eggs were smashed against the windows of a Number 23 trolley I was riding as it tried to pass through a far South Philadelphia Caucasian neighborhood. The trolley pole was pulled off its track, and the operator darted outside to replace it, only to have the Halloween "tricksters" yank the pole off again. This time the operator remained on the trolley and turned on a revolving light above the vehicle which summoned police. With police protection, he was able to reset the trolley pole on its track and resume his journey.

Trolley operators who followed him were less fortunate. Goons in the same area smashed eggs against trollies, yanked trolley poles off their tracks, and when operators attempted to reset them they were personally assaulted with barrages of raw eggs.

I didn't see any headlines saying, *WHITE TEENAGERS GO ON VIOLENT HALLOWEEN RAMPAGE IN SUBURBS AND SOUTH PHILADELPHIA.* Nor did I see news stories praising Black teenagers for their peaceful, civilized celebration of the holiday. It is customary for the Black community to be hit with big headlines for negative behavior, and to be completely ignored when its behavior is on a higher plane than that of the white community, *which is often.* It is mind-blowing to consider the improvement in the image we have of ourselves, and the image others have of us that would result if this were not true. A lion share of our problems in the Afro-American community can be traced to our "bad" image, and much of this image is the result of our "bad" press.

I think Halloween has outlived its time. It is a holdover from a heathen era, and I would like to see it replaced in our community with a holiday that has constructive relevance to our lives.

Nevertheless, when children came through our neighborhood asking "Trick or treat?" I was waiting inside my house with a bag of apples to give away, but nobody rang my doorbell. I was disappointed. I didn't get a chance to show our youngsters how proud I am of them.

Next Halloween, I just might sit on my steps with a bag of apples and offer celebrating children a treat as they pass by whether they ask me for one or not.

February 1978

WHAT'S IN A NAME?

The graffiti scribbled on the wall of a study booth in Paley Library at Temple University started me thinking. It said:

"ALL NEGROES SHOULD BE SHIPPED BACK TO AFRICA. WE DON'T WANT THEM HERE."
"THEN WHO WOULD TAKE THEIR PLACE AND BE NEXT TO BE HATED? THE JEWS? THE ITALIANS? YOU?"

> "I AM A NEGRO. AFRICANS COME FROM AFRICA. 'BACK' REFERS TO THEM, NOT US!"
> "IF YOU ARE A NEGRO, YOU WERE MAN-MADE IN THE U.S.A. I AM AN AFRO-AMERICAN!"
> "YOU TWO ARE LOST." [Arrows were drawn from this comment to the two immediately above.]
> "YOU'RE NOBODY 'TIL SOMEBODY LOVES YOU . . . "
> [This was written beside a cheerfully scrawled musical score.]

What is in a name? Nothing? An African-American is an Afro-American, is an Aframerican, is a Black American, is a black American, is a Negro, is a negro? Not so!

Some ancient societies considered a name all important. This society places little overt emphasis on names. Nevertheless, studies have shown they are important, that individuals tend to behave in accordance with a psychological image of the name they bear. Also, that many people react to an individual on the basis of his or her name. (According to one research project, grades given to students with unusual names such as "Egbert" were ten percent lower than grades given students with common names.) Although American society has never verbally stressed name significance, even a casual review of the history of the Black race in this country reveals that from the beginning, the importance of names was recognized and ruthlessly used in vicious psychological warfare against African captives. Also, that the strategy continues to be a factor in racial relationships today.

Historically, when an African was captured, brought to this country and enslaved, his name was changed at once. The purposes were basic to making a successful slave. It stripped the African of his personal and national identity. It also made it possible for the enslaver to pretend he had not enslaved a human being, since in addition to changing the captive's personal name, the individual was no longer called an "African," but a "negro," which was considered something sub-human.

Had the African been allowed to retain his name, it would have remained a constant reminder to all that Africa was his motherland. Also, since African names often reflect nationality, family history, and family role, an African name would have kept alive the link between the bearer, his original country, and his original culture.

The result could have been disastrous to the slave system that depended for its existence upon convincing both captive and captor that prior to enslavement, the captured person had been uncivilized and without a culture, virtually a part of the animal kingdom.

To destroy in everyone's mind the connection between Africa and its civilizations and captured Africans, the name "negro" was invented for them. On the evolutionary scale, a negro was said to be a bit above an ape, but somewhat lower than a man. A negro was specifically defined as a life form equal to three-fifths of a human being.

The captured Africans' concept of themselves as descendants of the originators of world civilization begun in Africa was destroyed when they were not permitted to call themselves Africans. Their feeling of self-value was further pulverized when the name "negro" with its dehumanizing definition was invented and applied to the captured race.

"I Told Jesus It Would Be All Right If He Changed My Name" is the most mournful spiritual I know. Our ingenious foreparents chose this way of sending a message down to the generations following them. The words were reassuring to the unsuspecting captors. But the severe minor key of the tortured melody wails across the centuries of the tormented suffering endured by captives forced to adopt a European interpretation of the Christian religion, an interpretation inimical to their interests.

The abiding symbol of the resulting inner disorientation, social revulsion, and rejection was a changed name. My penname is Mmayen. In the Nigerian culture from which it comes, the name means "A Loving Child" or "A Loving Mother." What is in a name? Everything! And I am an African-American, or any name that means the same proud thing!

January 1979

ABOUT THE "HOLY SPIRIT" NOBODY COULD QUENCH BUT "THE MAN"

It was long past midnight, but loud noises from the hotel room next to ours were keeping us awake. My daughter, my sister, my niece and I were attending a church convention. Presumably, so were the people next door who had kept a noisy disturbance going for two nights. We wondered about their lack of concern for others. Because of it, we thought the people in that room might have no connection with the church. This was the last night of the convention, and although the others disagreed, I thought the noise was worse than before.

About 1:00 A.M., someone entered our part of the building through the doors at the end of the hall and knocked at the room next door. We heard a female voice say, "You all are making too much noise!" Then the footsteps retreated out of the area. Obviously, the rowdyism was upsetting people on other floors, or on the other side of the building, or both. Still, the complaint had no effect.

"What are they doing? It sounds like they're throwing the TV set against the wall," my sister said. We speculated that they were playing ball, ping pong, or gambling because of some yelling about a bet. Finally my daughter started next door hoping to reason with our neighbors. My sister objected, afraid she might be harmed. "Marian, you are a teacher and a counselor, you should go."

I was silent. I didn't want to go. I thought of calling the desk clerk. But it sticks in my craw to call an outside authority to solve problems that should be resolved through mutual respect. Suddenly my niece ducked outside, knocked several times on the door of the next room. The occupants could see her through the "eye" of their door. At last a voice asked, "Who is there?"

"It's going to be the police if you don't quiet down," my niece answered sternly. The room was quiet for about five minutes, then the bedlam resumed. At 1:30 A.M., my daughter went to their door. She, too, had to knock over and over. Questioned through the door, she pressed them to open it, then reasoned with the ladies inside for about five minutes. This earned us about ten minutes of peace.

At 2:00 A.M., I knocked on their door. And knocked. And knocked. Finally, admitted to the darkened room, I introduced myself to two teenage girls, neither of whom was the leader of the activities. She was lying on the floor hidden between the bed and the wall. When it appeared I was going to be a real nuisance, she surfaced and blurted out, "Y'all put on the light and let me talk to this lady." Heavy-set, about 20, what a battle she gave me! To begin with, she would not give her name, or that of her church until I said I didn't blame her for being ashamed.

Indeed she was not ashamed! She said I was wrong to come in and try to quench The Holy Spirit! "I don't know what church *you* go to, but at our church we *never* quench The Spirit!" she lashed out at me. She and her friends had been praying and singing hymns. This was the last night of the convention, and she was a "night person" and couldn't sleep, so they were enjoying themselves. I should be glad that they were young and enjoying themselves in The Lord, and not out in "the world" getting high on drugs!

I talked of self-discipline, consideration for others, a time and place for everything, and made absolutely no impression. Finally, I asked her to explain what had happened to her pastor and ask for guidance. After some twenty minutes, the young lady apologized "for being rude" and promised to be quiet. When I left the room, it was filled with young women who had apparently "taken cover" when I arrived earlier.

Their room remained quiet for about an hour. Then they began a loud prayer meeting that included whooping, crying, groaning, an apology to The Lord for being rude, with an explanation that the devil was loose and needed to be bound. Two mature women entered the room, and I expected them to correct the situation, but the uproar continued unabated until a Caucasian man knocked on the door and spoke to the person who opened it in an extremely low key, almost indifferent way. "We've been getting complaints. Please, be quiet."

The boisterous, inconsiderate folks in the room next door had received innumerable, earnest pleas for quiet from fellow guests and ignored them all. This latest, offhand request came from a stranger who seemed bored almost to the point of yawning as he made it. We believed it was a waste of time. We were wrong.

When he spoke, the racket in the room which was booming in volume and zooming in momentum stopped immediately, as though his voice had pushed the "off" button on a blasting radio. The emotional outcryings did not take a moment and come to a halt as might have been expected. The praying, groaning, shouting and weeping "stopped on a dime"!

For the next hour there was no noise in that room. NONE! Now, nobody in our room could go to sleep because it was eerie! Incredible! How could there be no sound whatsoever from a room crammed with people? For at least one hour we heard no one murmur, or move, or turn over in bed, or leave the room quietly, or cough, or sigh. "I wish they would sneeze, or do something so we'll know they're all right," my niece quipped. "Maybe that man threw some chloroform in there!" At last, a faint rustle of movement from someone in the room confirmed the existence of life. Then it became a tomb again, and it remained a tomb until we left the next afternoon.

The experience was shattering. The man who had worked this miracle had given no credentials, not even his name. He had not been wearing a uniform. Although a uniform means nothing without credentials, if had he been wearing one, we might have thought our neighbors had been struck with fear at the sight of his official outfit. The man had knocked only twice, presumably unheard the first time because of the commotion. Someone had obviously looked through the "eye" in the door panel, seen his white face and promptly opened their bedroom door to him at 4:00 A.M.! Others of us who had attempted to talk with them earlier had been forced to knock repeatedly. We had then been asked who we were, and what we wanted. Even so, the door was opened only for those who pleaded that it be opened to make a conversation possible. By comparison, when the Caucasian gentleman knocked, the door was opened swiftly. He was not asked his name, his reason for knocking, if he represented the management, or anything else. He could have been a rapist and a murderer roaming the halls, but he was white, and the door was opened for him without question! And because *he* spoke, the prayer group instantly "quenched" the "spirit" in their room, promptly became orderly, and behaved with consideration for other people for the remainder of our stay.

I was left wondering how long some African-Americans will continue to respect a white face, ANY white face, above themselves, and the interests and needs of their fellow human beings. We had tried hard to share with the people in the next room ideas about showing self-respect, mutual respect, and consideration for each other. We had failed miserably. But a man had succeeded, not through love, which we felt, not through reason, which we had tried, not through caring, as we did so deeply, but through the color of his skin!

Later, thinking about what had happened, I faced a truth. There are people inside the church, just as there are those outside of it, who are "over loud, over fed, over dressed, and under bred." And such folks need teaching as well as preaching.

September 1978

AFRO-AMERICANS CRITICIZE *ROOTS*, DOCILE ABOUT INSULTING TV SHOWS

Part two of *Roots* failed to draw the record-breaking numbers of TV viewers attracted by the original program, and that was to be expected. However, I did not anticipate the large-scale criticism and carping against the telecast that I encountered in the African-American community. I heard it panned over and again by public personalities, and private individuals. But their objections were seldom clear or substantial. Frequent complaints were that *Roots, Part Two* was unrealistic in places; also that contrived situations were sometimes projected while accurate history was neglected. Actually, these faults were present in both segments of *Roots*. For example, in Part One, the character of Old George and much of the plot surrounding him were unrealistic, contrived, and unbelievable. Also in Part One we are told that Kizzy, on a plantation a few hundred miles from her father, did not know of his death for a number of years.

From stories passed down in my own family, I believe that Kizzy would have learned of her father's death in a matter of days, perhaps even hours. News traveled swiftly among the plantations: by spirituals sung as messages, by talking drums, by smoke signals, by underground messages. But the mistakes and misconceptions apparent in *Roots*, Parts One and Two, are minute considerations compared to the towering, positive contributions the telecast made to America by showing the African-American to the entire country for the first time as a dignified, productive human being before and after being captured and enslaved; also by exposing to the world the stupid, subhuman mentalities of the enslavers. Some contrived situations and lack of realism in the story line were a small price to pay.

What puzzles me is that I hear little or nothing said about regular programming on TV for and about African-Americans. Without exception, *ALL* of it is horrendous with no redeeming features that I can see. In the "entertainment" programs, the "entertaining" is at the expense of African-American culture. The focus of ridicule is always on something generally projected as an

Afro-American value, or attitude; or upon speaking, thinking, or behavior patterns popularly alleged to be Aframerican. *Good Times* may be the best example because there is no attempt at camouflage. The character J. J. could be inserted into the racist scripts of the earliest *Amos 'n Andy* radio shows with no changes whatsoever. Many Caucasians and Black Americans accept the role he plays as typical for a person of his race and age. Young people wear T-shirts with J. J.'s picture, and J. J.'s words. They also adulate and imitate his behavior, including the constant insults, disrespect, and verbal violence to which he subjects his sister and brother.

The Jeffersons is an example of the same thing more subtly, and thus more dangerously projected. George Jefferson is portrayed as an African-American who used Caucasian standards, values, and methods to become a rich, successful businessman. However, whenever George "reverts" into "Black" standards, values, or methods, he is a buffoon! Yet, I am not hearing criticism of *The Jeffersons* or *Good Times*, I am hearing criticism of *Roots*, the finest TV programming about the African-American sub-society ever produced!

Instead of non-stop complaining to each other about the flaws in *Roots*, we should be flooding ABC with letters commending the network for its pioneering efforts in producing interracial understanding in this country. Such letters need not say the telecast was perfect. Constructive criticism incorporated into positive correspondence is the best means of assuring attention from producers. Inundating the network with this type of correspondence from masses of people is the way to inspire more productions with the fine qualities of *Roots,* which could include improvements suggested by the letter writers, and be without the flaws they have pointed out.

May 1979

MODERN WOMAN vs. "TRADITIONAL LADY"
A Comparison of Roles

I agree wholeheartedly with Equal Rights Amendments advocates that women doing the same work as men should receive the same pay. Beyond that, the feminists and I part company on a great many issues. Quite often I think they are wrong, when some of them insist, for example, that there is no difference between men and women in their physical capacity for work. But even when they are right, sometimes I find it hard to care about what they're telling me I should care about.

For instance, the failure to allow upper-class women free participation in the business world has been misguided, as has the failure to allow women of every class upward mobility in the business world. Business genius comes in both sexes, and free expression of it should be encouraged in both for the good of society, and to allow every individual the maximum opportunity for personal development. Also, the tradition of giving women total responsibility for their homes and children was not ideal. Men certainly should be involved as well. And, perhaps it was unfair for some women to be economically dependent upon men. But I must admit that when these ladies start to plead their case, I turn an "almost deaf" ear.

Poorer class ladies have never been excluded from the business world of wash tubs, cook stoves, ironing boards, scrub brushes, file clerks, and factories. In fact, I've been "enjoying" full and free participation in this business world for so long, I can't quite comprehend why the upper-crust ladies are fighting for the privilege! I suppose it was difficult for them having to stay home and raise their children, and having to depend upon their husbands for food, clothes, and shelter. However, though I can imagine how the ladies feel, my own experience has left me unable to empathize, or even sympathize with most of their complaints. Quite frankly, I would be overjoyed if I could experience many of the circumstances about which they are unhappy. Still, they could be right, and I don't want to judge unfairly.

Tell you what. Somebody arrange the following swop for me: I'll relinquish my place in the "dog-eat-dog," "try-to-get-ahead-while-we-push-you-back" business world to one of the oppressed ladies who has been denied full participation in it. In her stead, get me out of my "free participation" in the work force, set me up in suburbia — or anywhere — where a gentleman expects me to care for a home and children while he provides everything all of us need. Let him demand that I stay away from work, stay out of taverns, and maintain old-fashioned standards while he opens doors for me, holds my coat for me, pulls out chairs for me, gives his seat to me, tips his hat to me, pays the bills for me, and does not swear in my presence.

Let me sample this life for as long as I've been "freely" participating in the hassling world of business. Maybe then I might join ERA ladies and vigorously protest and demonstrate for my "equal rights."

Maybe. I might. I really might . . . but don't count on it!

June 1979

A PROBLEM WITH BLACK WOMEN

Many African-American wives, secretaries, and sweethearts of businessmen in a position to help schedule, organize, and smooth activities instead act as a buffer between the man and any non-bureaucratic contact, especially if it is new — most especially if it is female!

Whenever I must contact an Afro-American businessman, I feel a special terror preparing to deal with the female "go-between" I expect to encounter. To begin with, I work on my voice, which is naturally a bit throaty or hoarse. Such ladies appear to associate it with the bedroom rather than the board room, and using it, I seldom get much past "Hello." So, I spend five minutes clearing my throat, as I think of ways to convince the female dragon I'm about to dare that I want to speak with the man she is guarding on a legitimate business matter. By affecting a brassy voice and matter-of-fact approach, I may get a brief hearing from the lady "stonewallers." Otherwise, they break the phone connection and blame it on the telephone company if I call back. Either way, affected or natural, I get nowhere.

Frequently I am requesting the participation of a businessman in newspaper or radio features or advertising. But I have come to anticipate that my access to such a person will be blocked persistently if one of my "sisters" makes his appointments. The first agony of trying to get past the "lady at the door" is special because I don't know which of many types of antagonists I must overcome — one that is openly rude, indifferent, sarcastic, hostile, jealous, or one who thinly masks these attitudes with pretended courtesies or office decorum. Once I learn how the lady operates, I must usually steel myself to withstand a series of "brush offs."

Recently, for instance, I phoned a restaurant repeatedly, only to have a female employee coolly refuse to allow me to speak to the owner every time. I left dozens of messages for him which he apparently never received. In desperation, I went to the restaurant, and I could tell from her end of a telephone conversation with him in his inner office that he was saying he would see me. Nevertheless, she hung up the receiver and said he was busy and it would be useless for me to wait. I then wrote a letter marked for his personal attention, and asked her to give it to him. She cooed sweetly that she would, and I left. Realizing I hadn't included my phone number with the information, I returned to find the lady eagerly reading the personal letter I had left for him! Ashamed and embarrassed on her behalf to have surprised her in such a breech of ethics, I excused myself (can you believe it?) and left quickly. However, I have no reason to believe that anyone other than she ever read my letter for I have yet to hear from the restaurant owner.

I also shrink from the memory of an African-American dental assistant stage whispering suggestively to the dentist working on my teeth, "I want to see you *alone!*" Since I was the only other person present, the remark assured my extreme discomfort. She had been alone with the dentist when I arrived as she would be again as soon as I left. But strapped in a dental chair, my mouth propped wide open, I could not easily leave the two alone at that moment.

However, for all I know they have been alone ever since, for once I was able to leave, you can believe I never returned!

This is not a problem exclusive to Afro-American ladies. In fact, my most horrible recollection of this kind is of telephoning the home of a university professor whose Caucasian wife answered the phone, slurred, insulted and attacked me, leaving me feeling as sick as she obviously was. But in my experience, Caucasian women in helping roles to men seem less ready to presume the caller will waste the businessman's time, or become a threat to their romantic interests in him.

There are African-American women who are intelligent, pleasant, cooperative assistants to businessmen. However, I have found them far outnumbered by Black American women with petty, "bedroom" mentalities who are more obstructionists than assistants, with no vision, overview, or interest in the business with which they are connected, and who desperately need to get their act together.

December 1977

AN OPEN LETTER TO BROTHER ———,
PRESIDENT, *PHILADELPHIA TRIBUNE,* INC.

On behalf of the African-American community, I want to touch hearts with you about the new editorial policy of *The Philadelphia Tribune*, and related matters. I understand that under your administration the *Tribune* has moved away from its previous commitment to serve the African-American community. The commitment is now to the total community. Since Black Americans are a part of that community, presumably we are entitled to fair and accurate representation of our views, interests, and concerns in the pages of the *Tribune*.

However, some of us believe this is not true — that the *Tribune* is now so oriented toward the status quo that it will not publish commentary relating to African-Americans that significantly challenges racist thinking, or behavior patterns, or explores major social problems.

Recognizing that the *Tribune* lacks columns that reflect our daily life, and expose the problems we encounter, I submitted three columns for consideration. One column exposed veterans' problems caused by lack of sanitation and inefficient record keeping at the V.A. Hospital. Another related a message from Alex Haley to Afro-American prisoners. The third called attention to the African heritage of southern European Caucasians.

After several months the managing editor tentatively accepted them, then gave them to you for review. Several more months passed after which the columns were returned to me without comment. Interestingly, these columns have since been published and drawn favorable response from Caucasian and Aframerican publishers and readers.

Since the *Tribune* continues to fill its pages with commentary that is virtually cowardly in its failure to challenge the minds of readers, or highlight important social problems, I must conclude that my columns were rejected because they challenged popular racist thinking, and detrimental practices of an establishment institution, and the *Tribune* was afraid of the consequences.

My experience was not unique. Ms. ———, Instructor at Temple University, offered to use her considerable writing talent to strengthen the *Tribune* commentary. She also was turned away.

The problem goes beyond what appears in the paper. For example, on *Telesis*, a talk show I help moderate on WDAS FM, Sundays at 9 a.m., a caller once reported a conversation with you in which you allegedly condemned the use of African names by African-Americans. I made no comment. I couldn't be sure the information was accurate. I also felt it would be unfair to give an opinion unless you could respond to the charge as you now may.

Actually, I had heard a similar accusation previously. I received a report that you had refused to accept the use of an African name by a young man inquiring about a job. According to the report, you asked his name repeatedly, and when he continued to give an African name, it is alleged that you demanded that he give an American name to apply for the job. I was told that the young man's shoulders drooped and his eyes clouded with pain as he finally murmured an American name which you then wrote down.

I hope this story isn't true because it reminds me of the scene from Alex Haley's story *Roots,* in which an overseer with the power of life and death over Kunta Kinte, a captured African, whipped him until he could not continue to say he was Kunta Kinte, the proud African name of his birth, but whispered what the overseer was demanding, that his name was "Toby," the American name he had been given as a captive.

The power of life and death over African-Americans is no longer held by overseers with whips. It is held by men with jobs to bestow. Such men who demand that an African-American deny his African name or be deprived of employment are the modern overseers, committed to making the African-American live in the shadow of his slave history, or die of starvation economically induced.

Many people feel that the use of an American name makes the person who uses it a living memorial to the man who once enslaved her or his ancestors. These people prefer to be memorials to their grand heritage that preceded the enslavement of their foreparents. Their right to name themselves from their majestic African heritage should be respected by all.

Although this is an open letter, I am sending it to you about two weeks before I plan to share it with the public to give you the opportunity to reply, so that I may share your response along with the letter. Please understand that I am looking forward to a future in which you and I are working toward an African-American community which takes pride in its own identity, in which we respect ourselves as individuals and as a group, in which we have unity, appreciation for our heritage, and more love for each other and all humankind.

Yours in the spirit of brotherhood,
Sister MMayen*

Note: *A copy of the above letter was hand-delivered to the offices* of The Philadelphia Tribune *December 7, 1977. Receipt of the letter was never acknowledged.*
*Penname for Marian E. Barnes

May 1991

Editor, Neighbor Section
Austin American-Statesman

Dear Editor:

In February, when *"Talk that Talk,"* the feature written about my storytelling career appeared in *Neighbor*, I was touring, and I did not read the story until today. While I thank your reporter for her outstanding effort, and very informative piece of writing, I am deeply distressed at the implication throughout the article that in speaking with her I used words that I tour the country lecturing against.

Under no circumstances do I refer to the ancestors of African-Americans as "slaves" because Africans captured and enslaved never accepted their captivity or enslavement as that word implies. The term "slave" — a key word in what I call "the language of subjugation" — was imposed upon captives to mask the state of their captivity and their ongoing resistance to it. Therefore, when referring to captured Africans and their enslaved descendants, I always say they were "captives" or "enslaved." In speaking of the master class of those days, I prefer the word "captor" to "master." And when I use the word "Black" to denote race, not skin color, I use a capitalized proper noun as should be used to define any ethnic group.

Having carefully explained during the interview the terminology that I systematically use, my reasons for it, and its vital importance, I considered it imperative that the published story accurately reflect this basic aspect of my work. Instead, readers of the article have cause to believe I freely used words and phrases during the interview that my oral presentations have waged war upon for years!

I ask that you publish this letter to help correct that impression.

Sincerely yours,
Marian E. Barnes

February 2, 1990
Austin American-Statesman
Austin, TX

Dear Editor:

I wish to address the decision of *The Statesman* to discontinue its policy of writing "Black" as a proper noun when the word refers to the race of a person or group.

While "white" is an adjective that describes the *color* of European races and nations, "Black" is a proper noun which identifies the *race and culture* of Africans and African-Americans who range in color from black to white.

Sentences such as the following which appeared in a newspaper story are offensive: "Irish, Polish, Jewish, Korean and black community residents attended the meeting." The grammar is indefensible, the underlying rationale insulting, and detrimental psychological fallout from reading such sentences affects people of every color.

It is distressing to see the long standing controversy over "Negro" versus "negro" still with us thinly disguised as "Black" versus "black." The word "negro" — which means "black" in Spanish — was contrived as a name for enslaved Africans to obliterate their connection with Africa and African civilizations, and to downgrade their status from human beings to what was defined by the U.S. Constitution as three-fifths of a human being. (No more to be capitalized in print than "lion" or "cow.")

When it was popular to use the Spanish word for "black" in referring to Africans and African-Americans, thoughtful, non-racist minds eventually rejected the lower-case "n" as being ungrammatical and racist. Now it is in vogue to use the same word in English with lower-case lettering. In time, thoughtful, non-racist minds will prevail again and reject the lower case "b" for the same reasons.

Very truly yours,
Marian E. Barnes
An Honorary Storyteller, City of Austin
Proclaimed by Mayor Lee Cooke, January 13, 1989

THE ROARING BOTTOM

*In honor of those African-Americans who survived
The Great Depression...
and in memory of those who did not.*

THE ROARING BOTTOM

Marian E. Barnes
Copyright © 1946 By Marian E. Barnes

"Come on and WALK for Papa! *Walk* for Papa now!" The sun was high and the crap game was just beginning. It would end by the light of two wax candles jammed against a brick wall, illuminating one foot of pavement where the dice fell.

Noisy little girls and boys played jacks, rope, and basketball, using a huckster's basket suspended from a telegraph post. Smoke from the railroad clouded the air. Shabby, unpainted wooden shanties, and overcrowded, poorly constructed tenement houses lined filthy streets. Women leaned through windows, resting their arms and elbows on pillows to cushion their endless vigil.

Where houses had caved in, or been torn down just in the nick of time, there were vacant lots. These served as public toilets for drunks, and private dumping grounds for lazy housewives. They reeked of rotting garbage and decaying matter. Often men congregated on these lots, playing cards and checkers, telling smutty stories and passing the bottle. High above it all, elevated trains rattled, rumbled, and thundered.

This was the huge slum area just west of the Schuylkill River in Philadelphia inhabited by African-Americans and known as "The Bottom." Originally the term related to the low numerical sequence of the streets in the section, beginning with thirtieth and continuing through forty-fifth, as compared with the indeterminate spot between forty-fifth and fiftieth, where "The Top" began. But gradually, imperceptibly, as years of deepening economic depression wore on, a more significant meaning crept into the expression. Man was at the lowest ebb of his fortunes in the roaring Bottom.

* * * * *

Chapter I

This was her baby. It was hideous. A howling mass of bone and pitifully creased and wrinkled skin. She knew it was hungry — had been born hungry in fact — but there was nothing she could do about it.

"Your name is Mary," she said, "after The Holy Virgin." Then she laughed, a choked, weak laugh that quickly turned to tears as she remembered standing before the sixth-grade class eons ago giving her "oral talk" on "When I Grow Up."

"I'm going to have a church wedding," she had told them. "My husband will be tall and handsome. I want two children, a boy, and a girl. I'll name the boy after him, and I'll name the girl 'Mary,' after The Holy Virgin."

But it hadn't happened that way. She hadn't had a wedding or a husband. She didn't even know the baby's father. She thought he was white, but she wasn't sure. He had been standing under the bridge at 33rd and Girard, and as she passed he had spoken softly. "Will ya — for a quarter?"

She had walked on. With a quarter she could buy a package of tea, sugar, a loaf of bread, and a basket of wood. *Mama doesn't get up anymore. She says it's because the bed keeps her warm these fall days. Only, she looks sick. And the food is all gone; we haven't eaten today.* A pebble pierced her foot through the hole in her shoe. She had turned around slowly. The man was still there, leaning against the bridge wall . . .

She had taken the tea, sugar, and bread home with her. A street vendor brought a ten-cent basket of wood into the house. When the water was boiling, she rinsed out the two baking powder tins that they used for drinking, and called her mother. She put a pinch of tea in the musty tea kettle, and called again. Then she went to shake her mother gently, and saw that her form was motionless with the stillness of death.

Now, nine months later to the day, she lay on a crude floor pallet. She had been alone when the baby came, one — two — three — perhaps four hours ago. It was raining, and water was coming through the soaked newspaper she had stuffed in the broken window pane. On the other side of the room a wax candle sputtered fitfully as the flame burned low.

She threw off her light covering and got up. "You wouldn't die! Why didn't you? I knew you wouldn't. I knew it." She muttered to herself, moving slowly about the room. "I could raise you — take the wrinkles out of your belly, put some meat on your bones. You'd be pretty; you'd have dreams. Then for a quarter . . . When you were fifteen you might need a quarter . . . a quarter. You might need a quarter." She picked the baby up, wrapped it in the covering she had used for herself, blew out the candle, and crept out into the black, wet July night.

Twenty minutes later she stood on the bridge above the river watching the inky water below. The baby cried fiercely. It was getting wet through the thin cover. "Half starved, uncared for, wet and crying. That's the way you'd end up." She stepped up on the iron bridge railing, leaned over, shut her eyes tightly, and dropped the screaming bundle.

The screaming stopped abruptly as the drop through space snatched the infant's breath. A splash far below; then only the sound of rain disturbed the quiet of the night. It was all over; this thing that was to plague her the rest of her days.

The young woman opened her eyes and peered down into black nothingness. "Mary," she sobbed. "Mary!" But the river gave no answer.

That night The Bottom was alive with her shrieking. "Mary . . . M-a-r-y! . . . M-a-r-y! . . ." Calling in vain to a tiny lost soul.

Chapter II

"Clifford, how could you?" Martha Hilton clutched the foot of the brass bed and struggled against rising emotion to keep her voice down.

Her husband was apologetic, and anxious, but he was also determined. "He didn't have anywhere to go, Martha. I had to ask him. He'll only be here until he gets enough money to go back home."

"That's what Reverend Mills said, and he's been here six long months!"

"It's not his fault."

"All right, all right, it's not his fault. I've never said a word in all these months. But how could you bring *another* man here? We're down to our last hundred dollars, you know that. We haven't got any money, and the money you get from the church is getting less all the time. It isn't enough to take care of *us*. Yet you insist on bringing home every stray evangelist that comes to the church."

"Martha, I might go off from home someday — you might yourself. We'd be glad to have someone take us in if we ran out of money."

"But we don't have anywhere to put him!" Martha said desperately.

"He can stay with Mills."

"Reverend Mills sleeps on the couch in the living room. It isn't big enough for two men."

"Then put two of the girls on the couch, and give the men their room."

"And food, Clifford! What about the food? Shall we give the men their food too!"

"Be careful, Martha, they'll hear you." He looked anxiously toward the door.

Martha felt suddenly weak, and older than her thirty years. She sat on the edge of the bed, then sank to a reclining position. Clifford came and knelt beside her. He felt keenly disturbed about having hurt her. He kissed her eyelids lightly while he searched for words of comfort.

"Little Girl," he stroked her head gently, "we'll come through this all right. I know you're worried, and frightened. I am too – all of our money going out, nothing coming in; all around us people being put out of their homes because they can't pay the rent. Honey, I'm scared! But as long as we have something, we have to share with those who have nothing. It's all a part of doing unto others as I would have them do unto me. I preach that, Martha. I've got to live by it. I feel if we trust God, He'll take care of us."

"Oh, Clifford, Clifford! It isn't that I don't want to help them. It isn't that."

"I know it isn't that." He kissed her forehead. "Let's go back downstairs."

When they got downstairs, tiny Reverend Mills was entertaining Reverend Bailey, the new guest, in a way with which the Hiltons were familiar. Pictures of the Mills family were spread out on a table. There was Mrs. Mills, big-bosomed and hefty. There were several little Millses – all ages, all sizes. Reverend Mills was crying. He always cried when he showed the pictures.

"This is my dear little wife. I wonder what she's doing now. And this is the baby. He's almost two years old now, but this is the size he was when I left home." Reverend Mills blew his nose hard, but the tears would come.

Clifford joined the two men. Martha went to the front door and called the children. She brought them into the living room, where they stood silently, waiting to meet the new guest.

"Well, well, well. So these are the children – four beautiful little girls." Reverend Bailey turned in obvious relief from the pictures of the Mills family. "And they all look just alike. How old are they?"

"This is Alice, she's twelve, and Jean, who is ten. Cathy, here, is seven, and Clifford is four."

"Oh, Clifford? Why, I thought you were a girl."

"She is a girl," Martha said.

"Who iss he?" Clifford asked. Her tone was unfriendly.

"This is Reverend Bailey. He's going to stay with us for a while."

Reverend Bailey smiled serenely, crossed his legs and poised a spatted foot.

The children greeted him respectfully — all but Clifford, who took advantage of her youth and walked away.

"Get ready for dinner now," Martha said to the girls. "Everything's done. I'm going in the kitchen to warm up the food."

"I'll help you," Alice said. "Wash Clifford's hands for me, Jean. And watch Cathy. She'll get water on her dress."

When they were all seated at the table, Reverend Bailey, with an epileptic jerk, and an enigmatic "*Ha como signi!*" began to pray. He thanked the Lord for "this beautiful Lord's Day." He thanked Him for "the wonderful message brought by this our dear brother this morning." He prayed long and hard while the food got cold, a prayer well punctuated with epileptic jerks and "*Ha como signi!*"

When he finished, he tucked a large, white handkerchief under his chin and reached for the mashed potatoes.

"Wha's ha-co-co sign, Mudder?" Clifford asked from her high chair beside Martha.

"Be quiet, Baby."

"Let the child talk. Let the child talk. You know the Gospel says 'a little child shall lead them.' Yes, yes. And there are all kinds of ways of leading. This little child may be leading you by her question." Reverend Bailey sawed away at his meat. "I knew the Lord had some plan in sending me here. Have you received the gift of the Holy Ghost, Brothers?" He looked from Clifford to Reverend Mills. They said they had.

"Well, in that case, you both have the gift of speaking in tongues." His statement was a question.

"No. I never spoke in tongues," Reverend Mills said. "As a matter of fact, I don't believe in them."

"Nor do I," Clifford said.

260

Reverend Bailey, who had been on the verge of openly attacking Reverend Mills' religion, thought better of it when his host spoke.

"I see," he said. "Well, it's all a matter of understanding. Lots of people will get into the kingdom without it, of course. But I'm so glad I prayed a little harder; oh, yes! — and went a little deeper. I wouldn't take anything for it. It's with me all the time; not just while I'm praying, but whenever The Spirit strikes me — *Ha como signi! Ha como signi!*"

Reverend Hilton's brow darkened almost imperceptibly.

"Hot cocoa signi!" young Clifford shouted, and her spoon clattered to the floor as she attempted to concoct an epileptic jerk.

Chapter III

Martha was on her way to the bank. It could not be helped. Reverend Bailey's enormous appetite was manifest in the food bill. More than that, the girls needed winter clothes. It was getting cold.

She was just about to turn into Citizens & Southern Bank, her mind greatly preoccupied, when a man dived directly in front of her and picked up a black purse.

"Any money in it, Mack?" A second man was at the elbow of the first as he groped about inside the handbag.

"Man! Look-a-here — *a hundred-dollar bill!*"

Martha stood transfixed by the sight of the crisp, green bill.

"Step over here in the shadow, Joe. You too, lady, you saw it." The three of them stepped into the shadow of the bank.

"Mack, if you ain't the luckiest — "

"Shh! Somebody'll hear you. And we got enough people in on this now."

"You mean — "

"I mean there's three of us saw it. I'm for splittin' this money three ways, and gettin' off of this corner before somebody comes back here lookin' for it."

"That sounds all right to me, Mack. How about you, lady?"

"Yes," Martha said nervously. "Yes — that is if you're sure there's no identification," she added, suddenly conscience-stricken.

Mack looked at her queerly, but rummaged through the purse once more. "Nothing's here, not even a wallet. O.K. now, if we're gonna divide this three ways we'll need change. You got any money on you, Joe?"

"Not a cent."

"You, lady?"

"No, I don't have any."

"Weren't you going in the bank?"

"Yes, but I was going to get some money out."

"Well, go ahead and get it. Maybe that'll help."

Martha disappeared into the bank and returned shortly with twenty-five dollars, which she gave to Mack.

"This ain't enough," Mack said when he had counted it. "Joe and I figured it out while you were gone. You need sixty-seven dollars. That would be thirty-three for me, thirty-three for Joe, we toss for the extra dollar, and I give you the hundred dollar bill. Twenty-five dollars ain't enough. I still have to find somebody to change this bill."

"Who, man? Who?" Joe seemed on edge.

"Y'all wait here. I'm goin' in that grocery store on the corner. They might have it."

Mack almost ran to the grocery store on the next corner. Ten minutes passed while Martha and Joe waited.

"He should be out by now," Martha said. "Do you think something happened?"

"I guess he had to wait," Joe answered. "That store has a lot of business." But when fifteen minutes had elapsed, he seemed to grow uneasy. "I wonder what's keeping him? Maybe I ought to go see if anything did happen."

"Maybe you'd better," Martha said anxiously.

Joe walked down the street and into the grocery store. Martha waited impatiently for the men to return. When another ten minutes had gone, impatience gave way to uneasiness. Five minutes more brought vague misgivings. Something must be wrong. She hurried to the store on the corner. Several people were in the store when she entered, but there was no sign of Joe or Mack.

"I'm looking for two men," she said to the storekeeper. "They came in here to get change for a hundred-dollar bill."

"*A hundred-dollar bill!*" The storekeeper turned away from the scale totally amazed. "Is this a joke? Somebody asked me that yesterday."

"I'm not joking," Martha said, cold terror tugging at her heart. "Two men came in here to change a hundred-dollar bill."

"Well, if they did, I sure didn't see them."

"But you *must* have seen them! I saw both of them go in here."

"Maybe they did, but they didn't say anything to me about changing a hundred-dollar bill."

"But they haven't come out. I've been watching for them."

"Maybe they went out that way." The storekeeper pointed with his scoop to a door that opened onto a side street.

"Thank you." Martha heard herself say the words. She turned and went out the side door. The street was filled with people, some hurrying, some loitering. But there was no one resembling either of the two men. She went back to stand in front of the bank. Perhaps they had gone to another store when they found the grocer busy. Maybe they had gone to several stores. That would take time. After all, money was very scarce. It would be difficult to change so much money even in a store.

Martha told herself these things as she waited; told herself over and over again, attempting to overcome her growing dismay. Dismay because a strange man had gone off with twenty-five dollars of her all too scarce money, and she might never see him again. Twenty-five dollars! Why had she given it to him? But he would come back. He *must* come back! It was only that they were having trouble changing the bill. She must wait for them.

And wait she did — until the bank closed its doors for the day; until the weak November sunlight faded out of the sky; until the shadows of evening lengthened and deepened; until the cold night wind whipped her legs and chapped her cheeks, wet by streaming tears.

So a big, blue-coated, ebony policeman found her. The sight of this lone, dejected young woman wrenched his great heart. He watched her silently for a while, searching for a tactful approach to the cause of her tears. Finally he decided on: "What's the matter, lady?"

Martha poured out her story at once, and with the telling the tears flowed more freely.

"That's a damn shame. I sympathize with you," he said.

"*Sympathize?* I want you to *do* something!"

"Lady, *I* can't do anything."

"Oh, but there must be something you can do."

"If there was, I'd be only too glad to do it. We'll catch them, all right. They'll try it just once too often. If I had been here earlier . . . But there's nothing in the world anybody can do now. I'll get one of the boys to take you home in a redcar."

"No. I'm going to wait a little while longer. Maybe they'll be back. Maybe —"

"They won't be back," he said gently. "You'd better go home now. It's getting cold out here; and they won't be back."

Martha was crying harder as she slowly left the corner.

It was drizzling when she reached home, tired and miserable. Cathy was already in bed on the unfolded couch in the parlor. Jean was huddled over a book at the dining room table. "Finish that chapter and come up to bed," Martha said to her as she passed.

She climbed the stairs to the back bedroom. Alice was putting Clifford to bed and having quite a time of it because Clifford was running round and round in her sleepers. Every time Alice laid hands on her, she squealed and slipped away like an eel.

"Mother, she won't say her prayers," Alice said when she saw her mother. "Make her say her prayers, please."

"What's the matter with you, Clifford?"

"Jean don' come to bed," she protested. "I want Jean come to bed wit me!"

"Kneel down and say your prayers first. Jean will come up as soon as you're in your crib." She led the child to the side of a large crib, and Clifford proceeded to pray.

"Now I lay me down t' sleep. I pray Thee Lord my soul t' keep — *Ha como signi!*" Her convulsive heave was perfect. "God, bless Mama an' Daddy an' make Cullifurt a good girl, Amen — *Ha como signi!*"

Martha thought it best to ignore Clifford's imitation of Reverend Bailey. "You forgot to say 'God, bless my sisters, and God, bless everybody,' " she said. Clifford corrected the oversight, and Martha kissed her and put her in her crib.

"You stayed such a long time Daddy was worried about you," Alice said.

"Where is he?"

"Sister Crawford is sick. They sent for him."

"Did he go alone?"

"Reverend Mills went with him. Reverend Bailey's in his room with a headache."

"All right. Tell Jean to come up to bed. And you go too. You have to go to school in the morning." Martha walked down the hall, past the room that Reverend Bailey and Reverend Mills shared, past the small bathroom, and into the front bedroom, where she immediately lapsed into tears.

Nevertheless, an hour later she made her rounds as usual; checking windows and doors, looking in on the sleeping children. Back in her room once more, she crawled into bed. The tears had stopped, only a terrible ache remained. She was torn now between longing for Clifford's return, and dread.

The light drizzle had turned into a steady rain. As always when it rained at night in The Bottom, the tormented, sobbing wail of a woman filled the darkness.

"*M-a-r-y . . . M-A-R-Y . . . M-a-r-y . . . M-A-R-Y.*"

Martha shivered and drew the covers closer around her neck. She sank into semiconsciousness. Although her thoughts were arrested, sleep did not come. She could hear the persistent cries of "Mary" rending the air. Now right in the room with her; now far, far away. She heard Clifford put his key in the lock, and came fully awake.

He came straight upstairs, and put his damp raincoat and hat in the closet. Martha sat up in bed, and saw that his eyes were gleaming, his lips drawn tightly together. He kissed her absent-mindedly, and she knew that he was greatly concerned about something. But she was not sympathetic nor even curious. The need to unburden herself was too great.

"Clifford —" she faltered, "today I lost twenty-five dollars." And the tears she had thought exhausted were perilously near again. He looked at her sharply but said nothing. He sat down beside her, waiting for her to continue.

"I didn't really lose it — It was stolen from me." Still Clifford said nothing. Nor did he speak when she had finished the sordid tale.

"Clifford, say something," Martha finally was forced to plead.

"It is unfortunate, Little Girl," he said quietly. "Twenty-five dollars now are like a hundred used to be. But let's not have more tears," he added as Martha's lower lip began to tremble. "They won't help. It could have happened to anyone. And don't forget, your planning and saving put that money there. If it weren't for you, we wouldn't have had twenty-five dollars to lose, or one hundred dollars in the bank."

Martha felt unbelievably relieved. Clifford always managed to make difficulties seem somehow less difficult. She slid under the covers, thinking that she was lucky to have him for her husband.

"From now on, however," Clifford continued, "we'll forget

about the money in the bank. We'll live as we would if we didn't have it. We've got to cut down in every way. Perhaps if the Crawfords had done that —" He seemed uninclined to finish the sentence.

"What about the Crawfords?" Martha prompted.

"They have all moved into one room — the whole family of them." Clifford began to pace the floor. "And there's going to be another baby. They gave me a drink of water in a milk bottle. And do you know what they eat, Martha? Oatmeal! Three times every day, they eat oatmeal!"

"I'll take them some food tomorrow."

"They'll have food tomorrow. I gave them five dollars. But what about all the other tomorrows — yes, and all the other families? I can't feed them. Worse than that, I can't even pray for them. I tried to pray for them tonight, and my prayer never left the room. All the while I was questioning a God that would let us suffer so." The palms of his hands were damp. He clenched and unclenched his fists helplessly.

"How can you say that, Clifford? You're a minister."

"I am a minister called by God," he answered harrowedly. "But tonight in that room, I doubted the call — I doubted The Caller."

"Oh, Clifford!"

"It's all right, Martha. I'm ashamed of myself now."

His drawn features told her that she was being pacified; that his doubts of the evening had not completely left him. Even so, she was pacified.

"But, I wonder," he continued in spite of himself. "Does a man — a thinking man — ever get to the place where he is free of these sudden attacks of doubt? I thought surely I was beyond them."

He was talking to himself now. Martha made no attempt to answer him. He sat down and pulled a pad and pencil from his inside coat pocket and began to figure. After awhile he said, "My income for the last three months averages about seventeen dollars a week. And things are getting worse instead of better." He pushed the pad and pencil away. "I'm going to have the gas cut off, Martha. You can cook on the coal stove." He hesitated, then added, "And the electricity. We'll use those old oil lamps."

Martha's heart missed a beat, but she said nothing. "We have got to economize," he explained, and reached for his pencil again.

"Come to bed now, Clifford. We'll go over it together in the morning."

When at last he lay beside her, halfway between wake and troubled sleep, he caught her fingers in his. "We'll make it, Little Girl," he mumbled. "Things look bad, but we have each other, and we have the children. Everything's all right." The words were still hanging in the room when someone screamed, once, twice, three times.

They were out of bed at once, running down the hall to Jean's room, from where the screams had come. They opened the door, snapped on the light, and were confronted by the lordly Reverend Bailey in gleaming white underwear!

"*Ha como signi! Ha como signi!*" he said, and blinked at the bright light.

Martha jammed her fist in her mouth and stifled a scream. She looked at Reverend Bailey's bare feet and thought, of all things, that it was the first time she had ever seen him without his spats on. Then she ran over to Jean, sitting wide-eyed in her small bed.

"Did he hurt you, Jean?"

"No. He scared me. I told him to go away, but he wouldn't. He kept coming closer."

Across the room, young Clifford, disturbed at last by so much commotion, sat up in her crib, rubbing her eyes.

"What is the meaning of this?" Reverend Hilton's voice was deadly grim. Deadly quiet.

"Brother, I must have lost my way. I got up to go to the bathroom — *Hallelujah!* And I had a vision — *Bless your name, Jesus!* There were angels all around me, and I saw the host that no man can number — *ha como signi!*"

"*Ha como signi!*" the baby mumbled an echo, her head lolling about on her shoulders, battling sleep.

"You'll be all right now," Clifford said to Jean. "Reverend Bailey was — confused." Then he walked out into the hallway, and Reverend Bailey followed him.

"It's raining now," Clifford said with taut control, "or I would insist that you leave at once. As it is, I shall expect to find you gone when I get up in the morning." He walked away from Reverend Bailey and into his own room. When he came back through the hallway, carrying Martha's robe which she had left behind in her haste, Bailey was gone.

Chapter IV

"Hell is gonna be full of these damn preachers! Drinkin' bathtub booze, an' sleepin' with everybody's woman, that's them." Ed slapped the leather arm of the barber's chair emphatically.

Rocky, the barber, looking into the wall mirror, stroked the sides of his face and decided he needed a shave. He hadn't had a customer all morning, but the shop was crowded. There were two checker games, a card game, and several conversations going. These last died away as Ed's vicious remark compelled the attention of others around him.

"I don't know, Ed," Rocky said, returning to the other barber's chair, placing a foot on the footrest, and propping one leg up with his knee. "They ain't all alike."

"I ain't never seed one yet as wouldn' drink a little likker on the q.t. *Hee! Hee!*" Pa, an ancient, formerly enslaved man rose from the bench along the wall as he spoke. The man seated next to him rose wordlessly and they exchanged seats. Pa always sat in the sunlight, and as the sunlight moved, he moved with it. It was understood.

"You said it, Pa! And I ain't never seen one that didn't go to bed with every woman on the choir." Ed leaned forward and his voice rose vehemently. "My wife wanted to join the choir, and I wouldn't let her. I made her quit going to church altogether because the very first damn time the preacher came to dinner, I'd kill 'em both!"

"That wasn't right," Rocky reprimanded. "She'd be better off in church than standing on the corners waiting for the lead to come out like the rest of these women."

"Ain't nothin' wrong with playing the numbers," Pa interjected. "I plays 'em. I plays 'em."

"There's good preachers," Rocky continued, forbearing comment on the well-established fact that Pa played the numbers. "Take that Reverend Hilton, visiting prisons and hospitals the way he does all the time. He's in and out of these shacks down here in The Bottom day and night, rain or shine, prayin' for the folks and givin' 'em a dollar when he ain't got it to spare. And can't nobody spot his life about women or booze. He's one preacher that's good through and through."

"You're right about that, and that's the truth," Pa said.

"And if there's one, there's more," Rocky summarized.

"Man, you can't tell me nothin'." Ed was unfazed. "Them kind you don't catch is the worst kind. They're slicker than most — " Whatever else Ed was about to add remained unsaid. His jaw dropped at the extreme shabbiness of diminutive Reverend Mills, who was entering the shop. The men greeted Reverend Mills with an affectionate lack of respect which the little man noted painfully.

"It's getting colder out," he said, smiling stiffly. "I wouldn't be surprised if we had snow before night."

"Man, ain't you got no other overcoat?" Ed asked, amazement creasing his face.

"Not just at present," Reverend Mills said, uncomfortably aware of many pairs of eyes upon his bedraggled overcoat, on his worn, scuffed shoes.

"Jesus Christ!" Ed gasped. Then suddenly: "I got a overcoat better than that I could give you."

"Oh, no indeed. I wouldn't think of it," Reverend Mills said in weak embarrassment.

"Wait here." Ed jumped from his seat and grabbed his coat from a hook on the wall. "I'll be back in a minute."

A heavy silence settled on the barber shop when the door closed behind Ed. It was accentuated by the flapping sound of cards as they hit the table, by the clicking of checkers as someone executed a three-man-jump. Pa changed his seat again.

"Hang your coat on a hook and sit down, Reverend. I'll trim your hair line for you," Rocky said a little too jovially.

"Well —"

"Sit down," Rocky raised the barber's chair, waving aside Reverend Mills' reluctance. "It won't cost you a cent. I'm glad for the chance to keep in practice."

Once Reverend Mills was in the chair, small talk flowed easily again. What had happened to that Reverend Bailey who disappeared so suddenly almost a month ago? Reverend Mills didn't know? Now wasn't that funny, though? The Depression was getting worse, and old Hoover still had two more years in the White House. And wasn't it terrible how these teenage boys were robbing and killing? Forty of them on the north side calling themselves "The Forty Thieves." People were scared to go out and scared to stay home. And here on the west side, they had two gangs, "The Top" and "The Bottom," making war on the city and on each other. And the cops couldn't do anything because the boys were too young to go to jail, and they didn't have any kind of institution for colored boys. Wasn't that a shame, though? A big city like Philadelphia too.

Rocky had intended merely to give Reverend Mills a "shape up," but once started, while the chit-chat flowed easily, the shears and clippers moved of themselves. When he finally whipped the apron away, Reverend Mills had a haircut, beautiful and complete.

Ed returned to interrupt the minister's expressions of gratitude. "Try this on." He unfolded a bulky overcoat and held it while Reverend Mills obediently slid his arms into the sleeves. Ed buttoned the coat deftly. Then, because it was dusty, he proceeded to hit the coat with his hands, evoking small puffs of dust. Then he stepped back to view the change in Reverend Mills' appearance.

An awkward quiet grew more awkward while everyone tried to see an improvement. But there was none. In fact, this overcoat, because it was dusty and slightly too large, looked worse than the first. Even Ed's highly prejudiced eyes arrived at this conclusion with little trouble. Reverend Mills sneezed convulsively, then continued to wait patiently for the barbershop opinion.

Ed clasped his chin pensively, surveying the dusty, threadbare, moth-eaten apparition that was Reverend Mills. "Man," he sighed softly, "this Depression is a dog!"

Chapter V

April found the Hiltons somewhat better off financially. Reverend Hilton now worked during the night; hard, back-breaking, stevedore's work, but he counted himself lucky to have obtained it. Martha, however, had been unable to persuade him to give up the church. Neither reasoning nor coaxing moved him in the least. Finally, not wanting to become a nagging wife, she was silent. Anxiously silent, for Clifford's tall body, always lean, grew skeletal. There were hollows in his cheeks, his cheek bones protruded, and his eyes were great holes in his head.

One morning, Martha heard his key in the lock just as she set a bowl on the table for his cereal. The huge coal stove had taken longer than usual to heat up this morning, throwing her behind time.

"Clifford, is that you?" she called.

"Who else?" He was in the room, kissing her with gaiety feigned to hide his fatigue.

Clifford set his lunch tin down, washed his hands, and seated himself at the table while Martha moved about quickly, apologizing for the delayed breakfast. She set a plate of toast in the center of the table and noticed that her husband's eyelids were drooping, heavy with sleep. These days whenever he sat quietly for a moment, he fell asleep. She poured a glass of milk, then began to fill his breakfast-bowl with hot cereal. This roused him. He opened his eyes and quickly stayed her hand. "That's enough." Then, apologetically, in answer to her alarmed expression: "I'm not hungry, Little Girl."

Just before he finished eating, the children came downstairs. Little Alice, who enjoyed her position as the eldest, had supervised their dressing, and they were immaculate.

"Why do you get up so early, Muggins?" Clifford said as he pushed his chair away from the table with one hand and tweaked the baby's nose with the other. "You aren't going anywhere." He reached for her, but she eluded his grasp easily, dashed across the room, and began to drag her high-chair toward the table.

"You didn't drink your coffee," Martha said.

"Save it for my dinner," he said, rising. "I'm going up now. Call me if anyone wants me."

Sometime later, Martha was alone in the kitchen. She was glad she had made the children prepare for rain. The threatening skies had loosed a deluge. A chill, April wind slashed the rain against the windows rhythmically. Now, in the kitchen made dark by the stormy weather, she gave up all thought of the weekly wash, picked up a basket of mending, and sat near the blazing coal stove.

"Rev'n Mills is cryin'. He's read' his letter an' he's cryin'!" the baby announced from the doorway.

"I hope you didn't watch Reverend Mills read his letter," Martha said sternly.

"No, I watch him cryin'."

"Clifford — "

"Every time," Clifford said emphatically, "every time he's readin' his letter, he's cryin'. Why? Why is he cryin'?"

"Well —" Martha faltered before the child's intense, questioning gaze. "Reverend Mills cries when he gets a letter from home because — well, because he's homesick . . . Yes, homesick — that means he wants to go home."

Clifford advanced toward Martha, her baby face twisted with intolerance. "Well then, why don't he *go*?"

Reverend Mills cleared his throat weakly. He was standing in the doorway. "I guess the ashes need to be taken out of the stove," he said, trying to look as though he hadn't heard.

"Had a letter from the wife this morning," he said when he was on his knees shaking the ashes from the grate. "Says she's glad the man said I was too small to be a stevedore. She agrees with him." He laughed dryly.

"The work does seem terribly hard," Martha said. "I think it's too hard for Clifford."

The jarring sound of the hand-operated doorbell cut off further conversation. "Now, who could that be?" Martha put her sewing aside. The doorbell shrilled again as she crossed the dining room. She opened the door, and a gust of wind dashed a sheet of rain inside.

"Come in." She led a young man into the hallway. He took off his water-soaked cap, and she recognized him as one of the Crawford boys. Martha's eyes widened. "Is something wrong?"

"It's my brother, Junior. He stole a loaf of bread off of the bread wagon for us this morning." The boy's voice jerked as he strained to control his feelings. "A cop saw him and hollered at him to stop. Junior threw the bread back, but he started to run and the cop shot him."

The youth turned his wet cap round and round in his wet, thin fingers. The room was silent except for the sound of the rain and wind outside.

"Shot him?" Martha was incredulous.

"He's dead."

"Dead?" The word had a numb, wooden sound on her lips.

"Mother sent me for Reverend Hilton."

"Is it someone for me? . . . Martha?" Clifford called from the head of the stairs.

It was a difficult moment for Martha. She was torn between not wanting Clifford to go, and a strong sense of guilt about her attitude. Why must they disturb him? The boy, Junior, was dead; Clifford couldn't help him now. If the family wanted a minister, there were others besides Clifford. Why weren't people considerate of him? He needed his rest. Oh, how he needed his rest! Did she imagine it, or were the hollows in his face deeper than they had been this morning?

Clifford was unaware of the suffocating conflict in Martha as she helped him prepare to leave. "Where's your umbrella?" she asked, buttoning the first button on his coat, the one he always left open.

"It's too windy for an umbrella," he answered, suddenly being unaccountably aware that Martha loved him very much. He saw now that she was concerned about him. Probably his lack of sleep, or appetite, or something. He drew her to him impulsively, briefly. "Little Girl, Little Girl. I'll be back in a few minutes; and I'm going to eat and sleep enough for two men." He kissed the tip of her ear and was gone.

Two hours later, soaked to the skin, his deeply sunken eyes fever bright, he entered the bedroom where Martha was putting fresh linen on the bed.

"Clifford!" His gaunt, haggard face sent a shaft of fear through her. "Here, I'll help you," she said as he slumped in a chair, fumbling with the buttons on his clothes. Her own fingers seemed awkward, leaden, clumsy.

"Yes, give me a hand, Little Girl. I don't feel so well," he said. Then he pitched forward headlong onto the floor.

Chapter VI

Depression stalked The Bottom. Pathetic heaps of junky furniture lined the sidewalks, mute evidence that families had been "put out." Homeless people lived on park benches and vacant lots, in public buildings and railroad stations. They ate from rat-infested dumps where large packing companies disposed of food declared inedible.

Clifford's illness was a spiritual blow to the stricken people. His tireless ministrations had made him a happy legend in The Bottom. All day long Martha answered anxious inquiries from people whom he had helped in some way, people who wished to help him now. They had no money, but was there something else? Could they wash or iron, cook or clean, mind the children or sit with the sick? The church members were especially helpful. However, income from the church had dwindled to almost nothing.

Meantime, while no specific illness had been diagnosed, Clifford lay barely conscious, in a world removed from problems. Sometimes, watching his still, wasted form, Martha choked with terrible apprehension. But slowly, almost imperceptibly, he improved, until toward the end of May he was well on his way to recovery. Martha was happy. Lack of income, and the extra expenses incurred by Clifford's illness, had eaten away the bank account. But no matter. He was going to be well! They would have to go on Government Relief temporarily, but things would straighten themselves out. It had been a month since she applied for Relief, and she watched the calendar anxiously. Did they always take so long?

Then one morning the doorbell rang, and Martha opened the door to a tall, sallow woman about her own age, wearing a cheap fur coat. "Martha and Clifford Hilton?" she asked abruptly.

"Yes."

"I'm the Visitor from the Lloyd Committee for Unemployment Relief," she said in a highly affected drawl. Martha led her into the parlor where Clifford, who now came downstairs, sat reading in his moth-eaten robe. She wasn't sure how their need for Relief had affected him. He had given no indication.

"This is my husband." Martha regarded him anxiously.

"Well, Clifford, I'm glad to see you're getting about. You were bed-ridden when Martha first came to us." The woman unzipped a leather record book. "I'm *Mrs.* Green." She said "Mrs." as though it were her given name. "I'm the Visitor assigned to your case." Clifford quietly closed his book. Mrs. Green sat down, being careful of the fur coat which she had declined to remove. Then came the questions: How old was Clifford . . . how old was Martha . . . where were they born . . . when were they married . . . the children's names . . . their ages . . . where were they born . . . what schools did they attend . . . how had they supported themselves for the past ten years . . . addresses for the past ten years . . .

Clifford's head began to swim. He closed his eyes and rested his head against the back of the worn arm chair. Through a maze, disjointed words and phrases reached him – Food . . . earn . . . relatives working . . . previous addresses . . . children . . . coal . . . did you burn . . . bank . . . definite amount . . . definite amount . . . definite amount . . .

"But there was never a definite amount." The desperation in Martha's voice cut through the haze in Clifford's mind. "The church just manages to take care of itself. Sometimes we get a small income from it, maybe two dollars, maybe five, occasionally ten. Sometimes, like for the last two months, we don't get a cent, and sometimes it is a liability."

Clifford opened his eyes to find Mrs. Green pacing the floor. "Now Martha, I can't accept that as an answer. You'll have to give the exact amount of income you received from the church. I certainly must say you're being most uncooperative. But you might as well realize that you won't get a cent, not *one cent* until you give a definite answer. How much income was there last week?"

"None."

"Then how did you buy food?"

"I drew money from the bank."

"The bank?" Mrs. Green stopped short. Her eyes narrowed. "Less than one minute ago you said you had no money in the bank."

"We drew the last of it out last week."

"I see." Mrs. Green resumed her pacing, and Martha saw that she was modeling the fur coat. "And how much of that money is left?"

"Ten dollars."

The Visitor inhaled deeply. "You have food in the house, and ten dollars, and you ask for Relief." She took her book from the mantle and put her pencil away. "When you have used all of your money," she said, buttoning her coat, "and eaten all of your food, your application for Relief can be considered. But I warn you —"

"Mrs. Green," Clifford interrupted hoarsely, "please go."

"But I warn you," Mrs. Green drawled persistently, "you will have to furnish us with specific information. You will have to give the definite amount —"

"Mrs. Green, will you please leave." There was something tragic about Clifford in this helpless, emotional state. Martha averted her eyes.

"The *definite amount* of your income each week." She drew on her gloves and started out. "Of course, I needn't tell you that your ill manners will be — remembered."

"Mrs. Green," his voice sounded foreign to his own ears, "please — please — go. And don't come back — ever."

Mrs. Green's visit left Clifford drained. The next day he did not come downstairs. He prayed almost constantly, despairing, pleading, until the significance of the act became vague and unreal. Once again he was wrestling with the problem of survival, this time seeing no way out. Gradually, without realizing it, he spent more and more of his daytime hours in bed.

Martha, however, was aware that his recently gained strength was slipping away. Uncontrollable panic seized her. Each night was a long succession of nightmares, in which Clifford stopped breathing, in which she stepped on a fierce rat while she gathered food at the dump, in which the children starved. The days were not less tormented. The nightmares seen in the light of day and cold reason were more horrible than dreaming.

Now, the thought of the money stolen from her at the bank returned to plague her. How they needed it now! A thousand times a day she berated herself. The family must suffer because she had wanted to get something for nothing, to make an "easy dollar."

About a week after Mrs. Green's visit, Pa came to see Clifford. He cleared his throat and looked about the bedroom uneasily.

"How nice to see you, Pa." Clifford shook the ancient hand. "My wife told me you were here once before. Take this chair by the window, the sun is here now." Pa crept across the room and stood in the sunlight.

"Ain't planning to stay. Just come to ask a sort of favor."

"Anything I can do, Pa. Anything at all." Clifford's face lighted at the thought of being able to help someone again.

"Well — these are times folk'll kill a man to get a few dollars. If they know you got money it ain't safe to keep it."

"Yes." Pa was having a difficult time of it, and not making much sense, but Clifford smiled encouragingly.

"Folks here abouts know all about it. News travels fast 'round The Bottom. And I don't trust them banks a-tall."

It was becoming increasingly difficult to smile encouragingly. A puzzled light shone in Clifford's eyes. Pa faltered, then cleared his throat raucously. "What I mean to say is, I come by a few dollars, and I want you should keep 'em for me."

"Why of course," Clifford laughed. "How many dollars did you come by?"

"Pa withdrew a fistful of crumpled bills from his pocket. "Five hundred."

The smile froze on Clifford's features. *"Five hundred!"* Something was amiss here. "Where did you get so much money?"

"I caught that 201," Pa mumbled guiltily.

"Two-O-one?"

"The figure yestiday."

"The numbers? You mean you hit the numbers?"

"That's right." The room seemed unbearably hot. Pa jerked at his frayed collar. "I reckon you might say it's the devil's money, but it'll spend. And I want you should use it 'til I need it. I don't reckon that'll be soon. I'm making out better'n most folks in this Depression. My pension takes care of me right smart."

Clifford held the soiled, rumpled bills in his hand long after Pa had gone. Strange indeed. Was this an answer to his prayers? What else? It wasn't at all the way he would expect God to work. Gambler's money. *But it'll spend* ... Pa's words re-echoed in his thoughts. Yes; it would spend, and spend well. Food, clothing, coal for his family; a little help here and there for the people in The Bottom; an investment — perhaps the grocery store he had thought of so often. Tears fell on the money he was holding. He crossed the room unsteadily and sat down at the desk in the corner. But his thoughts were muddled. Figures swam dizzily. Sums refused to tally. What was the matter? Then it struck him. A man must have food to work. He hadn't eaten a decent meal for days. He was hungry! He was hungry!

Chapter VII

At first The Bottom flocked to the new grocery store. A new store was rare indeed when people were going out of business on every hand. Furthermore, it was located across from Blotky's Grocery, in a store front which remained untenanted because no one had been able to survive Blotky's forceful antagonism. Clifford and Reverend Mills managed the store. Pa spent a great deal of time there, making suggestions and lending a feeble hand now and then. The new business had not opened its doors when Blotky's ugly influence was first felt. The sturdy oak on the front sidewalk was condemned by the city as a public menace. One of the neighbors, Mr. Blotky, had complained. It must be uprooted and carted away at Clifford's expense. It was the beginning of an insurmountable problem, for Blotky was determined to force the Hilton grocery store out of business. His efforts were audacious, unpredictable, and endless.

The first influx of trade brought the Relief checks, and orders of the curious; the panorama of life in the grocery store began to unfold:

A jobber refused to sell Clifford meat. "I can't do it," he

shrugged. "If I sell to you, Blotky won't buy from me. He gets a big order. A man's got to live . . ."

"You say our jobber wouldn't take your order for meat? . . . Mr. Blotky? . . . Is Mr. Mahoney the jobber for your section? . . . We'll speak to Mr. Mahoney about it, and he'll be out again tomorrow. We'll be happy to fill your order." The voice came over the telephone, impersonal and friendly.

"Our salesman wouldn't take your order for milk? . . . Mr. Blotky? . . . Perhaps you can get milk from another company. We've served Mr. Blotky for quite a long time . . ." The voice came over the telephone, impersonal and friendly . . .

"No, I don't want any meat," a customer said. "I buy all of my meat in white neighborhoods. They send the inferior meat to the colored neighborhoods, and make you pay more for it."

"My mother said to put these things on the book, and she's sorry she couldn't pay you this week, but she'll pay you next week . . ."

"I sure am glad to see your business doing so well. Mr. Blotky told me if I came over here, not to come to his store. These Jews sure have got nerve. But I'll always be one to help my own color."

"I asked you before to leave more whole wheat and rye bread."

"I'm giving you two of each, Reverend Hilton."

"That's not enough. I get calls for it all day long. Is there a shortage or something?"

"No. But this is a colored neighborhood. They like white bread; they don't eat much whole wheat or rye. I'm giving you two of each. That'll be enough . . ."

"Don't say I told you, but Blotky paid those boys to break your store window . . ."

"How come you buy at Blotky's all the time? It looks like Reverend Hilton's gonna have to close his store since so many folks started staying away."

"Now ain't that too bad."

"I believe you're jealous."

"I'm not jealous."

"Well, why don't you help your own kind, somebody who'll help you? Reverend Hilton'll help anybody that needs it, and it's surer'n hell Blotky won't!"

"Just the same, I'm not taking no more of my money there.

First thing you know he'll be ridin' 'round in a car and I'll still be walking!"

"Well, I'll be damn! How 'bout when Blotky starts ridin' 'round in a car?"

"That's different . . ."

"Reverend Hilton, is it true Blotky tried to buy the store out from under you? . . ."

"This Depression is getting worse. I counted ten of us selling apples in one block. You make thirty-five cents a crate, but it takes me two days to sell a crate. I stayed out last night 'till the cold turned my skin ashy, and my nose started running, and my hands were so drawn up I couldn't use my handkerchief. Then when I got home the kids wanted an apple and I couldn't let them have one . . ."

"Where've you been that you haven't heard about the Crawford baby? Not the one that's a year old, she had one two months ago. Well, the baby was asleep in the basket they fixed for it, and one of these great big, giant rats ate off half its face. Must have smelled milk on the baby. Those Crawfords have worse luck than anybody else in The Bottom, and let me tell you that's saying something. They tell me Reverend Hilton paid for the baby's funeral . . ."

"I'm glad business is getting better, Reverend Hilton. Some of us colored folks stuck by you all the way; that's to be expected. What surprised me was those Jews. You'd think they'd go to Blotky's . . ."

"That house the Crawfords live in is going to fall over. It's built on wooden blocks, and they been hacking wood off them blocks for the longest."

"They had a time keeping warm this winter. The last time I was there, they had burned all the banisters and the doors in the house, and chopped down the cellar stairs. If they wanted to go down cellar, they jumped . . ."

"Did you hear the good news? Reverend Mills earned enough money to go home! Working right there in the store . . ."

Pa sat on an orange crate – in the sun.

Chapter VIII

The middle-thirties brought a measure of relief. The Bottom had turned out in record numbers for the presidential election, waiting for hours in snake-like lines to "get old Hoover out." While the mark of Depression would never entirely leave The Bottom, the apple-sellers disappeared from the streets, and there were jobs to be had. Almost immediately, the new president became a demigod, trusted and loved because "he took my feet out of the miry clay and planted them firmly on the WPA."[1]

For Clifford, the Depression was over. The extreme pennypinching of the last few years was no longer necessary. It was strange to live without the old, fearful anxiety. Sometimes, without reason, it returned. But the church, at last, was providing a small, steady income. The grocery store was thriving, and once more there was money in the bank.

The changed pattern of life was pleasant. It was good to sleep and rest, to wake without a heavy foreboding of doom. It was good to reawake to things in life beyond mere survival. The beauty in a budding tree, the pleasure of watching the children grow. Beyond duty, there was joy in being a minister. And there was the soft glow of renewed pride, sweet and warm and strong. There was satisfaction in buying attractive clothing, though they cost a little more or might not wear so well. There was the sound of children's roller skates. There was the autumn smell of leaves burning. There was the laughter of women.

This last, Clifford heard often, in particular from the women he encountered at church. Was it a minor, but happy result of the improved economic situation, he asked himself, or had it always been so? Had those dreary years of Depression been filled with silvery laughter? He didn't think so.

Martha, however, had a better memory. "Nonsense! Economic improvement indeed," she laughed. "Nothing has changed at Saint Luke's but you. The women have always laughed and always flirted, but you were too worried and harassed to notice." Then as his eyes flashed in questioning surprise: "Yes, flirted." She sat on his lap and wound her arms around his neck. "They blink their eyes, and lower their eyelids, and talk in husky voices," she mimicked the women quickly and accurately as she spoke, "and they twist when they walk. I may be a little prejudiced, and of course I

---

1. Works Progress Administration, an agency established as part of the Emergency Relief Appropriations Act of 1935. Among the measures enacted during the administration of President Franklin Delano Roosevelt designed to counteract The Depression.

can't blame them, but I think they're all in love with you. All of them!" she nodded in playful conviction.

"You're teasing me," he said, stunned.

Martha kissed him, her lips sliding quickly from his mouth to his cheeks, his nose, his ears, back to his mouth, while he neither responded nor resisted. "Well, perhaps not all of them," she murmured between kisses, "but those who aren't are fools!"

"It makes me feel — odd." The word seemed a lame description of the unprecedented, tingling, warm feeling. He must be more observant, he thought. There were other things. The doglike deference to his every wish he had so recently noticed on the part of his congregation. Had Martha noticed it too? Perhaps this also was not new. He was about to broach the subject when he suddenly became very much aware of her clinging arms, her soft lips. "Little Girl —" His arms tightened, and his mouth sought hers. Then, woman-like, she darted up. He must chase her 'round and 'round the crowded bedroom, and finally pin her down wrestler's fashion on the great brass bed.

"Little Girl, you're not really a little girl, you know. Act your age," he said, breathing heavily. Her arms were tight around his neck and she was blowing her warm breath on his left temple, searching for the gray hair she had discovered there . . .

Chapter IX

A few weeks later, Clifford announced happily that besides the money set aside to send Alice to college, there was money enough to begin buying a home of their own. Martha was overjoyed. The neighborhood, poor to begin with, was now revolting. Recently at one intersection she had observed a crap game and a man masturbating on one corner, while cultists with foul mouths proselytized passersby on each of the other corners. Each corner drew an audience; and seeing the children among them, she feared for her own girls, young and impressionable. She was glad that strong spirited, resourceful Alice, who abounded in character and common sense, was the eldest of the children. At seventeen, Alice still seemed untainted by the ugly environment of The Bottom. This, despite Martha's fear that her daughter's innocence, preserved by a closely guarded childhood, might be transformed into a sullied, unhealthy adolescence as Alice awakened to the sordid realities of The Bottom.

Jean, two years her junior and also in the dangerous adolescent stage, likewise seemed to have remained unharmed. Her love of books and knowledge had proved a form of protection. So engrossed was she in the lives of fictional people, and in amassing incredible amounts of academic knowledge, that the development of her own personality had been grossly retarded. To Martha, this almost complete character amorphousness did not augur well. So far, even a potential for strong character traits was not discernible in this child. When Jean emerged from her world of books, there would be little of Alice's strength in her to withstand the influence of The Bottom. But now, before this happened, before Cathy and young Clifford reached an age when they could no longer be so closely supervised, they were to move. The thought of leaving The Bottom sent her spirits soaring.

But it was not to be. To her dismay, Clifford declined to even consider leaving The Bottom. He belonged here among these people. To move elsewhere would sever his tangible links with The Bottom, and The Bottom, in turn, would sever the intangible ones. Trust, confidence, sympathy would no longer be extended to him. And he must have these. How else could he help them?

Martha reasoned, entreated, and pleaded by turn, but it was no use. He turned a deaf ear. Only when she mentioned their children did the determined lines around his mouth soften. But even this did not move him. Their new home would provide a better environment for the girls, he said. It would be in a better neighborhood, but it would be in The Bottom.

The house on Westminster Avenue was in a better neighborhood. There were no tenement houses, and the people seemed quiet. There was a wide front lawn, and a long back yard with a tiny fish pond, a tinier bird bath, and an exquisite rock garden. The floors were of shining hard wood, the rooms were spacious and lovely, and there were two bathrooms glistening with white tile. It was indeed a beautiful house. It was, however, in The Bottom.

Martha viewed her new surroundings with a mixture of pleasure and pride, sadness and misgivings. Their new bedroom suite was both comfortable and handsome; but, my how she missed the old brass bed!

Each of the girls now had a room to herself. Martha was happy about that. But as she looked in on each of them before going to bed at night, their individuality impressed her as it never had before. The four girls no longer bore the marked family resemblance of their babyhood, and they were still changing. They were growing up. Each of them had a life to live. Was she preparing them properly for that life? Was she failing them in any way? Now was the time to think. *Now!* Their future was her responsibility.

Whenever Martha reached this point in her thinking, lucid thought was replaced by fearful foreboding — disjointed, vague, unaccountable, and shot through with visions of The Bottom.

Chapter X

It was September, and Alice was going away to college. Before going downstairs to the farewell party her parents were giving her, she was carefully, almost objectively, studying her reflection in the mirror. She was eighteen, a woman, or nearly so. Not tall or short; not fat or thin, for which she was vaguely glad. She had small bones, but there was the suggestion of strength in her young body. Her skin was fair, lighter than any of her sisters'. And unlike them, her black, shoulder-length hair had a natural wave. *I'm not pretty,* she decided, frowning at a few barely noticeable freckles on her nose. Her skin was too yellow, her mouth too wide. But in her flowing, white graduation gown, she looked pretty.

However, for the first time in her life, she was at cross purposes with herself. She wanted to go to college more than anything in the world. She wanted to prepare herself to teach. It had been her dream since early childhood. But now, on the brink of realization, she didn't feel the rapture she had anticipated. Sickening waves of nostalgia were sweeping over her, memories of life here at home. She wouldn't be a part of it anymore. Of course, Cheyney College wasn't far away; she could come home for weekends. But she would be a visitor. She tried unsuccessfully to visualize her new life. The future was a formless void; and she was leaving the only life she had ever known to step into it.

Alice rubbed her powder puff across her nose in a final, thoughtful gesture, and started downstairs. Tomorrow she would begin a wonderful new life. Tomorrow, college. A few short tomorrows away she would be a teacher. But tonight there was the party. Her schoolmates would be there, and they would have fun as always. She quickened her step, held the white gown a little higher so the hem wouldn't get caught by the heel of her shoe, and tried to swallow the tension that gorged her throat.

She did have fun. Marty Johnson, who had fought her battles

in grammar school and carried her books in high school, brought her a corsage. The weight of sadness and doubt lifted temporarily while she laughed with her school chums and danced with Marty.

Martha, who was busy in the kitchen, appeared in the doorway smiling at the young people. Clifford joined her, and she slipped her arm through his. "The girls look nice, don't they?" she said with maternal pride.

"Yes. Yes, they do. Jean is going to be tall," he mused, his eyes on the younger girl's slim, straight form. "She's taller than Alice already."

The doorbell rang and Martha hurried to answer, expecting another guest. But it was Sena Williams, Saint Luke's leading soprano. She was heavily painted, as usual, and Martha's quick eyes noted the cheap, new suit she was wearing. Sena preferred quantity to quality in clothes, Martha thought acidly. Since Sena had left her husband, her visits to Clifford for "spiritual guidance" had steadily increased. Now, she minced into his study, and Martha went to get him. In a secluded corner of the large hallway she informed Clifford, an unaccustomed edge on her voice, that Sena was waiting to see him. "Don't be long," she said anxiously. Clifford's smile was noncommittal as he started toward the study. When the last youthful guest had departed, he was still there.

When at last Sena had gone, he joined Martha in the bedroom. She confronted him fully clothed, eyes blazing. "May I ask what happened to you?" she said angrily. A startled expression flashed on his face for a moment.

"I think you know," he answered evenly.

"I know that it's Alice's last night home, and you weren't with her though you could have been. You should have been there to meet her friends. You should have been there to give her our gift. You should have been there to talk to her later as a father. We should have done these things together, but I had to do them alone while you spent the evening with Sena Williams!" She spat the words at him.

"Your choice of words is unfortunate," he said crisply.

"But very accurate," she countered.

"Sena Williams came to me as a minister for — "

" '*Spiritual guidance.*' " Martha snatched the words from him.

"Spiritual guidance," he repeated deliberately.

"Oh!" She clenched and unclenched her fists. "Tonight," her tone became one of desperate reasoning, "just for tonight, couldn't the spiritual guidance have been postponed, especially since she'll be back again very soon?"

"Your tone is insinuating and insulting. We'll discuss it at another time." He turned to the closet to hang up his coat.

"We'll discuss it now! Clifford!" She flung herself across the room and pulled him around, tearing his immaculate shirt. He glanced quickly at the tear and back to her, a stranger to him now. "Sena came as always to throw herself at you. Her need for 'spiritual guidance' as you call it is a *pretext*. Do you deny that?" He hesitated briefly, looking deeply into her eyes before answering softly.

"No."

Her hand that still clutched his torn shirt sleeve dropped to her side. "Then why didn't you send her away — not tonight, but many, many nights ago?" she hissed.

"Because I'm trying to help her. Trying to help her in spite of herself, if you can understand that."

"Which I can't!"

"Sena needs help. Not for the reasons she gives for coming here — as you say, they don't exist; but because of her actual reasons for coming. That's the real problem. And since she is not aware of it, and I am, I can help her."

Martha's eyes widened in amazement. "You mean you think she's in love with you, but you're trying to help her plant the love of God in her soul. You're trying to show her that He will fill her life and bring her happiness," she mocked.

Clifford jerked his tie off, the muscles around his mouth twitching.

"Sena isn't in love with you," Martha continued. "She'd be the same toward any man in your position. I don't think she *could* be in love with anyone. Help? She doesn't need help. If anyone needs help, it's you! She's just a scheming, admiring woman like the others, only she's got less sense and more nerve than they have!"

He flinched at the harsh words, the harsh, unfamiliar voice.

"You're not helping them, you're encouraging them. I can remember when you didn't have time to encourage admiring women."

"I have come to accept 'admiring women' as a problem, which is the first step toward an intelligent solution."

"You say you've come to expect admiring women?" she asked sweetly.

"I didn't say that at all."

"You might as well have said it. You *have* come to expect

them. More than that, you enjoy their admiration." She was surprised at her own words; the ugly, insidious suspicion that had rankled just beyond the grasp of her conscious mind for so long, blurting its way into the open to confound her, alarm her. She wasn't sure she believed it. Nevertheless, she knew the accusation would hurt.

For the same reason, as they lay in bed later, she broke the tense silence between them. "Darling," her voice came out of the darkness, falsely meek, "could you find time to drive Alice to the train station tomorrow if I entertain the women for you?"

Meanwhile, Alice, unable to sleep, was visiting her sisters' rooms. She ran her hands lovingly over pieces of furniture. She picked up Imogene, Clifford's doll, from the floor, and traced the crack in her head with a gentle finger. Clifford and Cathy slept soundly, undisturbed by her light footsteps or her parting kiss. The light was on in Jean's room, however, and she entered without knocking. Jean was propped up in bed, book in hand. "What are you reading?" Alice asked as she sat on the foot of the bed.

"*For Freedom*." Jean carefully dog-eared her page and closed the book.

"You ought not to do that. It ruins a book."

"I guess you're right, school marm."

Alice flushed in unaccustomed embarrassment. "I guess I am 'a natural'."

"Does the ring fit?" Jean asked, looking at the new birthstone ring on Alice's finger.

"It's perfect. I wonder how Mother and Dad knew what size to buy?"

"By the way, what happened to him tonight?"

"I'm not sure. I think there was someone in his study."

"They're proud of you going to college."

Alice suppressed an impulse to correct her sister's grammar. "I know. What are you going to do?"

"Me?" Jean said blankly.

"You."

"You mean when I finish high school?"

"Of course."

"I don't know."

"You always say that. You must have some idea what you want to do. Everybody does." Jean looked vague. "Don't you ever think about it?"

"No. Well, at least I haven't so far."

"O.K. So what would you like to do?"

"Like?" The vagueness increased. "I don't know. As I said, I never thought about it."

"Well, it's certainly time for you to think about it. Anyway, if you really like something, you don't have to think about it, you just like it. I never thought about becoming a teacher, I just began teaching my dolls. Weren't you ever that way about anything?"

"Not that I remember."

Alice looked puzzled. "You'll probably win a scholarship," she said finally. "By that time I guess you'll know what you want to do."

Chapter XI

Alice was right. When Jean graduated, she was offered two scholarships. She accepted the one from the teacher's college at Cheyney because Alice was there.

"So you want to be a teacher," Alice said when she arrived.

"I'm here," Jean's voice was happy, but not enthusiastic.

"You wouldn't be here otherwise," Alice persisted.

"I don't know. It's an opportunity to study, and it doesn't cost me anything. I'd be foolish not to be here. Teaching? I won't mind it. One has to do something."

Jean studied hard, making the honor roll consistently. However, Alice watched her anxiously, knowing there was something wrong in her sister's complete lack of purpose in life. Jean was young. Perhaps she needed time. Yes, perhaps in time . . . in time . . . But finally she came to believe that knowledge itself was Jean's only goal. As the certainty grew upon her, she sought constantly to correct this basic flaw in her sister's character. It seemed that only she recognized the weakness, and Alice was convinced that she was the only person who could help Jean. It was for her young, inexperienced hands to remold, reshape, redirect a mind which, though less mature, she knew to be stronger in many ways than her own. Nevertheless, she tackled the problem ceaselessly, from every angle; forsaking tact and diplomacy when they failed, for forthright appeals to Jean's reason which proved equally futile.

"Knowledge is unimportant unless it is applied in some way," she would say. Jean would agree apathetically, and Alice would feel rebuffed. It was a painful undertaking, doomed to failure from its inception.

Socially, Jean had no problems. At nineteen she was extremely tall, and she wore her abundant hair on top of her head, making her look even taller. She was slender and well built. Her skin was a smooth, rich brown. She was outstandingly attractive in a sophisticated way that immediately captivated the young men of Cheyney, particularly Eugene Abbot. Jean spent many hours helping him with his studies, which he found difficult. Afterwards, he dogged her footsteps about the campus.

"Jean, let's get married," one day he said abruptly.

"What?" Despite Eugene's ubiquitousness, there had been nothing to prepare her for this.

"I said, let's get married."

Jean had never considered her own marriage. Now, though she quickly refused, the idea struck her forcefully. She was old enough to be married, to fall in love. Memories of great love stories crossed her mind; for the first time she was aware that a similar thing could happen to her. Was she in love with Eugene? Sometimes she thought him stupid, and very untidy. But certainly she felt like a feather in his arms when they danced. She liked his dog-like devotion to her, and she was jealous if another girl dared interrupt it. Also it gave her a thrill for him to be jealous of her. She must be in love with Eugene.

"Why not?" he countered her refusal forcefully.

"I have to finish school and be a teacher."

"You can't be a teacher. I don't want my wife to work."

Jean thrilled at his possessiveness. "I have to finish school anyway," she said.

"Why?"

"I like it. I like to study more than anything else in the world."

"You could study at home — even better, in fact. Then you could study just what you want to study."

"Mama and Papa wouldn't approve," she said, hoping to forestall further argument; inexplicably reverting to the names she had called her parents as a baby.

"They don't have to know 'till it's done."

"Mama and Papa want me to finish school and be a teacher."

" 'Mama and Papa! Mama and Papa!' " he jibed. "Do *you* want to be a teacher?"

Jean considered this question a moment. "I guess not, really. But I won't listen to you," she added vehemently. Eugene, however, was not to be so easily put off.

The next June, the surface calm of the Hilton household exploded. In the midst of frantic preparations for Alice's graduation, Jean, frightened and harassed, divulged a startling piece of news. She had married Eugene in November on her twentieth birthday, intending to keep the marriage secret until her graduation. But now she was going to have a baby. She must leave school; and alarmingly, in view of his new responsibility, so must Eugene, who had "flunked out" again this semester. The truth of the matter was that they needed financial help badly.

Martha, although she was horrified at her daughter's predicament, was immediately sympathetic. Clifford, however, questioned Jean and his unkempt son-in-law laconically, pointedly. Then he wrote a generous check and gave it to Eugene.

"For this we raised her," he said slowly when the door had closed behind them. Was it love in his voice, chagrin, or contempt? Martha couldn't be sure. He was growing increasingly difficult to understand.

Chapter XII

Alice began her teaching career at John Adams Grammar School in the heart of The Bottom just as war, making no momentous changes in the congested slums, came to the country. The school was made of drab, ugly brown bricks that perhaps had been red in the indeterminable past. The pointing had long since fallen out, leaving gaping spaces between them. Here and there great, dangerous-looking cracks split the walls. Inside, little light or air came through the high, poorly spaced windows. The rooms were gloomy and depressing. The paint had long gone from the walls, and the wood itself was peeling. Overhead there were huge holes where plaster had fallen out. The stairways, the halls, the ancient sliding doors — everything, including the narrow steps of the fire escape, was made of wood.

Alice soon discovered that her youth was a problem. Because of it, the children loved her dearly; in fact, they considered her one of them. This would not do at all. She drew her loose curls into a severe bun at the nape of her neck, and removed all but a touch of color from her lips in the classroom. She was able then to command more respect from the children. Still, she was often embarrassed when they asked, "Teacher, are you a girl?" In the halls and schoolyard her students said to other children, "*My* teacher's pretty." This did not set well with other teachers. They frowned their bitter disapproval.

"Too young," they said. "Much too young." There was no youth or youthfulness in them. Their minds and their hearts were older than their bodies. Nobody called them pretty anymore. In fact, the children habitually made such hurtful comments on the looks of their teachers, that the teachers genuinely dreaded overhearing them and usually provided the little ones with loud evidence of their approach. This way they spared themselves anything more than several *"Hsssts"* and *"Cheese-its,"* to the effect that here comes "old lady" So-and-So.

They were decidedly cool to their new member. Coolness gave way to ill-concealed hostility when Leslie Hammond, Adams' only male teacher, sought to ease the plight of the friendless, bewildered girl. This was not at all what the other teachers had intended, an entirely unforseen development. Mr. Hammond was indeed adopting a "most injudicious" manner. Pointed phrases such as "judicious behavior," "bearing becoming to one's position," and "undue familiarity" began to be bandied about the teachers' meetings.

At these times, Alice's face, neck, and ears flushed to the vast satisfaction of her co-teachers, but Leslie sat unmoved, seemingly unaware of the thinly veiled reproaches.

He was not a handsome man: small-boned, and slender to the point of seeming frail, slightly taller than average, a prominent forehead, and a small head well sprinkled with gray hairs, though he was not yet thirty. He was without a single striking feature, yet he himself was striking, compelling. His presence overwhelmed a gathering, dwarfing or obliterating other personalities. He was never completely still; his slender, expressive hands moved nervously, a long leg slung over one knee swung rhythmically, or he paced the length of a room in precise, energetic steps, physical expressions of the ceaseless agitation of a phenomenal mind. He was a man electrified by his love of mankind, singly and collectively. His hours at school were spent trying to implant this love of his in the broken, bitter hearts of youngsters from The Bottom.

Now, he proposed to address the problems of their parents through a Home-School Association program to be carried out during hours when the school was closed. The idea was unpopular with the other teachers, but they lacked the courage to oppose him forcefully.

"It's a wonderful idea," short, stubby Mrs. Root said, "but I'd never be able to participate. It's all I can do to get to school in the day." They were at a teachers' meeting seated in the customary semicircle around the principal's desk. The married teachers let it be known that Mrs. Root had voiced their sentiments exactly.

"It's a good idea, but it would be wasted on these people," Miss Granberg said. She wore silver-rimmed glasses, was nearing fifty, and she was an inexorable old maid. Unlike the other unmarried members of the faculty, she entertained no romantic notions about Adams' male teacher. However, she felt grossly inferior to him, and in an attempt to disguise and submerge the feeling, she was forever delicately implying her own superiority. "These people," she said, emphasizing the words ever so slightly, "would never appreciate an organization of that kind."

Leslie Hammond, legs crossed, arms folded tightly across his chest, gave a particularly vicious kick with his swinging leg, and wrenched his mouth quickly to one side in a grim gesture characteristic of him.

"Why not?" He addressed Miss Granberg, his features as devoid of expression as he could make them. However, there was no hiding the sternness in his rather small eyes. He looked away from Miss Granberg, waiting for her answer. His all-seeing glance slid lightning-swift over the faces of the other teachers, included Mr. Barbour, the tired old principal, and returned to Miss Granberg briefly.

"Well," she spread her knotted fingers against the ancient handbag in her lap, knowing she must say something, not knowing what to say. Caught, trapped in a self-created situation, her heart pounded. She felt dangerously near making a fool of herself or being made a fool of. "It's obvious —" she was striving to keep from sounding lame.

Miss Loeffler came to the rescue, seeing a chance to impress Leslie with her intelligence. "I'm afraid it *is* obvious, Mr. Hammond," she said, running her hand through her bleached blonde hair in a Hollywood gesture. She was thirty-nine, and of the opinion that she looked much younger. She had a beak nose and lemon-colored skin, which she had bleached her hair to match. The overall effect was a little frightening. "These children don't come from homes at all. Most of them are uncouth and dirty, and the parents are dirtier and more uncouth than the children. They send their children to school in order to be rid of them for a few hours. They aren't interested in bettering the children or themselves. They're of low grade intelligence, and it's just impossible to get that kind of mind to cooperate on a thing like this. Impossible! You couldn't get even one of their parents interested."

"It would seem that the same thing is true of their teachers," Leslie said grimly, his face inscrutable.

"Oh, no!" It was Alice, at the far end of the semicircle, directly across from him. "I think it's a fine idea. And I'd be glad to help. Some of the parents will take a little coaxing, and some may not come, but there'll be others enthusiastic from first to last. I'm sure of it."

"Good." Neither Leslie's facial expression nor his voice had changed in the least, but his gratitude was unmistakable.

Jane Loeffler's reddish-brown eyes focused on Alice and narrowed. She dropped them quickly to the page of notes she was taking. *That wench! That silly, tricky, scheming wench!* she thought. *Pretending to be interested in those snotty-nosed brats just so she could worm her way in with Leslie.* She had been stupid not to think of it herself. Why hadn't she? If she had agreed with him tonight, there would have been countless opportunities as they worked together later on to show him how intelligent she was, she scoffed at herself. *Now this silly little fool will have him all to herself.* The point of the pencil which Jane was holding against the notebook snapped sharply.

"Then, if you have no objection, Mr. Barbour, Miss Hilton and I will proceed to organize the Home-School Association," Leslie said.

"Certainly. Certainly." The feeble figurehead nodded approvingly. "If I were younger, I myself would help you organize it. As it is, you may count on my full cooperation. There'll be no official connection with the Board of Education, of course. But we'll hold the meetings here at the school, and I'll help in whatever way possible."

"Thank you, sir."

Jane Loeffler cleared her throat. "What I said wasn't meant to be a refusal," she said a trifle weakly. "It was only my opinion. However, that won't stop me from being of help if I can."

Miss Granberg and the others kept silent, having too much pride to do such an immediate about-face. Nevertheless, when the

Home-School Association held its first meeting with Leslie as chairman, and Alice as his administrative assistant, they were there — all of them.

They resented the fact that Alice was Leslie's assistant. Immediately there were impromptu caucuses in hallways and doorways. How did *she* get that position? She was green as grass. There should have been an election! Some experienced teacher should have been given the job. "*You* would have been much better as the administrative assistant," they told Jane Loeffler, who agreed wholeheartedly. However, in Jane's absence the tone was somewhat different, for Leslie had asked Jane to be treasurer in case the need for handling money arose. Just how did *she* get to be treasurer? they wanted to know. There were many teachers more qualified. They really should get together as soon as possible and force the organization to hold a proper election so that more appropriate officers could be put in place!

And there were strenuous objections to the all-inclusive program Leslie had planned for the organization.

"I think we should confine ourselves strictly to problems involving the children," Mrs. Root said at the second meeting. Her statement, having been rehearsed at several hallway caucuses, found immediate favor.

Leslie, however, was not to be swayed. When the nodding heads and assenting voices were still, he rose and stated flatly: "The purpose of the Home-School Association shall in no way be limited. We shall be interested in anything and everything either directly or indirectly concerned with the home or the school."

"Thus," now he began to gesture energetically and rise feverishly up and down on the balls of his feet, his voice musical and compelling, "we'll devote our attention to the truancy, lateness, absenteeism, or emotional problem of one child, but on the other hand, we'll establish committees for clean block campaigns, and better housing projects."

"One of our first jobs will be to form a committee of parents and teachers to go to the mayor himself about having a traffic light put at that intersection two blocks from here where little Johnny Gates was killed last week on his way to school. People have been being killed at that corner for years, and will go on being killed unless you and I get busy and *do* something!

"The city officials over the years have time and again flouted their complete indifference to the problems of The Bottom. But we will go to the mayor and say: 'Mr. Mayor, no longer will we stand for this indifference. We *demand* protection for our children and ourselves.

" 'No longer will we endanger the lives of our children by sending them to school in a fire trap. We must have a new school, a safe school for our children. We must have an adequate supply of teachers for them. Away with this damnable system of having from three to six grades in one room! You can, and you will, correct all of these things because we, tax-paying citizens, demand that you do so.' These things and many more we will concern ourselves with until anywhere you look in The Bottom, the effects of the Home-School Association will be seen."

There was a clamor of approval. Heads that had nodded agreement with Mrs. Root nodded vigorously now. Mrs. Root, looking shame-faced and sheepish, was determining at this moment never again to be spokesman for her traitorous comrades.

Like everyone else in the room, Alice had been borne aloft, fired by the magic of a voice. But now, as she looked about her, a tiny chill closely akin to fear tingled along her spine. Suddenly, she was terribly aware of the man who had spoken. Long ago she had recognized in him a prodigious mind. His memory was infallible, the scope of his reading so great as to be unbelievable; he could figure mathematical calculations with the rapidity of a machine, and early in their acquaintance she had been astounded at the realization that of every subject, no matter how deep, how rare, how new or how old, he had more than average knowledge.

At first, she had been completely in awe of this impressive, superior person. But a little time had proved Leslie Hammond to be painfully modest, and more than a little shy. Alice found these very "human" traits, as she thought of them, most reassuring. They served to put her at ease with him from which it was a short step to discovering his easy laughter, his love of simple things — baseball, movies, small talk — and his great, overwhelming love of people.

But tonight she was seeing him with different eyes. She had seen his mind at work before this. And she had watched his voice sway a group of people as one man to his will. Tonight, for the first time, she became aware of Leslie Hammond's ability to rule and control, entertaining no opposition to his will. It was strangely frightening to see in this man, in whom until now she had seen only perfection. She bent her head low over the tiny table that separated them, mechanically taking notes. She had never thought he was perfect, she told herself untruthfully.

Everyone had faults. Leslie's was unyielding willfulness. It might be a terrible fault, but if so, it was greatly mitigated by the fact that his will would always be unselfish. If, as she thought, tonight had brought only a small indication of the power he might unleash, there was still nothing to fear. His purpose would always be good. It was well to have power to direct it.

Chapter XIII

Almost overnight the Home-School Association became the most important organization in the life of The Bottom. The association grew from bi-monthly sessions of the teachers and a few parents gathered in one room, to weekly meetings held in a huge assembly room made by opening the sliding panels which closed off the individual classrooms of the entire first floor. Before long, the parents filled all the seats in the huge room, and late-comers had to stand. They brought their problems large and small. As HSA grew, the quantity and variety of the problems grew until they were swamped in troubles, and sometimes it seemed the organization would disintegrate in chaos. But Leslie's willfulness, his power, his smooth direction mastered every situation.

They accomplished things on every hand. The traffic light was installed at the fatal corner. The Clean Block Campaign was a rousing success. The youngsters themselves swept the streets so consistently ignored by the street cleaners. They hosed the pavements and whitewashed the curbstones. Their parents put up new curtains and set flower pots on the steps. Truancy and absenteeism were all but abolished as parent and teacher worked together.

It was little Buddy Crawford, twelve years old, who indirectly started the association on its most lasting problem. Walking down an apparently deserted hallway one morning, Alice heard a mysterious noise underneath the wooden stairway. She had been called to Mr. Barbour's office, where the parent of one of her pupils had come to see her. The meeting had taken some ten minutes, and her class, unavoidably left alone, was having a high time. She had in fact been able to hear them in Mr. Barbour's office. Now, with her hand on the doorknob, she hesitated. The noise under the stairway conjured up unpleasant visions: a huge rat, an unpleasant stranger. She didn't want to investigate it.

Through the window in the door to her classroom she saw Betty-Ann Schofield streak to the front of the room, climb on top of "teacher's desk," and fling herself into a wild tap dance. Alice's fingers tightened on the doorknob, but just before she turned it another sound came from below the stairway. She paused indecisively, duty calling her from two directions. Glancing once again at Betty-Ann's abandoned dance, she released the doorknob and hurried down the hall, squelching visions of rats and strangers. It might be a truant boy returned to the scene of the crime as they so often did.

She approached the back of the stairs, bent slightly, supporting herself by holding onto the base of the stairway above her head, and peered into the semidarkness, horrified. Little Buddy Crawford was settling a bundle of oily rags on the floor beneath the stairs. Then he reached in his pocket and withdrew a tiny packet of matches. He struck one, its light illuminating his intent face and Alice's distorted one. He was so engrossed that he did not see Alice though her head was directly in front of him, apparently suspended in midair because of her unusual position. His arm, and with it the deadly match, descended toward the oily rags.

Instinctively, without thought, Alice reached out and enclosed his wrist in her slender, vise-like fingers. The boy gave a hoarse yell of surprised fright. Alice, her fingers tightening, her face terrified, was slowly drawing him from beneath the stairway. His frightened eyes were fastened on her; the flaming match glowed in his fingers. If he dropped it even now, even as she held him, the stairway would be a blazing sheet of flame before the alarm could be sounded. She heard the crying, the frightened shrieks of trapped children; she heard the hungry roar of the fire; she heard the rumble and crash of the flaming stairway as it caved in, saw the coughing, crying children shrink away from it, shrink toward other flames. And still she had not drawn Buddy the three endless steps from beneath the stairs; still the match flared in his hand; still he might drop it in the oily rags. One last step and he was out. Somehow she was powerless to move beyond that.

They were as if cast in stone; the frightened boy held in the grip of his teacher's unrelenting fingers, and piercing, probing eyes, the match still burning brightly as she closed the distance between them. Suddenly, Buddy yelled hoarsely as the match burned his fingers. It fell to the floor and instantly Alice's foot was upon it.

Doors were opening along the hallway. Faces appeared. Mrs. Root, Betty-Ann Schofield, peeping stealthily, then others of Alice's students, Mr. Barbour, Leslie Hammond.

Leslie persuaded Mr. Barbour to let him handle the situation, and after school he and Alice went home with Buddy. The house smelled strongly of urine and boiling cabbage. Mrs. Crawford ushered them through a dark hallway, past a stairway from which the three bottom steps and the banister had disappeared, through a doorless doorway, into a combination parlor and bedroom. The wallpaper had been torn from the wall in many places, and pencil scribblings decorated the bare plaster. Over by the bed a baby boy sat over a bucket. "You finished?" Mrs. Crawford asked him. She jerked the child up and peered into the bucket, then kicked it underneath the bed.

"What's the trouble?" she asked, turning to Alice and Leslie. She was a woman who looked as though she struggled with life's problems incessantly, and was never victorious. Her skin was leathery, and a permanent frown ridged her forehead. "What's the trouble?" she repeated. Her voice was wooden, without alarm.

Leslie put a stilling hand over Alice's as she started to speak. He rose from the sofa beside her and was soon pacing the floor in measured steps, telling of Buddy's dangerous escapade.

"How did he get out in the hall?" Mrs. Crawford asked, though Leslie had already told her.

"He asked me if he might be excused from the classroom. The children are given perfect freedom in that," Leslie reiterated.

"Where'd you get all them rags?" she said, turning to Buddy. He stood beside her, his eyes bulging with fright, sobbing and choking back his tears, yellow mucous rolling from his nose. His plight had drawn a room full of his sisters and brothers, cruelly unsympathetic and curious.

"I know. I seen him," one of his siblings sing-songed, taking advantage of Buddy's inability to answer. "He took some to school every day, and he wouldn't tell me what he was doin' it for. He must ha' been hidin' 'em at school."

"Is that so?" Mrs. Crawford asked Buddy. A whining sound came from his mouth which hung open, incapable of speech. He inclined his head slowly in answer to his mother's question. She raised her arm, and with a tremendous swing, smashed the back of her coarse-knuckled hand in his face. Leslie stiffened, and deftly interposed his body as the hand descended from the other direction aimed at Buddy's head. He pulled his sparkling white handkerchief from an inside pocket and used it to clean Buddy's nose.

"You sot them other fires, didn't you?" Mrs. Crawford leaned over, the better to see Buddy across the bulk of Leslie's figure.

"Were there other fires?" Leslie asked calmly. Only his shrewd eyes, invisible to the others as he leaned over Buddy, gave any hint of the flood of thought and emotion that had been touched off in him.

"We've had fires in this neighborhood once and twice a week for the last couple of months. Everybody knowed somebody was settin' them, but nobody knowed who. This house here caught on fire three times. Just lucky we found it early each time, but we could have all been kilt or something. And he sot 'em. He sot 'em all. Didn't you?"

Buddy began to blubber again, admitting his guilt. "You! You might have kilt somebody!" She thrust at him under Leslie's arm. He lowered his arm slightly, and the blow glanced off his side. There was something unfathomable in Mrs. Crawford's great concern. It existed alone, completely divorced from alarm, fear or anger. She jabbed at Buddy mechanically.

Leslie told the boy to sit beside Alice. Then he stood facing Mrs. Crawford, chin in hand. "Where is the boy's father?" he asked.

"He's in jail. Didn't you know that? I thought everybody knowed that. It was in all the papers, white and colored. Miss Alice, here, knowed it. We belong to Reverend Hilton's church. I haven't been lately because Esther is sick, but I'm going to call your father. I think I got his phone number here." She walked over to the pencil-marked plaster and traced a lingering finger through the jumble of numbers and the children's artistic efforts until she located the Hilton phone number.

"That's the whole trouble," she said, reverting to the original conversation. "I got to be father and mother to all these children. You see how it is." She swept her hand about in a broad gesture, indicating the many noisy children in the room with them. She was still for a moment, giving prominence to the wild shrieks and rumblings of other children throughout the house.

"God knows this ain't no job for no one woman. I'm not getting any younger. I get a little order from the Relief. They won't give me much because they say I ought to take the older children out of school. But I don't want to do that. I want every one of them to finish school if they can. They makes a few pennies by working at odd jobs after school, and that helps a little bit, but it ain't a drop in the bucket."

"How much longer does your husband have to serve?"

"They give him five years. Some say they'll let him out sooner; some say they won't. It don't matter when they let him out. I couldn't have him back after what he done. I guess you weren't here in The Bottom then. It was when I was in the hospital with this last baby." She pointed to the child who had been sitting over the bucket when they entered. "I left Crawford here with the children, and while I was gone, he raped Esther. Every day for ten days he slept with his own daughter.

"I was in the hospital while all this was going on, see. I didn't know nothing about it. When I come home, Esther was sick. She wasn't but nine years old, you see. It was enough to kill her. She ain't never been right since. Anyhow, every time I asked her what was wrong, Crawford said it wasn't nothing wrong with her, and kept chasing her outside to play with the other children, when I could tell all the time she was sick. Then I found the bloody sheets where he had hid them, and I put two and two together. I took Esther to the hospital, and that's when the whole thing came out. So you see, I couldn't never have him back here."

While she talked, the children pursued their antics unrestrained. Alice watched them, her nerves taut, waiting for the mother to take them in hand. However, Mrs. Crawford's eyes followed the children indifferently. Two of them stabbed at each other's eyes with sticks. The baby retrieved the bucket from beneath the bed and pushed it along the floor playing "choo-choo train" with the contents of the "train" splashing precariously. The twins sang "Row, Row, Row Your Boat," banging time on the room's only remaining window pane.

All at once, an older boy became envious of the baby's "choo-choo train." Grabbing the bucket from the baby, he began to push it, whereupon the baby began to squall. A girl older than either of the two snatched the baby from the floor and carried him screaming and kicking to the end of the sofa. There she dangled him by his feet over the sofa-arm until the squalling gave way to choking, sputtering gasps. Mrs. Crawford watched unperturbed, and it was Alice, having stood as much as she could, who rescued the baby. She smoothed his head and held him close, feeling the frightened thud of his little heart against her blouse.

"That's the way I make him stop crying," his sister protested violently.

With the baby in her arms, Alice crossed the room and succeeded in ending the eye-stabbing duel, and quieting the twins. Afraid to come near the "choo-choo train," she attempted, from a distance, to entice the "conductor" away from it and was unsuccessful.

"I quite agree with you," Leslie was saying. However, the fact that you're alone now makes it more difficult to manage the children. Tell me, what kind of child has Buddy been until now?"

"I never had no trouble out of him before," Mrs. Crawford said.

"How does he spend his leisure time?"

"Leisure time?" Mrs. Crawford looked perplexed. "I don't know."

Leslie glanced up, startled into stillness for a brief moment. Then: "What does he do when he's not at school? Where does he play, and with whom?"

"I don't know." There was an edge of impatience in her voice. "I don't have time to keep up with every one of these children all the time. I try to be a good mother to them. I see to it that they're warm, and ain't hungry. And I get them off to school. What they do after that, I don't know. As I say, I can't keep up with them. Buddy, he plays in the street with the others, I guess. They don't have no certain place for children to play." These last words rang in Leslie's ears as Mrs. Crawford spoke them. They were still ringing when he and Alice stepped out into the dark winter evening.

They walked in silence, each sunk in heavy, unhappy thoughts. On a corner of Lancaster Avenue they waited for the traffic light to turn green. Several boys from about fourteen to twenty years old stood talking, their conversation studded with "Man" and forced, harsh laughter. The March wind flapped their coats about their thin bodies as they stood in groups, lounged in doorways, leaned against the wall of the building. Their faces had a lean, hungry look. Hungry for food, yes, but also hungry for love, and light, and beauty. A pot-bellied Irish policeman appeared, swinging his club ostentatiously. "Break it up," he said without kindness. "G'wan, beat it! No loitering on the corner."

The boys moved away silently, their bodies bent slightly against the wind, their hands pushing forward in their pockets trying to close the gaping, blowing coats, trying to keep the wind out, trying to generate heat from their frail bodies.

Leslie's fingers were tight on Alice's arm as he led her across the street. She looked at him and saw that his lips were clamped together, his mouth drawn slightly to one side. "Stand right on this spot," he said when they had crossed, "and start walking in any direction you choose. I guarantee you, you'll walk for five miles — I'm tempted to make it ten — without finding one place of wholesome recreation for those boys."

It was a split-second calculation, seemingly little more than a rough guess. But invariably Alice had found Leslie's split-second calculations and rough guesses to be infallible. Now, she knew surely that within a radius of five miles — perhaps ten — there was, as he had said, no place of recreation for these youngsters.

"You'll find pool rooms," Leslie continued, "that are nothing more than gambling dens. You'll find bars and houses of prostitution waiting with open arms to welcome them. But you won't find one playground, or baseball diamond, or tennis court, or gymnasium for these kids to use. And then we're amazed when a twelve-year-old youngster takes to setting fires — when older boys form gangs and make war on each other. You heard what Buddy said. He set the fires for fun. In another year, he'll belong to one of the gangs in The Bottom, also for fun.

"What else is there for him? The gang will be other boys just like himself, like those we just passed; living in pool rooms and on corners, spitting through their teeth; adrift, not knowing how or why, in a world that has no place for them; frightened; fighting their arch enemy — life. Then one day, just for fun, they'll fight another gang, or rob the corner store."

When they reached Alice's home, his thoughts were still plaguing him. He followed Alice into the living room, accepting her dinner invitation absent-mindedly.

"A child is a delicate, sensitive mass of energy," Leslie said, more to himself than to Alice. "Children need constant attention and guidance. Buddy is typical of many of our kids in The Bottom. He doesn't feel loved, or special, or important to anyone. Does his mother love him? Probably, but in a strictly matter-of-fact way. She doesn't have time to show him that she loves him; there are too many others to be thought about. And she certainly doesn't have time to give him special attention. Guidance was out of the question at home. We gave him guidance at school — in a classroom with four classes and one hundred-twenty-six children. My God! Alice — " He broke off, waving his hand in a helpless gesture.

"I know," she said. "I know. The kids don't have much of a chance."

"No." He sank into a chair. "The kids don't have much of a chance . . . They enter the world as human mishaps, and they go through life the same way."

"And they're filled with hate." Alice's sister Cathy had entered unobserved. Her voice came from the shadows just inside the doorway. "I watch them on their way home from school. They chalk walls and break windows. They enjoy chasing the white children home with stones and sticks and penknives. They fight each other.

"Once I saw a fat, happy-looking white fellow try to intercede in one of their fights. He came down the street smiling and swinging a big umbrella. 'Don't fight, boys,' he said. 'It isn't nice. Go on home.' The boys turned on him, and the children who had been laughing and egging the fight on turned on him, snarling, hurling stones, calling him filthy names. They backed him into the corner of a building, and I'll never forget the sight of him there, clutching his big umbrella, his fat face terrified. He was as helpless as a baby, surrounded by a hundred young devils, dancing and hooting, with clenched fists and obscene oaths.

"I went to call the police and left him there. He was very close to tears, apologizing and pleading with the mob of children that had him cornered."

"It's a matter for the Home-School Association," Leslie said. "We've helped some of the children individually, and most of them generally. But I see now that a full scale program is needed. We want to reach the children before they're born — through their mothers. Then after they arrive, it's our responsibility to provide them with the love, the guidance, the care they need to mold them into worthwhile human beings.

"We must have boys clubs and girls clubs. We must have meetings of mothers, and expectant mothers. We must have a meeting of all the doctors in The Bottom — and one with all of the ministers. There are so many things to do," his hand thrashed the air briefly, "I hardly know where to begin. I'll have to call Jane. She loves to work with the kids, and she's invaluable. We must call her at once."

"Of course," Alice said, her voice betraying no hint of disapproval. He was always this way about Jane Loeffler, and it was wise to agree. Jane had worked hard and enthusiastically for HSA. Alice, however, remained unimpressed, certain it was a pose, a thin camouflage for Jane's unrelenting campaign to capture Leslie Hammond. Leslie alone was unaware of it. It seemed to Alice that his brilliant mind waxed positively stupid where people were concerned, having no ability to analyze them beyond their own interpretations of themselves.

"I believe Jane lives for those children, she's so fond of them," he was saying.

Only when you're around, Alice thought. *Otherwise, they are "those snotty-nosed brats."* She smiled at Leslie, feeling the sharp twinge of jealously his constant praising of Jane evoked in her, knowing he did not suspect it. "Tell Mother Leslie's staying for dinner," she said to Cathy.

Hammond was moving about restlessly. "Leslie." Alice broke the silence softly. He set a china figure back in its place on the mantle, listening for her to continue, and when she said nothing more, he faced her inquiringly. "Sit down. No, not there, over here." She led him to a low sofa before the fireplace, where gas flames leaped beautifully about simulated logs.

"You said sit down, not lie down," he protested as she pushed him back against the cushions.

"Put your feet up," she commanded, "and don't move until I get back." She crossed the room and lowered the lamp light, and pulled the yarn rug over by the sofa. Then she settled herself on the floor beside Leslie. "There, now, be perfectly still. I want to see if it's possible for you to relax." Happiness surged over her. The scene was exactly as she remembered it from a hundred dreams. The yarn rug, the hall light shining in, the firelight casting shadows, and Leslie on the low sofa relaxed and still — or nearly so. His hand was idly removing the hairpins from the knot in her hair.

"I'll relax better if you look less like a school marm," he said when she turned to him.

"Anything to help you relax," she said, a queer feeling at the pit of her stomach. "I don't know how you expect to last at the rate you're going. You never let up. The only time you rest your mind or your body is when you sleep — if you sleep."

"Oh, I don't" he teased. "Very little, that is. You see, I have insomnia. And when I finally get my eyes shut, I don't think I really sleep at all. I toss and turn, and open them at the drop of a pin."

"It's nothing to joke about. You must know you're wearing

yourself out. Why? Since I've known you, I've yet to see you really let loose and have a good time. Even when you're supposed to be enjoying yourself, your mind is full of committees to see the mayor, and Better Health campaigns."

"I can't help it. As long as there are maladjusted Buddy Crawfords feeling unloved and unwanted, or actually so, as long as there are filthy streets and bodies and minds here in The Bottom, I don't have the time to frolic and enjoy myself. In fact, I don't feel I have the right to enjoy myself."

"Everyone has the right to enjoy himself," Alice said quietly. "And you — have you ever thought that perhaps for a few hours of real enjoyment, your mind might be keener, your body more able to work?" Leslie did not answer. "You should have —" she hesitated, unsure of herself, "married someone —"

"Ha!" The monosyllabic laugh came from deep inside him. She was baffled, resentful.

"Someone to make life easier for me. Someone to bring me my slippers at the end of a weary day. Someone to fuss over me, worry about me?"

"Yes," she faced him defiantly. "That's it exactly. But I suppose you didn't have time."

"No," he said, some of the teasing gone from his voice at the unexpected feeling in hers. "It wasn't that at all. I couldn't ask anyone to share such a hectic life."

"That's only an involved way of saying the very same thing."

"I've been trapped," he murmured.

"You didn't have time," she insisted.

"Oh, I resent your keeping it in the past tense that way," he protested. "I know thirty must seem terribly decrepit to you, but I still have time."

"Oh, I didn't mean —"

"And though I may not have anyone to bring my slippers to me, you worry about me, so I'm not doing too badly. What shall I do with these hairpins?" he asked, retrieving the last one. She reached for them without thinking, still sputtering apologetically, and he dropped the hairpins in her hand.

Then on something half-impulse, half-instinct, his hand closed over hers, and pulled her toward him. Her mouth grew still under his. The union of their lips was cool and sweet. He felt fatigue leave his body. The visions of the hapless inhabitants of The Bottom disappeared, and he thought of nothing. When it was over, he could not believe it had happened. He kissed her again, and it was the same — like a gentle breeze on a hot afternoon, like cool water in a parched throat, like a soothing poem at the end of a day.

"And, so I need you," he said, his head back among the cushions. "I really do."

Alice's eyes shone in the semidarkness, and her breath came quickly. "I think I heard Cathy call," she said.

He hadn't spoken of love, but Alice knew he hadn't kissed her lightly. That he needed her she had known even before the soothing revelation of their first kiss.

His attachment to her increased with time. More than ever before, he sought her company. In the midst of controlling some stormy session of HSA, his tired eyes rested on her, quite obviously. So obviously, in fact, that Jane, bitterly jealous, dropped the last semblance of civility toward Alice. The other teachers became openly resentful and spiteful. They pointedly ignored and isolated Alice, continually making her aware that she was without a friend at Adams School, except for Leslie Hammond.

Alice did not mind.

Chapter XIV

There were five clubs in all, not a great many, but the Home-School Association was proud of them. It now busied itself with persuading the boys and girls who most needed these clubs to join them for, perversely, those who came were those who least needed them. There had been a series of meetings of parents and expectant parents in which teachers, psychologists, and doctors had lectured on such things as Home Education, Your Child, Your Baby, and Birth Control. There had been a meeting of all the doctors in The Bottom, and one of all the ministers. In this latter gathering, the clergy had determined, as had the teachers and doctors, to take a more personal interest in the people of The Bottom. The religious difficulties of birth control were discussed and resolved to the satisfaction of the majority, and the men of the cloth departed with new inspiration and new hope for their ministries in The Bottom. However, conspicuously absent was the pastor of one of The Bottom's largest church congregations, Reverend Clifford Hilton.

Full of enthusiasm, Alice had broached the subject to her father, only to find him coolly unreceptive. Surprised, and not a little perplexed, she had asked her mother to intercede, feeling certain he would listen to her.

Martha was softly aging. Though her shoulders were erect, and her gait graceful, she walked a little more slowly. Her eyes, now seen from behind glasses, were seldom happy, attuned with her entire being to a dire sense of foreboding that now preoccupied her life.

Her husband, on the other hand, had ripened with age. A few more gray hairs that became him well, a little more weight on a frame once too spare. Still, in some way that was not clearly definable, he had changed, was still changing. Martha wasn't as certain as Alice was that he would listen to her. Nevertheless, she introduced the subject one evening as he sat reading before the fireplace.

"I'm not going, Martha," he said, closing his book, "because I feel it's nothing more than a waste of time. I know you think I should go. Alice thinks I should go; my absence will prove embarrassing. How will she explain it to her foolish Mr. Hammond, who dashes about trying to rectify the ills of The Bottom single-handedly? Well, tell her to send him to me. I can tell him that these people won't be any better off after that meeting than they were before it. They aren't helped that easily. I've given my life to them, and I wish I could see that even that had done some good. Many of them aren't worthwhile helping, if the truth were told. There's a war on, for instance, but you wouldn't know it. The eternal crap game never even slowed down. There's a war to be fought, there're jobs to be had, and I haven't missed one man or boy from that corner. It's sickening."

"They may be hopeless incompetents, physically and mentally, but they don't represent all the people in The Bottom."

"I'm not as sure of that as you are."

"What do you mean?"

"I mean, I don't want to discuss it further. My own thoughts are confused — perhaps I'm wrong at that. But, nevertheless, my present state of mind won't permit me to go, Martha."

"Martha . . . Martha . . . Martha . . ." Her name as he had spoken it in that distant dismissing tone reverberated in her mind. She was always "Martha" to him now, it seemed, never "Little Girl."

She ached to pursue the discussion further, but his tone had been final, and the makings of a quarrel were present. The atmosphere recalled vividly the night of Alice's farewell party, when they had quarreled bitterly, irrevocably, about Sena Williams. That quarrel had resulted in a tiny breach between them, the breach she realized was still there, ever widening . . . widening. For Clifford had persisted in his guise as spiritual counselor to Sena; and through the years, Martha had watched other Senas come and go, while her husband obviously grew fond of the attention they lavished on him.

But it wasn't this that had brought the look of fearful foreboding to her eyes. His fondness for these attentions seemed to her to be dwindling, as she had always felt they would. However, at church there was a different, and even more disturbing, situation. The congregation had long met his smallest wish with the greatest respect, a fact which had caused Clifford surprise and concern some years ago. But his concern had vanished in time, and now he had grown the least bit demanding, the least bit disrespectful of those who so willingly performed his bidding. The people seemed not to mind; in fact, seemed to enjoy placing themselves in subservience.

But what was happening to Clifford? Was this merely a transitory headiness, or was it the first evidence of a change — permanent, inexorable, horrible? What then would happen to their home? She thought of her daughters, especially of the effervescent Clifford, who at sixteen was more headstrong, wilder than any of the other girls had been, whose sole stability was her love of home and family. Even more than her sisters did, Clifford needed her father to be sympathetic, understanding, loving as she had always known him. He mustn't change. Perhaps he hadn't. Surely it was all her imagination.

Clifford did not attend the meeting of ministers. Martha was ashamed and humiliated. Home-School Association meetings which she had so enjoyed became unbearable, and she no longer attended them. Alice and Cathy, though their embarrassment was keen, continued as members of HSA. Alice had tried to explain her father's action to Leslie one evening as they walked home after a meeting. He had plainly not understood — and after that it was a closed subject.

Chapter XV

About this time, it was apparent to the family that Alice was in love. She was glowingly happy in the quiet, gentle love that she and Leslie shared. For the first time in her life she gave herself over to thoughts of her own future and forgot her mothering of the younger Hiltons, unmindful even of Clifford's atrocious grammar. To that young person's unbounded joy, her grammar, her tomboy behavior, her rolled-up trousers, "sloppy joe" sweaters, and "dirty saddle" shoes went unmentioned. Alice was in love, and she, Clifford, hoped she stayed that way forever! Not that she was fondly impressed with Leslie. Cathy and Alice had taken her to a Home-School Association meeting with them once, and afterward she had treated them to an energetic monologue, mimicking Leslie's rapid, authoritative public speaking voice, interspersed with a ridiculously meek version of her own. "If he told me milk was black," she said, "I would agree with him! I would know he was wrong, but I couldn't defend myself. He'd say, 'White reflects all the rays of the light—and something or other, and so and so, isn't that right?' "

"Yes, sir."

" 'Whereas, black absorbs all colors—and something-or-other, and so and so?' "

" 'Yes, sir.' "

" 'Then, you are contradicting yourself!' "

" 'Yes, sir.' " Clifford drooped her head in hang-dog humility as her voice trailed away.

"Why, he'd never do anything like that!" Alice said. "In a group of people you'd think he knew less than anyone there. He's *very* modest. It's one of the nicest things about him. Don't you think so?"

"No!"

Alice's voice had grown soft, her eyes a little dreamy, and at first thought Clifford had been inclined to agree with her, like Cathy, who was smiling her approval. Her explosive negative answer was a little surprising, even to herself, but she supported it well. "He downplays himself to be a moron, then he thinks that makes *you* comfortable," she said diabolically.

Suddenly, Cathy laughed in appreciation of this quaint complaint. The giggling of both girls finally proved too much for Alice, and reluctant laughter forced its way through her lips.

* * * * *

Martha watched Alice bloom under the touch of love. Her beauty in this new radiance rivaled that of sandy-haired Cathy, the prettiest of the girls. Martha approved of Leslie. He was good for her daughter; she would be happy with him. Clifford, however, spoke neither one way nor the other. He said little on any subject these days.

One evening, Alice and Leslie left a particularly hectic HSA meeting. The warm, gentle breath of the night was a welcome thing.

"Where's Cathy tonight?" Leslie asked.

"One of her friends at the war plant was hurt in an explosion. Cathy went to the hospital to see her."

"That's too bad. Cathy's quite faithful to the association for a youngster. Most kids of nineteen don't think beyond jitterbugging."

"Not Cathy. She feels deeply about other people's problems, always has. And it's out of sympathy for them that she always wants to help. Although, don't think she doesn't jitterbug." She smiled up at him, finding no answering smile in his drawn face that looked straight ahead of him. Had it only been last year they had met? His temples were graying. The tiny wrinkles at the corners of his eyes were deeper. She tucked her arm through his protectively, and shut her eyes briefly at the warm thrill. "It's a beautiful night," she said. "I'd like to walk for a while."

His features relaxed, and he smiled. "So would I, 'Mrs. H.' After tonight's meeting, it'll be good for us."

He often called her "Mrs. H." It was his way of preparing her for his proposal, she thought. But she was sure he would continue to call her that long after they were married.

"We're not going to think about the meeting," she said. Arm in arm, almost without speaking, they strolled through the Indian summer night. They walked as far as the river, stopping in the middle of the bridge. A soldier walked by, his battle shoes clumping the length of the bridge. Far below, a sailor and his girl were barely discernible walking along the river road. High above them an airplane hummed, its lights reflected in the muddy water below.

"Have you ever been kissed on a bridge?" Leslie asked softly as his arms closed around her. As always their kiss was very nearly passionless, very nearly unbearable in its breath-taking sweetness.

"Not before," she murmured, her ear close to his heart. She

saw the sailor and his girl disappear, a bend in the road and thick foliage blotting them from view. "You know, Leslie," she said, looking into his eyes, her hand lightly along the side of his face, "this is heaven — right here — right now."

The walk home was over much too quickly. The brown stone house loomed ahead of them, and Alice found her feet involuntarily moving more slowly. She heard a rush of footsteps behind her and half turned in the direction of the sound. She got a confused impression of a ridiculous "zoot" suit leaping toward her, a face that was not really a face, twisted with hate, looming over her. Then her knees buckled under the weight of a man's body. The stranger yanked her up before she touched the ground. His hand swooped toward her face, and she felt a swift sting. Her knees gave way again, and this time Leslie quickly released his hold on the struggling stranger to catch her.

There was blood on Leslie's coat, and her muddled mind wondered why. She wanted to cry out, to somehow put an end to this wordless nightmare of struggling and grunts, and bewilderment, but no sound came from her lips. It was the zoot-suited stranger who spoke, himself bewildered now, his eyes darting from one to the other of them in dismayed lack of recognition. "Oh, *excuse me*," he breathed. Then he fled.

Chapter XVI

Cathy worked in the laboratory of a munitions plant. She had disappointed the family by refusing to go to college for no better reason than that she didn't consider herself "college material." She was charming, and pretty in an unusual way. Her hair was the color of dark sand; it framed her oval face in short curls. Her skin was a delicate brown, her dark eyes full and deep set, her nose and mouth strongly chiseled. She thought quickly, but she much preferred not to think. One got results by appealing to her feelings rather than to her reason. Above all she liked to laugh. However, it was becoming increasingly difficult to laugh. The happy atmosphere at home was altered. Alice's accident was greatly to blame; she had but to close her eyes and the ugly newspaper headline appeared: SCHOOLTEACHER'S FACE SLASHED BY MISTAKE. But there was something more than that, deeper and less tangible.

Leslie had asked her to act as HSA secretary until Alice recovered. It was proving a great strain on top of the tiring war-schedule of seven days a week, nine hours each day that she worked. Finally, Leslie himself mentioned it as they were walking home from a meeting. He was thinner, if that were possible, more nervous.

"I'll be glad when Alice is completely well," he said. "I miss her terribly. Then, of course, I realize it's hard on you, taking her place with your working hours."

They had reached the brown stone steps, and Cathy felt a twinge of remorse, thinking how always before she had gone inside quickly, leaving Alice and Leslie a few minutes to themselves.

"Les—" he had objected to her calling him Mr. Hammond, probably visualizing his future as a member of the family. "There's . . . something I ought to tell you."

Whatever Cathy had to tell him wouldn't be good. There was sadness and fear in her eyes that searched his uncertainly. So there was more bad news. It didn't seem possible. He felt he couldn't stand to hear what she had to say. Still, from the depths of dread where her frightened words had plunged him, he was able to feel wretched for Cathy. Her charming laughter, once heard wherever she was, had become subdued and infrequent, and there was a constant shadow in her eyes. "What is it, Cathy?" He tried not to sound alarmed.

"Alice—is— Alice *is* completely well."

His hand caressed the roughness of the handrail. "Of course she is," he said. "I know the wound has healed, that is. But your mother said she wouldn't eat for quite a while, and naturally that weakened her. It'll take time for her to regain her strength." He was feeling relieved.

"You don't understand," Cathy spoke unevenly. "She isn't in bed anymore. She's well—all well." Then at the question on Leslie's face, "She doesn't want to see people. You know, she wouldn't see you after the bandage came off. Well, she doesn't want to see anybody. Not even us."

"But why not?"

"I don't know. I think it's—the scar. She stays in her room all the time, with the shades drawn; and she comes down to eat when everyone's in bed or something."

"That'll pass," Leslie replied after a moment of stunned silence. "She has to make a difficult adjustment, and this is one of the earlier stages."

"That's what we all thought. But the other day she sent for a machine."

"A machine?"

"One of those power sewing machines that they let people have. The company sends you the machine and the material and you sew at home instead of at the factory."

"Did she say why she did that?"

"No. But—I don't think she's going back to school."

"Nonsense." Leslie tried to make his voice sound reassuring, but he was finding it difficult to breathe. "Where did you get such a foolish notion? If it weren't quite so late, I'd go in and see her now. As it is, tell her I'll stop by tomorrow evening."

Cathy toyed with the idea of not telling Alice; of simply announcing Leslie's presence when he arrived. But the next afternoon she returned from work and went straight to her sister's room. Alice received her quietly, without looking up from the skirts she was seaming.

"Leslie asked me to tell you he'd be here tonight," Cathy said.

"I told you I didn't want to see anyone."

"Yes I know, but Leslie—"

"I don't want to see anyone—especially not Leslie."

"But—"

"Please don't say any more. I won't see him." Alice continued to seam skirts until Cathy, miserable and ill at ease, went away. Then she left the machine and stood before her mirror. The fading light gave but a hazy view of her features. She put on the electric light, and its harsh rays cruelly illumined her face. Only, it wasn't her face at all. She didn't look like that. The woman in the mirror was at least ten years older than she, ugly and hideously scarred. The ugly singularity of the scar spoke of a razor wound. It began just inside her hairline, crossed her eyebrow in a wide hairless gap, somehow skipped the eye itself to continue along the side of her face and come to an end at the line of her lip. It was "the mark of The Bottom," a keloid scar. One saw it everywhere. The moment of nightmarish unreality persisted. That woman wasn't she. She wasn't that woman. Then who was she? Where was she? She was sleeping. She would awaken in a moment covered with sweat from an overly long, horrible dream. Tomorrow she'd tell everyone about it, so glad that nothing had really happened to her.

Then her identity returned to her in an overwhelming flood of certainty. The woman in the mirror was Alice Hilton. *She* was

Alice Hilton. And something *had* happened to her. A man in a zoot suit, whom she didn't know, and who didn't know her, had sliced her face with a switch-blade razor. Her wound had healed, leaving her with the jagged "mark of The Bottom" on her face; robbing her of beauty and love. There would be no safe, relieved awakening for her tomorrow. This nightmare was forever.

She wondered if it were possible for this strange face to take on familiar aspects. Slowly she removed the hairpins from the knot in her hair. Her eyes burned dryly, and she ached physically, remembering the fireplace, the yarn rug, and Leslie's fingers in her hair. She parted it on the right side and combed it into a ring of small curls just above her shoulders—the way he liked it. Then she brushed it until it crackled and shone. Powder—lipstick — a touch of rouge which she had never used before, but which might now serve to subdue the scar. Eyebrow pencil, also unused before, she put on her brows, blackening the hairless gap where the scar seared the right one. She fastened a single drop pearl to each ear. Leslie had delighted in watching them dance and sparkle as she moved her head. He had given them to her last April on her birthday.

Slowly, hopefully, desperately, she raised her eyes to the mirror. The face there had indeed been transformed. Why, she looked like — quite consciously she withheld the thought for a moment — a *whore!* Coarse, wicked, vulgar, cheap — one after the other the adjectives crossed her mind—*and* ugly. She covered her face with her hands, blotting out the horrible thing in the mirror. Tears ran down her fingers; rouge, powder, and eyebrow pencil dissolved and ran together. She glimpsed her face now. It looked like something from a horror movie. In a spasm of revulsion she dropped her head to the dressing table, snatching at one of the pearl earrings. It fell to the floor, rolled a trifle, and lay there sparkling.

When Leslie arrived that evening Cathy met him and nervously explained that Alice still refused to see anyone.

"But tell her it's *I* who wish to see her," he said. Then she was forced to tell him that Alice had said she especially did not wish to see him. For a moment she thought he was going to cry. However, he picked up his hat, turned it around in his hands, then softly said goodnight.

Leslie did not give up easily. When Alice didn't answer his telephone calls, he wrote to her. Every day for months she received some kind of communication: a card — flowers — a letter begging her to see him. On her birthday in April he sent her a single strand of pearls that perfectly matched the earrings of last year. Shortly after this he received a brief note from her. She would see him the next evening at five o'clock.

Promptly at five he rang the doorbell. Cathy led him into the living room, where he supposed Alice would come. But in a few moments she returned to say that Alice would see him in her room. Cathy led him up the stairs and left him before the door of the back room on the second floor. He raised his arm to knock on the door that stood slightly open, and Alice spoke to him.

"Come in, Leslie."

The room was long and wide, and crossed by the shadows of dusk. At first he did not see her.

"Won't you sit down?" Her voice came from a shadow slightly to the right of the four windows at the far end of the room. Facing that way, he saw her dimly; the curtain blowing from the window sometimes concealed her entirely. Nevertheless, he could see that she was thinner. Her features were a hazy blur, but when the curtain moved away from her he could discern the outline of the scar. He took a few steps toward her, and halted as she stiffened.

"Alice—" He wanted to lead up to it gently, but there seemed to be no way of doing so. "I came here to ask you to marry me."

The curtain moved, blotting out the still form; moved again, revealing the scarred face immobile. "It isn't a recent idea. You must have known before," he said.

"Perhaps."

"Then—"

"The answer is no."

Leslie had expected difficulty, but he had been certain that face to face with Alice her determination would prove no match for his own. Now, here in this shadowy room, he wasn't quite so sure. Her voice was still and detached and unfamiliar. She herself seemed so.

"I need you, Alice. We need each other."

She allowed herself a dry laugh. "You need someone all right. But you don't need me. Let's not pretend that nothing has happened. I would be a hindrance to you now."

"Nothing *has* happened. We're the same two people, you and I—"

"Leslie—I've ignored your letters and gifts hoping that you

would discontinue them. However, it has been several months now, and they continue to arrive. I asked you here today in order to tell you personally that I do not wish to receive them."

"Listen to me, Alice." Though the words came with little difficulty, he felt that he was floundering. "Are you going to let an unfortunate accident ruin your whole life? It doesn't matter to me. I didn't fall in love with your face; I fell in love with you. I'm still in love with you. I feel now as you would feel if the situation were in reverse. Would it matter so much if my face were scarred instead of yours? Would you cease to love me?"

"No."

He paused, his confidence soaring. Her voice was as remote as ever, but he had gained a major point.

"Then, darling," he said softly, "marry me. Marry me."

"I wouldn't have ceased to love you if your face had been scarred. But I did cease to love you when mine was." He was totally unprepared for this. "I don't love you, Leslie. I don't love you, or anyone, or anything." The color receded from her face, making the scar more hideous even in the half light. The apathy disappeared, and her voice became ugly. "There is no love left in me—only hate. I hate The Bottom. I hate people—all of them. I especially hate the people around me. I hate the most high, the just, and almighty *God* who visited this fate upon me! But most of all—most of all I hate life. Life that hangs on when all else is dead!"

Leslie was subdued and silent. The room vibrated with hate; the lengthening shadows seemed its visual product.

"If you don't love me—" his chest heaved painfully, and his throat contracted. The words of this last desperate plea came with extreme difficulty, "Come back to the kids whom we both love. They love you, and they need you. No other teacher can fill your place."

There was a short pause, then her answer came, studied and venomous. "I don't care about the kids. They're damned, every last one of them!"

There was nothing left for him to say. This was a stranger speaking. Had he ever known her? He peered into the corner where she stood. The shadow had completely blotted out her face. Her form was dim, almost indiscernible, and headless. He turned, and stumbled on his way out.

Cathy was waiting at the foot of the stairway. She had been unable to move beyond this spot from which she could see the door of Alice's room as she hoped and feared for what was happening there. Praying that Leslie would come out smiling, successful where she and her mother had failed, Cathy clutched the banister at the sound of his footsteps. "Les—"

He brushed past her without speaking, and she saw that there were tears in his eyes.

Chapter XVII

"I've been halfway around the world, fought in three battles, spent six months in a German PW camp, and let me tell you, it sure feels funny to be back in this barber shop cutting hair, with everything exactly the same as before," Rocky said.

"Everything isn't as much the same as it seems," Ed answered.

"Practikly the same." Pa took an endless time to rise and creep ever so feebly to a seat in the sun.

"No, indeed," Ed insisted. "Take me. I'm here just like old times, but look what's happened to me since them times, though. I wasn't on no sight-seeing tour like you guys in the Army. The Navy won the war. And LSI[1] where I was is the toughest part of the Navy."

"The Navy won the war?" A man wearing a Marine uniform asked incredulously. "I still can't figure out what the Navy did. Every time you saw them they were in dry dock painting! You guys kill me. I enlisted with the Leathernecks because that's the only place to see action. We fight on land, on sea, *and* in the air."

"Man, you ain't saying *nothin'*! I got a Silver Star, and a Bronze Star, and the Purple Heart. How much action did *you* see? But we were talking about how much things had changed," Ed said, unfairly depriving the Marine of the opportunity of answering. "We're sitting here like old times, but don't forget Chestnut won't be coming in to sit with us—I hear he burned up alive on Guadalcanal; and Frankie got it in Europe, nobody knows how; and there's Lovejoy, psycho over in Lions, New Jersey."

"I didn't mean changes like that," Rocky said. "Those are changes in people who went to war. It's the people who stayed here I was talking about, The Bottom itself. The bums are still hanging on the corner—the same ones. Everybody I left here looks the same, talks the same, they get their hair cut the same way."

---

1. Landing Ships Infantry.

"If it comes to that, a haircut costs you eighty-five cents now," Ed said, picking up a newspaper. "Who's this paid fifteen hundred dollars for a wedding? Somebody Crawford . . ."

"That's them same hard-luck Crawfords," somebody said.

"Hard-luck? With fifteen hundred bucks to waste on a wedding?" The conversation became general.

"How did they get money?"

"Oh, some of the children are in the service, some of them got good war jobs."

"Let me get a look at that gal." This was the Marine; he looked over Ed's shoulder at the picture. "Oh Baby, why didn't I get to you first? Is that the old buzzard she married?"

"No. This one over here. That other one's her Pa. Says here he give her away."

"I wouldn't have let that rascal come to the wedding after what he did," Ed said.

"I don't guess you heard. That Mrs. Crawford took that man back the day he got out of jail."

"Oh, no! You hear that, Rocky? I never would have believed it. What did they do with Esther?" Ed asked his informer.

"She's still there. She's real fat, and sloppy, doesn't say much, no boyfriends or nothing. She's older than this girl that just got married, or the other one that's married, but she looks a whole lot older than she is."

"Read about the wedding," Rocky said.

"Oh, I can't read all this. Says here what she had on—Jesus! Could they see her under all that? They had the reception in a ballroom, no less. Had an orchestra, entertainers—you still think everything's the same around here?"

"Not hardly. Where're they living?"

"Says here they have 'an apartment at the home of the groom.'"

"Yes sir! 'Three rooms and *private* bath,' Mrs. Crawford told my wife," the informed gentleman contributed.

"What else is in that paper?" Rocky asked.

"Here's something about Saint Luke's and Reverend Hilton. They think he might be going to give up the church. Let's see; it says they had a near split last year. 'Some of the members accused the pastor of being a smug, domineering tyrant.' Gee, that's a surprise."

"Not to me it ain't. He's done some changing, that man. Money don't agree with some folks, and he's one of 'em," someone said.

"They tell me he treats those people at Saint Luke's shameful. Won't let them say a word. Runs the church by himself. I heard he insults them in the pulpit, then tells them, if they don't like it there, go where they like it. And he used to be a right guy. He ain't the same as he used to be, you can bet on that. Ever since he sold that store — and even before that, 'cause he stopped Pa from going there."

"Is that right, Pa?"

Pa looked around feebly. A gray film clouded his eyes, and his hair was cotton-white. "Said it didn't look good for me to be settin' 'round all the time," he said.

"Damn! And you give him his start."

"That's gratitude for you."

"Whatever happened to that oldest girl of his?" someone asked after a time.

"Nothing. Not since she was cut that time anyway. She stays up in her room at the house. I hear she acts kinda queer."

Chapter XVIII

The telephone was ringing. Clifford lifted the receiver and spoke into it in the impressive resonant bass he often assumed. "Reverend Hilton."

"Rev'ren Hilton, this is Mrs. Crawford." As always Mrs. Crawford's voice came loudly over the telephone. Across the room Martha heard her distinctly. "I want you to come over. Esther's taken real sick."

"I'm sorry," Clifford rolled the word, "the Reverend isn't in."

"What's that?"

"Reverend Hilton isn't here. He went out of town on business." There was an extended silence. Then: "All right. I'll call later on in the week."

There was a slow click as Mrs. Crawford hung up, and Clifford followed suit. Martha turned on him incredulously, this stranger to whom she was married. He had surrounded her and their children in comfort and luxury. Then he had drawn into himself, saying little, never participating in the life of the family. What good were two cars and a summer home when one had no husband? Often she remembered wistfully the years when they hadn't known if they'd eat the next day, but she'd been his "Little Girl." They had loved together and lived together. He had been husband and lover. There had been no life apart from the one they shared. Now, his thoughts, his activities, his life were his own, walled in by silence so formidable it imposed a like silence on her and on the children. To them he was scarcely more than a stranger whom they dared not question, though he often acted questionably. Martha saw that he didn't expect to be questioned now. As she stood staring at him, he turned to leave the room.

"In all the years we've been married, I've never known you to lie," she said angrily. He paused for a moment, apparently considering an answer, then without speaking he continued on his way. He went up the stairs and into his room. Without knowing that she did it, she followed him.

"I didn't hear you knock," he said quietly. Suddenly, resentment that had smoldered for years flared. She slammed the door, jarring the white telephone beside his bed. They would quarrel. She knew, and found herself welcoming it. He looked at her sharply, unaccustomed to her anger.

"I said," she repeated as though there had been no interruption, "I've never known you to lie."

"You're offended?"

"Mrs. Crawford needed you."

"Mrs. Crawford always needs me. I'm sick to death of it. 'This one's in jail; that one's been hurt; the other one's been murdered.' "

"You used to enjoy being able to help."

"I used to be a fool. These people are beyond help. Only a fool could fail to see it."

"How can you, of all people, say that?"

"I, of all people, am fit to say it. I know! From twenty-five years of 'helping' in The Bottom, I know."

"Leave The Bottom out of it. Mrs. Crawford needs you because Esther is sick. That has *nothing* to do with The Bottom."

"I didn't mean to imply that it did. That's the old excuse, the old scapegoat. Blame everything on The Bottom. The Bottom doesn't make the people in it, they make The Bottom."

"And *they* are beyond help? Why?!" Her eyesight was blurred with driving emotion as she sought to wrest his innermost thoughts from him. She must draw him out. He must talk and talk until he was stripped of some of the mystery surrounding him.

"They can't surmount their racial heritage, their limited imagination, their inferior intelligence—"

"*Racial heritage?*" She was incredulous. "If there *is* such a thing, it certainly doesn't result in inferior this, and limited that. Given a chance, Negroes equal any other men on the face of the earth!"

"Don't tell me anything about the Negroes!" He pronounced the word "Nigrers." And now he began to look unfamiliar and even dangerous to her. His eyes flashed, his words tumbled over each other, and he executed a maniacal jig as he talked. "Don't I know them? Haven't I given my whole life to them? Give them food and clothes and soap one week. The next week they're hungry and naked and *stink*, having sold the soap for liquor or worse. Try giving them money to help them out of a rut; the next week they come back to borrow more. Open clubs and gymnasiums—and baseball diamonds like that fool Hammond wants to do—the crap game goes on!"

The impact of his words dazed her. Her answer was instinctive, requiring little thought, but she felt that she was losing control of herself. "That's true of the Negroes here in The Bottom, but it's just as true of the Chinese in Chinatown! Every slum area in the world is exactly like every other slum area—no better, no worse. Race doesn't make one particle of difference."

"I've had more dealings with Nigrers than you have. I wasted my time, my money, my life trying to improve this 'race'—as you call it—of talking gorillas. And that's all they are! They're incapable of one sensible thought, one decent emotion."

Watching Clifford's frenzied jig, his glazed, bright eyes that didn't really see her, it occurred to Martha that he might be mad. "How about the people at Saint Luke's? They've certainly loved and respected you," she said.

"Love! Respect! They don't understand the meaning of the words. I *loathe* them; their groveling, their vying with each other for the privilege of being my lackey! There isn't a white congregation like that in the world. There isn't, and there never could be—never. Never! They have too much sense. But Nigrers were made for bowing and scraping and grinning, and carrying out someone else's commands, with never an independent thought in their stupid gorilla minds. When they're sick let them die! They should never have been born. To die is the next best thing that could happen to them. It took me twenty-five years to realize that you can't civilize them, you can't teach them sense, you can't even teach them morals. Those things belong to white men. Nigrers will never have them."

"Since all Negroes are immoral gorillas, I'd like to know where that leaves you."

"I'm not a Nigrer. The law says I am, but it's a lie! I have Nigrer blood, unfortunately, but it's in the minority—I traced it back. I'm more white than Nigrer. White and Indian," he said proudly.

"*Indian!* Since when? And now *Indians* are superior!" she taunted, ignoring the stab from her conscience. "But anything is better than being a Negro, isn't it? And your white blood, how did you get it? I'll tell you how. Your moral white grandfather raped your immoral slave grandmother, who couldn't help herself!"

"I'm glad he did! Otherwise I'd have been just like the rest of the Nigrers. As it is, I have enough of his blood in me to overcome hers."

Something happened inside Martha. It was like a bridge collapsing, a dam giving way. She straightened up to keep from visibly slumping, and turned toward the door. Clifford's voice halted her.

"Martha—" She turned quietly, standing straight and still. "I hadn't planned to tell you just now, but since you're here we may as well get it over with. I'm planning to leave Saint Luke's. That shouldn't surprise you. I'm sick of Nigrers. I find them disgusting and revolting. When I leave Saint Luke's, I'll be rid of my last connection with them. Then, there's the matter of my life here . . . with you. Well, it must have been apparent to you for a long time now that we no longer have anything in common. We're not old. We still have the chance to make a new life apart. The wise thing to do is to separate legally before it's too late. I'm speaking of—divorce."

Martha thought it strange that she felt nothing. She wasn't surprised. She didn't feel wronged. "You'll be well taken care of," he was saying. "The house is yours, this one and the summer one. You'll never have to worry about money."

She waited, expecting to feel something. Nothing happened. Clifford seemed to have no more to say. Once more she approached the door. "There's something else," he said. "You're entitled to know." She turned her head, her hand still closed over the doorknob, her eyes squinting, feeling strained without the glasses to which they had become accustomed. "As soon as I'm free I'm going to be married. She's Joan Alexander. I don't think you know her." Martha's face relaxed. It was as though an invisible hand passed over her features smoothing away the squint, relaxing the tired mouth. She looked down at her hand as it tightened on the doorknob. Joan Alexander? Joan Alexander. Ah yes. The newspaper reporter, almost two years ago. She had come to Clifford for a story, something about Christmas baskets for the poor. Martha had seen her twice. Red hair, well shaped, not pretty, but not unattractive, less than thirty, well dressed. A white girl.

"I'm glad," Martha said. She turned the knob gently and closed the door quietly behind her.

That night it rained. The rain slapped the window panes monotonously. Outside, the cold blackness of the July night resounded with the sobbing, tragic moans: *"M-a-r-y . . . M-A-R-Y! . . . M-a-r-y . . . M-a-r-yeeeeeeeeeee. . . ."*

A train whistled mournfully.

Martha lay in her bed, sleepless and lonely.

Chapter XIX

Leslie was a different man after he visited Alice in her room. His hearty, monosyllabic laugh became a thing of the past. He was morose and bitter. It tugged at Cathy's heart to see him so. She wanted to help him, not knowing how. He invariably rebuffed her awkward attempts. There was but one answer — Alice. One day she steeled herself, quieted her fears, and went to Alice.

"If you could see him now, harried and — and irritable. He hardly seems the same person. He doesn't look well. HSA is famous since that last court case. It brought new members, a great many of them white, some out-of-towners even. Anyway, there's more work than ever, and it's all Les thinks about. I don't think he eats or sleeps or does anything as he should. If he keeps on this way he's going to make himself sick — or worse. I've tried to tell him, but — he needs you, Alice. I don't think anyone else can help him."

Alice listened intently. Her face was calm and inscrutable. She watched her sister's face, lined with concern, naively revealing. Her heart lurched queerly, and she marveled that her expression did not change. *Cathy! Little Cathy!* At last she was gone, downcast, dejected, depressed.

Alice fell across her narrow bed, pummeling the pillows, weeping bitterly.

* * * * *

That night Leslie's restless eyes fastened themselves on Cathy. She was quietly, intently taking notes on the meeting that was in progress; notes she had hoped Alice would be taking tonight. There was something forlorn about her. She had grown sober in a way that ill became her. Her childish levity, once so prevalent, showed itself rarely, only to be quickly dampened by conflicting dispiritedness. Poor kid! There must be something he could do to help her. His helplessness weighed heavily upon him. She raised her head, and he shifted his gaze slightly in order not to see the shadow in her eyes. It was a useless gesture. He saw it anyway. It occurred to him that he was always seeing Cathy's eyes. He saw them now, though he wasn't looking at them; they followed him home; they followed him beyond his waking world; he woke to find himself gazing into them through the darkness. Why? Why! *Why?*

The answer thundered; startling not because he hadn't known it, but because he *had* known it long ago. The inkwell on the table near his hand went crashing to the floor. *She was just a child!*

When the meeting was over, Cathy, still tormented by disturbing thoughts, waited at the rear of the auditorium for Leslie. As always, she had finished first, but it seemed to her he was taking an unusually long time. She was tired, a cold night wind was blowing outside, and she wished she were already at home.

Leslie, turning around in circles at the table up front, spoke an extra amount of time with each of the women gathered around him. There was Jane Loeffler, Miss Granberg — the others were all white. Vague, indefinite resentment stirred Cathy. It had been this way for a long while. Every new victory, or even defeat, for HSA brought more of them. They surrounded Leslie; admiring him, adoring him, walling him in. One by one the women who were not white dropped into the background, feeling unequal to the competition. *I often wondered why so many "big" colored men married them,* Cathy thought. *By the time they're really important there's probably nobody else around to marry.*

323

"Oh, Miss Hilton." A silver-haired little lady approached her briskly. "Mr. Hammond asked me to take you home in my car."

"That'll be nice," Cathy said. "He doesn't seem to be ready yet, though."

"Oh, he isn't coming with us. He'll be going home later, I guess."

"Later?" Cathy was confused. It had never occurred to her that she could leave without Leslie, or he without her. Someone might drive them, or they might walk along with other people, but they always left together. The habit had persisted unbroken since the days when he, Alice, and she had walked home together.

"It certainly is cold," the little lady said, shifting the gears with difficulty. Cathy hadn't felt the cold, although now she supposed that was why her face was burning. Her mind was wrestling with a slippery, elusive problem. Something was wrong and she didn't quite know what. It was a problem that was to grow.

* * * * *

To Leslie the realization that he was in love with Cathy was a source of great remorse. How could he have allowed himself to love her? He tormented himself continually. She was a child of twenty-one; he was thirty-three. When had he ceased to love Alice? Had he ever loved her? Certainly being with Alice was unlike being with anyone else in the world. She had brought him peace, relief, welcome rest. The same had never — would never — be true of Cathy. Alice had given; he had taken. He had taken from her selfishly, gladly, giving nothing. But to Cathy, who meant not peace, but torment, not rest, but agitation, he wanted to give. He wanted to make her laugh again, to take the shadow out of her eyes. He wanted to make her happy. If only he could take all the sadness out of her life, wall her in from future sadness, encircle her life with his protective love!

Strangely, in view of this, he grew increasingly less considerate of her. He wouldn't love her, he told himself. Love could be killed, *should* be killed when it was as wrong as this. More often than not, after HSA meetings he was "busy" at the front table with the ubiquitous circle of white women, who now aroused in Cathy jealousy — bitter, unreasonable, unreasoning; and he sent her home without him. There were other things, small things, peculiar and unfathomable even to him. He was cruelly polite at one time, unkindly inattentive at another. Why had he behaved so, he asked himself afterward, the pain of her bewildered, hurt eyes haunting him, hurting him still. He seemed unable to help himself, to have no control over his actions. The ever present shadow deepened in Cathy's eyes. Now rimmed by faint hollows. He had put them there. He knew it when her eyes followed him with that bewildered, lost expression — when her tentative, pathetic gestures of friendliness were repeated despite his rebuffs. He had hurt her. He wanted only to love her, to shelter her from the hurt of a sometimes brutal world. He had hurt her; the knowledge was a raw wound in his heart.

He had failed, he told himself, walking in a mad circle about the living room of his apartment. He had wanted to spare her pain by estranging himself, but he had hurt her anyway. He had sought to kill his love; avoided her spiritually and physically. *Kill it?* He flung himself on a chair, covering his face with his hands, the nails digging into his flesh. He had only whetted his craving for her. It had become a live, wild, uncontrollable thing, savage and demanding. Throttling his mind, usurping his life, claiming his soul. This had been his sole accomplishment.

He was wrong. He had accomplished something else. A few days later there was a knock on his door. He opened it, and Cathy came in. While he stood immobile, his weight against the door, she slipped off her coat and dropped it over the back of the sofa.

"You shouldn't be here," Leslie said at last, making a move toward her. She moved away from him. How often she had wondered what this room was like. Now she took it all in, touching things thoughtfully. There was a clock on the shining mahogany desk in the corner. She picked it up, holding it gently between her hands. It wasn't running; she wound it slowly and listened to its soft tick before setting it down. When she turned around, Leslie caught his breath. Her pale blue dress, made of some soft stuff, and her short sandy curls, blown by the spring wind, accentuated her youth. But something in her face set his mind seething. He smashed the fist of one hand into the palm of the other and turned away.

"Les." Her voice halted his footsteps, turned him around. "There's something I have to tell you. I think perhaps you've known it — but I just found out. When things changed between us, when you began to be a little — unkind — and I saw so little of you,

I felt like I was dying inside. Even then it took me such a long time to realize why. I'm in love with you."

He struggled to control his features while she searched his face, seeing there the answer to all her questions. He loved her then. She waited for him to speak, to tell her so. But he said nothing; and Alice appeared between them, poignant, nearly visible. Each of them felt her, her arms outstretched, pushing them apart.

"Feeling as I do," Cathy said somewhat desperately, "I don't think I should see you at all anymore. I'm going to resign as secretary of HSA."

Again she waited for him to break his silence, feeling that he must speak now. Leslie did not trust himself to speak. He lifted the clock from the desk, knowing that her eyes were boring into him, and its soft ticking filled the room. She was right, he told himself. Now that this thing was in the open, the situation was impossible, with the right and the wrong of it forever clashing between them; drawing—irresistibly, inevitably; driving—madly, relentlessly. Yes, she would have to leave HSA; it was best. He set the clock aside, preparing to tell her so, but when he looked at her the words wouldn't come. He clenched his teeth, and the muscles of his face worked powerfully, conveying his answer without words. Then Cathy saw a glint of the old unkindness in his eyes. She turned and almost ran to the door, snatching her coat as she passed the sofa.

But somehow he was there before her. His arms closed around her, and for a moment she couldn't breathe. The rough wool of his suit scratched her face; she wanted to laugh and cry at the sweetness of it.

"Oh, Cathy! Cathy! It isn't your fault—or mine." His hand was tracing her features, not gently, but heavily, as though her face were an art treasure seen for the first time. His thumb halted at the corner of her mouth, and his eyes fixed themselves hungrily there. Blood thundering in his ears, he ground his lips on hers with all the passion of self-inflicted deprivation. He released her and picked up her coat from the floor. Then he sat on the sofa, his eyes screwed tightly shut, his head pressed against clenched hands.

"It's Alice, isn't it?" Cathy said, sitting beside him. He turned, clutching her fiercely, trying to blot out thoughts of her youth, her extreme youth, with his savage kisses. Trying to blot out memories of Alice: Alice's face, radiant on the bridge, Alice's face, scarred, in a darkened room. Alice's face . . . Alice's face . . . Alice's face ... Somewhere in the dark recesses of his mind he was afraid of frightening Cathy. But there was no fear in the lips that answered his, in her tiny nails that stung his flesh. He heard the soft material of her dress rip as she strained toward him. The sound was an alarming danger signal. His hands clamped on her shoulders, forcing her body away from him, until she understood. Then his arms went around her gently, his head sank to her breast. Fighting the passion that boiled in him, he was still. Through it all the awareness of Alice had never left him. He felt that in the ultimate consummation of their love she would be there.

"Yes," he said at last, "it's Alice."

"Les..." She hesitated a moment, and he thought how he liked to hear her call him that. "She'll have to be told—first."

"I'll tell her," he said heavily.

"No." Her voice was soft, fighting the tears. "I will."

Chapter XX

Things were different when you grew up, Clifford realized. When she was a very little girl she had sat on Papa's lap, and twisted the curls in his hair; and she had been proud because her name was the same as his; and he had tossed her high in the air while Mama protested that he played too roughly. Later on he had taken them all for car rides, and helped with her homework, and talked to her about life. But Papa was gone now. He didn't care about them anymore. Perhaps he never had, or how could he have left them? Her mother, Alice, and Cathy were silent, unfathomable strangers. It all went to prove you couldn't believe in people. They changed, or weren't what you thought they were in the first place. Who would have thought Papa would do such a thing, or that the others could become such complete strangers.

It all made Clifford feel devil-may-care, and reckless. It was nothing to her what they did, how they felt. When you were little, families and homes were sacred. But when you grew up—that's when you found out. *Home* was just a house. Her family was a lot of people she didn't know. They were nothing to her; she was nothing to them. Then let them remember that! Her life was her own. Nobody was going to dictate to her how to live it like her mother was always trying to do. "You must go to college, Clifford ... You must be in before eleven, Clifford." But worst of all were the restrictions placed on where she could go, and with whom, lest she come in contact with "the wrong kind of people." She was damned sick and tired of that phrase. "You can't go there, Clifford . . . the wrong kind of people . . . You can't go *here*, Clifford . . . the wrong kind of people . . . the wrong kind of people . . ." Damn. Damn! *Damn!* There was perverse pleasure in thinking the forbidden word.

Clifford turned down Westminster Avenue instinctively, and her step slowed. She had stopped by Jean's house on the way from school, just to postpone going home, but it hadn't helped much. In a way it was worse than going home. Jean was disgusting. She had succumbed to the environment of her slovenly, almost stupid husband, and her in-laws with whom she lived. Clifford had been repulsed by her soiled dress, the thick roll of flesh about her middle, the omnipresent book; today a coarse novel, tomorrow a literary gem. She read indiscriminately, pointlessly, while her children ran about dirty and ill-cared for.

"You don't *have* to have children if you don't want them," Clifford had once said, half-resenting, half-pitying the hapless youngsters. But Jean had shrugged and said she was too young to understand.

Clifford reached the inevitable brown stone steps and took them two at a time. She flung her books on the flower stand in the hall and started for the kitchen. Her mother appeared from nowhere. "That isn't the place to leave your books, Clifford. You're late," she questioned. So, right away she started! Clifford clamped her thin lips together, gathered her books from the table, and started away.

"Clifford," Martha said patiently, "why are you late?"

Clifford whirled at the foot of the stairs. "I stopped at Jean's for fifteen and one-half minutes," she said impudently. "I don't see why you insist on treating me like a baby. I won't stand for it! I'm seventeen, old enough to be married, to be a mother, to do anything; and I won't be timed and restricted like a child."

"I don't mean to time or restrict you like a child," Martha reasoned. "I've explained to you often enough that when you stop off this way I have no way of knowing what happened to you. It doesn't matter how old, or how grown one is. I, myself, never leave the house without telling one of you where I'm going, and when to expect me back."

Clifford stared relentlessly at her mother, then without further comment tramped up the stairs. When she turned at the head of the staircase, she glimpsed her mother's face peering after her, strained, nervous and worried. An indefinite pain clutched Clifford. She wanted to run down the stairs and throw her arms around her mother, to kiss the troubled expression from her face, the sorrow from her eyes. But her feet continued unhesitatingly, resolutely, until she was in her room. Why was she feeling this way because her mother seemed hurt? She couldn't let herself be soft. She, herself, must learn to understand that her life was her own. Her mother was merely the instrument that nature had used to bring her here, and there was no cause for sentiment in that. And there was no cause for love.

"Live for yourself," she told her reflection in the mirror. "When you love people, you get hurt." And somehow she was thinking of Papa, and blinking back tears.

* * * *

She picked up the invitation from her dresser — the invitation that said Sparkle Beauty Products was inviting her to a party, given in honor of the winners of the Sparkle beauty contest for beauticians. Her beautician, Gertrude, had sent her the invitation with the scrawled notation that she had won first prize, so would Clifford please try to come. But Clifford couldn't make up her mind to go; to flaunt the Hilton tradition and cross briefly into that other world. All week long she had been telling herself that her life was her own, but she remained unconvinced, and the party was tonight. The mirror reflected her soft, black skin, her even features, her straight black hair, as she continued to gaze at the tiny white card. Here was an opportunity to see what the outside world was like.

Thoughtfully, Clifford lay down the invitation. She could say she was going to a movie. That would mean she couldn't stay long. But even so, suppose the family found out — her mother, Cathy. What then? Clifford's gentle brown eyes hardened. The sweet child's mouth came together firmly. Let them find out! She was tired of being sheltered and protected. Their loving care was costing her — her life. Why, she was seventeen years old, and as innocent as a baby! She'd be dead before you knew it, and she had never been *anywhere*. All her life she had missed out on dances and parties, and moonlight boat rides, because she might meet "the wrong kind of people" — people from The Bottom. Well, she lived in The Bottom — had always lived here. If the people were good enough to live among, they were good enough to live with. Her sisters might stay here and mold away, never knowing what life was about, if they wished. She wouldn't. The Bottom was alive with danger, but anything was better than dying of old age at seventeen!

With one swift motion she caught all of her hair at the top of her head and held it there. Yes, she looked older this way. . . .

Chapter XXI

The Haven was a neighborhood "beer joint," indistinguishable from the hundreds of its kind that cluttered The Bottom; The Haven Ball Room was a "hole in the wall" just behind it. Here the young sought entertainment, the old sought youth, and the frustrated sought release.

When Clifford arrived at eight, she was scarcely able to push through the door of the Ball Room. "Come right in, there's always room for one more. Here's a door prize for you." The man shoved a jar of Sparkle Hair grower into Clifford's hands, ignoring the invitation she extended. "Do you belong at the reserved tables?"

"I really don't know. My hairdresser invited me — Mrs. Brown."

"You belong at the first table, all the way up front."

Clifford began to push her way through the crowd. The distance to the table seemed to grow. Finally she reached it, and Gertrude was there, smiling.

"Glad you could come, Clifford. Here, sit down." Clifford squeezed around to the far side of the table to sit beside Gertrude.

"Do you know everyone? This is my husband. Fix a highball for her, Frank, while I introduce her to the others."

"I — I'm not quite used to drinking," Clifford said. "Make the highball weak, please."

"Yes, of course."

When she had been introduced around, she settled back in her corner with the highball that Frank had said would be weak. This was the first opportunity she had to observe her surroundings. It was infernally hot, for there were no windows to open. Her eyes smarted from the acrid smell of whiskey and smoke and overheated bodies. The room was small. At one time it had been the kitchen and dining room of a private home. By craning her neck, she could see through a small doorway to what had been the living room, and was now The Haven. The "reserved" table at which she sat was one of two long tables that ran along one side of the room. On the other side of the room was a bar. There was less than three feet of space between the bar and the tables. A five-piece orchestra occupied the stage, which once had been half a shed kitchen. The other half was taken up by two cubby-holes, crudely marked "MENS" and "LADIES." People were everywhere: on circular stools around the bar, on the edge of the platform, behind the bar, in every inch of the narrow aisle.

A heavy sinking sensation of guilt and fear settled at the pit of Clifford's stomach. It was to grow sickeningly all during the evening. She sipped her highball, and stifled a cough, just as the music the band had been playing ceased.

"Ah, yes. Ah, yes!" The master of ceremonies stepped forward. He was a man in his late thirties, wearing an extreme "zoot" suit, with a head full of long, gummy hair plastered to his scalp. He looked as though he had run the gamut of vice, but his voice was so refined that it seemed misplaced in him.

"Can the boys play?" he bellowed.

"Yeah, man!" the crowd answered him.

"Well, tell them about it!" A deafening shout went up.

"Well, all right then! Folks, your host tonight is The House of Sparkle. Your M.C. is Harold Harold. Eat, drink and be very merry. *Everything* is free, *everybody's* happy, for The House of Sparkle is giving a party. An' lemme tell y'all somethin'." Suddenly he rolled his eyes, pushed his mouth off, and lapsed into an atrocious vernacular, made more atrocious by the natural refinement of his voice. "They knows jus' how to give a party, too." The narrow room resounded with hearty laughter.

"All right. All right. I'm just Harold Harold, but I'm feeling mighty good tonight. In fact, have you heard the news? I'm a mighty man!" At once the orchestra began to play, and the whole house began to chant in complete abandonment.

> *Have you heard the news,*
> *There's good rockin' tonight!*
> *I'm gonna hol' my baby tight as I can,*

*Tonight she'll know I'm a mighty, mighty man,
Have you heard the news,
There's good rockin' tonight!*

They rocked their bodies and banged their hands together. They pounded the floor with their feet until the flimsy building shook.

*Meet me in a hurry behind the barn,
Don't be 'fraid, I'll do you no harm,
I want you to bring my rockin' shoes,
'Cause tonight I'm gonna rock away all my blues,
Have you heard the news,
There's good rockin' tonight!*

*Deacon Jones, an' Elder Brown,
Two of 'em sick an' can't skip town,
They'll be there jus' wait an' see,
Stompin' and jumpin' at the jamboree,
Have you heard the news,
There's good rockin' tonight!*

*Sweet Lorraine, Sioux City Sue,
Sweet Georgia Brown, Caldonia, too,
They'll be there, shouting like mad,
Oh, Sisters and Brothers, ain't you glad—
Yes, we'll rock tonight!
Hoy! Hoy! We'll rock tonight!
Hey! Hey! We'll rock tonight!*

A sad-faced little Jewish man weaved about with a decanter of whiskey, offering to fill all empty glasses.

"That's Mr. Sparkle," Gertrude whispered in Clifford's ear. "He's always giving something like this."

Clifford did not answer. Her eyes were fastened fearfully on a man standing on top of the bar. He was focusing a flash-bulb camera.

"Turn your head," Gertrude ordered. "They're taking pictures for the paper."

"The *paper?*" Clifford was terrified. This possibility had never entered her mind.

"I don't like it any better than you do," Gertrude said excitedly. "This is the first time I've ever been in a hole like this in my life, and they want to advertise it! Me, a respectable businesswoman. If

I had known this, they could have *kept* first prize – Duck!" The camera flashed.

"Yes, yes, yes." The song was over, and Harold was speaking. "Y'all kep' sayin' rockin.' Ain' s'pose to be rockin.' S'pose to be – " The piano player jumped up and clamped a hand over Harold's mouth, to the uproarious delight of the audience. "All right, all right. I'm just Harold Harold. Play, boys, play." Once more the music began.

A boy, slight of build, who appeared to be somewhat younger than Clifford, stepped forward on the platform. He was blowing a brand new saxophone. The instrument slowly distinguished itself from the others until they only formed an obscure background for it. At the first plaintive, whispering note, the men in the narrow aisle clutched the nearest woman in an attempt to dance.

"How in the world can they dance standing in one spot? Look at that faye boy getting his kicks! No matter where you go, you'll find them." Gertrude directed Clifford's gaze to a bespectacled white lad in the midst of the dancers.

"Oh, yes."

"There's the man with the camera again. He's trying to get a picture of us," Gertrude warned. "Sit back in your seat."

The beat of the music was changing. The delicate, sentimental strains gave way to a strong, steady rhythm, then to a fast, wild, savage bleat that found ample response in the feet, the hands, the bodies of the hearers. On and on the saxophonist played. He might have been born with the horn in his mouth.

"He's just a kid," Clifford whispered to Gertrude.

"They're all kids."

"But, I thought there was a law – "

"There *is* a law!"

"He's been playing too long. He ought to stop." Clifford spoke anxiously. Still, the boy played on; and in spite of her growing discomfort, despite her concern for him, she must keep time with her toe. He played until glistening sweat rolled into his eyes, down his cheeks, onto the floor, and Harold Harold must wipe his face for him, and adjust the dark glasses that he wore. He played until a dark, wet circle of perspiration grew outward from the center of his back, and spread until the whole shirt was wet and sticking to him. Now Harold Harold must wring out the handkerchief and wipe his face again. He played until saliva driveled from the mouth of the horn; until every jagged, heaving breath from his frail body was a jagged, heaving breath from his audience.

When finally the last note died away, the audience was spent. "Do you know who this is?" Harold pointed to the retiring saxophonist. "This is little Jimmy Shultz. Say something to the folks, Jimmy."

Jimmy stood up, visibly exhausted, mopping his face. He spoke in an immature, winded voice. "There isn't much I can say. I'll introduce you to the boys. This is James Williams, Johnny Rogers, Bobby Mason, and Mat Brown. We're all boys from 'round the neighborhood. We get together and practice wherever we can. We aren't professional show-men like Harold Harold, but we hope to be someday."

"Just keep on blowing that horn, boy!" someone shouted. "They don't have anything like you in the big name bands."

"The boys are going places. I'm sure of it." Harold spoke above the noise. "They can't lose with the stuff they use. Right now we have another treat for you. You all know Baby Zelda. You've followed her career ever since her days on the radio with the Colored Kiddie Hour. Well, Baby Zelda is in the house tonight. She's come all the way here just to do a number for you. Isn't that grand? Give her a hand as she comes up here to sing."

Zelda was twenty-two years old, and hard lines of ill-acquired wisdom were beginning to show in her face. As yet they did not detract from her appearance. In fact, they added strangely to her sensual type of beauty. She was dressed simply, as were most of the women present, in a well-fitted peasant skirt and blouse. Her legs were bare, and her bleached blonde hair was piled on top of her head.

The band was playing the introduction as Zelda sprang onto the platform, planted her feet wide apart, and began to hunch her shoulders, and snap her fingers. A very drunk little man, with wrinkled skin and frizzled, white hair lurched forward to stare.

"She ain't got on no brassiere," he said, and reached out to paw her. Zelda side-stepped.

"And no girdle either, Pop," she drawled huskily. "I find they get in the way."

A roar went up as the song began. Her strong, low voice had no beauty, but like everything else about her it was sensual. She sang in an excited, frenzied way.

That's all right baby, baby that's all right for you,
That's all right baby, baby that's all right for you,
Treat me low down and dirty, yes, that's the way you do.

I love to hear my baby call my name,
I love to hear my baby call my name,
He calls it so easy and oh, so doggone plain.

Meet me in The Bottom, baby, bring my boots and shoes,
Yes, meet me in The Bottom, baby, bring my boots and shoes,
Hurry, hurry baby, I ain't got no time to lose.

Let's drink some mash, an' talk some trash this mornin',
Let's drink some mash, an' talk some trash this mornin',
I wanna be lovin' you when the rooster crows at dawnin'.

'Cause I love you, baby, better than I do myself,
Yes, I love you, baby, better than I do myself,
And if you ever leave me I don't want nobody else!

Now Zelda closed her eyes and shivered. Still with her eyes closed, she removed first one, then the other of her high-heeled shoes, and tossed them behind her to stand shivering in her bare feet. She seemed to be holding some invisible part of herself very still, while the long shiver stole over her body until every part of her moved. The crowd yelled. The white-haired, little man stretched out his arms and started for her. Someone yanked him back.

Zelda's dance elicited uncouth noises and obscene expressions from the audience. She wrung, and squealed, twisted and groaned, jerked and grunted. Hairpins tinkled on the floor, as her hair fell down her back and in her face. She dropped to her knees and shivered. Then she lay on the floor. She moaned, and gasped, and wallowed in imitation of a snake, hips and stomach rolling. Then came the long, endless shiver, and she lay still.

The old man broke away from his captor and would have joined Zelda on the floor, if Harold Harold hadn't grabbed him. "If you touch her, I'll kill you," he said and shoved the old fellow back.

Zelda shivered once more, and the old man began to cry weakly, reaching for her through the restraining arms of his friends. One more long, provocative shiver, and the dance was over. Harold Harold helped her to her feet. Her clothes were disordered and soiled. She had smeared her lipstick. Her straggling blond hair was streaked with dirt it had wiped up from the floor. Still, the old man blubbered softly and reached for her.

Clifford felt sick. The gnawing, nauseated feeling of fear and guilt gorged up and threatened to choke and smother her.

"Later, later. She's tired now," Harold said to the people who clamored for more. "Somebody give the little man his bottle so he can stop crying, and we'll go on with the party. Isn't this a party though? And we're just getting started. Mr. Sparkle has planned lots more for us. By the way, does everybody know Mr. Sparkle? Step up here, Mr. Sparkle. Say something to the folks."

"I'm very glad to be here," Mr. Sparkle recited sadly, "and I'm very glad to have you here." He stepped off the platform to great applause.

"He sure is a good Jew," somebody said loudly. "This liquor costs twelve dollars a bottle."

"I have to go," Clifford said. "I wanted to see the prizes but it's after ten o'clock."

"I sure wish I could go with you," Gertrude said. "You'd better leave before they start another number. And be careful. There's that determined man with the camera."

There were more people now than when Clifford had entered, and they were less inclined to move. Her progress was painful. One of the boys was singing.

"Somebody's got to go! She's gettin' careless with my lovin'," the boyish voice cracked, and the people laughed.

Suddenly, rough hands were digging into Clifford's flesh. She recoiled in horror. It was the little, old man, drunker than ever. She tried to break away, but his strength and the pressure of the crowd rendered her helpless.

"Take your hands off me!" His hot, stinking breath enveloped her.

"Aw, don' be shtuck up. Gimme a li'll kish." She struggled as he tried to pull her head down on a level with his. The nightmare was complete when she felt his wet, slimy mouth on her throat, drawing the flesh inward. The photographer! His camera was focused on them, and there was nothing to shield her. The camera flashed just as a man stepped between her and her assailant, blotting out Clifford's face.

"Stop that, Pop." He pushed the old man away. "He don't mean no harm, Miss. He's drunk." Clifford sobbed, and redoubled her effort to get out.

"Damn!" the photographer muttered.

"So your little birdie is flying the coop." A man leaned over, whispering nonchalantly in his ear. "Why did you want her picture anyway? Who is she?"

"I don't know who she is. She's some chicken. *Some* chicken. And she didn't belong in here. A blind man could see that. You can't tell who she might be—or get to be. I wanted her picture. I'd have had it, too, if it wasn't for that damned, big ape!"

Outside at last, Clifford all but stumbled over a small boy who, with one knee in his wagon, was just beside the beer garden entrance. A woman stood over him brandishing a huge stick. A razor cut scarred her face, her hair stood on her head in vertical upheaval, and she was drunk, almost to the point of oblivion. "Come on home, Mama," the little fellow whined.

"Who the hell are you to come here looking for me? You ain't no man of mine, God damn you! I'll bust your damn head wide open. Go on home before I kill you!"

"Come on home, Mama," the boy pleaded. He was frightened and he was crying, but he made no move to go. He raised his eyes to his mother's face, but what he saw there, and the great stick thrashing the air, frightened him even more. He dropped his head; his tears fell on the floor of the little red wagon, so he shut his eyes tightly. "Come on home, Mama. Please. *Ple-e-e-se, ple-e-e-e-ese,* come on home!"

"God damn you. God damn you! You ain't no man of mine. You little son of a whoring bitch! I'll kill you. God dammit! You see this stick? *You see this stick?* Get on back to the house, or I'll split your damn head wide open. God damn you! God *damn* you! I said . . . ."

"Come on home, Mama. Please, Mama. *Please!* Please, come on home. *Ple-e-e-e-ese.*" He sing-songed persistently, his small body rocking to and fro on the wagon. It seemed to Clifford that the woman had some reluctance about using the stick, actually hoping to frighten the child into going home. But the youngster did not move. He rocked and pleaded monotonously through his tears. And now the woman lapsed into language foul beyond belief, and her drunken furor increased. Clifford walked away hastily as the stick came closer and closer to the small bowed head.

She groped in her purse for a tissue to wipe the burning wet spot on her throat, where she could still feel the slimy, drunken lips. She felt the spot would always burn, always be unclean. A man stepped out of the shadows and joined her. "Let me walk with you." She did not answer; nor did she heed his further attempts to engage her in conversation. In the middle of the block he left her as he had come, abruptly. His form merged with the shadowy forms of other men.

Clifford's relief was short-lived. She had not gone far when a milk bottle came hurtling through the air, missing her by inches. She began to run. The tears she had been holding back all evening began to fall.

She reached home panting and disheveled, and started eagerly to let herself in. Then she realized the consternation her appearance would cause. She stood on the front porch and composed herself before opening the door.

"Is that you, Clifford?" Martha called from the dining room.

"Yes."

"Make sure the front door is locked."

Clifford climbed the stairs slowly, her head swinging from the highball. So this was what the kids meant when they said they'd "pitched a ball" the night before. The revolting atmosphere of The Haven clung to Clifford, leaving her subdued and unlike herself in the days that followed. She wanted nothing more than the security, the protection, the blessedness of home.

Chapter XXII

Home, however, was a quiet, empty shell offering little comfort, no understanding. It wasn't long before its security and protection again began to chafe and ceased to appear so blessed. Though she shrank from the thought of venturing once more into the world of The Bottom, her vigorous spirit returned before long, to rise and struggle, demanding a thousand outlets.

Only at school, however, was any release possible. She danced, and flirted, and stayed just the right side of impudence with her teachers. Nevertheless, she continued to feel bound, frustrated. Life seemed somehow to be cheating her, passing her by.

Until the day she met Nicholas Bradley.

There was a photographer, the teacher told the class, who wished to take pictures of all the colored graduating students for the newspaper. Clifford stopped by the girls' room to fix her face. All over the school she was known as "Black Beauty," and she was extremely proud of the nickname, and of her good looks — the soft black skin and dainty features, the slanted, oriental eyes making her appear strangely exotic. She wore her hair long and straight with cut bangs to further this impression. She wasn't going to be tall, and she was glad; she could wear to advantage the clothes in which she gloried.

She was the last girl to leave the washroom. Even when they were all lined up to take the picture, she wasn't satisfied with herself. While the photographer fiddled with the camera she turned aside, finding her reflection in a dusty picture on the wall, winding a contrary piece of hair around her two index fingers.

"*You!*" It was the photographer's voice, surly, cutting. Clifford whirled, blood rushing to her face. Their eyes met — and clung. The photographer at The Haven! "Do you mind stepping back in place?" he said finally, some of the surliness gone from his voice.

"I hope you're not mad with me," he said after the picture had been taken, and she was signing her name and address for publication. Clifford, looking at him defiantly, put the pencil down with a deliberate clack and walked away without answering.

That evening, as Clifford was drying the supper dishes, the doorbell rang. There was someone to see her, Martha said. Cathy offered to finish the dishes by herself.

Clifford thought it was probably one of her classmates. If it was a boy, he wanted to go to a movie. If it was a girl, she had news. Either way, it was good to get out of doing the dishes; and she dashed into the living room, discarding her apron. There, hat in hand, stood the photographer.

"*You!*" It was all Clifford could say.

"The name is Nicholas Bradley," he said.

"Well, *Mister* Nicholas Bradley, you can just leave."

"But — " he continued unperturbed, tossing his hat on the piano, seating himself on the low sofa, "my friends call me Nick." Clifford maintained a baffled silence. She felt unable to cope with the situation. "I'd like you for a friend," he added.

"I don't know how you figure you can come in here and act like you own the place. I don't know you, and I don't want you for a friend. So will you please go!"

Nicholas Bradley lit a cigarette, his eyes fastened on Clifford. They were large and dreamy, set in a yellow face. He inhaled deeply before shifting his gaze to the fireless fireplace before him. "I came to 'pologize. I shouldn't have squawked at you like I did this afternoon."

"I blamed it on your home environment," Clifford jeered.

"That's enough of that," Nicholas said, looking at her sharply. "Don't get fresh with me — now, or ever. You're no better than I am. You may have a little more education than I have — not much. You may have a little more class — whatever that is. But, where it counts, *I* know — and you don't. I'm twenty-three years old, which ain't so old, but it's a lot older than you. I been halfway around the world, and I know all about life — first-handed. So never mind the cracks about home environment, which maybe I don't have. You got enough of it for both of us. And come to think about it, that's what's wrong with you."

"What's *wrong* with me?" Clifford moved further into the room, struggling to maintain her poise in a situation that had gotten completely out of hand.

"That night at The Haven was your first night out, and your last," he said matter-of-factly. "You been penned up in this joint — *house* — your whole life long, and if I hadn't come along, you wouldn't ever get out. But, I'm here now, baby! And don't you forget it."

"That night at The Haven . . . ," Clifford said, circling the room coquettishly, "how did you know — about it being my first night out?"

"And last? Easy. By the look on your face when you came in, I knew you'd never been out before; and, by the look on your face when you went out, I knew you'd never go out again. But you went to the wrong place," he explained easily. "You should never have gone to a hole like that, especially alone. Things were bound to go wrong. You should have gone someplace like Sunset Inn. Ever been there?"

Clifford pirouetted about, refusing him the benefit of a flat denial.

"I'll take you there," he said. "I'm going to take you lots of places. Introduce you to the world outside. I'll show you everything there is to see in Philly, take you everyplace there is to go."

Clifford's eyes shone, and her breath came quickly at this chance to *live* that fate was dumping in her lap. Still, it was not well to appear overanxious. She turned, trying to conceal the eager look on her face, and said nothing.

"There's just one thing." Nicholas rose and lifted his hat from the piano. "It's easy to see you're used to having things your way." He took her pretty fingers in his, examining them objectively. Then he looked at her pointedly. "It won't be like that with us."

Clifford withdrew her hand, a mild gesture of protest. He retrieved it leisurely. Just as leisurely, he brushed his lips against her hair.

"Now, listen, Nicholas—" she protested.

"Just, Nick, baby. Just Nick. I got to go now. I'll be back Sunday night."

"You can't come Sunday night."

"Get rid of him, baby. Like I said, I'll see you Sunday night."

That was the way Nick was. Insistent. Yet Clifford liked him more than any boy she'd ever known. The boys at school, naive and clumsy, were a sad comparison. He was different from them, older, less polished; occasionally he was crude, or his grammar was careless. Still, there was something about him. He made her feel feminine and wanted, and fully grown, the way he held her coat for her and fixed it around her shoulders, the way he brought flowers, and pinned them on her, the way he told her what to wear, how to fix her hair. Then, too, he knew his way around. He took her to clubs, good ones and bad ones. But with him there as protector and guide, it was always fun, always exciting. This was living. This was *life!* At Sunset Inn he ordered a Pink Lady for her, and laughed when the bubbles tickled sliding down her throat. She had wanted a cigarette and he had lighted it for her just as they did in the movies, but later he had taken it away, saying half a cigarette was enough to begin with.

For a while Clifford had feared the difference in their two ways of life, or his unconventional ideas would lead to an impasse between them. But though he was given to lauding the merits of free love, he never made it an issue between them. And though he lived faster than she could, or even wanted to, he never demanded that she keep up with him. Instead, he enjoyed himself immensely—roller skating and dancing with her, making her the envy of the girls at school with his easy charm. He taught her to bowl and to ride horseback, and to play tennis, infecting her with his enthusiasm for the game. Until at last Clifford relaxed, her doubts dispelled. After all, he had turned out to be a nice guy, full of fun.

At the class prom, it seemed to Clifford he was the best-looking boy there. Nick, as usual, had shown perfect taste. The red roses blushed beautifully against her white frills, as she glimpsed their forms dancing in a mirror. It was a perfect evening, one that she wished could go on and on. But it came to an end with Nick framed in the doorway, watching her through the glass panel as she moved away from him, into the house and up the stairs, his light kiss still on her lips.

June came, and graduation. Nick gave her a photograph album, filled with pictures he had taken. "It's not so much," he explained, "but I'm planning to get you something nice for your birthday. And I don't want you squawking about me spending too much money."

Her birthday. The Fourth of July. Less than a month to wait. But it proved to be eons. Nick must have an engagement ring for her. He hadn't spoken to her of marriage, but it would be like him to plan without her consent.

Her mother, on the other hand, was planning a college career for her, and Clifford, no longer able to avoid the issue, rebelled. "I don't want to go to college. I never have. I just want to — to settle down and get married like other girls do. I don't need a college education for that."

Get married? Not go to college? The planning of years would be rudely upset. However, Clifford was not to be moved, and any idea of college was abandoned. Martha had no concrete objection to Nick. He seemed, in fact, rather a nice young man. But to be worthy of Clifford was something else again. She could not easily see all her lifelong hopes for Clifford supplanted by him.

"Suppose you stay out of school for the fall term, while you make up your mind definitely," she suggested to Clifford. "And just in case you should change, we'll plan for the next term."

It was a small thing to promise, and Clifford promised readily, hoping to brighten her mother's face, glad when she saw the slow light kindle in her eyes. Yet secretly she was glad of something quite different. By the "next term" she'd be safely married to Nick.

The Fourth of July dawned clear and bright. When Clifford saw Nick arrive without a package, her hopes soared. One carried a ring in one's pocket. They spent the day together; a picnic lunch on a sunny hill, popcorn and ice cream, an amusement park, and waterworks on the river bridge. Through it all she couldn't persuade him to reveal her gift any earlier than the time he had set, the last event of the evening.

They were seated on the divan when he drew it from his inside pocket. A small oblong box; small, but too large for a ring. She seemed unable to control her fingers. They opened the package slowly, awkwardly. It was a watch, gracefully formed, its tiny dial smaller than a dime.

"Oh, Nick, it's lovely," she breathed. She tried to put it on, but her fingers wouldn't work at all now, and Nick had to put it on for her. There didn't seem to be much she could say after that. She looked at the watch, turned her wrist this way and that, listened to its tiny tick. "It's beautiful," she murmured.

"How well do you like it?" Nick asked, a thinly veiled invitation in his voice. She turned quickly, her arms reaching toward him. He caught her wrist, arresting her briefly, bringing a question to her eyes. Then he kissed her lingeringly, his lips murmuring over hers. "How well do you like it, Clifford? How well do you like me?"

It was hard to understand what he meant. She tried to move away, but he caught her chin in his hand and kissed her again.

"Nick?" She pronounced his name in two syllables, making a long, drawn out question of it. He didn't kiss her again. Nor did he release her. Finally she was quite still in his arms, the unanswered question filling the room. Perhaps this was Nick's way of proposing to her. For a moment she had thought he meant something quite different. Something awful. Perhaps her imagination was running away with her, and he hadn't meant anything at all. Her throat was dry, and she felt queer. She wished Nick would say something.

He dropped one arm away from her and rolled his head back on the cushions. The arm around Clifford relaxed. "Get one thing straight," he said. "The watch is yours — no strings attached. I give it to you 'cause I want you to have it, and whatever else comes up don't have nothing to do with that." Clifford felt relieved. She stirred slightly, and his arm tightened. "But I don't know how long you expect us to go along like we've been doing."

This was it. Clifford raised her head from the curve of his shoulder, and they faced each other. No, he wasn't asking her to marry him. The look on his face told her that.

"When I first met you I thought you'd be like this," she said. He moved his arm and folded his arms in front of him.

"When you first met me you were scared to death I was trying to rape you or something. I didn't. I never even kissed you like I meant it before tonight. I never pawed you, or mauled you around, 'cause I knew you didn't want to be pawed and mauled. And it's the same thing now — I know it is, only I kinda forgot. But you don't have to worry, I wouldn't touch you unless you wanted me as much as I want you . . . That's the whole thing in a nutshell. I like you a lot. And I want you. If you liked me . . ." He made no attempt to finish the sentence.

"I do like you, Nick. More than that. But there's a right way and a wrong way to do things."

"Right and wrong! Who says right and wrong? Your mother? Some book you read? That's what they tell kids in Sunday school, but you're a big girl now. Big enough to know that no matter what anybody says — if I got up and walked through that door, *that* would be wrong. And this — *this* is right." He kissed her roughly, his lips sliding down her throat and up. She felt the tears smarting beneath her closed eyelids.

"Clifford, any girl can say she likes a guy. How do I know you mean it?"

After that things were different between them. Nick was the same, and yet not the same. They did the things they had always done just as they had always done them. They never referred to the clash of wills, but when he kissed her the conflict was there, naked and undeniable, speaking of itself.

As a matter of course they went to the movies every Friday night. Then, one Friday evening he failed to appear, and though Clifford called his house, she got no answer. Saturday passed; and it was Sunday afternoon before he came.

"What happened to you?" Clifford wanted to know.

"A friend of mine died, and I went to his wake."

"A friend of yours?"

"Yeah. Jimmy. You ought to remember him. Jimmy Shultz, the guy who played the sax that night you went to The Haven."

Jimmy Shultz. Clifford envisioned a hazy face in dark glasses, the shining saxophone, and a shirt wet with perspiration. "Jimmy Shultz? He was just a kid."

"He was a kid, all right. He was sick when you saw him, though. T.B. I'll always believe blowing that horn give him that. Didn't have but one lung when he died."

"Is that what he died of?"

"No. Dope. Don't you read the papers? They found him with a heroin needle in his arm. Him and three others guys in the back of that pool room on Thirty-fifth Street."

"Still, you could have let me know you wouldn't be here," Clifford said, trying to shut out the picture of four bodies in back of the pool room by returning to the original subject.

"I guess I could have. But you know how it is."

It was no explanation at all. But it was typical of many she received thereafter. Other movieless Friday nights followed; other dates unkept. And now Clifford was worried. Was she losing him then? Had she done the right thing in not giving in to him? She had been remembering the things her mother and her father, and even her sisters, had taught her—forgetting that her life was her own, her decisions, hers to make. Nothing was right if it cost her Nick's affection, Nick's love. For, of course, he loved her. Had he not proved it a hundred different ways? He had planned to marry her; she knew that even though he had never spoken of it. When he gave her the watch he had been thinking of marriage. Yet, if you looked at it one way, you couldn't blame him if he never spoke of it. "Any girl can say she likes a guy," he had said. "How do I know you mean it?" And how indeed would he know? She had delighted in having him take her out, basked in his charm, and accepted his tokens of love just as any other girl would have done. There was only one way a girl could prove she loved a man; and, when it came to that, she had backed away, talking of right and wrong. Right and wrong. Wrong and right. Just as Nick had said, once you had grown up, who was to say which was which except you? Well, with any other man, right and wrong was as it had always been. But when the man was Nick, whom you loved — Nick, whom you couldn't live without — right and wrong reversed itself, just as he had said.

He came the next Friday night. Clifford greeted him a little breathlessly. "I was afraid you might not come."

"Would it have mattered?" he asked lightly.

"Yes." Her voice reflected none of the lightness of his own. "Tonight more than ever." He turned to her questioningly. For answer she wound her arms around his neck, forcing his mouth down on hers. "You were right," she said when she relaxed.

He released himself and took her hand, carefully separating the fingers on it as he spoke slowly. "Is it what you want?"

"It's what I want."

His hand tightened on hers. "Let's get out of here," he said.

Chapter XXIII

Instead of going to the movies that night they went to Ma's.

All through high school Clifford's friends had attempted to lure her to Ma's house with fantastic tales of what happened there on days they played hookey. But she had never gone with them. Now, as she made her first trip to Ma's, she seemed to step out of herself and become two people. She watched herself enter the house and looked around while Nick made small talk with a number of people.

It was a large house somewhat like her own but quite bare of furniture. They moved out of the lighted vestibule, which resembled a small lobby, and went through a door on the left. For a moment Clifford couldn't see; everything was completely black. Her eyes became used to the darkness gradually and she saw that she was in a huge, bare room, so large that it seemed a separate building from the lobby they had just left. It was lighted by a single dull, red light far up in the ceiling. A jukebox glowed at the end of the room, and Clifford could just make out several shadows around it.

As her eyes became more adjusted to the dark, she saw that giant posts supporting the ceiling lined the room. Against one of these posts, exactly in the center of the room, a girl was leaning, silent, her legs crossed languidly. She was pretty, and young, not more than fifteen. And she looked like a picture Clifford had seen on the jacket of a book, perhaps, or on an advertisement for a play. Several shadows were dancing to the soft music of the jukebox, and now she saw that other shadows were huddled together on benches that lined the walls.

At the very end of the room she saw something that startled her. On a panel of fibrous, brown, ragged-edged sackcloth stretched from floor to ceiling was a remarkable portrait of the actor Raymond Massey, the haunted eyes of Abraham Lincoln staring from his face. *My, but it would give Mr. Massey a turn to find himself here,* she thought. And it was her other self thinking this, even smiling a bit. The one who had not come along but stayed behind to watch.

"This way," Nick said. He led the way to the portrait of

Raymond Massey, lifted the coarse material, and opened a door behind it.

They were in a cozily furnished dining room.

"Ma!"

An elderly woman, her beautiful hair almost silver, looked up from the bedspread she was busily crocheting and abruptly stopped her rocking chair. "Nicholas, my boy! How are you?" She dropped her crocheting, extending her plump arms. Nick let himself be hugged affectionately.

"You'll fix us up, Ma?" he said.

"Why, of course." She smiled at Clifford. "I'll do it myself." She rose, dumping the bedspread in the rocker. There was another couple in the room. The boy, about Nick's age, had been talking to Ma when Clifford and Nick came in, and had since grown silent. The girl sat at the table, her head dropped on folded arms, quietly crying. Ma went to her now, placing an affectionate arm around her, smoothing her jet black hair. "There, love. There — there. Don't take on so. Everything's all right."

"They're like that the first time," she reassured the boy as she left the room. By the time she came back, the girl was crying harder, and Ma tried again to soothe her. "Now, you listen to Ma. It ain't anything so terrible." But there was no quieting her. She only cried harder and harder. "Is anything wrong, honey? Tell Ma what's the matter."

"There's nothing wrong with her," her companion answered. At this the girl shuddered and gave a low scream.

"The room's ready, precious. You go on up. You'll be fine in a little while, believe me." Ma administered a final pat. Now one low scream followed another. The girl raised her head, rolling it from side to side, for the first time showing her red and swollen face.

"I can't. I can't!" she sobbed. "Jimmy, I *can't*."

"What's the matter with her?" Ma wanted to know, her concern finally aroused.

"Nothing. There's nothing wrong with her. Cut that out, Pat; and come on."

"I'll tell. I'll tell! I'll *tell*!"

"Shut up." Jimmy half helped, half dragged the girl off the chair, apparently in a hurry to get her out of the room.

"No wait a minute," Ma said. "Let her talk."

"She ain't got nothing to say. There's nothing wrong with her."

"Never mind. Let her talk," Ma said arbitrarily.

For a long moment the room was filled with Pat's stormy crying. Jimmy made a desperate grab for her, increasing her alarm. She pulled away from him and forced herself to speak. When she spoke she could hardly be understood; her broken crying rendered the words almost unintelligible. "He's my brother. He's my brother. This man is my *brother*!"

Ma looked from one of them to the other. The same olive skin; the same silky hair. "Oh, no. No indeed! I'm sorry. You'll have to go somewhere else. I can't have anything like that in my house," she said. "You can go up now," she addressed Nick, still looking askance at the crying girl, the irate young man.

Clifford was feeling a little nervous now. But it helped a great deal to be not really there, to be somewhere else watching herself climb the stairs and enter an immaculate bedroom.

* * * * *

Ma was alone in the dining room when they came down. "I see our friends are gone," Nick said, indicating Pat's empty chair, and fishing in his pocket for change. "I was kinda surprised at you turning them away."

"It don't pay to court trouble," Ma replied. Nick put the change on the table beside her. "You'll have to get those sheets washed," he said. "She's just a baby."

"Bless her little heart." Ma smiled at Clifford and dropped the change into her apron pocket.

Chapter XXIV

The 8-ball trembled, hesitated, trembled, then rolled deliberately into the pocket. Nick's partner surveyed him from across the pool table, his mouth curled in surly disgust. Then he threw his stick down. "I quit! This ain't no game at all with you making shots like that three games in a row. You better go home and finish out your morning nap, I think you got up too soon."

Nick drew up and rested dreamily on his cue stick. "Yes," he said suggestively, "I got up too soon." He moved over to the slot machine, his erstwhile partner close on his heels.

"Who was she?" he wanted to know.

"Man, I copped a cherry last night!"

"A cherry! In The Bottom! I thought they were born without them down here. She young?"

"Eighteen."

"I guess you think that's helping you get rid of your bad blood."

"I *know* it is. Every person you give it to, takes that much away from you. You just gotta watch out you don't get somebody that has it. I make sure about a woman before I touch her."

"One of the guys told me you told him that."

"You sound like you don't believe it."

"It don't help you to give what you got to somebody else. According to the doctors, you just keep on getting worse."

"Sure that's what the doctors tell you. They don't want you to give it to anybody else."

"Where's your conscience?"

"They can get rid of it like I did."

"This girl—the one last night—"

"Hmm—the one last night. I don't always have that luck, I can tell you."

"She don't know what it's all about. Anything can happen to a girl like that. I feel real sorry for her. She needs a husband or something to look out for her."

"Want her address?" The screen of the slot machine twinkled with lighted signals: a series of numbers blinking quickly on and off—JACKPOT—then, TILT. "You can't beat this thing," Nick said.

On Sunday night he phoned Clifford to say he had a cold, and feared to expose himself to the misty weather. "Of course, I'll come if you want me to," he added.

"No. You'd better stay home if you're not feeling well," Clifford told him. But as she hung up the receiver she was stabbed by disappointment and fear. Then she told herself she was being silly. Of course he had a cold, and of course it was better for him to stay indoors. Everything was settled between them now. There'd be no more cat and mouse, or broken dates.

She was wrong. Before long Nicholas stopped coming altogether. Clifford was bewildered. What was wrong? He loved her, she was sure of it. And hadn't she proved that she loved him? Time and again she telephoned him, wrote to him, to no avail. Once, timid and frightened, she had gone to his house. A big-bosomed woman with a front tooth missing had told her curtly, "He ain't here. He don't live here no more." And with that she had found herself staring at the paint-chipped door panels.

And now she had a terrible secret. It harassed her days, haunted her nights. She told no one, sought no help. The secret was hers alone, too awful to be shared with a living soul.

Martha was happy that Nick no longer kept company with her daughter. It meant that Clifford would continue her education after all. February and the new school term were approaching, and one evening Martha went to Clifford's room to have the matter settled. The sound of muffled crying reached her ears, and she entered without knocking.

"Clifford? Is something wrong?"

"Go away, Mother. Go away." Clifford's head was buried in a pillow that muffled the words. As her mother approached the bed, Clifford's hand reached out, dragging a book that lay beside her toward the concealing bulk of the pillow. Martha laid hold of the book, prying loose Clifford's clinging fingers. *Facts About Venereal Disease*. Martha read the title aloud. However, it didn't tell her at all why Clifford was crying—not for several minutes.

Chapter XXV

Alice looked up from the gathers her fingers were expertly working into a piece of fancy work. She didn't shrink from the sunlight that illumined her face; and Cathy, watching her, thought how she had become quite her old self with the family, unashamed, even unconscious of the scar. The two were in Alice's room, each consumed with her own thoughts beneath their light, insignificant conversation.

"There's candy in that box on the dresser," Alice said.

"Thanks, but I don't want any."

"It looks like my little sister is really growing up. I can remember when you'd eat chocolate candy all day long if I didn't watch you. But then, you're almost twenty-three now," Alice sighed. "Quite the young lady."

Cathy smiled. She was thinking that she'd picked the wrong time to tell Alice. But no time could ever be the right time, and she couldn't put it off any longer. Still it had been foolish of her to come to Alice's room. Anywhere else in the house it would have been easier to say what she had to say. This room recalled that other time when she had come to Alice for such a different reason. Perhaps now, Alice would think that even then —

Alice's fingers paused momentarily while she contemplated her sister's disturbed features; then she carefully lowered her eyes. So. She was going to tell her. At last she was going to tell her. Poor Cathy! She was suffering so; had suffered so. Often Alice had seen it in her eyes, heard it in her voice, and she had wanted to make this easier for her sister. She could have had it over with quickly — long ago. Just a few words — the truth — spoken sympathetically, convincingly. But some instinct, perverse, diabolical and deep-seated, had overruled all tenderness and sealed her lips. It was with her even now, though sympathy for Cathy was a vague ache pervading her body. She wanted to toss her needlework aside and cross the room to say, "*Cathy, honey, I know. **I know**. You're torturing yourself for nothing!*"

"You haven't told me about HSA for a long while, Cathy. How's it going?" she said.

"HSA's all right."

"What's happening?"

"The usual thing. Les is working hard — as usual." She was moving about the room, fingering Alice's needlework wherever she found it. "He looks older, I think."

"Oh. Is Miss Granberg over her sick spell yet?"

"He's quite gray at the temples."

Alice looked up but said nothing. She turned and adjusted the curtain so that the light fell across the work in her lap.

Silently, a feeling of doom at the pit of her stomach, Cathy took a cushion from a chair and placed it on the floor by her sister's chair. She sat on it, curled her legs beneath her, and looked up to find Alice smiling at her. Cathy turned away. It didn't seem right that Alice should smile at her now.

"There's something I want to tell you. I should have told you long before now." She faced her sister, and finding that the smile had disappeared, she felt both relieved and anxious that it had. "It's about Les — Les and me."

Alice broke off a thread between her teeth. "About Leslie and you?"

Cathy looked down at her hands folded over the arm of the chair, then back at her sister. "We love each other." Her voice was so low that Alice had to strain to catch the words. She threaded her needle with a steady hand, without answering. "Alice, we didn't *want* it to be this way! But I didn't know. I didn't know until it was too late to do anything about it. Believe me, I didn't want to hurt you like this." Cathy's head dropped to the arm of the chair. Her own breath was stifling her, and she fought the tears, but they came anyway.

Alice rested her hand on her sister's curly head; self-reproach welled accusingly. Her silence had been crueler than she had known. The sight of Cathy as she was now was more than she could bear.

"Listen to me, Cathy. You're not hurting me. That's all over, do you understand? Do you understand? You're not hurting me. You didn't know, I know that. But I did. I knew long before you did." Cathy raised her head, her face wet and miserable, her eyes unbelieving. "Yes," Alice said firmly. "When you came to me before—when you pleaded with me on Leslie's behalf, I knew. I knew then. That was the hard time for me. Cathy, if I was hurt—as you put it—it was then. But, it's all over now. I don't feel anything at all now except happiness for both of you."

It was unforseen and it was unbelievable, but Alice's voice had the convincing ring of truth. Cathy took her sister's hand and laid her cheek against it. "I'm glad," she said simply. "I'm so glad."

"And now let's plan the wedding." Alice sounded more enthusiastic than she had about anything in years. "Leslie's going to have a pretty bride." The words hung in awkward significance for a moment. "I—I'll make your wedding gown."

"Oh, we're not going to have a wedding."

"Not have a wedding?"

"We thought we'd just get married."

"Even so, I can still make your dress. But I don't see why you can't have a wedding. What does Mother say?"

"I haven't told her yet."

"When are you going to tell her?"

"Any time, now that I've told you."

"Well, let's tell her now." Alice went to the door and called her mother. Martha pretended to be more surprised at the news than she actually was, for Cathy, always easily read, had given herself away a hundred times a day. And Martha had come to expect this "news" long ago. She was much surprised, however, and vastly relieved at Alice's genuine tranquility.

"She says she doesn't want a wedding, Mother. Can you imagine! I wish you'd talk to her. I'd make her wedding gown."

"Of course you must have a wedding. I wanted that for all of you girls. Every girl should have a wedding. It gives her something to look back on for the rest of her life."

In the end the two of them proved too much for Cathy.

"It's for their sake," she told Leslie later. "Mother and Alice want me to have a wedding, and I felt as though it was the least I could do for them."

"A church wedding, I suppose?" He was pacing the floor.

"No. They wanted a church wedding, but we finally agreed to have it at home. All this providing you agree, of course. Alice is going to make a gown for me."

"*Alice?*" Leslie stopped short, hoping he hadn't conveyed his thoughts to Cathy. He wanted to be married. He wanted no further delay. No wedding. No wedding gown made by Alice to serve as a painful reminder even as they made their vows.

"I know," Cathy said quietly. "But it'll give her a little happiness. We can't refuse her that, Les."

"No. We can't refuse her that."

He sat down beside her. "Is it always going to be this way, Cathy? Will we ever be behind closed doors with the world and everyone in it on the outside?"

"Things will straighten themselves out. Just a little while longer."

She put her cheek against his, anticipating the sweet thrill before it came. As always the touch of her soft young body was electric. His arms closed around her in a tightening circle. "Give me your lips," he murmured. Then, "There's nothing soothing in kissing you."

"I wouldn't change that if I could," she said.

Chapter XXVI

It was cold the day of the wedding, and toward evening it began to rain. The atmosphere of the Hilton house in the bustle and fuss of wedding preparations was strange and unfamiliar to its inhabitants. Cathy was a beautiful bride.

"You're the loveliest bride I've ever seen," Alice told her. She stood at the head of the stairs, prayer book in hand, the heavy, creamy satin of her gown billowing around her.

"I wish you'd come down, Alice—just this once."

"I'll be watching you from here."

The wedding march began, and Clifford, having been coaxed by her mother into being a bridesmaid, descended. Then *Lohengrin*, and the two sisters embraced. To Cathy it seemed that when she let go of Alice she would be losing her hold on everything she had known and loved until now to step off into an unknown, and for the moment unwanted, future.

"Keep sweet," Alice disengaged her sister's clinging arms. "You'd better go now."

The long walk down. Her father, now grown unfamiliar to her, waited at the foot of the stairs. Then Clifford, removed and sober-faced, came into view. There was her mother, unaccustomed happiness lighting her face through her tears; and Jean with the look of someone "cleaned up," in clothes not made to accommodate the roll of flesh around her pudgy middle.

She was at the foot of the stairs. She took her father's arm and looked up. Alice was still there, smiling at her. Cathy smiled nervously for a brief moment, until she felt the tears smarting beneath her eyelids and turned away, holding on tightly to her father's arm.

Then there was Leslie — handsome in his well-cut tuxedo, his gray temples glaringly incongruous with his lithe, youthful figure, his almost boyish face.

The ceremony was simple and profound. It was over quickly, and there were kisses for the bride: Leslie's — her father's — her mother's. The evening dissolved into a maze of pictures taken . . . guests . . . congratulations . . . their two hands cutting the cake . . . more pictures . . . rice and confetti . . . the change into street clothes . . . goodbyes . . . the run from the house to the waiting car through the rain . . . rice and confetti . . . the train rumbling out of nowhere . . . rice and confetti . . . goodbyes . . . rice and confetti . . . the train rumbling into nowhere . . .

* * * * *

The black night cried with a woman's screaming. "M-a-r-y . . . M-a-r-y . . . *M · a · r · y* . . ." The last guest had gone, leaving the rooms abysmally dreary with chaotic remnants of a gaiety now dead; the house was asleep and Martha stood looking out of the window, watching the driving rain. She was tired, she told herself. Tired and lonely. The depths of her soul cried out in longing for her husband. Not for the pompous, paunchy, overbearing person who had given Cathy away this evening. He was a man she didn't know, or even want to know. But for Clifford, *her husband*, as she had known him, and loved him. She needed him now. Oh, how she needed him! She needed his arms around her; she needed his comforting voice—"Little Girl . . . Little Girl . . . It's all right. Don't cry, Little Girl . . ." Tears slid down Martha's cheeks. She heard it so clearly, the voice in her mind. *His* voice. But he wasn't here. The Bottom had robbed her of him. The Bottom! It had snatched life, and love, and happiness from Alice. And young Clifford, the spirited "little firecracker" they used to call her, without health or happiness, downcast, dejected, her spirit irrevocably broken. The Bottom had done that. And for Jean there'd be another baby, and another, and another; and she'd get more stupid and less clean, until she, like her husband, became the muck and the mire that was The Bottom. Cathy alone of all her children would have any happiness. A happiness that must sour slightly whenever she remembered it was built on the broken life of her sister. The Bottom. The Bottom! The *Bottom!*

Martha's tears fell faster, and it was no relief to cry. The burning, aching emptiness was still there—grew worse. The sound of that other woman crying in the night came closer. "M-a-r-y . . . M-a-r-y . . . *M–a–r–y* . . . ."

Closer . . . Closer . . . Closer . . . Martha held the curtain aside, and for the first time she saw the woman who had haunted seventeen years of rainy nights in The Bottom. The light from the street lamp fell across her face, hideous, puffed, bruised and scarred. A rough stubble of hair covered her scalp. The cold rain had plastered her thin dress against her skin, and she shivered as she looked up and saw Martha standing at the window. Her eyes were terrible, stupid, senseless, like some beaten brute's. Then she smiled through her tears, a loose, toothless, monstrous leer. Martha returned the smile as best she could through her own tears. They were sisters, this woman and she. Two of the countless who had been beaten, ravaged, sucked under by The Bottom. It was right that they should smile encouragement at each other through their tears.

Then, the woman remembered her mission and went on, her hoarse cries ringing through the night . . . echoing in the distance . . . .

Epilogue

John O'Neal, Junebug Productions

When John O'Neal ambles onstage as Junebug, audiences hear poignant stories of the people who live in Junebug's world. The plays are a rich, folkloric history of African-American life. They are also powerful cultural implementations of the oral tradition.

The following rap summarizes You Can't Judge a Book by Looking at the Cover: Sayings from the Life and Times of Junebug Jabbo Jones, Volume II.

> You can't judge a book by looking at the cover
> You can read my letter
> But I betcha can't read my mind
> If you want to get down, down, down
> You got to spend some time
> I want to walk with you
> I want to talk with you
> I want I want I want I want to rap with you
> Hey.............Hey hey hey!

> I done told you a story 'bout my old friend Po
> 'Bout tings he tried to do, places he had to go
> 'bout home boy going out, to get some money
> If it wasn't so sad, it really might have been funny
> told all about the way he tried to make it in the city
> told you everything although it wasn't pretty
> told all about the way that he was misunderstood
> by his family and his friends — thought that he was just a hood

told how the man misunderstood himself
he went to get some knowledge, left the book upon the shelf
He got the cover of the book, but didn't get what it had in it
what should have took a week, he tried to do in just a minute

You can't judge a book by looking at the cover
You can read my letter but I betcha can't read my mind
If you want to get down, down, down
You got to spend some time
I want to walk with you
I want to talk with you
I want I want I want I want to rap with you
Hey.............hey hey hey!

When you grow up in the country, things are hard and times are tough
take to growing your own food, but it never seems enough
think you're too smart for the country and you gotta get away
gonna move up to the city, got to be a better way
Then you move up to the city, put the country stuff behind
But when you hit the city, it starts messing with your mind.
You get on the straight and narrow and you follow all the rules.
You figure you're the one that's going to outdo all the fools.
You struggle and you scramble just to do the best you can.
You think you're working for a living, find you're working for the man.
People stacked like chickens on the way to meet the slaughter.
They flopping all around the ground like fishes out of water.
A blind man begging on a corner, holding up a sign
It say "No more water, the fire next time!"

You can't judge a book by looking at the cover
you can read my letter
But I betcha can't read my mind
If you want to get down, down, down
You got to spend some time
I want to walk with you
I want to talk with you
I want I want I want I want to rap with you
Hey.............hey! hey! hey!

Afterword

Compiling this anthology was a labor of love, conducted because I found little literature depicting the African-American life experiences it portrays. It troubled me that the "sanitized" version of the American slavocracy generally promoted was widely believed, while the horrendous reality of U.S. slavery remained largely unacknowledged, and all but unknown. Further, I found little written that reflected what I knew of the suffering, triumph, and defeat that crowned the lives of African-Americans during the Great Depression.

It is satisfying to know that depictions of African-American life in this anthology will be part of the future. In time, the book may be obscurely shelved in a few libraries. Still, it will stand in contradiction of the concept of the American slavocracy as "benevolent"; it will provide insight into feelings, behaviors, speech and contributions of Aframericans; and it will remain a valuable source of information about African-American life during the Great Depression.

I would welcome a letter from you with your reactions, questions, and suggestions relating to this work. Write: P. O. Box 14-3262, Austin, TX 78714-3262. I also invite your publishing suggestions and input into anthologies I am now compiling: **What in the World is God Doing?,** an anthology of sermons by renowned ministers and feature stories about their work; **Let the Church Say Amen!,** sermons from the Black clergy; and **A Different Kind of Storybook for Children,** a collection of autobiographical stories about present-day and historical Afro-Americans.

Marian E. Barnes

About the Authors

Leon C. Anderson, Jr., is a poet, musician, and artist. Selections in this anthology are from his book *So Kwame Can Read.* He and his wife, Evelyn Martin-Anderson, operate LAEMA Enterprises, Inc., Austin, Texas.

Will Angst is a Liberal Arts Academy student of Johnston High School in Austin.

Alli Aweusi, poet, artist, puppeteer, and historian is co-author of a volume of poetry, *Words Never Kill.*

Dorothy Charles Banks, a Texas newspaperwoman, says of her poem, "This poem grew out of the quiet times I shared with my granddaughter, Nartarsha, when she combed my hair, and I combed hers."

Marian E. Barnes was graduated cum laude from an Honors Program at Temple University with a B.A. in communications (radio, TV and film). As a scholarship intern at Villanova University, she earned a B.S. degree in counseling and human relations, and was graduated Kappa Delta Pi. A nationally published feature writer and columnist, she co-edited *Talk That Talk, An Anthology of African-American Storytelling* in 1989. In addition to her primary profession as a counselor, her career has included international storytelling, writing and reporting for Philadelphia's ABC-affiliated television station, hosting radio talk-shows, and directing the Public Relations and Volunteer Services Departments of a Philadelphia hospital.

J. Mason Brewer (1896–1975) was one of the nation's leading folklorists. Named in *Who's Who in America,* Dr. Brewer devoted much of his life to collecting and preserving the oral tales and folklore of African-Americans. J. Frank Dobie, among the most outstanding folklorists in Texas, once called Dr. Brewer the best storyteller of Black folklore anywhere in America.

Dr. John Henrik Clarke is a world-stature historian who says, "I always liked to collect and explain information, just for myself, and I learned to read well because I wanted to teach the junior Bible class in the local Baptist church. This is where my search for the identity and place of African people began, and where a conflict started within me that took me twenty years to resolve. Although most of the Bible stories unfolded in Africa with African references, I saw no African people in the printed and illustrated Sunday school lessons. I began to suspect at this early age that someone had distorted the image of my people. My long search for the true history of African people the world over began."

Eartha Colson, an Austin poet, is known for her vibrant, historical poetry and her moving performances.

Dottie Curry is an Austin homemaker. Her poem evolved from feelings of frustration experienced when an organization of artists rejected her membership application, saying she lacked creative abilities.

Kyisha Diefenbach, Austin student.

Michelle Dion, Austin student.

Paul Laurence Dunbar (1872–1906), prolific poet and literary author best known for poems that depict Aframerican life.

Sean Erickson, Austin student.

Dr. John Hope Franklin is among the world's greatest historians. His book *From Slavery to Freedom* has been called the best history of Black Americans ever written.

Dr. Wacira Gethaiga is part of the largest national group in Kenya, the Kikuyu. His writing reflects traditions and traditional stories of his people.[1] A second post-colonial generation Kikuyu, he has first-hand knowledge of European missionaries and decries the passing of the old ways.

Jennifer Hansen, an Austin student, says, "I write what I feel."

Jessie Mae Hicks founded Hicks Beauty School in San Antonio,

---

1. See *"Warigunga,"* Wacira Gethaiga, *Talk That Talk, An Anthology of African-American Storytelling,* eds. Linda Goss and Marian E. Barnes (Simon and Schuster, 1989), 247.

Texas, with one student. In operation continuously since 1941, the school was once the largest African-American institution of its kind in the country. She holds a bachelor of science degree from Huston-Tillotson College, and a bachelor of divinity degree from Howard University.

Langston Hughes was one of the most prolific authors of his time (1902–1967). His poetry splendidly expresses what Aframericans must do to present the world with a true picture of themselves, and correct the distorted image of the group generally popularized by others.

Mark Hyman has written many historical volumes, including *Blacks who Died for Jesus, Blacks Before America Volumes I, II, and III, Blacks Among the Seminole Indians, Famous Black Women from World History, Five Hundred Facts About Blacks, Blacks in the American Revolution,* and *Blacks in the War of 1812.* In 1958, he founded Mark Hyman Associates, Inc., a public relations and advertising firm headquartered in Philadelphia.

Trice Ijeoma, a student at St. Andrews School in Austin, wrote the poem in this volume when she was six.

Jawara, a name which means "peace-loving" in Swahili, was selected by Janice E. Bishop to be used in storytelling because of its message. An educator in the Philadelphia School System, she directs a unique team of students in competitive rope jumping. Her first published story appears in this anthology.

Amanda Johnson, Austin student.

Dr. C. Eric Lincoln, internationally recognized authority on the sociology of Black religion, is professor of religion and culture at Duke University. He is author of some twenty books, including the highly acclaimed work *The Black Muslims in America.*

Evelyn Martin-Anderson is the founder of Catfish Poets Society, which sponsors weekly public readings for Austin area poets.

Christina Mayne, Austin student.

Christina Mullins, Austin student.

Joseph Mwalimu is a pen name for a South African playwright.

John O'Neal, nationally known storyteller, is celebrated for his interpretation of folk character Junebug Jabbo Jones. He is the founder of Junebug Productions, which tours three plays including *Ain't No Use in Going Home, Jodie's Got Your Gal and Gone.*

Deborah Orr-Ogunro has written a book of short stories, *I Opened my Trunk*. She is co-author of two books of poems.

April Parra, an Austin student, says her poem in this volume resulted from attempts to understand her relationship with her mother.

Colly Patton wrote "Song of Myself" following her mother's death. The Austin student says, "I had grown tired of pretending that everything was fine and decided to vent that through this poem."

John F. Phillips, Major General, U.S. Air Force, is commander of the Joint Logistics Systems Center, Wright-Patterson Air Force Base, Ohio.

Doris Barnes Polk, homemaker and mother of four with three grandchildren, writes poetry sporadically. Her poem in this book was written some forty years after the incident described occurred.

J. Diego Prange, an Austin student, was inspired by the Persian Gulf War to write the poem in this anthology.

Farhana Qazi, an Austin student, says, "I wrote 'Warm Thoughts' thinking of my dear grandfather, Rahmatullah Qazi, who sits wrapped in scarves and quilts in mild weather." She explains that to her, "Farhana Qazi" is a sacred pen name because it is the name of her grandfather.

Cedar Sexton, Austin student.

Jonathan Sheppard was a ninth-grade student at Kirby Hall School in Austin, Texas, when he wrote the poem included in this anthology.

Ada DeBlanc Simond was an educator, historian, writer and storyteller.

Rebecca Sims, an Austin student, says, "A few years ago I went back to Ohio to attend my great-grandmother's funeral . . . the house had that empty feel to it that 'peopleless' houses get. I was the one person in my family who didn't have memories associated with the things in the house; I could barely even remember the woman that had lived there all those years ago. I came to know her through the place, which is something I tried to capture in the poem."

Ana Sisnett is a Black West Indian Panamanian who lives in Austin with her daughter and son. Her poetry reclaims the West Indian rhythms of her voice. A frequent performer at poetry readings, she thanks the people who attend, and credits them with inspiring her creativity.

Jimmy Stanley, Austin student.

Joan Barnes Stewart is an Austin attorney who developed her story from a Haiku she had written in high school about her grandmother.

Temujin the Storyteller (Temujin Ekunféo) is a lecturer, workshop developer-leader, musician, dancer, instrument maker, and singer. Dressed in West African garb, he performs as the character "Apalo," an itinerant who hails crowds with his "talking drum" and is known for his extravagant exaggerations. Based in Pittsburgh, Pennsylvania, Temujin vigorously promotes and lives up to his slogan: *Temujin will tra-vell!*

Dr. Margaret Wade-Lewis is assistant professor of linguistics and literature at the State University of New York, College at New Paltz, where she also chairs the Department of Black Studies.

Michelle Wilkinson wrote the delightful spoof on American politics chosen for this anthology as a student at Johnston High School, Austin.

Ruthe Winegarten met Annie Mae Hunt through a mutual friend and learned that a biographical manuscript begun by Ms. Hunt at fourteen had lain in a cardboard box for over fifty years. The two women completed the story together, and *I Am Annie Mae, The Personal Story of a Black Texas Woman* was published. The book became a best-seller and was produced on the stage.

Christine Wright is a student at Bowie High School in Austin, Texas.

About Illustrations

1. *Coming to America,* page 4. An illustration of the lower-deck plan of eighteenth-century merchantman Brookes. Used by permission of Carnegie Institution of Washington and Schomburg Center for Research in Black Culture, New York Public Library, Astor, Lenox and Tilden Foundations.

Although it was built to accommodate 451 persons, documents for the Brookes show 609 Africans transported on one voyage despite lack of rudimentary space and toilet facilities. Such ships and the captives they carried were hosed down periodically as a sanitary measure. However, sailors as well as captives often sickened and died on these disease-ridden vessels, the stench of which fouled the air for miles around.

Africans captured in battles or purchased from brokers were horded into prepared booths or prisons. Then they were brought to a large plain "where the surgeons examine every part of every one of them, to the smallest member, men and women being all stark naked."[1]

Those without physical or mental imperfection were branded with a red hot iron that imprinted the logo of a French, English, or Dutch Company on their chests. "In this particular, care is taken that the women be not burnt too hard."[2]

Chained together, the captives were rowed on small boats to the "Slave Ship" for the dreaded Middle Passage, the six- to ten-week voyage across the Atlantic Ocean. Once aboard, they were stacked like books into holds sometimes sixteen to eighteen

---

1. *Before the Mayflower, A History of the Negro in America, 1619–1964* (Revised Edition), Lerone Bennett, Jr. (Penguin Books, 1973).
2. *Ibid.*

inches high. "They had not so much room," one captain said, "as a man in his coffin, either in length or breadth."[3]

Wedged immovably, and chained to the deck by the neck and legs, captives would frequently go mad before suffocating or dying. "In their frenzy, some killed others in the hope of procuring more room to breathe. Men strangled those next to them, and women drove nails into each other's brains.

"It was not unusual, John Newton said, to find a dead and living man chained together. So many dead people were thrown overboard on slavers that it was said that sharks would pick up a ship off the coast of Africa and follow it to America."[4]

2. *Whip-scarred flesh of an African Captive Named Gordon*, page 5. Used by permission of Schomburg Center for Research in Black Culture, New York Library Astor, Lenox and Tilden Foundations, and Culver Pictures, Inc.

The lash of the bullwhip flayed, slashed, and sliced the flesh of African captives during U.S. slavery. The punishment was central to a program of vicious physical and psychological battering inflicted upon Africans from the moment they were captured. This combination of physical violence and mental terrorization was designed to terrorize captives and dehumanize them in their own minds, and in the minds of the master class.

An enslaved person was often first whipped without cause as part of a "breaking in" process. According to former captives interviewed after the Civil War,[5] the whip was laid on regardless of gender or age. A hole was dug in the ground to accommodate the swollen area of a pregnant woman's body so she could be whipped without injuring or killing the unborn child and causing her captor an economic loss.

In one method of whipping, a person was stripped naked, stretched face down on the ground, and staked to four posts in a "tanning" position. *Slave Narrative* interviews describe beatings where "hide and blood flew" with up to 2,000 lashes intermittently laid on sometimes over a period of days. The interviews explain further that clothing was removed from a person about to be whipped because "hide would grow back." If a captive survived a

---

3. *Ibid.*
4. *There is A River, The Black Struggle For Freedom in America,* Vincent Harding (Harcourt Brace Jovanovich, Inc.), 1981.
5. *Slave Narratives* (Scholarly Press, reprinted 1976).

whipping, it was customary to rub salt and / or pepper into the wounds.

Front cover photos:
Line 1 – **Rev. Richard Allen,** founder, African Methodist Episcopal Church (Illustration by Reginald Smith); **Dr. John Henrik Clarke,** historian, author, educator (Photo courtesy John Henrik Clarke); **Dr. Mae Jamison,** astronaut, physician (Photo courtesy NASA)
Line 2 – **Dr. Maya Angelou,** author, educator, actress (Photo courtesy Jill Krementz, 1975); **Theresa Bender** and son **Benjamin** with **Dr. Benjamin S. Carson, Jr.,** director of Pediatric Neurosurgery, Johns Hopkins Hospital, following surgery separating Benjamin and Patrick Bender, born joined at the skull (Illustration used by permission of Johns Hopkins Children's Center / illustration digitally composited by Reginald Smith); **Dr. Martin Luther King, Jr.,** leader of the Civil Rights Revolution
Line 3 – **Dr. John Hope Franklin,** historian, author, educator (Photo courtesy Graham Photography, St. Petersburg, FL); **El-Hajj Malik El-Shabazz (Malcolm X),** leader of African-American Islamic Movement; **Professor Barbara Jordan,** stateswoman, educator, writer (Photo courtesy Barbara Jordan and the University of Texas at Austin)

Back cover photos:
Line 1 – **Marian E. Barnes,** counselor, writer, storyteller (Photo courtesy John Watson, Philadelphia)
Line 2 – **Dr. Bill Cosby,** entertainer, educator, philanthropist (Photo courtesy *New York Journal American* and Harry Ransom Humanities Research Center, University of Texas at Austin)
Line 3 – **Dr. C. Eric Lincoln,** historian, educator, author, literary agent (Photo courtesy C. Eric Lincoln); **Oprah Winfrey,** TV talk show moderator, actress, businesswoman (Photo courtesy Arthur Shay, Click/Chicago); **Michael Jordan,** athletic superstar (Photo courtesy Daniel/Allsport Hall of Fame)

Bibliography

Adams, Russell L. *Great Negroes, Past and Present.* 3rd ed. Chicago: Afro-Am Publishing, 1969.
Barnes, Jack. *Malcolm X Talks to Young People.* Young Socialist Alliance, Merit Publishers, NY, 1969.
Behr, Robert. *The Search for Black Identity.* Wellesley Hills, MA: Independent School Press, 1970.
Bennett, Lerone, Jr. *Before the Mayflower, A History of the Negro in America 1619–1964.* Rev. ed. Baltimore: Penguin Books, 1964.
Blassingame, John W. *Slave Testimony, Two Centuries of Letters, Speeches, Interviews and Autobiographies.* Baton Rouge: Louisiana State University Press, 1977.
Burton, Art. *Black, Red, and Deadly.* Austin, TX: Eakin Press, 1991.
Carson, Benjamin, with Cecil Murphy. *Gifted Hands.* Grand Rapids, MI: Zondervan Publishing, Review and Harold, 1990.
Carson, Benjamin, and Cecil Murphy. *Think Big.* Grand Rapids, MI: Zondervan Publishing, 1991.
Chapman, Abraham. *Voices.* New York: New American Library, 1968.
Cheek, William F. *Black Resistance Before the Civil War.* Beverly Hills, CA: Glenco Press, 1970.
Ciardi, John. *A Second Browser's Dictionary and Native's Guide to the Unknown American Language.* New York: Harper & Row, 1983.
Diop, Cheikh Anta. *The African Origin of Civilization, Myth or Reality.* New York: Lawrence Hill & Co., 1974.
Cloyd, Iris, ed., Wm. C. Matney, Jr., consulting ed. *Who's Who Among Black Americans.* Detroit, MI: Gale Research, 1990.
Federal Writer's Project. *Slave Narratives, Texas,* and *Slave Narratives, South Carolina.* A Folk History of Slavery in the U.S. from Interviews with Former Slaves. St. Clair Shores, MI: 1936; Reprint, Scholarly Press, 1976; assembled by Library of Congress, Works Projects Administration for D.C.
Franklin, John Hope, and editors of Time-Life Books. *An Illustrated History of Black Americans.* New York: Time-Life Books, 1970.
Franklin, John Hope. *From Slavery to Freedom: A History of Negro Americans.* 5th ed. New York: Alfred A. Knopf, Inc., 1980.
Ginzburg, Ralph. *100 Years of Lynching.* Black Classic Press, 1962.

Goss, Linda, and Marian E. Barnes, eds. *Talk That Talk, An Anthology of African-American Storytelling.* A Touchstone Book, Simon & Schuster, 1989.
Greig, Mary E. *How People Live in Africa.* Chicago: Benefic Press, 1967.
Gutman, Herbert G. *The Black Family in Slavery and Freedom, 1750-1925.* New York: Pantheon Books, 1976.
Harding, Vincent. *There is A River, The Black Struggle For Freedom in America.* Harcourt Brace Jovanovich, 1981.
Kunjufu, Jawanza. *Countering the Conspiracy to Destroy Black Boys, Volume II.* Chicago: African American Images, 1986.
Logan, Rayford W., and Michael R. Winston. *Dictionary of American Negro Biography.* New York: W. W. Norton & Co., 1982.
McGovern, James R. *The Anatomy of a Lynching: The Killing of Claude Neal.* Baton Rouge: Louisiana State University Press, 1982.
Miers, Earl Schenck. *The Story of the American Negro.* New York: Wonder Books, Grosset & Dunlap, 1965.
Peterson, Robert W. *Only the Ball was White.* Englewood Cliffs, NJ: Prentice-Hall, 1970.
Ploski, Harry A., and Ernest Kaiser. *Afro USA, A Reference work on the Black Experience.* New York: Bellwether Publishing, 1971.
Pruett, Jakie L., with Everett B. Cole. *As We Lived, Stories by Black Storytellers.* Burnet, TX: Eakin Press, 1982.
Robinson, Battle, and Robinson. *The Journey of the Songhai People.* Philadelphia: Farmer Press, 1987.
Rogers, J. A. *Sex and Race.* Volumes I, II, and III. St. Petersburg, FL: Helga M. Rogers, 1968, 1970, 1972.
Stampp, Kenneth M. *The Peculiar Institution, Slavery in the Ante-Bellum South.* New York: Vintage Books, Random House, and Alfred A. Knopf, 1956.
Stewart, Paul W., and Wallace Y. Ponce. *Black Cowboys.* Phillips Publishing, 1986.
Sullivan, Leon H. *Build Brother Build.* Philadelphia: Macrea Smith Co. , 1969.
Temple, Robert K. G. *The Sirius Mystery.* New York: St. Martin's Press, 1976.
Walker, Margaret. *Jubilee.* Bantam Books, 1969.
Wells, Ida Bell. *Crusade for Justice, The Autobiography of Ida B. Wells Barnett.* University of Chicago Press, 1970.

Oral Resources

Some of the information presented in this anthology was secured by the editor through consultations and special instruction in Black heritage from historians as follows:

Esteemed Elder, Alli Aweusi:	Historical consultant, heritage ceremonies specialist
Esteemed Elder, Baba Atu:	Historical consultant
Dr. Yosef Ben Jachannon:	African heritage classes
Esteemed Elder, Charles Blockson:	Historical consultant

Dr. Wacira Wa Gethaiga:	Kikuyu culture and Swahili language consultant
Dr. Vincent Harding:	Afro-American history instructor, Temple University
Dr. Makedi KunTima:	African heritage instructor, Temple University
Dr. C. Eric Lincoln:	Cultural-historical consultant
Dr. Edward Robinson, Jr.:	Historical consultant; corrective history instructor
Dr. Melvin Wade:	Historical consultant
Dr. Margaret Wade-Lewis:	Consultant, African languages, African-American English
Esteemed Elder, Merzie Wilson:	Historical consultant

Suggested Reading

Adams, Russell L. *Great Negroes Past and Present.* 3rd ed. Chicago: Afro-Am Publishing, 1969.
Angelou, Maya. *I Know why the Caged Bird Sings.* New York: Random House, 1969.
Aptheker, Herbert. *A Documentary History of the Negro People in the United States.* New York: Citadel Press, 1951.
Bastide, Roger. *African Civilisations in the New World.* New York: Harper & Row, 1971.
Burton, Art. *Black, Red, and Deadly.* Black and Indian Gunfighters of the Indian Territories. Austin, TX: Eakin Press, 1991.
Carson, Benjamin S., with Cecil Murphey. *Gifted Hands, The Story of Pioneer Surgeon Ben Carson.* Grand Rapids, MI: Zondervan Publishing House, 1990.
Carson, Benjamin S., with Cecil Murphey. *Think Big.* Grand Rapids, MI: Zondervan Publishing House, 1992.
Chapman, Abraham. *Black Voices, An Anthology of Afro-American Literature.* New York: New American Library, Mentor Book, 1968.
Clarke, John Henrik. *Rebellion in Rhyme.* Prairie City, IL: Decker Press, 1948.
———. *Harlem, a Community in Transition.* New York: Citadel paperback, 1964.
———. *American Negro Short Stories.* New York: Hill & Wang, 1966.
Dunbar, Paul Laurence. *The Complete Poems of Paul Laurence Dunbar.* New York: Dodd Mead, 1913.
Gates, Henry Louis, Jr., and Charles T. Davis. *The Slave's Narrative.* New York: Oxford University Press, 1985.
Goss, Linda, and Marian E. Barnes, eds. *Talk That Talk, An Anthology of African-American Storytelling.* New York: Simon & Schuster, 1989.
Haley, Alex. *Roots.* New York: Dell Publishing, 1976.
Hemenway, Robert E. *Zora Neale Hurston, A Literary Biography.* Chicago: University of Illinois Press, 1977.
Hughes, Langston. *The Panther and the Lash.* New York: Alfred Knopf, 1985.
———. *Selected Poems of Langston Hughes.* New York: Vintage Books, Random House, 1959.

Kearns, Francis E. *The Black Experience, An Anthology of American Literature for the 1970s.* New York: 1970.
Kunjufu, Jawanza. *Countering the Conspiracy to Destroy Black Boys.* Volumes I, II, and III. Chicago: African American Images, 1986.
Lincoln, C. Eric. *The Black Muslims in America.* Rev. ed. Boston: Beacon Press, 1973.
McGill, Alice. *The Griot's Cookbook, A Storytelling Cookbook.* (African, American and West Indian stories and recipes.) Alice McGill, P. O. Box 1607, Columbia, MD.
Rogers, J. A. *Sex and Race.* Volumes I, II, and III. 1968, 1970, 1972. Helga Rogers, 4975 Avenue South, St. Petersburg, FL 33715.
Pitre, Merline. *Through Many Dangers, Toils and Snares: The Black Leadership of Texas 1868-1900.* Austin, TX: Eakin Press, 1985.
Robinson, Battle and Robinson. *The Journey of the Songhai People.* Philadelphia: Farmer Press, 1987.
Sullivan, Leon H. *Build Brother Build.* Philadelphia: Macrea Smith Company, 1969.
Temple, Robert K. G. *The Sirius Mystery.* New York: St. Martin's Press, 1976.
Winegarten, Ruthe. *I Am Annie Mae, The Personal Story of a Texas Black Woman.* Austin, TX: Rosegarden Press, 1983.
Malcolm X. *The Autobiography of Malcolm X.* Alex Haley, ed. New York: Grove Press, 1965.

Audiocassettes*

Barnes, Marian E. *Black Heritage Remembered: From African Civilizations to African-American Contributions.*
——. *The Blue Jackal, Anansi's Riding Horse, and Other Folktales.*
——. *Talk That Talk Some More: On the Cutting Room Floor,* 1993. Selected stories from the anthology *Talk That Talk Some More: On the Cutting Room Floor.* A slice-of-life anthology on the Black experience.
——. *Talk That Talk and Walk That Walk: The African Roots of Storytelling,* 1987.
——. *Out the Lamp: Supernatural Tales* (some from personal experience).
——. *Wade in the Water.* From *Talk That Talk Some More: On the Cutting Room Floor,* 1993. The truth about slavery brought to life as never before! (All cassettes by Marian Barnes are available from Black Expressions, P.O. Box 14-3262, Austin, TX 78714-3262.)
Imhotep, Akbar. *Stories from Africa, Georgia, and The World.* Akbar Imhotep Connections, P. O. Box 11386, Atlanta, GA 30310.

Counseling Cassettes

Successfully Guiding the Very Young: Pre-birth to Age Ten.
Successfully Guiding a Modern Teenager: Preteenage and Teen Years.
Improving Your Self Image in a World That Puts You Down.

Relaxation Techniques.
Contact: Marian E. Barnes, P.O. Box 14-3262, Austin, TX 78714-3262.

Videocassettes*

Barnes, Marian E. *The Blue Jackal,* 1992. A folktale from India dramatically related to the Black Experience.
——. *Talk That Talk Some More: On the Cutting Room Floor,* 1993. Selected stories from the anthology *Talk That Talk Some More: On the Cutting Room Floor. A* "slice of life" anthology of the Black experience.
(All cassettes by Marian Barnes are available from Black Expressions, P.O. Box 14-3262, Austin, TX 78714-3262.)
McGill, Alice. *Sojourner Truth Speaks.* 1986. Alice McGill, P.O. Box 1607, Columbia, MD 21045.
Robinson, Edward. *The Songhai Princess,* a drama for children. VHS digitally recorded. Set in the grandeur of 15th-century Songhai, West Africa; shows Timbuktu "arched in gold and clothed in education." New Dawn, Inc. Film Production, 219 E. Clividen St., Philadelphia, PA 19119.
——. *'Twas the Night Before Kwaanza.* New Dawn, Inc. 219 E. Clividen St., Philadelphia, PA 19119.

For the Very Young

Adams, Barbara Johnston. *The Picture Life of Bill Cosby.* Watts, 1986.
Adoff, Arnold. *Malcolm X.* Trophy, 1988.
Davidson, Margaret. *Frederick Douglass Fights for Freedom.* Four Winds Press, 1986.
Greene, Carol. *Desmond Tutu: Bishop of Peace.* Children's Press, 1986.
Greenfield, Eloise. *Rosa Parks.* Crowell, 1973.
Lillegard, Dee. *My First Martin Luther King Book.* Children's Press.
Mitchell, Barbara. *A Pocketful of Goobers: A Story About George Washington Carver.* Carolrhoda, 1986.
——. *Shoes for Everyone: A Story About Jan Matzeliger.* Carolrhoda, 1986.
Purcell, John W. *African Animals.* Children's Press, 1982.
Stein, R. Conrad. *Story of the Underground Railroad.* Children's Press, 1981.
Wilson, Merzie. *Merzette Coloring Book (Inventions).* 1986. 4221 Otter Street, Philadelphia, PA.
——. *Merzette Coloring Book (Bessie Coleman).* 1990. 4221 Otter Street, Philadelphia, PA.

*Most stories in *Talk That Talk Some More: On the Cutting Room Floor* are available on audio and / or videocassettes. **Contact Black Expressions, P.O. Box 14-3262, Austin, TX 78714-3262.**

Index to Authors

Anderson, Leon C., Jr., 92
Angst, Will, 103
Aweusi, Alli, 149–151
Banks, Dorothy Charles, 73
Barnes, Marian E., xiii, 12, 24, 43, 56, 60, 66, 76, 79, 80, 82, 85, 86, 95, 103, 106, 109, 118, 123, 126, 129, 135, 142, 143, 145, 146, 151, 153, 154, 161, 167, 169, 170, 172, 183, 198, 204, 206, 224–254 (columns/letters), 256, 358
Brewer, J. Mason, 19, 22
Clarke, Dr. John Henrik, ix, 120
Colson, Eartha, 3
Curry, Dottie, 151
Diefenbach, Kyisha, 97
Dion, Michelle, 100
Dunbar, Paul Laurence, xiii
Erickson, Sean, 96
Franklin, Dr. John Hope, 14
Gethaiga, Dr. Wacira, 172
Hansen, Jennifer, 96
Hicks, Jessie Mae, 66
Hughes, Langston, xx, 120
Hyman, Mark, 23
Ijeoma, Trice, 101

Jawara, 78
Johnson, Amanda, 102
Lincoln, Dr. C. Eric, 9, 12
Martin-Anderson, Evelyn, 142
Mayne, Christina, 99
Mullins, Christina, 98
Mwalimu, Joseph, 170
O'Neal, John, 356
Orr-Ogunro, Deborah, 172
Parra, April, 75
Patton, Colly, 98
Phillips, Maj. Gen. John F., 93
Polk, Doris Barnes, 102
Prange, Diego, 100
Qazi, Farhana, 74
Sexton, Cedar, 99
Sheppard, Jonathan, 93
Simond, Ada DeBlanc, 117
Sims, Rebecca, 74
Sisnett, Ana, 72
Stanley, Jimmy, 96
Stewart, Joan Barnes, 77
Temujin, 122
Wade-Lewis, Dr. Margaret, 188
Wilkinson, Michelle, 120
Winegarten, Ruthe, 58
Wright, Christine, 74

Index to Articles/Poems

About the "Holy Spirit" Nobody Could Quench . . ., 242
African-American Contributions Get Us Through the Day, 183
Afro-Americans Criticize *Roots* . . ., 246
"A republic is an elephant?," 120
America's Black Holocaust Museum . . ., 151
Answers and Questions, 100
Black American Cowboys and Cowgirls, 153
Black English Expressions, 206
Black Man, 142
Black Woman, 146
"Black Women . . .," 149
Black Muslims in America After Elijah Muhammad, The, 9
Chance for the Fire Department, A, 98
Combing Grandma's Hair, 73
Creativity, 151
Crumb Snatchers, The, 78
Death of a Kikuyu, The, 172
Deeper Look at Aesop, A, 23
Depression Love, 79
Dr. C. Eric Lincoln: Early Roots, 12
Doris ("Dorie") Miller: Pearl Harbor Hero, 95
Eagles, 92
East Meets West, 109
Enslaved: Former Captives Tell About Slavery, 45
"Everyone thinks," 96

Exiled From South Africa, My Home, 170
Fifty Men of Color Who Changed the World, 143
Fifty Women of Color Who Changed the World, 146
For Anna Mae, 74
Gone With the Wind: Jessie Mae Hicks Remembers Times Past, 66
"Goodie Two Shoes," 123
Grandmother's Room, 77
Grannie Jus' Come, 72
Hospital Corpsman Battlefield Hero, 154
How a Hoe Became a "Ho" and Turned Into a Rake, 129
How a Horse Spoke to Me, 118
I Can't Forgive Her, the Way She Used to Beat Us, 19
I Like Spiders, 117
I Must Speak Out!, 172
In Spite of Myself, 97
Juneteenth, First African-American Holiday, 56
Just Another Soldier, 100
Knife in His Hands: The Story of Dr. Benjamin Carson, 106
Langston Hughes and Jesse B. Semple, 120
Language and the African-American, 198
Lessons, 135
Letter, The, 85

Letters to Editor, 251–254
Love and Respect Beat a Bloody Paddle, 86
Mama, What Don't White Boys Have?, 99
Merry Go Round, 101
Minister Farrakhan Challenges Black Men, Defends Black Women, 224
Modern Woman vs. "Traditional Lady," 247
Monster Children "Unreal" Horror Story, 226
Morning Dew Drop, 96
Mother, 75
My Day as a Migrant Farm Worker, 161
Negro, 150
Notes on the Psychological Use of Language as a Tool of Oppression, 204
Philly's Aframerican Youth Have Peaceful, Civilized Halloween . . ., 238
Poor Sonny Boy Died in Vain, 126
Portrait of Segregation, Discrimination and Degradation, A, 14
President Johnson's Gift to Me, 167
Problem With Black Women, A, 249
Progress . . . Or Ode to a Cynic, 93
Racist Insults Please a Listening Audience, 234
Reconstruction Days: Ku Klux, 22
Reverse Racism: New Problem in the New South, 229
Ride, The, 92
Roaring Bottom, The, 256

Round and Round, 102
Scenes from the Life of Malcolm X, Martyred Muslim Leader, 169
School Play Audition, 102
Slavery Time Party, 43
"Someday somebody'll . . .," xx
Song of Myself: A Requiem, 98
Tears of the Atlantic, 3
"The pale cloud swells," 99
The Way It Is: African Words and Creative Expressions in English, 188
To Joan, My Loving Daughter, 76
To Martin, 93
Tonka Truck, 103
"Uncle Tomahawk" — "Apple": Sad Moment in a Sad Life, 237
Urban Life and Depression Years: Thoughts of North Philadelphia, 82
Vaseline, 142
Voices, 103
Wade in the Water, 24
Warm Thoughts, 74
Wartime Trolley, 60
We Met a Little Tragedy on a Navasota Plantation, 58
We Wear the Mask, xiii
What is a Grandfather?, 74
What's In a Name?, 240
White Angel Learns Her Proud Black History, 231
White Pawn, 96
Who Needs Richard Pryor?, 225
Willi and Joe Joe and the Pamper Diaper, 122
Wood Bowl, The, 80
"You can't judge a book . . .," 356